The New Middle Kingdom

The New Middle Kingdom

China and the Early American Romance of Free Trade

KENDALL A. JOHNSON

Johns Hopkins University Press

Baltimore

This book was brought to publication with the generous assistance of the
Johns Hopkins University Press General Humanities Endowment.

Johns Hopkins University Press
2715 North Charles Street
Baltimore, Maryland 21218-4363
www.press.jhu.edu

Library of Congress Cataloging-in-Publication Data

Names: Johnson, Kendall, 1969– author.
Title: The new Middle Kingdom : China and the early American romance of free
trade / Kendall A. Johnson.
Description: Baltimore : Johns Hopkins University Press, 2017. | Includes
bibliographical references and index.
Identifiers: LCCN 2016040202| ISBN 9781421422510 (hardcover : acid-free
paper) | ISBN 1421422514 (hardcover) | ISBN 9781421422527 (electronic)
Subjects: LCSH: United States—Commerce—China—History—19th century. |
China—Commerce—United States—History—19th century. | Free trade—
United States—History—History—19th century. | Merchants—United
States—History—History—19th century. | China—Foreign public opinion,
American—History—19th century. | Printing—Social aspects—United
States—History—History—19th century. | United States—Territorial
expansion—History—19th century. | Free trade—United States—History—
History—19th century—Sources. | Free trade in literature. | China—In
literature. | BISAC: HISTORY / United States / General. | HISTORY / Asia /
China. | LITERARY CRITICISM / American / General. | BUSINESS &
ECONOMICS / Economic History.
Classification: LCC HF3128 .J76 2017 | DDC 382.0973/051—dc23
LC record available at https://lccn.loc.gov/2016040202

A catalog record for this book is available from the British Library.

*Special discounts are available for bulk purchases of this book. For more information,
please contact Special Sales at 410-516-6936 or specialsales@press.jhu.edu.*

Johns Hopkins University Press uses environmentally friendly book materials,
including recycled text paper that is composed of at least 30 percent post-
consumer waste, whenever possible.

To my sisters, Christine and Stephanie

CONTENTS

This book springs from the experience of moving back and forth between Philadelphia and Hong Kong during interesting times. Its ideas began germinating a decade ago at Swarthmore College with the intellectual and moral support of Peter Schmidt and then provost Connie Hungerford. During this time in Philadelphia my scholarly curiosity was nurtured by the collegiality and friendship of Nathalie Anderson, Elizabeth Bolton, Hester Blum, Timothy Burke, Martin Brückner, Rachel Sagner Buurma, Edmund Campos, Max Cavitch, Jeanine DeLombard, Christopher Densmore, Joseph Dimuro, Allison Dorsey, Bruce Dorsey, Chuck James, Nora Johnson, Anthony Foy, Adam Hotek, Edward Larkin, Carolyn Lesjak, Bakirathi Mani, David McWhirter, Kyoko Miyabe, Mark Rifkin, Martha Schoolman, Bethany Schneider, Sunka Simon, Eric Song, Gus Stadler, Phil Weinstein, Patricia White, Craig Williamson, and Christina Zwarg.

During 2008–9 as a Fulbright Scholar in the American Studies Program at the University of Hong Kong's School of Modern Languages and Cultures (SMLC), Dixon Heung Wah Wong supported my research efforts, and Glenn Shive of the Hong Kong–America Center helped orient me to scholarly networks in Guangzhou, Hong Kong, and Macao, where I was fortunate to meet May-bo Ching, John R. Haddad, Takeshi Hamashita, Sibing He, Vincent Wai-Kit Ho, Rogério Miguel Puga, and Paul Van Dyke. After relocating to Hong Kong in 2010, my horizons continued to expand in conversation and travel with historians, literary scholars, political scientists, and friends, including Stefan Auer, Katherine Baxter, Tony Carty, Evelyn Chan, Stuart Christie, Wayne Cristaudo, Cosette Cheng, Stephen Y. W. Chu, Maureen Chun, Frank Dikötter, Michael Duckworth, Louise Edwards, Staci Ford, Wendy Gan, Otto Heim, Elaine Ho, Julia Kuehn, Yeewan Koon, Angela Ki-che Leung, Andreas Leutzsch, Kam Louie, Andrew MacNaughton, Christopher Munn, Timothy O'Leary, Michael O'Sullivan, Priscilla Roberts, Elizabeth Sinn, Helen Siu, Facil Tesfaye, Q. S. Tong, Scott Veitch, Roland Vogt, and Marco Wan. At key junctures, John Carroll, Douglass Kerr, James Fichter, Tim Gruenewald, Selina Lai-Henderson, Charles Schencking, Shu-mei Shih, John D. Wong, and Guoqi Xu took the time to read portions of the work in progress and offer substantial feedback. From an early stage Gordon Hutner was generous and patient with advice that helped keep me on track, as did the encouragement, in later stages, of Gordon H. Chang, Shelley Fisher Fishkin, Sander Gilman, Josephine McDonagh, Donald Pease, John Carlos Rowe, Ivy Wilson, and Rob Wilson. In the bigger picture I remain deeply grateful to Eric Cheyfitz, Nancy Bentley, Elaine Freedgood, Farah Griffin, Eric Haralson, Chris Looby, and Scott Manning Stevens. I wrote most of the book while serving as the head of the School of Modern Languages and Cultures; special thanks go to

Shirley Chan, Zena Cheung, Alice Tse, and Yvonne Yeung, and all the members of the SMLC's administrative staff who helped make this possible.

As unexpected continuities wove through archives and cultural heritage sites on both sides of the Pacific, I enjoyed the intellectual hospitality of research librarians at the Independence Seaport Museum (Philadelphia), the Institute of Culture (Macao), the Library Company of Philadelphia, the National Archives of Singapore, and the Swarthmore Friends Historical Library. Support from Hong Kong's Research Grants Council of the University Grants Committee and from the University of Hong Kong enabled travel to conferences, talks, and research trips to Beijing, Guangzhou, Jakarta, Lhasa, Macao, Ningbo, Xiamen, Jakarta, Malacca, Penang, Rome, Seattle, Singapore, Taipei, Tsukuba, Ulaanbaatar, and elsewhere.

Elizabeth Sherburn Demers has been a stellar editor at Johns Hopkins University Press, and I deeply appreciate her initial enthusiasm for the manuscript and her advice in its final stages. Thanks go to Meagan Szekely for all her timely reminders during production, to Andre Barnett, for her care of the manuscript in its final stages, and to the managing editor Juliana McCarthy for overseeing the entire process. The book has benefited from Brian MacDonald's keen eye as a copyeditor and reader.

My heartfelt thanks go to lovely Puujee whose deep spirit and warm sense of humor often lift me out of bookish self-absorption. At times Hong Kong can feel too far from my parents Frances and Karl, who recently celebrated their fiftieth wedding anniversary, and from my wonderful sisters Christine and Stephanie, their husbands Sean and René, and their sons Evan, Grayson, Jarret, Kurt, and Lukas, my five very fine and energetic nephews.

The New Middle Kingdom

Prologue

The American romance of free trade with the Middle Kingdom of China was a quest narrative of the young nation's potential accomplishment in the global marketplace. Versions of it began to circulate after the Revolutionary War (1776–83), when the harbor of Canton was a destination for ambitious merchants capitalizing on commerce that extended beyond the transatlantic trade and through the Indian and Pacific Oceans. Influential biographical accounts presented the successful merchant princes as heroic philanthropists whose mastery of trans-hemispheric finance had enabled them to establish foundational cultural institutions back home and to plot the westward continental advance of communication and transportation.

As American missionaries and diplomats followed the merchants to China, these quest narratives of Far Eastern commerce proliferated during the nineteenth century, boldly asserting the rising nation's world-historical importance. However, because the fortunes amassed in the China trade often depended on opium smuggling, gunboat diplomacy, and disregard of Chinese sovereignty, these narratives also justified commercial practices and diplomatic policies that defied the principles of democratic republicanism and liberal economics upon which the new nation had been founded. Through literary historical analysis of the writings of these American merchants, missionaries, and diplomats, this volume tracks the cultural impact of the China trade on the developing United States to offer a shared early history of the two countries.

As the Civil War (1861–65) split the nation into warring halves, romances of free trade lived on in China. After the war, as grief-weary Americans followed news reports of President Andrew Johnson's impeachment trial, these romances offered pathways to national reunification and redemption. A southern Democrat who had supported the Union throughout the war, Vice President Johnson had risen to the presidency with the assassination of President Abraham Lincoln in April 1865. As president, Johnson ran afoul of the aggressive Radical Republicans because he refused to prosecute Confederate leaders for treason. In mid-May, he dodged removal by just one vote. Looking out from Washington, DC, in the early phase of Reconstruction, the national prospect seemed dreary. The New York–based political newspaper *Harper's Weekly: A Journal of Civilization* lamented in the lead article "Party Terrorism" (30 May 1868) that "party-spirit, inflamed into ferocity, lost to reason and moral sense is the perpetual menace of free institutions. We are at this moment seeing it in its worst aspect."[1] And yet, as partisan recrimination menaced Washington's "free institutions," there was reason for great hope. An American romance of free trade came to the rescue.

Harper's Weekly conjured hope in commerce with China to counteract potentially existential disappointment over party conflict within the nation. Spotlighting the intercontinental routes of international trade, the same *Harper's* issue enthused over the global centrality of the United States in a network that connected the Far West of North America to the Far East of Asia. The grand geographic scale of this hope extended the nation's commercial influence from sea to shining sea, through the hemispheres of the Americas, and across the Pacific Ocean, from California and Oregon to Hawai'i, Australia, Japan, and China. By looking west to the Far East of China, *Harper's* directed readers' attention outside national borders, transcending the war-scarred sectional territories, to a world of commercial adventure that promised capital for the re-united states.

Matching historical depth with geographic expansiveness, *Harper's* framed the vision in the achievements of two men: the Spanish–employed explorer from Genoa Christopher Columbus and the American diplomatic minister Anson Burlingame. It was not enough to tell their stories. Dynamically coordinated pictures and words drew readers into a shared national future. The cover of *Harper's* displays an epic scene of Columbus reporting back to King Ferdinand and Queen Isabella his discovery of an eastward sea route to what he mistakenly believed to be the East Indies. Steadying the map with his hand that anchors the represented world like a compass, Columbus charts a westward course that promises imperial ascendance to recently united Spain. A century later Spain's rising imperial rival Great Britain would plant American colonies that, in the revolutionary course of human events, bucked the yoke of colonial subordination to become a national republic. Having looked back to Columbus, *Harper's* looks ahead to a pax Americana of confederated postcolonial nations networked in global commerce and overlooks the pall of destructive sectional resentment in the Washington of May 1868.

Harper's celebrated Minister Burlingame as the modern and liberal incarnation of Columbian commercial adventure. President Lincoln appointed him the U.S. minister to China in 1861, but it is ironic that Burlingame spent most of the war outside the United States. As an ardent and outspoken member of the antislavery

"Columbus explaining his discovery of America to King Ferdinand and Queen Isabella of Spain." *Harper's Weekly* 12.596 (30 May 1868). Wood engraving from drawing by John Gilbert.

Free Soil Party in Boston, he had won election to the U.S. House of Representatives, where in 1856 he denounced the brutal caning of Massachusetts senator Charles Sumner on the Senate floor. And yet, as the first battles of the U.S. Civil War raged, he voyaged to China where he set a respectful tone in dealing with the Imperial Court at Peking. Aided by his diplomatic secretary Samuel Wells Williams, a missionary printer and translator with decades of experience in China, Burlingame gained the trust of China's Office for the Management of the Business of Foreign Countries, the Zŏnglĭ Yámén (總理衙門). Upon Burlingame's retirement from diplomatic service in 1867, the Imperial Court enlisted him to represent China in its first diplomatic envoy to Western nations.

The first stop was the United States. Burlingame and the Chinese diplomats landed in San Francisco to gratifying fanfare and a celebratory dinner. The embassy traveled on to Washington, DC, where in June 1868 Burlingame finalized a treaty that promised to open China to expansions of rail and telegraph, while merely acknowledging the Chinese emperor's consent as a condition of this projected Western investment. Celebration of the Burlingame Treaty picked up steam through the summer months in New York City and Boston. Praise was effusive. Mark Twain penned the *New York Tribune* article "The Treaty with China: Its Provisions Explained" (28 August 1868), heralding the Burlingame Treaty as the "broadest, most unselfish, and the most catholic treaty yet framed by man"; the treaty presumed that China had "supreme control over its own people" but also promised to "[lift] up of a mighty nation and [confer] upon it the boon of a purer religion and of a higher and better civilization than it has known before."[2] As Burlingame opened China, Twain pitched the revival of America's rise to world-historical prominence.

Reading about Burlingame and Columbus in *Harper's*, the nation seems to have moved beyond the crises of treason and the enduring sectional animosities that would bedevil Reconstruction. Rather it seems poised to complete a revolution in the world-historical cycle of human progress, powered by the interlocking gears of Christianity and commerce. Dispelling partisan shadows of "Party Terrorism" with the rays of transnational commercial hope, *Harper's* lauded Burlingame for realizing the "union of the Oldest Empire and the Youngest Republic."[3] The magazine's centerfold illustrated the result, laying out Burlingame's accomplishment. The collage juxtaposes scenes (including Hong Kong's harbor and North American railway construction) that encircle the "Map of the World on the Mercator's Projection, Showing the Geographical Relation of New York and the Rest of the Universe."[4] The ribbon of news print announces the paradigm shift: "The United States have become the great highway between Western Europe and Eastern Asia," with New York rising to become "the world's great mart" — "the center of the commercial world."[5] The following chapters are an intercultural history explaining how and why *Harper's* countered the "Party Terrorism" of postwar Washington, DC, with a glorious vision of a heroic Burlingame forging a commercial highway that connected Asian and Europe and repositioned the United States spatially and historically as the world's new Middle Kingdom.

But the free trade in these romances was not free. Beyond serving as an ideological blueprint of national redemption, *Harper's* map obliquely registers the social and economic distress in China after Western nations pried open the doors of

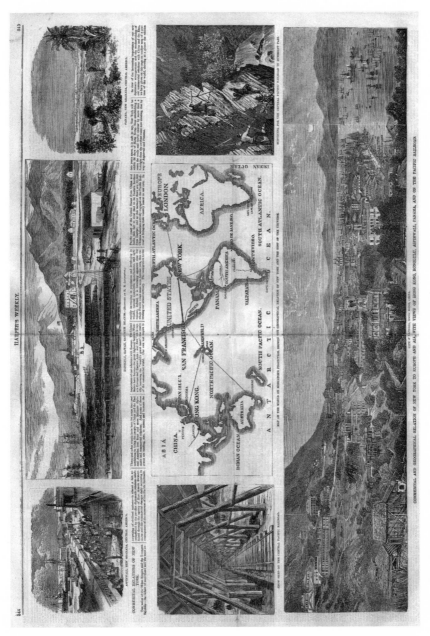

"Commercial and Geographical Relation of New York to Europe and Asia, with Views of Hong Kong, Aspinwall, Panama, and on the Pacific Railroad." *Harper's Weekly* 12.596 (30 May 1868).

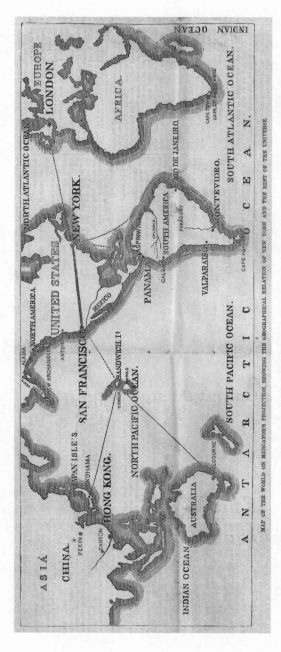

Centered "Map of the World on the Mercator's Projection, Showing the Geographical Relation of New York and the Rest of the Universe." *Harper's Weekly* 12.596 (30 May 1868).

commercial regulation with opium in the name of free trade. The First (1839–42) and Second (1856–60) Opium Wars are the backstory of the map's bold labeling of British-controlled Hong Kong and the diminutive designation of Canton. By mid-century, the treaties that ended the opium wars also dismantled the Canton System of commercial regulation, which early American merchants had navigated in hope of national recognition and economic credibility. The circumvention of Canton's imperial regulations also echoes in the unintended consequences of U.S. missionaries, whose printing and preaching helped to inspire the Taiping Rebellion (1850–64), during which 20 million Chinese people lost their lives. Finally, Burlingame's romance of free trade in China was short-lived. After his death in 1870, the U.S. merchants, missionaries, and diplomats to China eschewed his cooperative example amid new rounds of hostility with Britain, France, Germany, Russia, and Japan that threatened China's legal sovereignty and territorial integrity. Back in the United States, federal laws of Chinese exclusion (1882) eliminated the Burlingame Treaty's guarantee to Chinese immigrants of free movement and legal protection, setting the precedent for subsequent exclusionary regulations.

The interwoven strands of national anxiety, commercial optimism, and diplomatic imperialism that resonate in *Harper's* May 1868 image of a world with the United States at its center are captured in the term *romance*. Romance registers the grandly speculative triumphalism of the nation's rising to oversee global flows of trade, the paradoxical blend of individualism and representativeness by which heroic merchants and diplomats exemplified the national promise of global trade, and the print cultural dynamics by which accounts of commercial quests in China reached layers of audience worldwide. Given the reach back to Columbus and the Spanish empire—the Holy Roman Empire of the mid-sixteenth century—the term *epic* might at first seem more appropriate, especially because the following chapters include writing that falls outside conventional literary designations of the realist novel or literary romance. But the term romance better fits how the magazine was making its claim, selling sensationally illustrated accounts of Burlingame's diplomatic adventures to postwar readers, inspiring them to self-realization as citizens through trade that connected the continental Far West to the Far East in China.[6] Romance also suggests the sentiments, desires, and idealizations of family that pervaded these early national ventures to win outside the United States fortunes upon which to establish a name and intergenerational legacy within it.[7] In the nation's early adventures of global speculative liberalism, China provided an exotic setting where the young, free-trading American hero faced an anciently pagan, despotic antagonist.

Introduction

[O]ur territory spreading from ocean to ocean, and placed midway between Europe and Asia, it seemed that we might with propriety apply to ourselves the name by which China had loved to designate herself, and deem that we were, in truth, "the Middle Kingdom."

COMMODORE MATTHEW C. PERRY, in Reverend Francis L. Hawks, *Narrative of the Expedition of an American Squadron to the China Seas and Japan . . .* (1856), 1:75

In the imaginations of early Americans, the Middle Kingdom was the wealthiest empire that the world had ever known. It was also very far away, on the other side of the globe. But this geographic distance did not deter commercial aspirations. It inspired them. The colonies had waged war to extract themselves from the British Empire. Soon after, merchants from New York, Philadelphia, Boston, Salem, Newport, and elsewhere cast speculative lines to China, striving to establish credibility in an international network of trade that linked ports of the world. The resulting fortunes shaped the cultural foundation of the early Republic and funded westward frontier expansion. For the merchant princes who speculated in the global Far East, Manifest Destiny promised not just the coalescence of the fractious regions of the continental Far West but also a golden gateway onto the Pacific Ocean. By proceeding through that gateway, the nation would realize its historical destiny as the world's *new* Middle Kingdom of commerce.

Following the path of the merchant princes, missionaries from the Boston-based association the American Board of Commissions of Foreign Missions (ABCFM) embarked for south China in the 1830s to save souls, investing their faith in printing as they preached the virtues of *free trade*. They went on to play crucial roles in helping diplomats negotiate treaties of "peace and commerce" after the First (1839–44) and Second (1856–60) Opium Wars—treaties that prioritized commercial opportunity over respect for China's legal and territorial sovereignty. The early commercial, literary, religious, and legal writings by these merchants, missionaries, and diplomats amplify what Lisa Low calls the "intimacies of the four continents" and offer new transnational perspectives on the place of China in the first century of U.S. cultural history when the new republic asserted, tested, and extended its economic influence in a world system stretching across the Atlantic, Indian, and Pacific Oceans.[1]

From the first days of U.S. independence, China inspired Americans to write, and the resulting documents compose a richly descriptive cross-cultural archive. The following chapters present key moments in early relations among the twenty-first century's superpowers through topical clusters of memoirs, biographies, epistolary journals, monthly magazines, book reviews, narrative fiction, travel narratives, and treaties, as well as literal images such as maps and engraved illustrations from books and magazines. Close attention to figurative language, generic forms, and social dynamics of print cultural production and circulation shows how authors, editors, and printers appealed to multiple overlapping audiences in China, in the United States, and throughout the world. The chapters as a whole highlight a generally overlooked aspect of early twentieth-century literary and cultural studies— the importance of China in antebellum U.S. culture.

The first two chapters consider how the genre of national biography personified the China trade in the antebellum period. Chapter 1 analyzes *The Journals of Major Samuel Shaw, The First American Consul at Canton: With a Life of the Author* (1847), published by the influential early national biographer Rev. Josiah Quincy. Having served as an officer in the Revolutionary War, Major Shaw embarked in 1784 for Canton, the designated trading port just outside the city gates of what has become today's mega-city of Guǎngzhōu (廣州) in south China.[2] His journals describe the initial challenges of securing China's recognition of the new nation as an independent and credible trading partner. Plotting his investment strategies, he warily admired the early success of the British East India Company (EIC) in shipping opium from colonial India, through ports of Southeast Asia, and to China, where it became powerfully transformative as a contraband commodity and currency. Major Shaw's observations are fascinating but take on added significance because Quincy published Shaw's journals in 1847, when the pursuit of Manifest Destiny justified war on Mexico and annexation of the Oregon Territory. Quincy's revision shows how editors amended early accounts of the China trade to inspire new generations of readers. The second chapter continues to trace U.S. trade with China by turning to the China trader Amasa Delano's *Narrative of Voyages* (1817) and Herman Melville's skeptical revision of it in the novella "Benito Cereno" (1855). The Canton trade with the interlocking regional economies involving enslaved people, seals skins and beaver pelts, silks, and silver specie connected Canton to the port cities of Batavia,

Lima, Boston, and Saint-Domingue. The chapter contends that Melville's novella criticizes not only Amasa Delano's willingness to overlook slavery as he pursued trade bearing on Canton but also the presentations in national biographies of early American merchant princes as models of virtuously ambitious commerce despite their involvement in the slave trade.

The third chapter highlights the notions of gender that pervaded trading activities in China and connected these activities to family life in the United States. It focuses on the fascinating epistolary diary of a young American woman named Harriett Low who accompanied her aunt and uncle to China in 1829 and lived there while her uncle ran Russell & Company, a firm that would play an influential role in U.S.-China relations for decades thereafter. During her four years of residence in Macao, she recorded firsthand observations of key historical figures and reflected on her affairs of the heart through accounts of what she read and saw in Macao. Her writing lends unparalleled insight into the gender roles that structured the trafficking of opium and the disciplinary terms of intimacy that enabled Harriett Low to dissociate such traffic from an idealized family life back home in the United States.[3] The chapter aligns her sense of "reproductive, family community" with an ideology of early national commercial patriarchy that pervaded interconnected zones of commerce stretching across Africa, the Americas, Asia, and Europe.[4]

From the early merchants and their rising companies the book turns to the aforementioned American Board missionaries who arrived to south China in the early 1830s. Funded primarily by congregations in the United States but also by the merchants, they pursued a grand project of extraterritorial printing, publishing for decades a variety of texts—including texts in Chinese—as they violated the Chinese laws regulating foreigners' presence in Canton. The fourth chapter considers the regional and international circuitry of their print endeavors as they collaborated with British missionaries in attempts to evangelize China and to contribute to centuries of scholarly compilations regarding Sinology, all the while appealing to congregations in the United States for funding as they wrestled with the ethics of opium traffic and the ensuing wars to which they were firsthand reporting witnesses.

The fifth and sixth chapters take up the diplomatic efforts that followed the First Opium War—efforts in which merchants and missionaries were crucially influential. The missionary printer Samuel Wells Williams became a key diplomatic aid, interpreter, and secretary to U.S. ministers, including Caleb Cushing, who signed the first treaty between China and the United States in 1844, and Commodore Matthew C. Perry, who headquartered in south China the U.S. East India Squadron during his 1854 mission to open Japan to free trade. These two chapters follow different tacks in considering the imperialistic terms through which the unequal treaties folded commerce into Christianity to trumpet the civilizing benefits of free trade. Chapter 5 considers Cushing's early career as a book reviewer and lawyer to explain how he developed a racial justification for asserting an absolute and unqualified extraterritoriality that exempted Americans from Chinese law in an extreme and inaccurate interpretation of the Treaty of Wanghia. Turning from Cushing to Perry, chapter 6 considers the copiously illustrated *Narrative of the Expedition of an American Squadron to the China Seas and Japan, under the Command of Commodore M. C. Perry* . . . (1856). Its images of extraterritorial burial imply an aesthetics of free-trade imperialism that memorializes patriotic sacrifice while equating national interest with corporate expansion into the pagan countries of East Asia.

The final chapter traces the imperialistic legacy of these antebellum endeavors in the cooperative diplomatic strategies of U.S. minister Anson Burlingame and the ultimately disappointing Burlingame Treaty of 1868, with its softer insistence that China open its ports to free trade and its heartland to railroad and telegraph construction. In tracing the hope and eventual disappointment of Burlingame's legacy, the chapter contrasts the triumphalist message of Walt Whitman's "Passage to India" (1871) in *Leaves of Grass* with the crises of faith evident in Samuel Wells Williams's revision of his two-volume *The Middle Kingdom*, first published in 1848 and revised for the last time in the final edition of 1883.

These seven chapters unfold in roughly chronological order though with some exceptions when developing intertextual frames of reference and intellectual influence for the editors, writers, printers, and cultural historians who have produced and revised the print record. Before considering Shaw's account of the first forays of U.S. merchants to China, it helps to understand the layers of commercial, evangelical, and legal meaning implied in the phrase *romance of free trade* that pulls together China and the United States.

The Romance of Free Trade

The term *romance* is fascinatingly complicated. I use it to refer to the optimism and energy of international commerce as it captured the imaginations of early American citizens striving for the fruits of free-trade liberalism after the Revolution. On an individual level, the international market presented a citizen with the opportunity to secure capital and establish a family. On a communal level, it promised to distinguish the nation internationally and pave the way for it to become the world's leading commercial republic in an increasingly secularized Christendom. The commercial dynamics of personal and national aspiration complement well-trodden paths of scholarship regarding the individualist legacy of social contract theory and classical liberalism.[5] To summarize broadly, in the post-Revolutionary United States, social status was not determined by aristocratic conventions that tied property to birthright and that regarded wealth as a buffer from the marketplace in guaranteeing the virtue of political authority. Instead, understandings of virtue adapted to what J. G. A. Pocock calls a "transactional universe" in which individuals upheld contractual obligations as they pursued with competitive vigor their economic self-interests.[6] In the parallel legal context of classical liberalism, Sir Henry Maine's *Ancient Law* (1861) formulated this prioritization of individuals' market ambition as a shift "from Status to Contract."[7]

The China trade was an endeavor that significantly broadened the early Republic's transactional universe of contractual obligation to the world networks of commercial ambition. With an eye to eighteenth-century Britain, Chi-ming Yang contends in *Performing China* (2011) that, as modes of consumerism developed, the idea of *China* sustained "imagined links and hierarchies between and among disparate parts of the globe" in changing configurations of a British Empire.[8] Similarly in the nineteenth-century United States, the China trade helped shape how American citizens related to one another across the sectional divides of national territory and how Americans imagined their nation beyond its borders in a world-historical community of empires and nations. Ralph Waldo Emerson's 1844 lecture "The Young American" offers a prime example. First delivered to the Boston Mercantile Library Association and later published in *Nature: Addresses and Lectures* (1849), the lecture ramps up a claim of national distinctiveness into exceptionalism by enthusing on the transformative effects of Far Eastern trade.[9] The quest of Columbus marks an origin point of epic reference as Emerson proclaims "trade" to be the "principle of liberty" that "planted America and destroyed feudalism."[10] Emerson predicts that through the commercial ambitions of its citizenry the United States will continue to rise relative to its peers and become the world's "leading nation" as the "development of our American internal resources, the extension of the utmost of the commercial system . . . are giving an aspect of greatness to the Future, which the imagination fears to open."[11] In the embrace of Columbus, Emerson invokes the conventional westward course of empire—the classical *translatio imperii et studii*—in a grand historical narrative of trade progressing to lift humankind to a new level of fulfillment in the commercial success of U.S. citizens.[12] Others would similarly characterize American trade as a revolutionary principle, derived from European precedent that generated a new nation with the potential to configure global commercial flows to the betterment of all.

The genre of literary romance is a prominent signpost in early twentieth-century scholarship that discerned a canon of American literature, but until recently China has seemed a world away from the early national experience that these romances

"Donald McKay, Builder of the Flying Cloud, the Sovereign of the Seas, the James Baines, and the Lightening." Daguerreotype by Southworth and Hawes; frontispiece to Matthiessen, *American Renaissance.*

represented.[13] Nevertheless, traces of the China trade run through paradigmatic formulations such as F. O. Matthiessen's monumentally influential *American Renaissance: Art and Expression in the Age of Emerson and Whitman* (1941), which begins with a daguerreotype portrait of shipping magnate Donald McKay (1810–80), "Builder of the *Flying Cloud,* the *Sovereign of the Seas,* the *James Baines,* and the *Lightening.*"

Although the China trade was crucial to McKay's success, it does not figure in Matthiessen's attempt to put a face on the American Renaissance. Representing the "common man in his heroic stature," McKay complements the literary masters Ralph Waldo Emerson, Nathaniel Hawthorne, Henry David Thoreau, Herman Melville, and Walt Whitman, who "all wrote for democracy in a double sense": "to give fulfillment to the potentialities freed by the Revolution, to provide a culture commensurate with America's political opportunity."[14] Adapting Benjamin Franklin's rise from poverty to affluence from the print shop to the shipyard, Matthiessen presents McKay as "the master builder of the clipper era, a farmer's son who reached his full fame when, the same year as *Moby-Dick*, he built the *Flying Cloud*."[15] "McKay's portrait," Matthiessen continues, "makes the most fitting frontispiece [to *The American Renaissance*], since it reveals the type of character with which the writers of the age were most concerned, the common man in heroic stature, or, as Whitman called the new type, 'Man in the Open Air.'"[16] The phrase "type of character" is a knot of relation tension by which the photographic image of McKay's singular face conveys a *uniqueness* of an individual character that paradoxically *generalizes* a national American type, which in turn *specifies* this American type as distinct from others in the world.

The irony of McKay representing the homegrown sensibility of a "farmer's son" is that the "open air" source of his wealth depended on the global networks of commerce stretching across the Atlantic, Indian, and Pacific Oceans. His ship the *Flying Cloud* was launched in 1851 and earned its reputation by logging the two fastest times between New York and San Francisco, just under ninety days on both runs (less than half the time that it would have taken Samuel Shaw on the first voyage to China in 1784).[17] As a representative of early Americans then, McKay could very reasonably allude to the U.S. merchants who were purchasing his ships to gain advantages in speed and reliability of transport that might yield advantageous positions of brokerage and credit in a global market. Such figures do not seem very "common," despite the best efforts of biographers who present them as models for young aspiring readers.[18] As Jacques M. Downs explains in *The Golden Ghetto: The American Commercial Community at Canton and the Shaping of American China Policy, 1784–1844* (1997), the speculative activities of the China trade led to "remarkable family complex[es]" that included "brothers, nephews, cousins and in-laws."[19] Their lucrative corporate endeavors built the fortunes of patriarchs such as Astor, Boit, Cabot, Cunningham, Cushing, Delano, Dumaresq, Forbes, Gardiner, King, Low, Orne, Parkman, Perry, Russell, Shaw, Sturgis, Wetmore, and Whitney, whose families would grow into prominence during the Gilded Age.

Matthiessen's canonization of American literature may seem outmoded, but his erasure of the China trade resonated for decades after as literary scholars reassessed his methods of literary and cultural studies and his struggle to explain "democracy" during the Cold War.[20] Of course, the proposition that the *genre of romance* is the most vital expression of U.S. culture has been extensively reconsidered by Nina Baym, Michael T. Gilmore, Myra Jehlen, Amy Kaplan, Michael Paul Rogin, and others who have shown that rigid distinctions between the American romance and the realist British novel of manners are better at registering anxieties over the young nation's cultural respectability than at establishing a generic basis for U.S. cultural production.[21] In *American Romanticism and the Marketplace* (1995), Gilmore considers how the themes by which twentieth-century scholars discerned American romanticism were nineteenth-century responses to changing social conditions brought on by a "market revolution" that transformed the United States from agrarian to industrial.[22] Maritime enterprises of the China traders are an important, albeit underappreciated, layer of this transformation in that merchant princes financed the spread of railways and telegraphy while aligning in their speculative plans the frontiers of the continental Far West, Caribbean ports, European metropolises, and the trading port of Canton. One could dedicate a book to how the China trade permeates the American romantics—for example, the ice cut from Thoreau's Walden Pond found its way to India and China—but this would unnecessarily limit the cultural impact of the China trade.

Furthermore, canonical American romances, rather than capturing the strident optimism of this commercial adventure, instead evince the authors' limits in imagining resistance and alternatives to lifestyles predicated on possessive individualism. As Jehlen explains, in their respective "heroic myths" Cooper, Hawthorne, and Melville seem to lament the hero's capitulation to "structural constraints of a hermetic cosmos" based in a national ideology that equates liberty with liberalism.[23] The flights of Hester Prynne and Ahab away from society and into the wilderness of land and sea neither inspire new potentials for self-realization nor escape a gravitational pull of national republican liberalism and individualistic self-reliance. Hester returns to live on the margin of the community that had punished her, defiantly wearing the scarlet letter in ways that inspire Hawthorne and his readers. Melville's Ahab does not return to Nantucket but offers little alternative to the ways of "the mutual, joint-stock world."[24] Instead, he is abruptly yanked off his boat into the watery abyss, leaving readers to contemplate the sublimely destructive depths that swallow his rage and the *Pequot*. Furthermore, national heroes such as Cooper's Natty Bumppo are impotent when it comes to cultivating the heteronormative "familial and social attachments" that premise procreative national futurity.[25]

To emphasize the cultural impact of the China trade in the antebellum United States, I lift romance beyond strict definitions of literary genre. The nonfictional prose of so-called merchant princes, missionaries, and diplomats was functionally descriptive in recording the mundane experience of travel (journals, letters), journalistic in reporting world events (newspapers), picturesque in its scenic execution of landscape description (the grand tour), and proto-ethnographic in describing people and environments of the world (natural histories). These writers blurred the boundaries of realism and idealism, venturing into interrelated fields of emotional force in what Lauren Berlant describes as the "National Symbolic," a "tangled cluster" of law, language, politics, ancestry, and experience.[26] Adapting Ann Laura Stoler's observation, such "blurred genres" do not indicate that a U.S. empire was "in distress" but instead imply "the active realignment and reformation" of its polities.[27]

China was a significant extraterritorial point of reference in this tangle, as writers traveled, lived, traded, and wrote in China, facing the monotonies and dangers of sea travel, the uncertainties of territorial and cultural dislocation, and moral concerns over how they were making money. Along the way they read and were inspired by books to which they referred as *romances*, modeling themselves in their own letters, journals, and memoirs after fictional characters. The writings of Sir Walter Scott, Lord Byron, and James Fenimore Cooper were popular, but so were the British travel narratives of Commodore George Anson, Captain Basil Hall, and Mrs. Fanny Trollope. In this context, Americans drew on the idea of romance as a multivalent theme across mixed modes of discourse as they fit personal circumstance to ideals of national type and the gender roles that supported an idealized national family.[28]

National biographies of the nineteenth century did not pass the literary muster that canonized the American romance, but these biographies best convey the hope that China trading would build a family and enhance the national reputation. Generally these biographies tended to "proclaim America's glory and virtue to the world (and to America itself) and to instill virtues in sons imperiled by their temporal and cultural distance from the founding."[29] Memoirs and biographical sketches that appeared in monthly journals such as the *North American Review* and *Hunt's Merchants Magazine* presented the lives of merchant patriarchs as models of virtue worthy of young readers' imitation.[30] Such life stories operated in a mode of literary historiography that Hayden White likens to the "archetype of Romance" for its power to explicate complex events of history and social occurrences through a dramatically paced story of a nationally representative individual whose narrated experience of personal development was meant to be morally instructive.[31]

Despite the frontispiece portraits that offer a secure visual reference for the life being told, these accounts contain a fair amount of fiction as editors and authors interpreted source materials (letters, diaries, travel writings, and natural histories) to script the moralizing success of individual national heroes. The biographers did not need to work very hard in conjuring national pride. In their letters, merchants of Boston and New York and Philadelphia reveled in the national significance of speculative success even as this success required coordinating movement through several zones of national jurisdiction. The biographies also informed readers about the powerful social influence that successful China traders enjoyed at home. They were influential members of discussion clubs that included Emerson, Hawthorne, Cooper, and Washington Irving, and they collaborated on cultural projects, such as the Boston Athenæum, with two presidents of Harvard College who had

Thomas Sully, "Colonel Thomas Handasyd Perkins" (1831–1832). Oil on canvas, 287 × 195.6 cm. Boston Athenæum.

major influence on early national literature, Rev. Jared Sparks and the aforementioned Rev. Josiah Quincy.

The early merchant prince Colonel Thomas H. Perkins (1764–1854) offers a prime example of the dense social and intellectual imbrications of commerce and cultural influence in national biographical heroism. With his two brothers he made a massive fortune by pivoting from transatlantic commerce disrupted by the Haitian Revolution (1791–1804) to the China trade, where he grew rich speculating on tea, silver, furs and skins, and opium. When Perkins stopped making voyages to China, he pursued additional domestic investment opportunities in real estate and transportation, incorporating in Massachusetts one of the first U.S. railway ventures and investing in ironworks, canals, and western land.[32] At his death he had amassed a fortune of more than 1.6 million Spanish dollars, giving him the economic power of a contemporary multibillionaire during a time when there were far fewer superrich.[33] When Perkins stepped down as president of the Boston

Athenæum in 1832, Thomas Sully painted his portrait, featuring an exquisitely illustrated porcelain pitcher in the foreground.[34] The setting is Perkins's "warehouse office on Boston's India Wharf."[35]

The beneficiaries of the Perkins fortune extended several generations. John Murray Forbes (1813–98) was one of several nephews to follow his uncle into the China trade. In 1830 at the age of seventeen he went to Canton, returning a decade later with a fortune that enabled him to become one of the century's celebrated railroad builders and a major figure in New England's Brahmin society. He joined the Saturday Club with Emerson, Louis Agassiz, James Russell Lowell, Hawthorne, and others. Fanny Kemble entrusted Forbes with her manuscript *Scenes of Georgia Plantation* (1863) for delivery to Harper & Brothers in New York.[36] During the U.S. Civil War, he supervised the acquisition of steamships for the secretary of the navy, all the while keeping abreast of the Russell & Company in China.[37] In his posthumous memoir, *Letters and Recollections of John Murray Forbes* (1899), he recounts managing recruitment of the Fifty-Fourth and Fifty-Fifth Massachusetts Regiments. Colonel Robert Gould Shaw was his younger cousin.[38] His son William Hathaway Forbes never went to China, but his father's fortune helped to pave his road to economic success and social prestige. After serving in the Civil War, he went on to become the first president of the American Bell Telephone Company, the precursor of the American Telephone and Telegraph Company (AT&T).[39] He married Edith Emerson, the daughter of Ralph Waldo Emerson. When John Murray Forbes died, Emerson's son Edward W. Emerson eulogized him the *Atlantic Monthly*, beginning the life summary with his making a fortune in the China trade, which laid the capital foundation for his westward accomplishments as the prime investor in the "great Chicago, Burlington and Quincy" rail system, "with its seven thousand miles of well-laid road, a perfect equipment and organization, connecting the great Indian-corn country with the markets of the world."[40] Forbes and his uncle Colonel Perkins were among several China traders who committed to railway development upon their return.[41]

Curiously, despite substantial social and familial connections to the Forbes family, Emerson's particular rise as a cultural icon tended to obscure early national connections to China in the early twentieth century. Scholars celebrated Emerson as the era's most intellectually respectable idealist, inspired by religious philosophy from India that enabled him to break out of the confining orthodoxy of Puritanism and Unitarianism. In contrast to Emerson, American missionaries who traveled and lived throughout the world were cast as small-minded and provincial Christians of little importance. For example, Arthur Christy begins *The Orient in American Transcendentalism: A Study of Emerson, Thoreau, and Alcott* (1932) by

John Murray Forbes at nineteen, "From a miniature by Chinnery about 1832." Frontispiece to *Letters and Recollections of John Murray Forbes*, vol. 1.

writing: "This book is a study of the beginnings of American interest in Oriental thought. Traffic with the Orient began when Yankee clipper-ships entered the China trade, but for decades the traffic was almost alone in economic values."[42] After dismissing the cultural impact of the China trade, Christy appreciates Emerson's "Transcendentalism" for not merely "breaking Puritan intolerance" but also for expressing an "inherent sympathy with Oriental thought" and "spiritual values."[43]

What are these spiritual values? Frederic Ives Carpenter explains in *Emerson and Asia* (1930) that Emerson was interested in Hinduism as "a symbol for the unknown—for the other half of the world—for mystery, and romance, and poetry, and love, and religion."[44] Eighty years later, David Weir insightfully notes in *American Orient* (2011) that interest in Hinduism rose at the turn of the century as Unitarian sensibilities gained firm cultural footing; however, Emerson's engagement with Hinduism was itself quite superficial, his idealistic energy trumping more

"J. M. Forbes, At 68." Frontispiece to *Letters and Recollections of John Murray Forbes*, vol. 2.

careful understanding.[45] John Eperjesi concludes in *The Imperialist Imaginary* (2005) that "the most coherent thing that can be said about the representations of Asia in Emerson's poems and essays is that they are marked by more than a few contradictions and inconsistencies. As a devout idealist, Emerson based his generalizations at first on secondary readings, and then on primary readings, of religious texts, such as the *Vishnu Purana*, the *Upanishads*, and the *Bhagavad Gita*, and therefore could do little but furnish his imagination with a highly abstracted and dehistoricized Asia."[46] Filtering an early national view of Asia through a transcendental movement inspired by Emerson's readings of the *Upanishads* makes China and the China trade seem quite irrelevant to Emerson's social and intellectual circles. However, missionaries—funded by the U.S. merchants with whom Emerson socialized—lived for decades in China and produced documents that set the foundation of United States–based Sinology and fill out the story of antebellum United States–China relations.

China and the Global Geography of Early American Missionary Printing

In U.S. literary and cultural studies, missionaries to China have received even less attention than the merchants. And yet the extent of their print publications expands the geographic perspective of early national faith, commerce, and diplomacy to a global scale. One such work is Samuel Wells Williams's aforementioned two-volume book, *The Middle Kingdom: A Survey of the Geography, Government, Literature, Social Life, Arts, and History of the Chinese Empire and Its Inhabitants* (1848; 1883).[47] After arriving in China in 1833, Williams spent the next forty-six years in Canton, Macao, Hong Kong, Peking, and Shanghai printing comprehensive commercial guides and compiling dictionaries. He dedicated himself to learning how to read, speak, write, and print Chinese, enabling him to serve as the secretary to the U.S. diplomatic legation during the momentous decades from the mid-1850s until his retirement from China in 1876.

Williams's *The Middle Kingdom* is especially salient to the romances of the China trade because it blends commerce and Christianity in the pursuit of extraterritorial print evangelism. The commercial assumptions behind Williams's printing endeavors resonate in the title of his book. Its various editions are loaded with civilizing implications that exceed any literal translation of the phrase *zhōng guó* (中國)—which one could render alternatively as *middle/central* and *state/people/ country*.[48] In 1848 Williams explains what is at stake in the title: "I have called [this book] the Middle Kingdom, chiefly that being the meaning of the most common name for the country among the people themselves; and also, from the Chinese holding a middle place between civilization and barbarism,—China being the most civilized pagan nation in her institutions and literature now existing."[49] By asserting that the Chinese people refer to themselves as the Middle Kingdom, Williams hints at the nefarious influence of ancient Asiatic despotism (viz. the works of Montesquieu and Adam Smith), the inferiority of which he goes on to catalog.[50] The phrase does more than merely refer to "China" (a word whose origin Williams also tries to explain). It assigns China's relative natural historical status, above the stages of savagery and barbarism in the lower tier of "civilization" but, as a "pagan nation," beneath any civilized Christian nation.

China's claim was not just a curiosity but a challenge, implying China's pagan disrespect for Christian nations. The phrase Middle Kingdom marginalized Western nations in the long history of human development, putting them on the periphery of the world's oldest civilization. China's history outstretched Greece and Rome. Centuries before the birth of Jesus, China had practiced "upon a vast scale all the industrial arts, whether rural or manufacturing" to "maintain the largest population ever united under one system of rule"; from a longer range and literally millennial perspective of "ten centuries" China was "the most civilized nation on earth."[51] In comparison, the thirteenth-century travels of Marco Polo were recent. Polo had moved eastward from Venice, across the Silk Road and through Kublai Khan's Cathay to a "Chinese Empire" that was "one of the most extensive domin- ions ever swayed by a single power in any age, or any part of the world."[52] Since Polo told his stories, three dynasties of the Yuan (1271–1368), the Ming (1368–1644), and the Qing (1644–1911) had governed shifting territorial boundaries that Williams attempts to survey as the Middle Kingdom. And so, long ago when China was the pinnacle of human accomplishment and wealth, its emperor had reasonably ad- opted the phrase "*Chung Kwoh*, or Middle Kingdom," believing himself to be "sit- uated in the centre of the earth" and deserving of the tribute of all other barbarian peoples who lay beyond its influence. However, times had changed. In the modern era the phrase was evidence of ancient China's "ignorance" of its true "geographi- cal position" and "rank among the nations."[53]

The once great civilization of China had become not only ancient but also stag- nant. Why, over the many centuries, had China not continued to develop? Wil- liams's answer was that it lacked Christianity, "the summary of all civilization."[54] His ideal brand of Christianity is a democratized Protestantism "of the people," unfettered by social "forms and contracted into a priesthood"; he asserts that, "without this spring of action," "the attainments of the Chinese in the arts of life are perhaps as great as they can be."[55] The book's subtitle echoes the geographic sensibilities by which Williams hoped to correct the situation. Spreading the good word would break down China's barbaric sense of world centrality. It would prove that Protestant Europe was at the center of the modern world and that the United States was on the rise. Recognizing this, China would open itself up to trade with the civilized nations of the modern world and reap the civilizing benefits.

Commercial activity ideally furthered Williams's religious mission. With tea God had put into motion a civilizing plan. By describing tea, Williams is able to admire ancient and pagan China while allegorizing the civilizing effect of a rela- tively modern synergy of Christianity and commerce. In both volumes of the 1848 edition, he invokes Francis Bacon's Aphorism 129 of *Novum Organum* (1620) to credit China as "a people, from whom some of the most distinguished inventions of modern Europe came (such as the compass, porcelain, gunpowder, and print- ing)."[56] In the second volume of 1848, he replaces porcelain with tea, ascribing to "China and Chinese ingenuity" the "four things which have worked marvelous changes in the social condition, intercourse, disputes and mental improvement of mankind," now listed as "Tea, gunpowder, printing, and the compass."[57] By adding tea, Williams conjures a fantastic commodity that serves divine intentions in bridging the East and West through reciprocal commercial flow, thus realizing a world system of Christian nations.

Williams's allegory of tea runs something like this. Two centuries after the fall of Constantinople had stymied eastward land traffic from Europe to China, Polo's *Il Milione* inspired Columbus to sail west. A century later the Dutch and British introduced Chinese tea to Europe, provoking a revolutionary change in world relations through the consumers' growing demand for this novel beverage.

> The demand for [tea] gradually encouraged the Chinese to a greater production, and then succeeded the consumption of one and another foreign article taken in exchange for it, while the governments of the west derive too much advantage from the duties on it lightly to permit the Chinese to interfere with or hamper the trade, much less stop it. Thus one influence and another, some beneficial and others adverse, have been brought into action, until the encouraging prospect is now held out that this hitherto secluded portion of mankind is to be introduced into the family of nations, and partake of their privileges; and these consequences have gradually come about from the predilection for a pleasant beverage.[58]

This description naturalizes commerce in the circulation of an indigenous Chinese commodity moving across the globe to meet consumers' demand for it. Tea springs from soil of the Middle Kingdom, appeals to the literal taste of civilized Christians, and solicits the speculative endeavors of Western merchants. Ideally, this demand for tea would then spur China to produce and to supply more, completing a mutually beneficial circle of burgeoning exchange. The results are as profitable as they are spiritually profound, leading to the world's "family of nations" to adopt China: "The gradual introduction and use of this beverage among the nations of the west, and the most important consequences of bringing the two into more intimate intercourse, and opening to Chinese the blessings of Christian civilization, resulting from the trade, is one of the most interesting results that have ever flowed from commerce."[59] The phrase "flowed from commerce" naturalizes the process of exchange and resource distribution, suggesting that commerce just happens, beyond political calculations, albeit in accordance with a divine design that Williams hopes to further through his missionary work as a printer.

A world economy centering on tea, however, was not so easy to navigate. To turn demand for tea into profits, U.S. merchants had to figure out how to purchase it. Standing in their way was China's Asian despot whose regulations monopolized the tea leaves as his pagan subjects cowered in fear. To this point, Williams invokes the virtuous revolutionary protest of the Boston Tea Party, asserting that nothing comparable had "ever occurred in China or any other Asiatic country."[60] In allegorizing tea as a divine seed of civilizing free-trade circulation, Williams does not mention silver or opium, or any of the controversies that precipitated the First Opium War between Britain and China. His vision of tea is a vehicle of profitability and spiritual enlightenment that builds up the United States as a commercial republic while ignoring the multiple political clashes and competitive tensions bound up in *trade* at Canton.

The American Romance of Free-Trade Imperialism in China

Williams's commercial allegory of tea's civilizing effects reflects several different meanings of the phrase *free trade* as it related to the dynamics of early U.S. cultural formation during a time when Britain, Holland, Portugal, and Spain controlled the networks bearing on the China trade. In the 1780s literal trade with China inspired post-Revolutionary Americans to express pride in their distinctiveness as a newly free nation that had broken the bonds of colonial subordination. By the letter of Britain's mercantile laws, the Navigation Acts of the 1650s and 1660s had restricted the colonies to trading directly with the imperial center, and monopoly companies such as Britain's East India Company were chartered by the Crown in order to eliminate competition in raising and directing investment capital. Resentment in colonial North America peaked before the Revolutionary War as various taxes highlighted the degree to which colonists were expected to accept any regulations dictated to them. As James Fichter explains, the Boston Tea Party protested the relegation of colonialists' rights: "For Patriots, tea signified monopoly as much as anything else—the monopoly of the East India Company, which engrossed all British trade with Asia."[61] As U.S. merchants invested in ships that proudly sailed unfettered by the British mercantilism and flew a new flag, free trade might be best rendered as the "freedom to trade." The bigger question was whether these ships could navigate waters and ports controlled by the Dutch, Portuguese, French, Spanish, and other powers without protection of the Union Jack.

The increasing success of private American traders reverberated in England to fuel arguments against rechartering monopolies such as the EIC.[62] In the wake of the Peace of Paris (1783) the sailing was not always smooth, but private U.S. trading firms developed a reputation as "free traders" because they operated outside any monopoly privileges or restrictions in establishing their global routes and networks of finance. U.S. merchants secured their company charters through individual states (e.g., New York, Massachusetts, Pennsylvania) as colonial merchants had through the individual colonies before the Revolution. As a rule, they received no exclusive advantages from the federal government.[63] Their businesses were called "companies" but were of a very different kind from the East India companies of Britain, France, and Sweden. Part of their success came from the relative advantage of having less administrative oversight.[64] In the words of the eminent early twentieth-century trade historian Hosea Ballou Morse, "The Americans were the 'free-traders' of the day, in the sense in which the word was then understood; in their country there were no privileged corporations to exercise any monopoly, trade was open to all on equal terms, and the merchants and sailors of Boston, Salem, and New York asked only a fair field and no favour."[65]

In Britain, this U.S. example of free trade garnered rhetorical force in Whig protests against the government's chartering of monopolies. Liberal British merchants and textile manufacturers (primarily the Anti-Corn Law League based in Manchester) saw more opportunity in a world without the EIC and used U.S. companies to make their point.[66] Their line of argument followed Adam Smith's criticism of mercantilism in *An Inquiry into the Nature and Causes of the Wealth of Nations* (1776). For Smith, stockpiling gold and silver in the imperial center did not foster commercial success.[67] He championed the free flow of goods in an international marketplace where competing actors pursued self-interest as individuals. Out of this national competition would arise a general system in which resources tended to balance equitably as if guided by an invisible hand. The aggregate effect of individual pursuits created efficiencies in capital flows born out of market competition, thereby stabilizing a general confidence in the system that rewarded those who invested their labor and resources wisely. Under these principles of liberal economics, the best prescription for growing national wealth was to avoid interfering with the marketplace energies of individual actors, unless to counter the artificial restrictions (tariffs and taxes) of competitor nations or to protect national welfare against rogue manufacturing and financial factions, such as joint-stock companies, that might compromise national defense.[68] The EIC was thus a relic of the past, an antiprogressive bulwark blocking the revolutionary tide of free trade that had lifted the economic prospects of U.S. merchants.

Embracing free trade as a national ideal, U.S. merchants, missionaries, and diplomats often portrayed China as the pagan adversary of commercial Christendom. In this frame, China resisted free trade not on the principle of maintaining sovereignty but because it lacked a civilized understanding of its place in the world and its obligation to facilitate the demands presented by Western markets. Accordingly, China's imperial laws—even those seeking to ban the traffic of opium—did not *regulate* trade but *restricted* it in an arbitrary and corrupt exercise of political and economic power that sought to monopolize trade itself. Adam Smith makes this point in *Wealth of Nations* (1776) by figuring water as commerce to allegorize China's fall from imperial glory into despotic stagnation. As an ancient agrarian empire, China had grown very wealthy but also self-satisfied in its insular refusal to open its literal channels to the free flow of world commerce.[69] Smith finds it "remarkable, that neither the ancient Egyptians, nor the Indians, nor the Chinese, encouraged foreign commerce, but seem all to have derived their great opulence from this inland navigation."[70] China's agricultural resources had made it "the most fertile, best cultivated, most industrious, and most populous country in the world," and this agricultural bounty had been possible because "several great rivers" "form, by their different branches, a multitude of canals and, by communicating with one another, afford an inland navigation much more extensive than that either of the Nile or the Ganges, or, perhaps of both of them put together."[71] Alas, these hydraulic resources had not carried China forward into modern history but instead now isolated it as a moat encircles a castle. Having "acquired that full complement of riches which the nature of its laws and institutions permits it to acquire," China is stuck with tyrannical rulers who look down on the world's free-trading nations as barbarians.[72] The renaissance of China depended on linking its waterways to the world and communicating commercially with Western nations rather than merely irrigating its degenerate garden plots.

Smith's water motif allegorizes more than the political tyranny of the Middle Kingdom. It also implied China's moribund relationship to print media and its cultural incapacity to create socially meaningful outlets of print publication. As an ancient civilization, China had essentially been frozen and static for centuries. Thus, although Marco Polo had visited China "more than five hundred years ago," his descriptions of the kingdom's "cultivation, industry, and populousness" were still accurate, replicated in accounts from "travelers in the present times."[73] For Smith stereotype printing plates symbolize the frozen state of China's commerce, politics, and religion under the dynastic authoritarian rule. Chinese writers were stuck in a rut; incapable of adding anything new to reiterated descriptions of China, they also avoided potential curiosity about peoples outside the empire. In contrast, the dynamically curious Western readers could read printed pages to understand a "China" that was as rigid as the stereotype plates that had printed them.[74]

As the brief overview of Williams's phrase Middle Kingdom indicates, Smith's characterizations echoed frequently in the 1830s before the First Opium War as U.S. merchants, missionaries, and diplomats protested China's refusal to trade opium with Western nations and rationalized the prosecution of war and its consequences. Behind the war was the general question of who would control the terms of trade for tea in China. In the late seventeenth century after the fall of the Ming Dynasty, the new Qing emperor had stopped hosting Western diplomats in Peking; in the eighteenth century, new imperial edicts established the Canton System that quarantined most Western traders (with the exception of the Spanish and Portuguese) to the southern port city of Canton (see chapter 1). The goal of the Canton System was to pull in silver while preventing foreign expansion into Chinese territory. In *Wealth of Nations* Adam Smith hones in on Canton when illustrating his stereotype of stagnant China. Despite the country's immense wealth, the "poverty of the lower ranks of people in China far surpasses that of the most beggarly nations in Europe."[75] He makes his point by positing a scene, describing the many "thousand families" who "have no habitation on land, but live constantly in little fishing boats upon the rivers and canals," on such margins of "subsistence" that "they are eager to fish up the nastiest garbage throne overboard from any European ship. Any carrion, the carcass of a dead dog or cat, for example, though half putrid and stinking is as welcome to them as the most wholesome food of other countries."[76] He later concludes that, because China "neglects or despises foreign commerce" and "admits the vessels of foreign nations into one or two of its ports only," it "cannot transact the same quantity of business which it might do with different laws and institutions."[77]

Smith's multisensory description of a clogged and poverty-stricken Canton harbor reinforced the stereotype of China as a literally stagnating empire that needed the rejuvenating flows of unrestricted trade with Britain. When Lord Macartney led an embassy to Peking in 1792, the emperor Qianlong treated him like a subject from one of the Middle Kingdom's many tributaries and dispatched him with a message to deliver to King George III. After thanking "the British monarch for sending an ambassador to pay tribute to the Middle Kingdom," the emperor declared, "We have never valued ingenious articles, nor do we have the slightest need for your Country's manufacturers."[78] Throughout the nineteenth century, Anglo-American writers such as Williams invoked the Macartney embassy to reinforce Smith's image of a stagnant China whose modern commercial potential was being stifled by a petulant emperor ensconced in moldering ruins of Peking's Forbidden Palace.

Western merchants appealed to principles of free trade as justification for violating Chinese regulations that banned opium, a commodity with which Britain and the EIC eventually turned the tables of commercial power in Canton. At the time of Lord Macartney's embassy, the EIC systematized opium production in colonial Bengal. The EIC did not directly export opium to China but supervised its sale and distribution to private British traders in a network of country trade extending from West Bengal and other parts of India, through Southeast Asia, and into China. By brokering opium, the EIC had found a way to secure tea without silver. Although before the Opium War, some British and American merchants and missionaries thought it quite reasonable that China would ban the importation of opium to protect its population, other merchants adopted the mantra of "free trade" to insist on their right to traffic the drug. They cast Chinese laws, the Cohong merchant associations at Canton, and trade regulations as an affront to British honor and freedom—as an affront reflecting the pagan chauvinism of the ancient Middle Kingdom. Conflict over opium culminated in the First Opium War in which Britain punished China for destroying British property and secured the concessions of the Treaty of Nanking (1842) and the Treaty of Bogue (1843). These treaties effectively ended the Canton System by opening four additional ports for commerce. The treaty also annexed Hong Kong and charged China 21 million Spanish dollars for war reparations, outstanding debts to the British merchants, and the opium that China had confiscated and destroyed as the war commenced.

In the twentieth century, economic historians focused on these bellicose undercurrents of Western commerce in the phrase *free-trade imperialism*. As John Gallagher, Ronald Robinson, and Bernard Semmel explain, in the early nineteenth century Britain reworked its "system of mercantile colonialism" to stimulate international consumption of British manufactured and agricultural commodities.[79] After the EIC charter monopoly became less effective and eventually defunct (expiring in 1834), the new "colonial and trade policy" fostered colonial networks of private traders that strengthened England's position as the "Workshop of the World."[80] In the 1830s and 1840s, Britain's colonial pursuits in India, outright war with China, and "informal techniques of free trade" in Latin America and North America worked to foster "complementary satellite economies, which would provide raw materials and food for Great Britain, and also provide widening markets for its manufacturers."[81]

The United States was technically a neutral party in the First Opium War, but American merchants and missionaries did not just stand witness. They profited from the economy around it and, in the aftermath, strategized on how to use Britain's victory to their diplomatic advantage. Similarly, missionaries relished the greater access to potential converts in China. In effect, the call for free trade deprived China of the sovereignty to control trade with Britain, France, the United States, and other nations that was transacted in its territory. Trade was an imperative presented by diplomats as an ultimatum, backed up by gunboats and even territorial occupation. Refusal was not an option, and attempts at accommodation were often overwhelmed by major social upheavals.

Rhetorically the phrase free trade packed a particularly powerful punch in the transatlantic press, mobilizing the virtue of Christian commerce to justify the violation of Chinese laws against opium traffic. The British parliamentarian John Bowring and the former U.S. president John Quincy Adams illustrate the moral tenor of exulting free-trade imperialism. Bowring was the editor of the liberal *Westminster Review* and a free-trade politician who became the governor of colonial Hong Kong in the 1850s before the Second Opium War. Campaigning for election to Parliament in 1841, he is reported to have summed up his liberal convictions with the stunning declaration: "Jesus Christ is Free Trade and Free Trade is Jesus Christ."[82] The same year, Adams matched Bowring for boldness of interpretive license in a lecture to the Massachusetts Historical Society. Blaming the war on China's disregard of the "moral obligation of commercial intercourse between nations," he asserted China's violation of the sacred "Christian precept": "to love your neighbor as yourself."[83] As the nineteenth century wore on, the opposition between the Christian and the pagan took on an increasingly racial logic that distinguished Anglo-Saxons as the world-historical carriers of civilization.[84]

For early Americans the phrase free trade was this skein of connotations that relished the revolutionary implications of early national commerce while embracing the chance to make a fortune in China by circumventing the laws of pagan China. The ostensible contradiction of imposing conditions of trade on the Middle Kingdom did not generally bother most who embraced commerce as a profitable and edifying endeavor that promoted Christian civilization and the nation's Manifest Destiny to stretch across North America. For example, in negotiating the Treaty of Wanghia after the First Opium War, Caleb Cushing mimicked British gunboat diplomacy to secure what he characterized as China's concession of *absolute and unqualified* extraterritoriality, meaning that U.S. citizens in China would be exempt from Chinese laws and judged exclusively by U.S. law.[85] This treaty—the first between China and the United States—influenced subsequent diplomatic and military initiatives to open China further to trade after the Second Opium War. The treaty was also significant in U.S. diplomacy throughout broader East Asia. In his 1854 mission to Japan, Commodore Perry not only headquartered his mission in South China but also used Cushing's treaty as a blueprint for presenting Tokugawa Japan with a free-trade ultimatum. At the end of the nineteenth century, U.S. secretary of state John Hay followed the rhetorically softer example of U.S. minister Anson Burlingame in penning the Open Door Policy to prevent outright land grabbing in China while ensuring that Western nations would direct the flow of commerce through China in developing the steamboat routes, railroads, and telegraphy. The U.S. stake in the China trade had come a long way from the first foray of Major Shaw to Canton in 1784.

Bridging American Studies and China Studies

In showing how commerce, Christianity, and diplomacy intersected in early China-U.S. relations, I will move between literary and historical studies to connect scholarship produced in the fields of American studies and China studies, two areas of study that ran parallel for much of the twentieth century as research models of area study achieved institutional standing.[86] To say that Samuel Wells Williams laid the foundation for academic study of China in the United States might be overstating his importance, but only slightly. In 1877 he took up the first professorial post dedicated to Chinese language and literature in the United States at Yale University, and his son Frederick Wells Williams became an assistant professor of "Oriental History" and chairman of the executive committee of Yale-in-China. Other influential scholars with missionary backgrounds followed, including Kenneth Scott Latourette (*The History of Early Relations between the United States and China, 1784–1844*, 1917) and Tyler Dennett (*Americans in Eastern Asia: A Critical Study of the Policy of the United States with Reference to China, Japan and Korea in the 19th Century*, 1922). At Yale University today, the China Records Project at the Divinity School Library and the Sterling Memorial Library continues to organize a massive archive, including much of the missionary writings over the past two centuries.[87]

In the early twentieth century, the historiography of the China trade promised new understandings of early U.S. cultural development. Summarizing the vast historiography of China is not possible here, but consider the China-based administrator-turned-scholar Hosea Ballou Morse, writing in the first decades of the twentieth century. Born in Canada and raised in Massachusetts, Morse worked for decades with the Chinese Maritime Customs Service in China under British inspector general Robert Hart and as an administrator in Shanghai and Canton.[88] After retiring, he settled in Britain and published extensively, including the three-volume *International Relations of the Chinese Empire* (1910–18) and five-volume *Chronicles of the East India Company in China, 1635–1834* (1926–29), which contain much about the United States.[89] In their study *Gold of Ophir: The Lure That Made America* (1925), Sydney Greenbie and Marjorie Barstow Greenbie build on Morse's work in making the bold claim that "the trade with the Orient is one of two great economic facts of the history of the United States between the Revolution and the Civil War, the other fact being the development and westward extension of negro slavery. This trade not only set the Atlantic coast states on their feet after the Revolution: it furnished capital which gave them their initial industrial impetus."[90] One should add a third major economic fact with unexpected connections to the China trade: the attempted removal of Native Americans into the Far West through war accompanied by unequal and broken treaties of "peace, friendship and commerce."[91]

During and after the Cold War as China went through various revolutionary events (the Great Leap Forward and the Cultural Revolution), the relationship between the United States and China continued to receive attention. The "Far Eastern Association" was founded in 1943 and took the name Association for Asian Studies (AAS) in 1956. At Harvard University, John King Fairbank, who studied under Morse, wrote his dissertation on the Customs Service and published *The United*

States and China (1948).[92] Over the ensuing decades he and many others played a major role in developing the Center for East Asia Research at Harvard, shaping generations of scholars.[93]

Meanwhile, early twentieth-century U.S. literary and cultural studies generally overlooked all of East and Southeast Asia when outlining the nation's genteel tradition, main currents of early American thought, the high literary expression of the American Renaissance, and the myths and symbols of the Far West.[94] In the wake of World War II, the area studies model in the United States cut across the disciplinary grain of departmental organization and brought both political and social sciences to bear on the study of national and regional cultures. The American Studies Association was founded in 1951.[95] During the decades of the Cold War, area studies approaches benefited from funding and civic initiatives coordinated in part by government intelligence agencies and corporate interests that hoped to enlist universities in organizing formal and informal foreign policy responses to the era's communist adversaries and in promoting the United States as a bastion of "free enterprise and individual liberty," both at home and abroad.[96]

Throughout this period, U.S. scholars of American studies were developing the myths, symbols, and generic contours of a distinctly national literature and culture with a focus on the North American continent. The classic works of twentieth-century American studies tended to stay rooted in developing central myths and symbols of continental nature, savagery, and the frontier. Henry Nash Smith, R.W. B. Lewis, Leo Marx, Annette Kolodny, Myra Jehlen, Richard Slotkin and many others have explicated figures of the *wilderness*, the *virgin land*, the *garden*, the *West*, and the *middle landscape* in differentiating American cultural identity from both Europe and Native America.[97] These insightful tropes powerfully focus the promise and violence of Manifest Destiny on the contestation and reconfiguration of continental territory, yet China rarely receives sustained consideration.[98] Especially during wars in Korea and Vietnam, it is surprising that scholars in the areas of China studies and American studies did not have more to say to each other.

In *Orientalism* (1978) Edward Said echoed the conventional wisdom that the United States and China had been a world apart in the nineteenth century, even as he turned a skeptical eye to the imperial premises of defining, observing, and classifying "the East" in academic contexts, whether through nineteenth-century paradigms of Orientalism (emphasizing language, history, literature) or twentieth-century models of area studies (emphasizing social and political sciences). Focusing on Britain and France, Said considered U.S. imperialism in the Pacific to be a phenomenon with significance for the post–World War II era.[99] However, as John Carlos Rowe notes, Said revised his observation, recognizing legacies of U.S. imperialism in the nineteenth century.[100] Furthermore, Said influenced American literary scholars such as Eric Cheyfitz, Amy Kaplan, and Donald Pease, who have redirected attention to the fundamental role of empire in U.S. cultural formation.[101]

Helping to rectify the lack of exchange between China studies and American studies, scholarship has resituated U.S. cultural development in transatlantic or hemispheric contexts that could very reasonably extend the frame to the Pacific.[102] In brilliant readings of Cooper, Irving, and Twain, Stephanie LeMenager reconsidered their renderings of "continental territory" as a "loose collection of local and international economies," overturning foregone conclusions that the Far West would be territorially consolidated to manifest the nation.[103] Scholars such as Richard Drinnon, Arif Dirlik, John Eperjesi, Yunte Huang, Lisa Lowe, Mark Rifkin, Malini Johar Schueller, Ann Laura Stoler, and Rob Wilson have rendered accounts of U.S. imperialism in Hawai'i, the Philippines, Samoa, and Guam, exploring the political implications of categorical terms such as China, the East, the Orient, Asia, the Pacific, and the Pacific rim.[104] Demonstrating the powerful allure of the East Indies in the early American imagination as an international zone of commercial promise centering on China, Alfred Owen Aldridge, John Kuo Wei Tchen, Jacques M. Downs, Malini Johar Schueller, Caroline Frank, John R. Haddad, Hsuan L. Hsu, Eric Dolin, Jim Egan, David Weir, Kariann Akemi Yokota, Teemu Ruskola, Guoqi Xu, Selina Lai-Henderson, Gordon H. Chang, and Michael Block have filled out the picture.[105] Their insight comes in part from developing the imaginative force of the U.S.-China relations that historians have extensively covered over the past century; in addition to the previously cited work of Jacques M. Downs and James Fichter, this impactful historiography includes works by Leonard Blussé, Paul Cohen, Jonathan Goldstein, Yen'ping Hao, Michael Hunt, Christopher Munn, Jonathan Spence, Elizabeth Sinn, Paul A. Van Dyke, and Frederic Wakeman.[106]

As for American studies, recent transnational critical approaches have complemented the interdisciplinary ones to bridge various area studies, especially in recognizing connections between the early United States and China.[107] The idea of the nation remains an insightful frame of reference or scale of comprehension, even if the conventional senses of national time and space can seem "glaring[ly] inadequate" in the terms Wai Chi Dimock explains in *Through Other Continents* (2006).[108] The writers here considered asserted the cultural significance of the United States in global geographies and in the *longue durée* of history, even as domestic events threatened the foundational premise of confederative union. Benedict Anderson's dynamics of imagining community have provided important frames of reference in reaching to the international contexts of print culture, and Giovanni Arrighi's *Long Nineteenth Century* (1994) and Andre Gunder Frank's *ReOrient: Global Economy in the Asian Age* (1998) have considered the span of historical frames to recognize world systems of overlapping sovereign states and the changing patterns of capital concentration and dispersal.[109] Henri Lefebvre's *The Production of Space* (1974) and Johannes Fabian's *Time and the Other: How Anthropology Makes Its Object* (1983) outline the intersecting relation of space and time for U.S. writers who objectified "China" as standing not just far away but long ago in the deep and ancient past, beyond the temporal pale of civilized history in which the putatively innovative, progressive, free-trading Christian nations realized comity through market-based competition.[110]

Of course, Edward Said's relational senses of orientialism remain fundamental. As Dirlik observes, moments of contact between peoples are rarely episodes of total "domination" and invariably involve degrees of "exchange, even if it is unequal exchange."[111] This is very true of the China trade, in which legal and political orders successfully controlled the terms of interaction until the early nineteenth century.[112] Canton and Macao were "contact zones" where people met in order to do business and to work in practical ways across differences of language and culture.[113] Appreciating the active role of Chinese people in these contact zones, Paul A. Van Dyke and John D. Wong have pursued deeply insightful studies of the Chinese merchants in South China; and, with an eye to the United States, Mae N. Ngai has looked back to the Philadelphia Centennial of 1876 to consider Chinese participation in shaping exhibits.[114]

Translation is an abiding and complicated concern in building a case for the relevance of China to the early United States, because one must not only consider actual moments of communicative interaction across languages and cultures but also how writers represented cross-cultural communication.[115] Lydia Liu's work is particularly important for debunking fantasies of transparent communication, especially in contexts of commerce, business, and trade—words with different connotations, enveloped by a general assumption of mutually beneficial exchange.[116] My U.S.-focused perspective may risk distorting Chinese history by exaggerating or misconstruing the importance of these merchants, missionaries, and diplomats in regard to the total history of China.[117] There is no easy way around this except to broaden the scope to an explicitly global history, and such a project would stretch many volumes instead of supplementing the literary historical record that it informs.

Finally, for early American writers striving to realize a distinct sense of national identity, the terms *European* and *Western* are slippery. In their writing these U.S. merchants, missionaries, and diplomats depicted Catholic empires of Portugal and Spain as old and degenerating, balanced admiration and affiliation with Protestant Europe (Britain and the Netherlands), and mythologized the Roman Empire's republic—shadowed by its eminent overrun by Germanic hordes—centuries before the advent of a united country of Italy. American distinctiveness resonated locally, regionally, nationally, continentally, and globally across the hemispheres and in relation to multiple Others (racial, cultural, religious, and linguistic). Thus, in foregrounding the layered audiences of these early U.S. texts, "Orientalism" might be best characterized as "a network of aesthetic, economic, and political relationships that cross national and historical boundaries"—a network in which authors, editors, publishers, readers, and teachers retraced dividing lines between East and West in a process of becoming American that continues to this day.[118]

CHAPTER ONE

Characterizing the American China Trader

The Global Geography of Opium Traffic in Josiah Quincy's
The Journals of Major Samuel Shaw (1847)

The philosopher and lover of man have much harm to say of trade; but the historian will see that trade was the principle of Liberty; that trade planted America and destroyed Feudalism; that it makes peace and keeps peace, and will abolish slavery. We complain of its oppression of the poor, and of its building up a new aristocracy on the ruins of the aristocracy it destroyed. But the aristocracy of trade has no permanence, it is not entailed, was the result of toil and talent, the result of merit of some kind, and is continually falling, like the waves of the sea, before new claims of some sort.

RALPH WALDO EMERSON, "The Young American" (1844)

Today Major Samuel Shaw (1754–94) is not widely known. But in his day he was well connected to men of political and financial influence, having served as the aide-de-camp to General Henry Knox in the Revolutionary War. After the war he wrote the constitution for an exclusive organization of war veterans known as the Society of Cincinnati. His first major sea voyage was to China when, months after the Peace of Paris, he accompanied Captain John Green on the *Empress of China* to the southern Chinese city of Canton, contemporary Guangzhou (Guǎng-zhōu; 廣州). As the ship's supercargo, he oversaw the payload of ginseng and silver on behalf of investors who included Robert Morris, the ill-fated early national financier and signatory of the Declaration of Independence. The *Empress of China* arrived in China in November 1784 and headed back to New York two months later loaded with tea. Shaw estimated the profit at an encouraging 25 percent and initially sang the high praise of ginseng as a wealth-generating commodity.[1] In total he made four voyages to Canton (in 1784–85, 1786–89, 1790–92, and 1793–94), becoming "the first American consul at Canton," an appointment President George Washington renewed in 1790. As a merchant, Shaw and his brothers enjoyed only modest success.

More important than making the four voyages, Shaw wrote about them in reports to the U.S. secretary of foreign affairs John Jay, newspaper articles, and a

Frontispiece to Samuel Shaw, *The Journals of Major Samuel Shaw*. Courtesy of the Kislak Center for Special Collections, Rare Books and Manuscripts, Van Pelt-Dietrich Library Center, University of Pennsylvania.

journal of his first two voyages.[2] The newspaper articles might have caught the eye of merchants such as John Jacob Astor, Stephen Girard, and Colonel Thomas H. Perkins who had turned to Canton in the wake of the Haitian Revolution (1791–1804), which disrupted their transatlantic operations. But Shaw's voyage journals are most valuable. They offer a fascinating overview of the Canton System through which China regulated trade with Western nations from the Portuguese enclave of Macao up the Pearl River to the harbor in Canton. They also reflect Shaw's broadening geographic understanding of the China trade as he moved beyond exchanging ginseng for tea and strategized on how to coordinate a basket of commodities in the commercial networks of South and Southeast Asia as opium traffic took off. Shaw even visited Bengal, where the British East India Company (EIC) cultivated opium and auctioned it to private British traders for transport to China in the country trade. He offers a firsthand account of how opium became a powerful commodity in the China trade. On his fourth and final voyage, he continued to probe how to integrate India into his commercial network, visiting Bombay on route to Canton, where he became very ill.[3] While rounding Africa on his return to Boston in 1794, he died at age thirty-nine.

Embedded in Shaw's description of trade logistics are his uncertainties over what it meant to be an American citizen of an independent national republic after the Revolution. He is sensitive to how he and the *Empress of China* present the United States to people across transatlantic and transpacific zones of commerce. Taking pride in representing the new nation for which he had fought, he proudly reports the respectful reception of the ship by the Chinese in Canton and gauges degrees of association with and distinction from British, Dutch, French, Portuguese, Spanish, and Swedish peoples along the way.

Today Shaw's journals and letters are especially important because subsequent editors revised them to tell new generations the story of the first interactions between China and the United States. Decades after his death, Shaw was back on the cultural radar due to the editorial work of two former presidents of Harvard College who had a particularly strong impact on early national literary culture. The first was Rev. Jared Sparks (1789–1866), the prominent Unitarian minister who became a professor at Harvard College and its president from 1849 to 1853. He was the founding editor of the *North American Review* and shaped the genre of early national biography by editing the Library of American Biography in two series of ten (1834–38) and fifteen (1844–47) volumes. Scott E. Casper explains that Sparks considered "biography a branch of history, with a mission akin to the state historical societies founded in these years: preserving America's fast-fading past, separating documentary 'truth' from unreliable 'tradition' or lore before it was too late."[4] After the U.S. Congress opened the diplomatic archive for Sparks to review for publication in the 1820s, Major Shaw's account of the first U.S. commercial voyage circulated nationally and internationally.[5] It found a particularly interested audience in Canton where the U.S. missionaries Elijah Bridgman and Samuel Wells Williams summarized Shaw's account in the *Chinese Repository*, a monthly journal.[6]

A decade later, Major Shaw resurfaced again. His adopted nephew Robert Gould Shaw had become a very successful merchant and preserved his uncle's writings, including the voyage journals and wartime letters that Shaw wrote to his father and brothers during the Revolution—letters expressing anger over war profiteers, desperation as his service left him without money to clothe himself, and doubts over the fiscal future of the United States. To honor his uncle, Robert Gould Shaw handed over his uncle's writings to Rev. Josiah Quincy III.[7] Quincy was also very influential. He preceded Sparks as president of Harvard College and served as a U.S. congressional representative of Massachusetts, the mayor of Boston, and the president of the Boston Athenæum (succeeded by the Boston merchant and philanthropist Colonel Thomas H. Perkins).[8]

Quincy synthesized Major Shaw's letters and journals in *The Journals of Major Samuel Shaw, the First American Consul at Canton, with a Life of the Author* (1847). The book, which begins with a preface and Quincy's "Life of the Author," casts Shaw as a determined Revolutionary War veteran who finds his highest distinction as an early national commercial hero of the China trade. In the editorial hands of Quincy, Major Shaw's account of the China trade does more than inform readers about the China trade or Shaw's life. The memoir bridges the historical distance between 1776 and 1847, redeeming Shaw's anxiety about national disunion in a romance of commerce with China. The book's very title designates Shaw as both a "Major" and as "the First American Consul at Canton," and the preface emphasizes China's importance in claiming that it "was [Shaw's] fortune and happiness during his residence in that city [of Canton], by his official influence, to give to its inhabitants the first impression of the character and resources of a new nation, of even whose existence the Chinese had previously no knowledge."[9] In the template of national biography promoted by Sparks and Quincy, Shaw's individual experience takes on nationally representative significance. His trustworthy "character" ("elevated and chivalric," "imbued" with a high "sense of honor") becomes a narrative "character" with whom readers can identify as fellow Americans.[10] In reviewing the book, the *North American Review* guided readers toward such identification, claiming that Shaw's memoir "illustrates one of the most pleasing characters that adorned the times of our great national struggle."[11]

As Shaw's individual success in China reflects national achievement, crises of national confederation seemingly dissolve in predictions of profits to come. Shaw's ruminations over wartime sacrifice, lingering doubts over national solvency, and shock over the brutal practice of the slave trade become tests that the nation passes with flying colors as Quincy molds the narrative trajectory of Shaw's China career. Reading about Major Shaw's early national struggle, readers in 1847 are invited to appreciate how much the United States had developed and to see present international speculation bearing on China as supporting future realization of continental Manifest Destiny.

Not everyone appreciated Quincy's attempt to recast Revolutionary War veterans as a heroic China traders or to idolize New England's merchant princes as paragons of virtue. Herman Melville was particularly cynical about the conditions of international commerce and the virtue of those who won fortunes in its pursuit. He wrote two works of fiction—*Israel Potter* (1855) and *Benito Cereno* (1856)—that criticize both the mercenary means of building wealth in China and the editorial transmutation of social crises into commercial quest narratives with happy end-ings; they are discussed respectively later in this chapter and in chapter 2.

Mapping a United "New People" for China

Planning the initial commercial venture to China after the Revolution, Shaw and his fellow investors were first challenged with securing a commodity to trade for tea. Silver was what China wanted, but it was scarce. Initial plans considered a payload of beaver pelts.[12] For the *Empress of China*, the solution was ginseng, an indigenous root harvested from the shaded mountainside forests of Appalachia.[13] In his journal, Shaw noted the economic potential of the exchange: "Soon after the close of the war between Great Britain and America, several merchants in New York and Philadelphia being desirous of opening a commerce with Canton, in China, a ship was purchased and loaded principally with ginseng, in order to ex-change it for teas and the manufactures of that country."[14] In newspaper articles and reports to Secretary of State Jay he went so far as to predict during his second voyage (1786) that "advantages which America derives from her ginseng" will gen-erate the wealth equivalent to "mines of silver and gold" controlled by Spain in the Americas.[15] Needless to say, the China trade proved much more complicated for the post-Revolutionary United States.

In 1784 ginseng helped the American voyagers meet the elementary challenges of trading for tea, but the challenge of explaining what it meant to be a new and unified nation remained. The *Empress of China* arrived in Canton to face initial confusion over whether the Americans were in fact different from the British—the ship's crew spoke English, looked British, and flew a flag of red, white, and blue. Shaw reports clearing things up with the map: "Ours being the first American ship that had ever visited China, it was some time before the Chinese could fully com-prehend the distinction between Englishmen and us. They styled us the *New People*, and when, by the map, we conveyed to them an idea of the extent of our country, with its present and increasing population, they were not a little pleased at the prospect of so considerable a market for the productions of their own empire."[16] In China, Shaw found a clarifying distance from which to idealize a more perfect union in North America. It is unclear whether Shaw is referring to a particular map prepared for the occasion or to "the map" as a practical technology of navigation and textual geography by which to represent the United States on paper, parch-ment, or vellum. Either way, thousands of miles away from Boston, Shaw oriented his "New People" in the world, projecting the extent of his nation's continental territory as a premise for portentous commercial agreements between the United

States and China. It is hard to say whether Shaw's interlocutors understood what Shaw claims that they did. A map of North American could easily have exposed the uncertainties of such a union that contradicted the presentation of a single market.

In utilizing "the map" to communicate with the Chinese, Shaw nevertheless suggests the global scale of the developing nation's spatial imaginary. The ginseng roots on which Shaw's voyage speculated had been pulled from the mountainside forests of Appalachia stretching from Virginia to Pennsylvania and New York. The goal was to insert this home-harvested commodity into a world market in ways that generated profitable exchange. The challenge of doing so echoes in the opening address of the odd letter that the Continental Congress provided to the voyagers; in requesting respect for the captain of the *Empress of China* in his efforts to "transact his business," it strains to address "Emperors, Kings, Republicks, Princes, Dukes, Earls, Barons, Lords, Burgomaster, Coucillors, as also Judges, Officers, Justiciares of Regents of all good Cities and places whether ecclesiastical or secular."[17] The letter is witnessed rather than signed by the president, Thomas Mifflin, echoing concern over centralized political authority that proved necessary for pulling the post-Revolutionary states together as a republic.

Presenting the United States as continuing to grow beyond its colonial borders, Shaw consolidated "a market," but what could he have exactly meant by the "extent of our country"? Before the U.S. Constitution was drafted in 1787, the Articles of Confederation guaranteed sovereignty to each of the states, thus crippling federal efforts to raise revenue through taxation, to finance a national navy, and to arbitrate interstate tensions regarding borders and tariffs. To paraphrase Noah Webster, the United States seemed but a fragile cobweb of a pretended union made up of thirteen nations with separate commercial agendas. Border conflicts loomed ominously in the Far West. There were severe financial troubles within each state as well. Farmers and bankers within Massachusetts disagreed on the proper role of government in a fiscal environment sorely lacking hard currency. During Shaw's second voyage to China in 1786, as various states' monetary notes competed for legitimacy, the former Continental Army soldier Daniel Shay and fellow farmers became so desperate for credit that they took up arms against the governments of State and Union.

When he had been a Continental army officer, Shaw had worried about the fiscal foundation of the new nation. In letters to his father and brothers, he rails against war profiteers, complains about the personal financial devastation of hyperinflation, and laments the general insolvency of a young nation that lacked a dependable currency. Financially adrift but socially connected, Shaw turned to the China trade rather unexpectedly. Distinguished service to General Henry Knox had left him penniless but well connected. After the war, he did not put his faith in schemes of representative democracy but in the Society of Cincinnati, which restricted future membership to society members' patrilineal descendants. Members of the Society of Cincinnati were well represented in the venture, including the ship's captain John Green and Shaw's junior supercargo Thomas Randall, with whom Shaw partnered on subsequent voyages. Benjamin Franklin even had a nominal investment of seven dollars that appears in Captain John Green's account book.[18] In any case, given Shaw's own anxieties over the financial viability of the nation, mapping out his fellow "New People" in a single "market" might have been as self-reassuring for Shaw as it was novel to the Chinese.[19]

Imagining ginseng's spectacular marketability in China also enabled Shaw to disclaim the brutality of the transatlantic slave trade. On the voyage out, he first witnessed its practice and it horrified him. Crossing the Atlantic in 1784, the *Empress of China* approached Port Pray on Portugal's St. Jago Island in the Cape Verdes Islands, where they stopped for repairs. Shaw sets the scene by explaining that "the trade of the island is conducted by a company, who have a factory not far from the fort. Their vessels arrive here from Lisbon, whence they go to the coast of Africa for slaves, which they dispose of in their other islands, and return here to complete their homeward cargoes."[20] While anchored off the island, Shaw observes a "French brig, on her way to Cape François, with a cargo of slaves, from Senegal."[21] Shaw's exposition suggests deep ambivalence. He hopes for national recognition from the French ship even as he registers his shocking impressions of slavery. Shaw reports that the French captain boarded the *Empress of China* to pay his respects but also mentions that his ship held "one hundred and twenty-three slaves, that cost [the captain], on an average, about five crowns a head, who he hoped would come to good market at the Cape."[22] The ship's departure on the next morning tests Shaw's powers of description:

> The French brig sailed the next morning, and in the passage gave us a salute of four swivels and *Vive le Roi!* which we returned with three cheers. A number of the naked blacks were on deck,— poor creatures, going to a state of hopeless slavery, and, torn from every tender connection, doomed to eat the bread and drink the water of affliction for the residue of their miserable lives! Good God! and is it man, whose distinguishing characteristic should be humanity and the exercise of every milder virtue, who wears sweet smiles and looks erect on heaven,— is it man, endowed by thee with a capacity for enjoying happiness and suffering misery, to whom thou has imparted a knowledge of thyself, enabled him to judge of right and wrong, and taught to believe in a state of future retribution,— is it man, who, thus trampling upon the principles of universal benevolence, and running counter to the very end of his creation, can

become a fiend to torment his fellow-creatures, and deliberately effect the temporal misery of beings equally candidates with himself for a happy immortality?[23]

Shaw hoped to relish the French ship's recognition of the American vessel but does not overlook the "naked blacks" on the ship's deck. With the refrain "is it man?" he questions the humanity of the French slavers who commit moral outrages in pursuit of profit, sounding more like de Crèvecoeur's narrator of *Letters from an American Farmer* (1782) describing "Negro slavery" in Charlestown than like a merchant adventurer.[24] In this context, ginseng helped Shaw delimit his participation in the world economy by fantasizing a cohesive United States flush with a desirable commodity that did not depend on slave labor as did cotton and tobacco. Over the next decade, the merchants who built great fortunes in Shaw's footsteps were much less sensitive to the cruelty of the slave trade as they brokered the sale of the enslaved and worked out ways of ensuring their transport, rationalizing their endeavors with very different senses of virtue and benevolence.

Over his four voyages Shaw surely recognized the hyperbole of comparing ginseng to silver. But there are indications that his promotion worked to fuel public optimism over the China trade, especially early on when the success of the first U.S. voyage to China reverberated in newspapers in New York, Philadelphia, and Boston. The early national poet Philip Freneau amplified the voyage's significance in the poem "On the First American Ship That Explored the Rout[e] to China, and the East-Indies after the Revolution" (1797). Its cadence of iambic tetrameter, chopped into eight short stanzas of four lines apiece, evokes the wobble of a rowboat, but it might have stuck in the head of newspaper readers in New York and Philadelphia. Freneau's *Empress* passes landmarks of the global commerce—around the "Stormy Cape," to the "countries plac'd in burning climes" and through Indonesian straits with "islands of remotest times."[25] And Freneau's "Chinesean shores" promise China's eager consent to mutually beneficial exchange.[26] Tea and porcelain are low-hanging fruit for courageous Americans with a ship, trading capital, and the national pride in no longer being repressed by King George and his court. Shaw's promotion of ginseng echoes in Freneau's verse. The root serves as a fantastical commodity of unbounded reciprocity, enabling perpetual exchange between the United States and China, smoothing out terms of exchange that would prove to be fraught with difficulties.

Freneau's poem makes another false claim in gloating that no foreigner had shown "our native oak its way." In fact, a French ship did precisely that, escorting the *Empress of China* through the archipelago of contemporary Indonesia. In August 1784 the Americans were anxious about navigating the straits where currents were swift and natives might be hostile. When happening to meet the French ship

Triton, Shaw was overjoyed to find it captained by M. d'Ordelin, a wartime acquaintance who had served in the Revolutionary War and who held the Society of Cincinnati in high regard. The *Triton* guided the *Empress of China* onward from the Isle of Gaspar. Nineteen days later Captain Green anchored in the shallow waters near small islands about three miles outside of the Portuguese-administrated port city of Macao at the mouth of the Pearl River. The *Empress of China* fired the ship cannons thirteen times in salute to signal its arrival and waited.[27] However, arrival to "Chinesean shores" was just the beginning of a regulatory process, as the Canton System moved foreign ships up the Pearl River to anchorage off the Island of Whampoa and traders to an area of quarantine called Canton outside the walled city of Guangzhou. Shaw's detailed description of his passage through the system demonstrates that it mattered symbolically to him in asserting the autonomy and commercial viability of his "New People."

New Americans in the Canton System

Movement through China's regulatory system from Macao to Canton opened Shaw to a deeper sense of world-historical geography. For centuries prior to Portugal's arrival in China in the 1500s, Canton had hosted sea-based trade extending from the Middle East and India in networks of coastal ports stretching through the straits between contemporary Indonesia and Malaysia. Ronit Ricci discerns in this movement of people and goods a pervasive "Islamic presence in maritime South Asia"; some of the oldest mosques in China are in and near Canton.[28] Before the fall of Constantinople (or rise of Istanbul) in 1453, trade routes extended eastward from Europe by land, across the Middle East and along the Silk Road through Central Asia and northern China. In the 1490s, after Columbus sailed west to meet the Grand Khan, Portugal's Vasco da Gama voyaged down and around the coast of Africa to the Indies, following the continental shoreline into the Indian Ocean to reach Goa on the west coast of what is today India. Very lucrative trade routes from Europe branched out to the so-called Spice Islands or Malaccas (part of contemporary Malaysia).

Portuguese ships first reached Guangzhou in the early 1500s.[29] Within a few decades, the Ming Empire pushed them down the Pearl River to Macao, about 195 kilometers or three to four days away by sailing ship. Portugal paid a fee to China in order to remain in Macao where it managed the arrival of foreign traders and patrolled for pirates who preyed on costal trade.[30] Elsewhere in the Pacific Ferdinand Magellan sailed under a Spanish flag to reach what he called the islands of San Lázaro in 1521, soon after renamed the Philippines in honor of King Phillip II. Lured by the China trade, European empires of Austria, Britain, Denmark, Estonia,

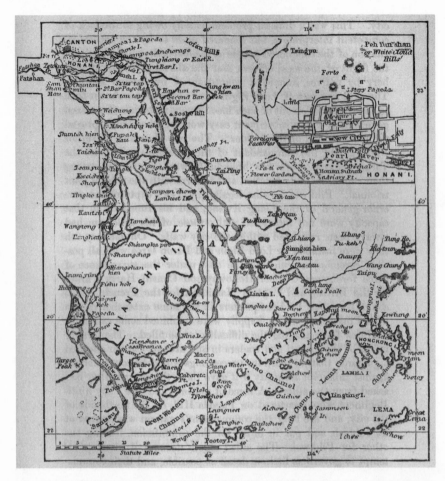

"The City of Canton and Adjacent Islands." S. Williams, *The Middle Kingdom* (1883), 2:645.

France, Portugal, and Sweden charted East India companies. At the beginning of the seventeenth century Britain's East India Company and later the Dutch East India Company (Vereenigde Oostindische Compagnie) superseded the Portuguese in controlling flows of trade in Southeast Asia. The Dutch company established Batavia (contemporary Jakarta) on the large island of Java as its major headquarters. At the intersection of Spanish and Dutch influence in the East, the Sultanate of Sulu developed a seat of power in Jolo that extended through an archipelago that is today part of Indonesia, Malaysia, and the Philippines.[31] From these positions, China's Canton remained a crucial destination for speculative endeavors, and traders coordinated multiyear voyages that moved through ports including Boston, Liverpool, Cape Town, Batavia, Singapore, Malacca, Pondicherry, Manila, and Nagasaki.[32]

In north China at the Forbidden City of Peking (Beijing; 北京), the Qing emperor and his mandarin advising councils sought to control how foreign traders approached and transacted business with China. In the late sixteenth century he designated four trading ports: Ningbo, Quanzhou, Xiamen, and Canton.[33] This changed in 1757 with the Canton System, which closed all the ports except Canton (although unique privileges for Spain were permitted at Xiamen via the Philippines, and different rules were established for Japan and Russia).[34] For decades into the eighteenth century, the Canton System worked to balance trade in favor of China, which pulled from Great Britain and other European companies tons of silver, usually in the form of Spanish dollars minted in Spanish-controlled South and Central America (contemporary Peru and Mexico).[35] Because silver was the key commodity and currency in Canton, Robert Morris and his fellow speculators made sure that the *Empress of China*'s payload included $20,000 in silver bullion, an impressive amount given the early national scarcity of specie.[36]

Shaw's journals document firsthand how the Canton System worked. After anchoring in the shallow waters of the Macao Roads a few miles outside of Macao, the ship blasted its cannons and waited for trade officials to register the ship with the Portuguese and Chinese authorities. As the ship's supercargo, Shaw was responsible for hiring a pilot, a comprador, a linguist, and a fiador. The pilot guided the *Empress of China* seventy-five miles up the Pearl River, avoiding shallow waters and pirates and navigating through a series of checkpoints, the most prominent of which was the Bogue or Bocca Tigris Forts at the mouth of the river. (Outside this area are the island of Linton and harbor of Cum Sing Moon that became relay centers for opium smuggling.) After navigating the Pearl River, the ship then anchored off Whampoa Island with its landmark nine-story pagoda, where the Mandarin customs official called the hoppo and associated government officials measured the ship, ascertained its cargo, and collected tariff duties in a ceremony called the cumshaw. As a token of respect, it was customary for the hoppo to receive gifts of "clock-work and other curiosities" for imperial authorities.[37] After completion of the measurement ceremonies and crosschecking of cargo at Whampoa, small boats ferried the merchandize to the factories or countinghouses ten miles up the river to an area outside the walled city of Guangzhou. In this process, the Chinese linguist was "absolutely necessary" for securing small boats or sanpans "for unloading and loading"; he was "always on call" while "employed in transacting all business with the custom-house,—which is in the city [of Guangzhou], where no strangers can be admitted."[38] As the supercargo, Shaw worked closely with a comprador responsible for supplying the ship during its anchorage at Whampoa Island and "furnish[ing] provisions and other necessaries, for which he contracts at certain prices."[39] There was also the Chinese fiador, the "principal [merchant]" through

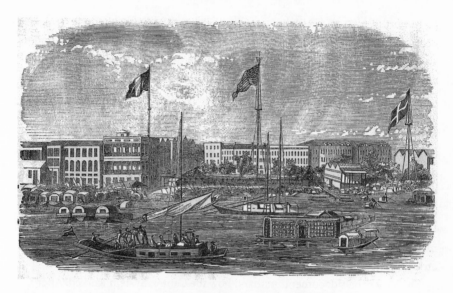

"Canton—Foreign Settlement. Before the Fire." Bridgman, *The Pioneer of American Missions in China*, 39.

"whom business [was] transacted"; as the middle person or intermediary, the fiador facilitated the connection between the foreign traders, the imperial official (or hoppo), and the Cohong or Hong (行; *hong4* in Cantonese; *háng* in Putonghua) organizations that controlled the warehouses, countinghouses, and living quarters known as "factories" in a designated area outside Guangzhou known as Canton.

The historian Jacques M. Downs called this warehouse and boarding area the "golden ghetto" because Western traders spent the trading season from October to March in hectic negotiation and account keeping while living in a rented factory house in front of which they flew a national flag.[40] Fires in 1822, 1841, and 1856 destroyed the factories, and the entire zone was eventually relocated "to Shamian Island farther up the river."[41] As business went on in Canton's factories, the ship and its crew bided their time at Whampoa Island.

The commercial strategy was rarely as simple as bringing in one thing (ginseng or silver) and trading it for another (tea) and then going back home. The factory area's small scale of apportioned space correlated to vast global networks in which merchants coordinated their transactions for goods and services, speculating on advantageous trading positions throughout the world. The maps of the global trade underlying their strategies underwent dramatic changes throughout the Napoleonic Wars (1803–15), the War of 1812 (1812–15), the series of Anglo-Dutch Wars, and later the Crimean War (1853–56), all of which realigned global alliances and transformed the nautical and financial networks. In a pretelegraphic world, information

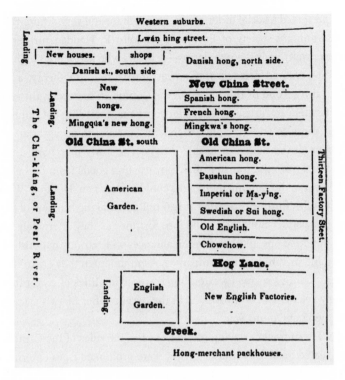

"The Thirteen Factories," *Chinese Repository* 15.7 (July 1846): 373. The occasion for this diagram is in locating the outbreak of "riots" by Chinese against foreign merchants and traders taking place in Canton in July, two years after the conclusion of the Opium War in 1844.

moved slowly across water and land by word of mouth and exchange of paper. Timely reports about political events, the dearth or glut of particular commodities, or the assurance of credit could make or break an investor in Canton. After a few weeks of trading, the foreigners repacked their ships and obtained the proper departure permits, culminating in a final permit or grand chop. They then sailed back down the Pearl River, past the various checkpoints and Macao, and out to sea.

At Canton, the Cohong merchants were very powerful in facilitating and brokering international trade. Specifically designated by the authorities in Peking, they handled all business with the foreigners, rented them their factory space, and paid a tax to the government for the opportunity of brokering trade.[42] Shaw estimates a total of ten or twelve Cohongs with the "exclusive privilege [from the emperor] of the European and country trade, for which they pay a considerable sum to the government."[43] In terms of Confucian social mores, the Cohongs were not a respected class and were subordinate to Mandarin officials, soldiers, and farmers. John K. Fairbank writes that "until after 1800 the agrarian-bureaucratic empire of

China . . . preserved a social order more ancient than, and very different from, the commercial-military society of Europe."[44] As John R. Haddad further explains, "Aside from royalty, only the mandarins—scholars who had scored high on a state examination—enjoyed privileges of power and class. . . . In theory, a merchant could not claim second or third place in the Confucian hierarchy, these being reserved for farmers and artisans. The latter vocations, according to Confucian logic, contributed more to society than a merchant because, in an agrarian economy, their labor produced edible or usable things. The lowly merchant, in contrast, merely profited from the transfer of already-existing goods from one place to another."[45] However, the Cohong merchants could be very rich. Houqua (Wu Binjian, 1769–1843) built a fortune estimated at $26 million, making him one of the richest people in the world.[46] Still, they could lose fortunes as they alternately competed with and supported one another, forging alliances with various nations' East India companies and private trading companies. As middlemen they ensured continuity between trading seasons by extending or receiving lines of credit that proved increasingly volatile and controversial in the decades after Shaw's account in the run-up to the First Opium War.[47]

As for Western traders staying in the factories, the rules of the Canton System strictly regulated their daily routines. They were prohibited from entering the city walls of Guangzhou. Government officials at various levels (provincial, urban) and the local population were vigilant in policing the foreigners' movements. During certain periods, foreign traders were permitted recreational strolls on nearby islands or the country area outside the city. An occasional dinner at the grand estate of a Cohong merchant was an opportunity to witness their business associates' extensive gardens.[48] Each year at the end of the trading season foreigners were supposed to leave Canton. Most set off on the high seas while others retired to Macao during the off-season. To discourage long-term settlement, the Canton System banned foreign women entirely anywhere beyond Macao. Imperial laws also forbade the teaching of the Chinese language to foreigners. Shaw also reports that the importation of opium was already forbidden.

Negotiating National Recognition and Market Credibility

Shaw's descriptions of the voyage to and through the Canton System register his aspiration to be recognized as a peer member of fellow Western Christian nations and empires. On the voyage out from New York, Shaw looked for respect from all the nations' ships that he encountered, indexing recognition of the "New People" across diverse languages and cultures, throughout the Atlantic, Indian, and Pacific Oceans and the continents of Africa, the Americas, Asia, and Europe. These international encounters began when Shaw encountered the French slave ship outside of the Portuguese port on his voyage out. By the end of the month of March, Shaw and the ship were headed south, around Africa's Cape of Hope and across the Indian Ocean. Moving through what today are Indonesian waters, Shaw notes the respectful reception by Dutch administrators and French sea captains. He characterizes non-European peoples as a different class of people, comparing the "natives" who greeted the ship from their canoes off the coast of Java to the "North American savage."[49]

As for the Chinese, Shaw's descriptions of Canton exemplify conventional orientalist ambivalence. He describes the wealthy Cohongs and Chinese mandarins with respect, while presuming either their complete understanding of issues relating to trade or their relative ignorance of civilized ways of life. Any ostensible confusion about commercial procedures seems but a minor impediment to shared goals of conducting business to mutual benefit. He notices and carefully explains the interlocking administrative roles of the Canton System with pride in having worked through them. However, in relishing the significance of Chinese trade, he overlooks all social differences of class and status in China. When reporting the challenges to his commercial ambition, Shaw homogenizes the Chinese as a static people whose history has stopped progressing. There is no evidence that Shaw read Adam Smith—he quotes Oliver Goldsmith and Lord Kames—but, like Smith, he figures China as a literal stereotype, an inflexible printing plate that stamps the same fading image over and over again. Thus, on his second voyage he dismisses the need for any further descriptions of China: "After the detail, in my former journal [during the first voyage], of such matters as occur among the Chinese at Canton, there can be nothing to remark, . . . respecting people whose manners and customs may be considered like the laws of the ancient Medes and Persians, which altered not. Consequently, any observations, on occasions succeeding a first visit, must be mainly confined to the foreign commerce."[50] In comparing the Chinese to ancient civilizations of Media and Persia (geographically, roughly comparable to contemporary Iran), Shaw pays them a measure of respect as noble precursors to innovative Western genius. The problem with these ancient empires is that they have stopped progressing historically. In 1847 Quincy, who never went to China, picks up this motif as he introduces Shaw's writings, fusing the literal and metaphorical sense of *stereotype* to advise his readers that Shaw's experience "throw[s] light on the commercial relations of our country with those of distant regions at that period, which cannot fail to be interesting," while "the unchangeableness of Chinese Habits and policy, . . . which, even at this day, is both useful and attractive."[51] Whereas the commercial relations of the United States ("our country") are an index of dynamic development, the Chinese habits are static, unchanging, and therefore a stable point of ancient reference. Such stereotypes might have been reassuring to Shaw's and Quincy's cultural egos, but the Canton System was much more complex than Shaw suggests.

Shaw's sense of American distinctiveness entailed multiple cultural Others in relation to which Shaw narrates similarities and differences. Categories such as "East and West," "Christian and pagan," "white and black," and others operated simultaneously in the logic by which he sought distinction as an American. However, the fulcrum of any particular categorical opposition does not hold in the broad context of his observations as differences of language, religion, and political history take priority in distinguishing the United States from Western nations. For example, consider the diplomatic protocols of arriving and anchoring near Macao on 24 August 1784. The French consul in Macao honored the Americans while visiting the *Empress of China* by inviting them to "pass the day" together on shores of Macao.[52] Unable to introduce the Americans to Macao's Portuguese governor, the French consul held his own honorary dinner with the officers of the *Triton* (the ship that had escorted the Americans from Indonesia) and the supercargoes of ships from Sweden and Germany. At the dinner, Shaw presented copies of the treaty papers that had ended the Revolution. A few days later Shaw met with the Portuguese governor and presented him with copies, but the new Americans did not yet warrant an official dinner.[53]

There are amusing moments when Shaw bristles at the Portuguese's lack of respect. With their eyes on the China trade, Portuguese administrators seem unimpressed by the American's arrival and dismissively uninformed about the American Revolution. Returning to Macao on the second voyage after he had been appointed the American consul to China, Shaw finally wins a place at the Portuguese governor's dinner tables of dignitaries but is insulted by their lack of interest in him or his new nation. In his journal he vents his feelings by belittling his host. Complimenting the governor's pretty wife, Shaw notes that she is "a European Portuguese, sensible, artful, and, when she pleases, very agreeable."[54] As for her husband, the governor of Macao, Shaw deems him unimpressive in several ways, punctuating his assessment by relating the governor's remarkable ignorance over the outcome of the American Revolution: "*His* Excellency appears to be under forty years of age, is a native of Goa, and in point of knowledge vastly [his wife's] inferior. To persons not acquainted with the Indian-Portuguese, so called, what I am going to relate of this governor may appear an illiberal sarcasm rather than the simple truth. But it is a fact, that he did ask an English gentleman, who sat between him and me at the Swedish table, whether the war between England and America was yet at an end!"[55] This complacent Portuguese governor has overlooked what Shaw regards as the era's most dramatically significant world-historical event. By 1847,

Shaw's readers must have seen this as richly ironic, evidence of a fading imperial Camelot of Portuguese-administered Macao. In 1786, Shaw chalks the governor's ignorance up to his relative youth, to his having been raised in Goa, and to being of mixed Indian-Portuguese parentage.

Shaw follows up by recalling another conversation from a diplomatic dinner party: "One of [Macao's] principle senators . . . betrayed an equal want of knowledge, when, the American Revolution being the topic, it was observed that the English had lost a great deal in losing America. 'Ah,' replied our politician, 'that may be; but they have taken Pulo Pinang!'"[56] This remark baffles Shaw, who responds with a rhetorical question: "When such are the rulers, what must the bulk of people be?"[57] He reinforces his judgment by appealing to "The united voice of the European residences," assumedly the British, Dutch, French, and Swedish, who proclaim "[the Portuguese] idle to a proverb, consequently poor, and superstitious in the extreme."[58] In Shaw's pecking order of Western Christendom, the Protestant United States sits ahead of the weak link of Catholic Portugal. It is possible that these two Portuguese officials were trying to get a rise out of Shaw. But, in any case, their nonchalance over the American Revolution also suggests their very different geographic perspective on world events—a perspective that would cease to baffle Shaw after he had voyaged through Southeast Asia to Bengal and learned more about the ongoing contests of commercial influence between Britain, the Dutch, and Portugal.

On Shaw's second voyage of three years from 1786 to 1789, he visited Bengal via the Straits of Malacca, adjusting his perspective on world-historical geography as he gauged how to augment his position in the regional trading network. During these travels, he realizes the significance of the port city of Pulo Pinang, where the British EIC planned to gain not only "the monopoly of tea trade for Europe" but also "exclusive commerce of this division of the globe"[59]:

[Britain's] new plan of government for Bengal and its dependences—their late establishments, both to the eastward and westward,—the prohibition to their subjects in India against selling their ships to foreigners,—and, in short, their whole conduct, strongly favor the suspicion. How far the Dutch, whom it most nearly concerns, will suffer attempts of this kind, a few years must determine. The settlement of the English at Pulo Pinang, which enables them to command the whole of the navigation from the peninsula of India, that of Malaya, and the island of Sumatra, has not a little alarmed them; and the settlement at Botany Bay, on the southeast coast of New Holland [contemporary Sydney, Australia], has increased their apprehensions.[60]

In light of Shaw's further travels, the Portuguese officials do not seem so clueless. After visiting Pulo Pinang, Shaw slips into an informative mode of travel writing to note that the British had renamed it Prince of Wales Island (and then later George Town) upon occupying it in early 1786. He continues with a description of the place itself, alluding to its strategic importance as a pivot point for regional commerce and to Britain's colonial tactics of taking control of it and augmenting that control inland and through the straits:

> [Prince of Wales Island] is between twelve and thirteen miles long, its medium breadth about five, and has a very good and safe harbor. It was given by the king of Queda to Mr. [Francis] Light, who, as captain of a country ship, had for a number of years been in the Malay trade, and was well known to his Majesty; for the Malay princes are the chief merchants in their own dominions. Its situation, near the west entrance of the Straits of Malacca, is so advantageous, in trading with the Malays for tin, pepper, canes, rattans, &c., that it has become an object of attention to the Bengal government. . . . the encouragement given to the Malays to bring their merchandise to this place, where they obtain the highest prices, and have the certainty of receiving either dollars, opium, or such commodities as they have occasion for, and without incurring any risk, has already much affected the Dutch at Malacca in their commerce with these people, and it is not improbable will in a short time deprive them entirely.[61]

Drawing on a classic script of the colonial American first encounter, Shaw describes how the tribal Malayan "king's" gifted land to the British country trader, who stands in for the broader colonial project of establishing colonial posts in a network of oversight reaching to Bengal. Pitting Malayan "princes" against one another, the British trick is to make its factories the relay points of exchange for the local and regional adversaries. After the country trader Francis Light establishes the island as a commercial outpost, the Dutch would lose their commercial leverage in Malacca.

In light of these observations, the Portuguese politicians in Macao seem less ignorant of the American Revolution than they are aware of the scale of commercial confrontation unfolding in South and Southeast Asia. From Pulo Pinang the EIC would indeed contest the Dutch East India Company for control over the Straits of Malacca. This control over the nautical traffic and inland trade was not only about controlling the centuries' old trade in spices but also about establishing the networks of warehousing and brokering necessary for the systematic traffic of opium as British private traders bought it at auctions in Bengal and moved, stored, and smuggled it along the way and into China. The abiding questions of Shaw's observations are: Where will U.S. traders fit into these developing networks? How will they find commercial positions in Southeast Asia as Britain's EIC dislodges Holland and Portugal? Shaw may have been reassured to know that they found a way. In 1786 Shaw estimates two thousand opium chests entered China per year.

By the early 1830s, the estimates had reached thirty-six thousand, and U.S. merchants were fully and profitably engaged. By the time Quincy published Shaw's journals at the expense of his successful merchant nephew, China had been defeated in the First Opium War, and the trade in opium continued to boom.

From Ginseng to Furs to Opium

Shaw was wrong about ginseng. It did not make him a fortune, let alone generate wealth on the scale of Spanish-controlled silver mines and mints in South and Central America. Ginseng's supply was soon depleted in the United States. As the quality of the harvest dropped, demand waned in Canton. Asian varieties from Manchuria and Korea remained more valuable and, over the next century, U.S. ginseng was just a blandly consistent item in a basket of many more lucrative commodities.

As ginseng fizzled in the 1790s, beaver and sea otter furs from the Northwest of North America and sealskins from the South Pacific took off. The rising fortune of Colonel Thomas H. Perkins exhibits the shift to fur as commercial ventures spanning the Atlantic Ocean widened across the Indian and Pacific Oceans. In 1789 Perkins made his first voyage to Canton aboard the *Astrea*, owned by the Salem merchant E. H. Derby and loaded with seventy-five thousand pounds of ginseng.[62] At Canton Perkins witnessed the arrival of the ship *Columbia* from the American Northwest during its first voyage (1787–90). The lucrative opportunity of trading beaver and sea otter pelts made a big impression. He voyaged back to Boston and by September 1790 had outfitted the ship *Hope* for the fur trade. By 1803, "the leading commodities in the [U.S.-China] trade . . . were [silver] specie and sea otter skins. The first trade on the Northwest coast had been British at the start; by 1798 it became principally American. Two years later it was almost a Boston monopoly."[63] As Frederick William Howay explains, during this period "the Americans had a perfect golden round of profits: first, the profit on the original cargo of trading goods when exchanged for furs; second, the profit when the furs were transmuted into Chinese goods; and, third, the profit on those goods when they reached America."[64]

The fur trade was relatively short lived. The historian Carl A. Trocki estimates that by the 1820s it was all but ruined.[65] In 1835 the U.S. missionary Samuel Wells Williams treats it in nostalgic terms for the *Chinese Repository* article entitled: "The fur trade: animals which produce fine furs; those producing hairy skins; the progress of the fur trade in Asia, America, and Europe; imports into China."[66] Williams explains that popular beaver pelts were hunted and purchased in the "wilds of Northwestern America"—"in the country west of the Rocky Mountains, and north of the Columbia river"—and sealskins were found on "many of the islands in the Pacific Ocean south."[67] However, "the exterminating policies of the hunters" had greatly curtailed supply of high quality pelts.[68] Furthermore, by the 1830s silk hats became more popular than those of felt, and the more plentiful South American river rodent called the nutria was cheaper than beaver.[69]

Even as the pelt trade flourished, silver remained the most important commodity that Americans brought to Canton, as the next chapter explores in greater depth through Amasa Delano's narrative.[70] In the first decade of the nineteenth century, the world supply of silver contracted dramatically in the wake of revolutions in Central and South America after the Napoleonic Wars (1799–1815). No amount of furs or sealskins or ginseng would have made up the deficit. The key commodity became opium, a tool with which the British EIC eventually reversed the balance of the silver trade with China. From a perspective looking toward the "trading world of Asia as a system of interdependent relationships, the role of opium emerges as a pivotal agent of change."[71]

Shaw's account offers a fascinating commentary on the emerging role of opium in the 1780s. He did not regard opium as a controversial commodity even as he warily envied the system that Britain was developing around it. He does not moralize over opium use or lament its sale in China, although he notes its strict prohibition by Chinese law. On his first voyage in 1784, Shaw observes that the "natives" in Java were "exceedingly fond" of the drug, which they chewed in large quantities without "bad effect."[72] As Frank Dikötter, Lars Laamann, and Zhou Xun note, opium had long served beneficial medicinal, recreational, and spiritual roles in China and in other cultures throughout the world.[73] Opium trade into China had existed for centuries, and before the 1500s "opium was just one of the many exotic chemicals that made up an element of the traditional long-distance trade."[74] In the sixteenth and seventeenth centuries, Portugal trafficked enough opium from Bengal (Patna variety) and Malabar (Malwa variety) into China to raise concerns in Peking, and in 1729 the Qing emperor imposed regulations, and the availability of gold and silver made up the balance to stabilize the markets.[75] From 1721 to 1740, "some 95 percent of British payments for Chinese exports . . . were made in silver dollars."[76] For most of the eighteenth century, two hundred chests of opium at most moved into China each year. By 1767, as gold specie became scarce and silver imports rose, opium was beginning to serve as a handy commodity for facilitating exchange. Opium imports into China jumped to one thousand chests per year and prompted renewed regulatory attention from Peking, but there was not yet a serious problem as China continued to pull in silver.

As mentioned, in the 1780s and after the EIC developed a colonial trade system that reversed the flows of silver exchange at Canton and won control of the strait settlements from Penang to Malacca to Singapore. This commercial influence was possible because in the 1760s the EIC had "gained de facto sovereignty over" the fertile regions of the Indian subcontinent's "Bengal, Bihar, and Orissam."[77] The India Act of 1773 formalized the triangulation of trade between India and China and Britain. By the time Shaw arrived in China in the mid-1780s, "most of the opium trade from Calcutta to China was left in the hands of private merchants working under EIC license."[78] By this arrangement the EIC obeyed the letter of China's Canton System that prohibited the importation of opium. The EIC did not send company ships with the drug, instead auctioning it off to private British traders who then smuggled it into China from the Pearl River and coastal ports.[79] Paul A. Van Dyke explains that the EIC "benefited from this commerce in two ways": the company made a direct profit selling opium to country traders from whom they received silver as payment.[80] The EIC then used this silver to purchase tea. Furthermore, the EIC developed the financial instrument of bills of exchange that promised bearers silver on paper, payable in London. The silver stayed in London or in EIC offices as bills of exchange moved through the trading system, offering parallel opportunities for speculative leverage.[81]

The particular power of opium as a commodity (i.e., something that could be bought and sold in relation to other commodities) came from its function as a sort of foreign-trade currency that shadowed the exchange of silver. Opium was compact and economical to transport and could last for years. It could be stored and stockpiled from one season to another. When world supplies of Spanish silver contracted, Britain used opium to fill the vacuum. Trocki writes that after "the collapse of the Spanish Empire in Latin America and the faltering production of [silver] mines of Mexico and South America," opium became a "medium of exchange for tea" and "for all other commodities as well, including silver"; "the years after 1820 saw opium production and exports skyrocket, and they continued to increase until 1880."[82] Exaggerated characterizations of opium as the cause of socially crippling addiction, beyond the agency of those using it, risk missing the strategic role that the drug played as both a commodity and a sort of currency, facilitating the exchange of a basket of commodities moving through Canton in violation of Chinese law. As opium washed over the Canton System, China pulled in less and less silver. Trocki gives a sense of the scale: "At the beginning of the nineteenth century, the Chinese were spending between 2 and 3 million Spanish dollars annually for about 4,000 chests of opium or about 160 metric tons"; a decade later, they were "spending about twice that, or between 4 and 5 million" for the same amount of opium.[83] This trend intensified, so that between 1814 and 1850, there "was a net outflow of something like $150,000,000 (Spanish/Mexican) from China," or "13 percent of China's total silver supply and 11 percent of the country's money supply."[84]

Shaw gives us firsthand account of how private British traders set up the colonial opium network. His observations in the late 1780s register the early realignment of commercial influence as the EIC began using opium to coordinate speculation in a colonial system that triangulated London and India and China. On the lookout for opportunities during his first and second voyages, Shaw was most concerned with the market advantages that British traders could derive from using opium to negotiate prices across a basket of commodities, buying tea on better terms than other European and American traders:

> The English derive considerable advantages from the permission granted [by the British Crown and EIC] to private ships, owned by their subjects in India, to trade with China. These vessels, besides the cotton, sandal-wood, putchock-root, ebony, opium, sharkfins, and birdsnests they bring from the coast, carry on a smuggling trade with the Dutch settlements in and about Malacca, and with the natives, whom they supply with opium, clothing, fire-arms, &c., in return for which they receive pepper, block-tin, and spices. The proceeds of these, with the silver and other articles they bring from India, are, to the amount of one third, carried back in such merchandise as will suit the India markets; and the remainder, either in cash or transfers from the Chinese merchants, is paid into the company's treasure, for which they receive bills on the company in England, at the exchange of five shillings and sixpence sterling for a the dollar, payable three hundred and sixty-five days after sight. This fund has for a number of years rendered it unnecessary for the company to export from Europe any specie for carrying on their commerce with the Chinese.[85]

Shaw is sensitive to British traders' potential to gain an upper hand not only in China but also in the pepper and spice trade, even challenging the Dutch control over "settlements in and about Malacca."[86] Estimating that two thousand chests are going into China on an annual basis, he describes the relative advantage the British traders are gaining over the Portuguese in Macao:

> Opium is with the Chinese entirely contraband, and cannot legally be admitted to their ports, under any conditions whatever. This prohibition does not extend to Macao, as belonging to the Portuguese, and the governor takes care to be interested in all that is brought there in Portuguese ships from Bengal, and, to a considerable extent, in what the English vessels bring. It often happens that these latter, on failing to obtain at Canton, where it can always be smuggled with the utmost security, the price they demand for their opium, make a deposit of it in some Portuguese vessel at Macao, in

order that they may not lose a season by waiting for the market to rise; in which case, the governor is either concerned as a partner in the business, or receives a handsome *douceur*.[87]

According to Shaw, the momentum of opium commerce was tilting in favor of the EIC in China. As Portugal's regional influence ebbed, Macao's governor seemed resigned to receiving kickback bribes for overlooking the warehousing of opium. The economic advantages that Portugal had enjoyed administering the Canton Trade in Macao continued to diminish as the British private traders set up smuggling stations on islands and ships at the mouth of the Pearl River:

> Instead of being concerned with [the Portuguese governor], as before, the English speculators now keep a vessel plying among the neighbouring islands, where are plenty of safe harbors, which vessel serves as a depository for so much of the drug as remains on hand when the time arrives for the return to Bengal of the ships that brought it. . . . The Chinese purchasers repair to this vessel, and pay the money before receiving the opium, in addition to which they pay twenty dollars for every chest to the mandarins, who in their boats always keep near enough to watch and receive the bribe.[88]

Beyond documenting the changing terms of the China trade, Shaw offers a fascinating perspective on the international geography of early national U.S. identity. As Portugal falls and Britain rises in the East, where will the United States find position and rank? As the following chapters show, these outlying positions of opium dealing at Lintin Island and Cum-sing Moon were crucial to the trade tactics of U.S. firms such as Thomas H. Perkins's organization and its successor, Russell & Company.

Opium and the Merchant Princes

By the time Shaw died in 1794, John Jacob Astor, Stephen Girard, and Thomas H. Perkins were already active in the South and Southeast Asian zones of Canton-based commerce. Sailing under an American flag meant they were locked out of EIC-controlled Bengal. Furthermore, as the Jay Treaty (1794) extinguished the border disputes that the Peace of Paris had left smoldering, it also stipulated that Americans would not trade between India and any other port of the world outside of "some Port or Place in America" for a decade to come.[89] However, the EIC monopoly framework also left opportunities for U.S. merchants who were not required to heed company regulations and unfettered by any government charters.[90] Private British ships could not move goods from continental Europe to China, and

EIC ships could not transport opium at all. This left American merchants with a wide commercial field in which to find alternative sources for opium without British commercial competition.

The earliest evidence of American involvement in the opium trade is from 1788 when Stephen Girard's (1750–1831) interest was sparked by the ventures of fellow Philadelphians Robert Waln and Benjamin Wilcocks. They found sources of opium in the Mediterranean port of Smyrna (Izmir), Turkey, and in the markets of Amsterdam and Hamburg.[91] Turkish opium was of lesser quality than that of Patna or Malwa and was usually processed into liquid forms of laudanum rather than smoked. Nonetheless, it was a lucrative commodity that was very useful in a basket of commodities. By 1806, Girard was heavily invested in opium and "diligently persevered" in its trade "with total disregard for the prohibited nature of the trade, not to mention its deleterious effect on the Chinese people."[92] His stake in opium "became so large that his representative in Hamburg suggested that he send out a separate schooner on a regular basis, carrying only opium from the Continent to Canton."[93] Girard's last voyage was in 1824. Afterward he retired in Philadelphia and focused on coal mining in Pennsylvania and construction of canals and railways (including the company that would become Reading Railroad); he also founded a school in Philadelphia dedicated to educating orphaned boys.[94]

John Jacob Astor and Thomas H. Perkins (with his brothers and cousins) also worked their way into opium.[95] After the Jay Treaty expired in 1804, Perkins & Company began transshipping opium from Bengal to Batavia, making a good turn of profit on the purchase of pepper.[96] Smyrna was also in the Perkins playbook. As Timothy Mason Roberts writes, Thomas H. Perkins's cousin George Perkins ("a British loyalist . . . who fled America during the American Revolution") was probably "the first American opium trader" in the Turkish port city of Izmir.[97] According to Roberts, "Ships from Philadelphia, Baltimore, and Boston began carrying Turkish opium in 1804," and in 1805 Colonel Thomas Perkins wrote that "the representative of the Perkins firm in Canton, averring that since opium could be bought in Turkey at $2 per pound ($8 less than in China), 'great profits can be made on it.' "[98] In 1816 the J. & T. H. Perkins Company opened an office in Izmir and "from these origins, trade in opium out of Izmir, bound for China, would become the main American export from the Middle East in the nineteenth century."[99]

The historian Charles Stelle estimates that by 1805 Turkish opium accounted for about 10 percent of the total 4 million Spanish dollars in total revenues from trade, around "fifty and one hundred dollars a season."[100] Because opium was being smuggled, it is difficult to estimate its revenue. In regard to scope, Stelle concludes that Turkish opium investments in the early nineteenth century amounted to "twenty to thirty percent of the value of the commodities which Americans carried to China," with "the greater portion of American shipments to China consist[ing] of silver dollars."[101] By the trading seasons of 1817 and 1818, opium consisted of as much as "half of the commodities which Americans used for the purchase of Chinese goods in the seasons 1817 and 1818."[102] When in 1818 China cracked down and enforced a long-standing ban on opium, Perkins doubled-down on the traffic, hoping that his competitors would flee the additional risks of confiscation. His gamble paid off and Perkins & Company built up a strong position over the next two decades, before merging in 1831 with Russell & Company to become even stronger. U.S. merchants developed new smuggling stations at the mouth of the Pearl River to store and broker opium. From ships anchored off Lintin Island, Perkins's young nephew John Perkins Cushing brokered sales and transfers from the company office in Canton. Trocki estimates that by 1832–33 nearly twenty-two thousand chests of Patna, Benares, and Turkish opium were shipped into Canton, for a value of 13.5 million Spanish/Mexican dollars; by 1838–39, the number exceeded forty thousand.[103]

In the 1780s Major Shaw understood that success required an international branching of financial positions across many ports and commodities. In the decades after his death, opium proved very useful and lucrative. Unlike slavery, Shaw seems not to have had much trouble with it, although he died before he could take advantage of the networks on which he commented. Astor, Girard, and Perkins put into action much of the insight Shaw generated as they branched out to the China trade from transatlantic commercial enterprises that included the West Indian–based slave trade that Shaw found so horrifying.

Coda: Herman Melville, Bunker Hill, and the National Biography of Merchant Princes

Dedicated to the granite stone memorial of the Battle of Bunker Hill, Melville's novel *Israel Potter: His Fifty Years of Exile* (1855) seems to have nothing to do with the China trade as it fictionalizes the pamphlet account of a destitute veteran of the Revolutionary War. However, it seems a critical rejoinder to Quincy's *Journals of Major Samuel Shaw*. The dedication and editorial preface of *Israel Potter* directly refer to Jared Sparks and allude to Thomas H. Perkins in offering a serious criticism of national biography for waving the bloody shirt of the Revolution to profitable ends in a global system of commerce.

Israel Potter is Melville's first work of fiction to revise an already-published, non-fictional document, the second being "Benito Cereno." It was first serialized in *Putnam's Monthly Magazine of American Literature, Science and Art* from July 1854 to March 1855 and then appeared as a book in London and New York.[104] In the decade prior, Melville had established himself as a novelist of first-person accounts based on his experiences as a sailor and castaway in the South Pacific, including *Typee: A Peep at Polynesian Life* (1846), *Omoo: A Narrative of the South Seas* (1847), *Mardi: And a Voyage Thither* (1849), *Redburn: His First Voyage* (1849), and *White-Jacket; or, the World in a Man-of-War* (1850). His reputation suffered after the 1851 publication of the colossal and philosophically expansive *Moby Dick; or, The Whale* (1851) and the bleak third-person novel *Pierre; or, The Ambiguities* (1852). His works *Israel Potter* (1855), *The Piazza Tales* (1856; short stories including "Benito Cereno" and "Bartleby"), and his novel *The Confidence-Man: His Masquerade* (1857) followed in quick succession.

Before turning to Melville's story, consider the posthumous national biography *Memoir of Thomas Handasyd Perkins: Containing Extracts from His Diaries and Letters* (1856), written by his son-in-law and business protégé Thomas Cary.[105] The book narrates Perkin's life as a rise from commercial enterprises in Haiti to early ventures in China as he travels throughout Europe to secure lines of credit during the French Revolution.[106] Encouraging his reader directly, Cary presents Perkins as a Franklinian role model for aspiring young American merchants who are seeking their way to wealth:

> Each day with him [Colonel Perkins] was the illustration of a thought which young men, and particularly young men entering on commercial life, will find to be a safe-guard against precipitation or perplexity, and against the irritation, as well as the miserable shifts, to which they sometimes lead. The Action of the mind in preparing with calm foresight what is to be done, before it is absolutely necessary, is widely different from its action when affairs are left until necessity presses, and the powers are confused by various calls on the attention in the midst of hurry and embarrassment.[107]

The *North American Review* raved about Cary's biography of his father-in-law, stressing the instructive value of Perkins's life for young American men looking to make their name as merchants. The magazine's editor Andrew Preston Peabody, a minister and a professor of Harvard College, characterizes Perkins as holding "a pioneer's place with reference to the mercantile profession as it now is in New England. Brought up under the old *régime*, he was the founder and for many years the leading mind of the new."[108] Peabody concludes that Perkins's "biography" is one that "ought to be in the hands of every young merchant and merchant's clerk in the country" because it "presents in many important aspects a model character,—not only that deserves to be, but one that can be, imitated."[109]

It is worth mentioning that, whereas Major Shaw had earned his title of major by serving during the Revolutionary War, Perkins adopted his title of colonel in the late 1790s after being "made commander of military corps,—the battalion which

Frontispiece to Cary, *Memoir of Thomas Handasyd Perkins.*

constitutes the guard and escort for public occasions of the Governor of the Commonwealth of Massachusetts."[110] The title was basically ceremonial. Today, Perkins is recognized as an exemplary early philanthropist, and he surely was beneficent. As Cary documents, Perkins funded the Massachusetts General Hospital's Asylum for the Insane, the Boston Athenæum, and the Perkins Institution for the Blind.[111] Cary also credits Perkins with building the nation's "first railroad."[112] Chartered by the state of Massachusetts in 1826, the Granite Railway Company had tracks extending two miles "from the [stone] quarries in Quincy [Massachusetts] to the water."[113] Curiously, Cary does not mention that Perkins started the company to move granite from a stone quarry in Quincy to the site of the Bunker Hill Monument. It was not coincidental that Perkins was one of the original planners, promoters, and financiers of the monument.

In contrast to Cary and Quincy, Melville did not idolize the China trade's merchant princes. Melville's grandfathers had also been heroes of the Revolutionary War. Major Thomas Melvill had taken part in the Boston Tea Party and joined the Society of Cincinnati.[114] But Major Melvill's son Arthur Melvill (Herman's father) had not flourished, failing to capitalize on his father's reputation after leaving Boston and floundering in New York.[115] *Israel Potter* is in part Melville's satire of early national biographies that celebrated international commerce as a means of establishing national virtue.

The source of *Israel Potter* is an 1824 "autobiographical pamphlet" by Israel R. Potter, a Revolutionary War veteran, wounded three times at the Battle of Bunker Hill.[116] Taken prisoner during the war, Potter spent decades after in London and Paris before returning to the United States in 1824 with the help of the U.S. consul, at about the same time as a group of Massachusetts politicians and businessmen (including Perkins) had begun to plan the construction of a monument to the Battle of Bunker Hill. Having returned to the U.S. poor and destitute, Potter worked with popular writer Henry Trumbull to publish a life account in hopes of securing a veteran's pension from the U.S. government; the long descriptive title gives an overview of his ordeal: *Life and Remarkable Adventures of Israel R. Potter, (A Native of Cranston, Rhode-Island.) Who Was a Soldier in the American Revolution, And took a distinguished part in the Battle of Bunker Hill (in which he received three wounds) after which he was taken Prisoner by the British, conveyed to England, where for 30 years he obtained a livelihood for himself and family, by crying "Old Chairs to Mend" through the Streets of London.—In May last, by the assistance of the American Consul, he succeeded (in the 79th year of his age) in obtaining a passage to his native country, after an absence of 48 years* (1824).[117] The pamphlet was somewhat popular in its day, but contemporary scholars have determined that it is very likely Trumbull's work rather than Potter's.[118] The printer Trumbull was known for his *Life and Adventures of Daniel Boone* (1824) and other "little books belong[ing] to a popular type that included the narratives of shipwrecked sailors, Indian captives, frontiersmen, criminals, runaway slaves, eccentrics, veterans of the American Revolution and other wars, and biographies of Founding Fathers."[119]

Recently, literary scholars have read *Israel Potter* as a genre-bending critique of national biography. Peter Bellis contends that Melville's revision purposely teases the conventions of sincerity and disrupts the authenticity upon which biographical and historical narratives generally derive their credibility as fact rather than fiction.[120] To establish their status as true, biographical and historical narratives contrast with fictional accounts, even though biography and history and fiction all rely on similar discursive strategies in building "mythic figures" that exceed reportage of facts as they become "large-scale" presentations of "national self-definition."[121] The clear line of narrative development in a conventional national biography starkly contrasts with the uncertainties, vagaries, and moral dilemmas of lived experience. The putative continuity of virtuous national "character" belies the selective, discontinuous, and deeply personal operations of memory. Whereas national biographies such as Quincy's *Journals of Major Samuel Shaw* and Cary's *Memoir of Thomas H.*

Perkins encourage readers to identify with the biographical model and idolize the subjects for their speculative adventures, Melville reads their life stories to index degrees of alienation from national belonging premised on commercial redemption.

Rewriting the 1824 pamphlet of a pathetically exiled and destitute veteran, Melville creates an unreliable editorial voice that augments the distance between the biographical model and the textual representation of that self. Ironically, Melville's Editor reassures his readers that Potter's literary monument of the rewritten and republished account "preserves, almost in reprint, Israel Potter's autobiographical story," which the Editor reports having saved from oblivion after obtaining a "tattered copy, rescued by the merest chance from rag-pickers."[122] The only change the Editor acknowledges making is the adjustment of the narrative's "grammatical person"—that is, the altering of Potter's first-person "I" to the new account's third-person "he." Of course, this pronoun shift is a fundamental matter for genres of autobiography and biography that depend on readers' willingness to trust that the narrative reflects the views of the person whose life is being recounted. The shift from first to third person enables Melville to structure dramatic irony that emphasizes the "gap between individual self-consciousness (autobiography), and the wider perspective of history as a whole."[123] And there are many obvious gaps between the two textual versions of Israel Potter, so many gaps that Melville's story is a new creation altogether. Nevertheless, the Editor assures fidelity to the original—a fidelity bordering on verisimilitude. Appealing for his readers' trust, he avers too high a respect for "the allotment of Providence" than to have embellished with any "poetic justice" the "hard fortunes of my hero."[124]

In regard to the book's relevance to the China trade's merchant princes, the red flag of irony is in the Editor's "Dedication" of *Israel Potter* to the memorial of the Battle of Bunker Hill with these words: "Your Highness' Most devoted and obsequious, The Editor."[125] The Editor then dates the prefatory dedication "June 1854," the eightieth anniversary of the battle. The Editor goes on to enthuse that "His Highness the Bunker-Hill Memorial" is more than a granite obelisk built to honor those killed in the famous battle on 17 June 1775.[126] It stands in for the veterans themselves. As the Editor personifies and addresses the granite memorial as his sovereign, the dedication extends the book's structural irony by offering hyperbolic praise to the biographical genre itself: "Biography, in its purer form, confined to the ended lives of the true and brave, may be held to be the fairest meed of human virtue—once given and received in entire disinterestedness—since neither can the biographer hope for acknowledgement from the subject, nor the subject at all avail himself of the biographical distinction conferred."[127]

Like the granite memorial of Bunker Hill, the generic form of biography seems to have subsumed the human life that it ostensibly celebrates. In a tone that upon second reading verges on sarcasm, the Editor analogies his new biography to Potter's own "private Bunker Hill" memorial, which promises to pay a "posthumous pension" every spring in "new mosses and sward."[128] The Editor also laments the literary neglect of Israel Potter's life, which he surmises the public was probably "astonish[ed]" not to see "in the volumes of [Jared] Sparks." In hyperbolic estimation, "Israel Potter" (the pamphlet) is wise beyond the limits of Israel Potter (the person) in having avoided Spark's attention, "purposely . . . wait[ing] to make his popular advent under the present exalted patronage" of the Bunker Hill memorial.[129] The screw of personifying hyperbole tightens as the Editor credits the Bunker Hill Monument with not merely financing the work of a Great Biographer (i.e., the "Editor") but actually being Potter's Great Biographer, authorizing Potter's Life as the "national commemorator" of "the anonymous privates of June 17, 1775" who died on the actual battlefield and who now receive their "solid reward of your granite."[130] The wounded and penurious veteran Israel Potter has been alienated several times over: by his government stranding him in destitution upon his repatriation, by a pamphlet that did not attract the attention of Jared Sparks, by an Editor who retrieves it from a trash heap only to rewrite it beyond recognition, and by the Editor's dedication that goes so far as to authorize the moss-covered Bunker Hill Monument as the sovereign author and caretaker of the deceased Israel Potter's life.

Melville probably could not have read Cary's 1856 biography of Perkins before writing *Israel Potter*, but Perkins seems to be in the background of Melville's satiric dedication. As Melville impugns conventions of national biography, he defies the authenticity of a Bunker Hill memorial built to honor those who had lost their lives while leaving the surviving veterans without a government pension. Melville could be objecting in principle to memorializing structures such as biographies and national monuments. But in the context of Perkin's life story of international commerce, Melville seems to resent the specific opportunism of the Bunker Hill Monument's construction and the realignment of Revolutionary War heroism with commercial adventure that served ideological promotion of free-trade imperialism.

Melville would have been well aware of how waving the bloody flag of Bunker Hill had served generations of merchants in promoting speculative endeavors that reached from Boston to Canton. As Hennig Cohen remarks, the preface to Melville's *Israel Potter* seems a "sarcastic comment on the oration that Daniel Webster delivered" at the dedication ceremony to begin construction of the memorial in 1824.[131] As the fiftieth anniversary of the Battle of Bunker Hill approached, a core group of politicians and businessmen formed the Bunker Hill Monument Association. On 17 June 1824, the forty-ninth anniversary of the battle, there was a grand fund-raising gala. President John Quincy Adams attended, Webster was the key speaker, and the honored guest was none other than Marquis de Lafayette. Josiah Quincy—Shaw's biographer— introduced Lafayette to the surviving Revolutionary War veterans, who formed a ceremonial reception line. At the proposed site of construction, Lafayette laid the cornerstone and speeches commenced. Reflecting back on the event in 1883, Josiah Quincy exclaims: "How can I give an idea of the freshness and feeling with which we celebrated the fiftieth return of the day when the great battle of our Revolution had been fought!"—"The day was simply perfect."[132] Melville's grandfather Major Thomas Melvill in fact met Lafayette during his visit to the United States, but it is unclear whether he attended the memorial's dedication ceremony as a representative war veteran.[133]

Construction of the monument lasted two decades, affording more opportunities to commemorate the veterans of the Revolutionary War. It is difficult to determine whether Perkins made a material profit from construction of the monument itself, but he definitely used the endeavor to start a railway company. Perkin's biographers Carl Seaburg and Stanley Paterson explain in *Merchant Prince of Boston* that Perkins saw "commercial possibilities" in the endeavor, "particularly since there was a captive customer, namely the Monument Association."[134] On 4 March 1826 Perkins incorporated the Granite Railroad Company to transport the stone from the Quincy quarry to Bunker Hill, and, in the decade before the steam engine, horses soon pulled the granite-laden railcars on the track. In 1827 Perkins became president of the Monument Association and took on other roles as well, achieving an "interlocking directorate": "As president of the railroad, he oversaw the sale of granite at a profit. As chairman of the building committee, he oversaw the railway work. As president the association, he oversaw the Building Committee."[135] In 1834 he "relinquished the presidency" of the Granite Railway but continued to influence operations through its new president, his son-in-law and future biographer, Thomas G. Cary. Over the next decades, the Granite Railroad Company linked up with other developing rail lines and proved to be a very profitable longterm endeavor.[136]

As the First Opium War concluded in 1842, China featured prominently in the ceremonies that re-celebrated the memorial. Given how Quincy linked Major Shaw's Revolutionary War service to his eventual success in the China Trade, this is not surprising. The dedication ceremony for the Battle of Bunker Hill memorial on 17 June 1843 provided President John Tyler an occasion to trumpet the extension of U.S. influence throughout the Pacific in what became known as the Tyler Doctrine (1842), penned by Secretary of State Daniel Webster. Along with the thirteen surviving veterans of the Battle of Bunker Hill, his cabinet attended the ceremony.[137] As the secretary of state, Webster again delivered the keynote, this one nearly two hours long.

Attending the banquet as a guest of honor was the new minister to China, the former Massachusetts congressman Caleb Cushing, who would negotiate the first treaty between China and the United States, the Treaty of Wanghia (1844). President Tyler introduced him at the banquet with this toast to "The Chinese Empire": "In all its celestial surface there was no mound like Bunker Hill."[138] In his remarks, Cushing proclaimed that "there is a glory above our field of battle—there is a glory in the teaming prosperity around us—in the smiling myriads who to-day assembled on Bunker Hill"; he continued, "I have myself been honored with a commission of *peace*, and am entrusted with the duty of bringing nearer together, if possible, the civilization of the old and new worlds—the Asiatic, European and American continents."[139] Cushing concluded by lifting the Bunker Hill memorial to grand humanitarian significance: "I go to China, sir, if I may express myself, in behalf of civilization, and that, if possible, the doors of three hundred millions of Asiatic laborers may be opened to America. And if there is to be there another Bunker Hill monument, may it not be to commemorate the triumph of power over people, but the accumulating glory of peaceful arts, and civilized life."[140]

In Cushing's imagination, the memorial to the Battle of Bunker Hill foretells a global pax Americana that stretches to and through China. Melville saw the world very differently. Israel Potter never made it to Canton and never secured loans for such commercial adventure during his peripatetic adventures in penurious exile. The American protagonist Amasa Delano of Melville's next novella, "Benito Cereno," did travel to Canton. Melville created the story by revising a chapter from the historical Delano's nonfictional account of three voyages to China in *A Narrative of Voyages and Travels* (1817) in which the American merchant and ship captain comes upon a distressed Spanish slave ship while desperately hunting for sealskins in the Pacific Ocean to take to Canton. The story highlights another reason that Melville resented the casting of U.S. merchants as virtuous national heroes: their participation in the slave trade ran parallel to speculations in the China trade.

CHAPTER TWO

Captain Amasa Delano, China Trader

Slavery, Sealskins, and Herman Melville's Dollar Signs of the Canton Trade

> To pass beyond the pillars of Hercules, that is, to sail out of the Streights of Gibraltar, was, in the antient world, long considered as a most wonderful and dangerous exploit of navigation.
>
> ADAM SMITH, *An Inquiry into the Nature and Causes of the Wealth of Nations* (1776), 1:30

Captain Amasa Delano (1763–1823) from Duxbury, Massachusetts, was a younger contemporary of Major Samuel Shaw. A decade after three extended voyages to Canton put him deep into debt, he wrote *A Narrative of Voyages and Travels, in the Northern and Southern Hemispheres: Comprising Three Voyages Round the World; Together with a Voyage of Survey and Discovery in the Pacific Ocean and Oriental Islands* (1817).[1] Delano's account extends Shaw's description of the China trade into the nineteenth century and permits a reinterpretation of Herman Melville's "Benito Cereno" (1855) as a satire of the era's prevalent free-trade rhetoric that glorified New England's merchant princes.[2]

Delano's account drew scholarly attention in the twentieth century as the source of Melville's story.[3] In both versions, Captain Delano boards a distressed Spanish ship and walks into the middle of a revolt masterminded by Senegalese and other West Africans who have survived the transatlantic Middle Passage and subsequent land passage across South America.[4] Instead of killing Delano, they feign subservience to the Spanish captain and crew, biding time to strategize a return to safe harbors of Africa. Wary of the circumstances but oblivious to the revolt, Delano spends the day conversing with the ship's captain, Don Benito Cereno, whose ostensible servant listens in, all the while intimidating his ostensible master. Delano realizes the situation only *after* his crew has retrieved him, at which point he orders them to salvage the ship and to re-enslave the Africans. When this is done, he sails to Concepción, Peru, expecting the Spanish courts to award him a lion's share of the recovered capital.

Frontispiece to Delano, *Narrative of Voyages and Travels*
in Northern and Southern Hemispheres.

Melville's story and the original *Narrative of Voyages* provide insight on the success of Delano's contemporary competitors, the first millionaires of the United States: John Jacob Astor, Stephen Girard, and Thomas H. Perkins. All three built their capital foundations in the West Indies and, after the Haitian Revolution (1791–1804), extended their speculative blueprints to China, where they coordinated ventures in sealskins, beaver pelts, silver, and opium. *Narrative of Voyages* describes the short window of time at the turn of the century when sealskins harvested from islands in the South Pacific commanded great profit at Canton where Western traders were limited to silver as the medium of exchange in purchasing tea. Unbridled killing of seals soon led to an oversupply of skins and the animals' near extinction. As both supply of and demand for sealskins waned in Canton, revolutions across South America severely curtailed the world supply of silver, posing a more serious threat to trade. As for Delano, he retreated to Boston, disappointed and in debt, not daring to undertake a fourth voyage. Conversely Astor, Girard, and Perkins flourished as their companies survived the silver contraction and subsequently thrived by turning to Turkish opium and transshipment services for British firms outmaneuvering the British East India Company's country trade regulations.

This chapter proposes the China trade as context for a new understanding of Melville's story. By juxtaposing Delano's *Narrative of Voyages* and "Benito Cereno," the goal is to highlight the dramatic irony that Melville generates in using third-person narration to recast Delano from being disappointed and indebted by his efforts to being optimistic and enriched (albeit "blunt-thinking").[5] The original's account also highlights the importance of the Spanish silver dollar in the trans-hemispheric slave trade stretching from the West Indies to Southeast Asia on the geographic periphery of Canton. The dollar's importance explains why Melville weaves allusions to the Spanish empire and Southeast Asia throughout the story in critiquing U.S. China traders for free-trade imperialism.[6] His critique is most pronounced in the story's final conversation when Delano enthusiastically personifies trade in the blue sky, blue sea, and gentle trade winds while remaining oblivious to the historical shadows of slavery that haunt his Spanish counterpart to his grave.

Sealskins and Slavery in the Southeast Asian Zone of the Canton Trade

In 1784 when Major Samuel Shaw set off to Canton on his first sea voyage, he was horrified to witness the misery of those enslaved on a French ship outside a Portuguese port in the Atlantic Ocean. In Delano's account there is no comparable complaint. Having been on several trading ventures in the West Indies, he knew what to expect in the transatlantic. Sailing in the Pacific and throughout Southeast Asia, he witnessed different modes of slavery.

On his first China voyage Delano coincidently accompanied Major Shaw on the ill-fated *Massachusetts*; once its cargo hold became infested with mold, any plans for additional long-haul voyages were ruined. From Macao Shaw helped Delano sign on with the British commodore John McClure as a volunteer officer at the rank of lieutenant for a two-year trading (1791–93) circuit to collect commodities, brokering trade in networks leading to the Cohongs in Canton.[7] McClure and Delano headed southeastward to the Philippines and the Pelew Islands (Palau), down to New Guinea (contemporary Indonesia and Papua New Guinea), and to the Spice Islands (in the Banda Sea). Then they proceeded southwest to the Dutch-controlled island of Timor (contemporary Indonesia and East Timor), whose "natives" he classifies as "Malays" and "Mahometans."[8] After stopping at the major port of Batavia (contemporary Jakarta, Indonesia), they sailed up the west coast of the island of Borneo (contemporary Brunei in Indonesia and Malaysia), through the Sea of Celebes and back to Pelew, and on to Formosa (contemporary Taiwan), before arriving back at Macao.[9]

On this long leg of the first voyage, Delano outlines the dynamics of slave trading that pervaded this maritime network of Southeast Asia. Influential regional leaders acquired, retained, put to work, exchanged, and ransomed human beings "astride the arterial trade routes near the eastern Malaysian seas."[10] Although enslaved people were not commodities traded into China, enslaved Malay and New Guinean people were bought and sold in Southeast Asian ports, including Dutch-controlled Batavia.[11] In Delano's time, Christians and Mohammedan Rajahs struck up alliances as Spain, Holland, and Britain vied with each other for influence across a watery geography populated by varieties of indigenous peoples. Rajahs ruled their sultanate territories and projected influence by collaborating with indigenous leaders in regional networks. Commercial reward depended on controlling the labor forces that harvested commodities and on overseeing the commercial exchanges that flowed through the region's archipelagos.

Reading Delano's account, it becomes clear that U.S.-based racial designations codifying slavery in terms of black and white did not effectively categorize the labor required to accumulate the merchantable goods such as pearls, tortoise shells, tripang (sea cumbers or beche-de-mer), shark's fin, bird's nests, wax, camphor, cinnamon, pepper, nutmeg, opium, and rattan wood. In these eighteenth-century zones of trade, the "clientage relationships" were based in shifting affiliations rooted in kinship and Islamic law.[12] Delano alludes to these relationships when describing "the natives" of Borneo as "Mahometans and Gentoos [Hindus]," noting "the Arabic [language] in some degree spreads with the extension of the Koran; but the Malay is the general language of the island."[13] He also alludes to various forms of captivity and slavery in Southeast Asia when musing over his personal safety and economic prospects. Western ship captains and their crews found themselves vulnerable to being taken captive around the thousands of islands that form the archipelagos of what have become the Philippines, Malaysia, and Indonesia, most often for eventual ransom in networks of political alliance similar to those of the Barbary States in the Mediterranean.[14] Acknowledging his vulnerability to enslavement, Delano suggests the limits of Western commercial power in South and Southeast Asia. He reports having "seen several Europeans, who have been in slavery in Borneo" and suffered treatment "far worse than the severities of Algerine captivity."[15] Delano's citation of David Woodard's 1804 captivity account corroborates James Warren's observation that, from a European perspective, this zone must have seemed "an Islamic world whose activities centered about piracy and slavery."[16]

Feeling vulnerable in the Pacific seems to inspire Delano to condemn any form of human captivity or commodification and to blame European traders from Portugal, Holland, Spain, and Britain for taking slaves from New Guinea for service, enjoyment, or brokerage elsewhere in the zone. He validates the New Guinean hostility toward "white people," explaining that Western traders "have too often, and to their everlasting disgrace, used their arts and force, as members of civilized society, to betray, to kidnap, or to seize openly and violently, the natives for most selfish and inhuman purposes."[17] Delano's employer, Commodore McClure, would seem a case in point. Delano writes that at Timor he purchased "three or four female slaves of Malay, from nine to twelve years old," along with some "males of Malay," "a Bombay female, born of European parents; and five or six male slaves, from different eastern coasts."[18] However, Delano never criticizes the commodore. Quite the opposite—he compliments him for being "uniformly just, honest, generous and friendly" in his dealings with "natives" in various places.[19] Assessing Delano's commentary during this first voyage, Sterling Stuckey and Joshua Leslie conclude that Melville must have "had serious reservations" about him "as a human being."[20]

Delano's first China voyage (1790–93) consisted of two parts. Returning to Canton after nearly two years, he "cashed out" from his service with McClure, taking "part of his wages in [opium], which he smuggled into China and sold, doubling his earnings."[21] He then partnered with a Captain Steward to command the ship *Eliza* for the influential Dutch merchant Andreas Everardus van Braam Houckgeest. They set off for Ostend, Belgium, from Macao in April 1793 but found trouble upon reaching the Isle of France (Mauritius). In the wake of the French Revolution, the Wars of the First Coalition (1793–97) had begun. France had begun confiscating Dutch property, and van Braam Houckgeest's cargo was particularly vulnerable. There were more immediate concerns too. The *Eliza* was leaky and worm-infested—a disaster waiting to happen. Delano and Stewart acted boldly, selling the ship, buying a new one, and then heading to Bombay, hoping to protect van Braam Houckgeest's property in British-controlled waters under cover of Delano's American citizenship as they circled back to Canton, thus salvaging the payload in the face of wartime adversity. It never worked.

Wind and rains wreaked havoc on their new ship. Authorities in Bombay (contemporary Mumbai) recognized the ship as sailing under the flag of a neutral country, but this did not brighten the prospect of getting back to Canton because France had begun seizing Dutch goods on any American ships passing through the Indian Ocean. Delano and Stewart tried to wait things out and resigned themselves to missing the trading season in Canton. Setting their sights on Calcutta, they navigated from colonial port to port down the southwestern coast (Malabar) of the Indian peninsula, past Goa (Portuguese controlled), and to Ceylon (British; contemporary Sri Lanka), and then northward up the eastern coast (Coromandel) of the Bay of Bengal, from Tranquebar (Danish; contemporary Tharangambadi), passing Pondicherry (French), to Madras (British; contemporary Chennai), and then to Calcutta (British; contemporary Kolkata) in Bengal, following landmark pagodas along the way.[22] Debts mounted. In the end, they accepted unfavorable loans on the collateral of their ship and its cargo. Flat broke and in debt, Delano headed back to Boston by way of Philadelphia. Describing his missteps in *Narrative of Voyages*, he mentions being impressed by the successful private British companies that had sprung up alongside the East India Company and the immense wealth accumulating in British-controlled Bengal through the country trade. Alas, his own "high hopes" had been dashed, and his "mind wounded and mortified" by his commercial failure.[23]

Delano's second voyage (1799–1802) was much more successful due to a bountiful albeit brutal harvest of sealskins. In Boston, Delano regrouped with his brothers, forming a company and building a small ship, the *Perseverance*. Setting out for the Pacific with a crew of thirty men in November 1799, they rounded South America at Cape Horn and sailed up the coast of Chile, taking note of various Spanish settlements and ports along the way. In November 1801 they had a full cargo of sealskins and left the Gallipagos Islands (contemporary Galápagos Islands, Ecuador) for Canton, stopping in Owhyee (Hawai'i), the "easternmost of the Sandwich Islands."[24] Delano estimates that at Canton each skin sold for as high as three or four Spanish dollars and as low as thirty-five cents, and usually around one dollar, with "three fourths of the payment . . . generally made in teas."[25]

Because of excessive killing of the seals, the bounty did not last. Outlining a tragedy of the South Pacific commons, Delano writes that when "the Americans came to [Más Afuera Island off the coast of Chile] about the year 1797, and began the business of killing seals, "there is no doubt but there were two or three millions of them on the island. I have made an estimate of more than three millions that have been carried to Canton from there, in the space of seven years. I have carried more than one hundred thousand myself, and have been at the place when there were the people of fourteen ships, or vessels on the island at one time, killing seals."[26] His prescription on how to best slaughter seals explains why they nearly disappeared: "Make a lane of men, two abreast, forming three or four couples" and "drive the seals through this lane," clubbing each on the nose, especially the "half grown, or what are called the young seals."[27] The club stuns the seals, at which point "knives are taken to cut or rip them down on the breast, from under the jaw to the tail, giving a stab in the breast that will kill them. After this all hands go to skinning."[28] Some men could skin sixty seals in one hour. The skin was then stretched, dried for market, and packed on the ship. After selling the sealskins for "teas, sugar, and other articles" at Canton, Delano was back in Boston by November 1802 after nearly three years at sea.[29]

From Boston the Delano brothers looked ahead to further success, but the windfall in sealskins did not extend to his disappointing third and final voyage. Delano embarked in September 1803, setting off for the Pacific's South Sea by way of Africa's Cape of Good Hope. Delano captained the refitted *Perseverance* and his other brother Samuel the newly built *Pilgrim*. A hapless year of searching for seals resulted in desperation. They reconnoitered the coast of Van Diemen's Land (Tasmania, Australia) and sailed up to New Holland's Botany Bay (Sidney, Australia), on to New Zealand, and then eastward to the coast of Chile. They could not find seals. To compound the troubles, Delano uncovered seventeen stowaways who had snuck aboard in Australia. Fearing mutiny, he meted out hard floggings. Delano sums up his feelings at the time of seeing the *Tryal*: "We were in a worse situation to effect any important enterprize than I had been in during the voyage [1803–7]. We had been from home a year and a half, and not made enough amount to twenty dollars for each of my people, who were all on shares, and our future prospects were not very flattering."[30] Growing more desperate, the Delano brothers decided to split up to reconnoiter islands off the coast of Chile.

At this point Amasa Delano came upon a ship drifting near the island of St. Maria.[31] It turned out to be a Spanish slave ship named the *Tryal* transporting seventy-two enslaved West Africans to Lima. Led by a group of Senegalese men, the enslaved had risen up and taken over the ship, killing their putative owner and demanding return to Senegal. Without realizing that a rebellion had taken place, Delano boarded the *Tryal* and spent the day talking with the Spanish captain, "Don Bonito Sereno," whose servant Mure seemed unrelentingly "officious," "subservient," and omnipresent.[32] When Delano's crew came to pick him up, Captain "Don Bonito" leapt into the boat. Delano soon understood the situation. After regrouping back on the main ship, he sent his crew to put down the rebellion, promising them shares of the expected compensation estimated at "more than one hundred thousand dollars."[33] After fierce fighting, Delano's crew re-enslaved the Africans.

At the Spanish courts in Chile and Peru, things did not go as planned: Delano is "mortified" by the spitefully ungrateful Captain Cereno, who sues him for privateering and, to attack his character, collects depositions from the most disaffected of Delano's crew, documenting his penchant for flogging.[34] Delano had to spend several months litigating in the Spanish courts.[35] He won the sympathy of the Spanish viceroy in Lima and his invitation to tour Lima's mint. In *Narrative of Voyages* Delano describes in detail the manufacture of Spanish silver dollars. But biding time in Lima, as the wheels of judicial administration slowly turned, was expensive because his ship and its crew waited in the port of Callao.[36] Eventually, Delano settled with Cereno for a disappointing eight thousand pesos in gold, which did not cover the voyage's investment.[37] Delano reports the president's and viceroy's assurances that "his majesty Charles IV [Carlos IIII]" would likely "do something more" to compensate Delano for his efforts in the *Tryal* affair.[38] Delano departed for Canton, arriving in July 1806 and waiting for two months to sell the skins that he had managed to collect. His brother plied the coast of South America for another year but lost his payload in a storm in the China Sea. Upon return to Boston, the steep debts of their failed voyage loomed for the rest of their lives.

Delano never received additional compensation from the Spanish king for salvaging the *Tryal*. Upon his return, a "polite letter" was waiting for him from the Marquis De Case Yruso of Madrid, who conveyed "the satisfaction of his majesty, the king of Spain, on account of your conduct in capture the Spanish ship Tryal."[39] The letter accompanied a gold medal with "the likeness of his majesty [Charles IV] on one side" and the "Reward of Merit" on the other.[40] This medal dashed Delano's hope of receiving a fortune in compensation. In *Narrative of Voyages* he muses over the more generous reward that he would have received if not for the "the unhappy catastrophe which soon after took place in Spain, by the dethronement of Charles IV, and the distracted state of the Spanish government."[41] The Spanish reign of Napoleon's brother Joseph Bonaparte lasted only one year before Charles's son Ferdinand took the throne. Despite the restoration, Spain lost control of the Americas as revolutions spread throughout Chile, Mexico, and Peru. Delano wrote *Narrative* in the wake of his personal disappointment over compensation for the *Tryal* affair and as these revolutions curtailed the world supply of silver to make the China trade even more challenging. When Delano died in 1823, his "total estate" consisted of "one thread bare hammock," "an old pine writing desk," and "seven hundred copies of *A Narrative of Voyages and Travels*."[42]

Herman Melville's Delano and the China Trade

In turning the *Tryal* episode into "Benito Cereno," Melville was not interested in fidelity to the original at the levels of fact, narrative exposition, or characterization. Three changes bring to the foreground the relevance of the China trade and Melville's corresponding critique of free-trade imperialism. First, he transforms Delano from a desperate and indebted merchant captain on his way to China into a successful, confident, and optimistic one, fresh out of Canton with a lucrative payload. Second, he adjusts the narrative perspective from first to third person, thus emphasizing the protagonist's blind spots and encouraging readers to think beyond Delano's impressions and inchoate formulations. The story's dramatically ironic structure immediately calls Delano's judgment into question, introducing him not only as "a person of a singularly undistrustful good nature" with a "benevolent heart" but also as "blunt-thinking" and "of such native simplicity as to be incapable of satire or irony."[43] This directs readers' attention to *how* the protagonist counters fear and confusion in the story's South Pacific scene with incongruous racial stereotypes related to transatlantic slavery. Third, Melville weaves signs of Spanish empire ("mythical or symbolic devices") throughout the story as realistic details that build a sense of place and as fixations in the minds of Delano and Babo, who relate to the signs in very different ways. A short summary of the plot highlights the dramatic contours of these key alterations.[44]

For Delano to be successful in his seal-hunting endeavors, Melville needed to move the *Tryal* incident earlier, to 1799 from 1805. After a winning season in Canton, Delano is sailing across the Pacific where he spies a ship drifting without a flag in becalmed waters near St. Marie Island off the coast of Chile. It turns out to be a Spanish slave ship named the *San Dominick* (rather than the *Tryal*). Approaching the ship through gray shadows, Delano sees the *San Dominick* as a "whitewashed monastery after a thunderstorm, seen perched upon some dun cliff among the Pyrenees," and the Africans on board as a "ship-load of monks" peeking out from the window of their cloister. Upon determining that it is indeed a "Spanish merchantman of the first class, carrying negro slaves, amongst other valuable freight, from one colonial port to another," Delano conjures a vision of "superannuated Italian palaces" that "preserved signs of former state" "under the decline of masters."[45] Moving closer, his eye is caught by the "principle relic" on the prow of the ship, "the ample oval of the shield-like stern-piece, intricately carved with the arms of Castile and Leon, medallioned about by groups of mythological or symbolic devices: uppermost and central of which was a dark satyr in a mask, holding his foot on the prostrate neck of a writhing figure, likewise masked."[46] Delano does not see the ship's "figure-head" because there is a canvas tarp wrapped around it; readers later learn that the tarp covers the skeleton of the executed slave owner—a skeleton that replaces the ship's original effigy of Christopher Columbus, "the discoverer of the New World."[47]

Boarding the ship, Delano spends the day conversing with Captain Benito Cereno, whose officious Senegalese servant Babo (rather than Mure) listens in on the conversations while orchestrating the broader masquerade. Due to Cereno's strange behavior, Delano relegates him to the status of a "paper captain," enervated and weak like the sixteenth-century "Charles V., just previous to the anchoritish retirement of that monarch from the throne."[48] Trying to understand the cause of the ship's distress, he asks him many questions. The original itinerary of the *San Dominick* was a routine, coastal transport along the colonial ports of Valparaiso,

Chile, to Callao, Peru, near Lima. But, as Babo listens in, Cereno claims to have rounded Cape Horn from Buenos Aires to Lima after "heavy gales" destroyed the lifeboats, carried off three crewmembers, and necessitated the casting of provisions overboard.[49] The damaged *San Dominick* drifted northwestward into the Pacific Ocean when "the breeze suddenly deserted her, in unknown waters, to sultry calms."[50] In Cereno's false tale of nautical woes, wind has not been a friend.

Throughout the day Delano entertains many suspicions, even likening Cereno to a Malay pirate plotting to take his ship. Delano feels that his story does not add up but never figures out that Babo is behind the ruse. In a famous scene, Babo takes Delano to a room where he shaves Cereno in a highly theatrical manner, placing Cereno in a chair with "a rude barber's crotch at the back, working with a screw" that "seemed some grotesque engine of torment."[51] Seating Delano in a Malaccan settee across from Cereno, Babo affixes to Cereno as a bib the Spanish flag—"a profusion of armorial bars and ground colors—black, blue, and yellow—a closed castle in a blood-red diagonal with a lion rampant in a white."[52] Upon noticing Babo's use of the flag, Delano addresses Cereno: "'The castle and the lion,' exclaimed Captain Delano—'why, Don Benito, this is the flag of Spain you use here. It's well it's only I, and not the King, that sees this,' he added, with a smile, 'but'—turning towards the black—'it's all one, I suppose, so the colors be gay;' which playful remark did not fail somewhat to tickle the negro."[53] Although Delano notices what Babo ("the black") is doing, he dismisses it as "an odd instance of African love of bright colors" rather than a conscious desecration of the flag.[54] As the shaving session continues, Delano presses Cereno on the ship's itinerary, even as he muses over the image of Babo holding the razor above Cereno's head and sees briefly "in the black . . . a headman, and in the white a man on the block."[55] The narrator dismisses this disconcerting impression as "one of his antic conceits, appearing and vanishing in a breath, from which, perhaps, the best regulated mind is not always free."[56] Nevertheless, as the scene ends, Delano comes back to the image: "Indeed, [Cereno] sat so pale and rigid now, that the negro seemed a Nubian sculptor finishing off a white statue-head."[57]

Delano survives in part because he does not register the revolt or Babo's visceral intimidation. When Delano's crew comes to retrieve him, Cereno desperately leaps down into the boat with Babo chasing after. As the Spanish sailors abandon ship, Delano realizes what is happening. He sends his crew to recapture the ship and promises each man a share of the reward. He then heads to colonial Spanish America. The story—like the original—shifts to court depositions that present the backstory of the rebellion and Babo's symbolically rich tactics of intimidation, which play on the symbols of a Spanish empire. After killing their owner (Cereno's friend Don Alexandro Aranda), Babo skeletonized the body and mounted it on the prow of the *San Dominick* to replace the effigy of Columbus. Beneath this skeleton, Babo chalked the message, " 'Seguid vuestro jefe,' (follow your leader)" and called "each Spaniard forward, and [asked] him whose skeleton that [is], and whether from its whiteness, he should not think it a white's."[58] To each, Babo repeated the chilling admonition: if you do not "keep faith with the blacks from here to Senegal," then "you shall in spirit, as now in body, 'follow your leader.' "[59] After the trial, Spanish authorities convict and publicly execute Babo, fixing his head—"that hive of subtlety"—"on a pole in the Plaza" of Lima to meet, "unabashed, the gaze of the whites."[60]

After being rescued, Cereno remains despondent. An exhilarated but concerned Delano tries to cheer up his Spanish counterpart, asserting: "The past is passed. Why moralize upon it? Forget it."[61] Exclaiming on the role of Providence in preserving his life, Delano finds inspiration in the "bright sun," "the blue sea," and "blue sky" that have "turned over new leaves."[62] Cereno resists the redemptive personification by frustrating Delano's figurative associations: the sky, sun, and sea have no memory and are not human. Delano presses the personifications by appealing to a sense of touch: "But these mild trades that now fan your cheek, do they not come with a human-like healing to you? Warm friend, steadfast friends are the trades."[63] Don Cereno refuses the saving hand of commerce, insisting that the winds only "waft me to my tomb." Delano makes a final appeal with the exasperated question: "What has cast such a shadow upon you?" Cereno replies with his final words in the story—"the negro"—and fades into deeper despondency culminating in his death months after Babo's execution.[64]

As Melville works signs of the Spanish empire into the story, the China trade may seem irrelevant. However, he pointedly maintains Delano's identity as a China trader in an early exchange that explicitly references Canton. With Babo eavesdropping, Cereno asks Delano in a "husky whisper":

> "Señor [Delano], may I ask how long you have lain at this isle?"
> "Oh, but a day or two, Don Benito."
> "And from what port are you last?"
> "Canton."
> "And there, Señor, you exchanged your seal skins for teas and silks, I think you said?"
> "Yes. Silks, mostly."
> "And the balance you took in specie, perhaps?"
> Captain Delano, fidgeting a little, answered—
> "Yes; some silver; not a very great deal, though."

"Ah—well. May I ask you how many men have you Señor?"

Captain Delano slightly startled, but answered—

"'bout five-and-twenty, all told."[65]

Delano's itinerary evinces considerable nautical expertise, and Babo might hope to use him and his American flag in plotting a route to Africa that avoids interception and recapture. Beyond indicating that Delano has concluded a successful season of trade, the conversation establishes Canton as a key point of dramatic reference, raising the question: How does it matter that Delano is on a China voyage when he encounters the slave ship (*San Dominick*) floating in the South Pacific?

One answer may lie in the story's social commentary on very wealthy merchants, such as Colonel Thomas Perkins. In the early 1830s Perkins decided to merge his company with another to form Russell & Company, the most powerful U.S. trading firm in China during the nineteenth century. When, more than a decade after the First Opium War (1839–42), Melville reimagined Amasa Delano as an optimistic and successful China trader in "Benito Cereno," the Second Opium War (1856–60) was about to begin. During the interwar period—from 1844 to 1856—opium continued to be extremely lucrative. In a historical irony of which Melville may or may not have been aware, Amasa Delano's descendants profited in China; Warren Delano Jr. and Edward Delano took turns directing the Russell & Company and winning their fortunes.[66]

Beyond biographical speculation, Melville's inclusion of the China trade stretches the early national commercial geography from transatlantic to the transpacific, from the West to East Indies, and from the silver mining capitals of Spanish colonial America to Canton. Melville criticizes Delano's behavior as a China trader in part by recasting him as a provincial nationalist who overlooks the Pacific context by falling back on simplistic racialist and racist stereotypes relating to the transatlantic slave trade. Here is the story's dramatic irony in action. The narrator offers a generalization: "Always upon first boarding a large and populous ship at sea, especially a foreign one, with a nondescript crew such as Lascars or Manilla men, the impression varies in a peculiar way from that produced by first entering a strange house with strange inmates in a strange land."[67] The narrator then continues by relating Delano's contrastingly simplistic conclusion that the *San Dominick* was "in the condition of a transatlantic emigrant ship, among whose multitude of living freight are some individuals, doubtless, as little troublesome as crates and bales."[68] At another early point in the story Delano wonders if Cereno had a "sinister scheme" like "the Malay pirates" who "lure ships after them into treacherous harbors" "by the spectacle of thinly manned or vacant decks, beneath which prowled a hundred spears with yellow arms ready to upthrust them through the mats."[69]

Signs of vulnerability pervade the scene in which Babo leads Cereno and Delano to the secluded cubby room, wraps Cereno in a Spanish flag, and cuts him during a shave. As Delano allays his fears through racial stereotypes, the narrator reports that Delano believed that "negroes are natural valets and hair-dressers" and that, "in fact, like most men of a good, blithe heart, Captain Delano took to negroes, not philanthropically, but genially, just as other men to Newfoundland dogs."[70]

Thus the story's narrative structure highlights Delano's misapprehension of the scene's commercial geography through his projection of stereotypes related to racial binaries of black and white. The reassuring effects of relating everything back to fantastical binaries of race that supported transatlantic slavery are obvious when Delano rebounds from his concern that he might be on a Malay pirate ship by conjuring a tableaux of rustic beauty; spying through the "lace-work of some rigging," he sees an enslaved mother dozing with her nursing child as an innocent, docile doe and faun, "naked nature now, pure tenderness and love."[71] Dismissing a suspicion that Cereno is colluding with the blacks, Delano asks himself rhetorically: "Who ever heard of a white so far a renegade as to apostatize from his very species almost, by leaguing in against it with negroes?"[72] This is not to say that transatlantic stereotypes of black and white were not culturally nuanced; Delano expresses a sense of whiteness that differentiates representative Americans and Spanish from "the blacks," while simultaneously distinguishing American commercial virility from the faded degenerative impotence of the Spanish.[73] But later, relieved at the sight of his crew approaching in a boat to retrieve him, Delano even pulls the pathetic Cereno up to his level: "Spaniards in the main are as good folks as any in Duxbury, Massachusetts."[74]

Melville leaves it to the reader to interpret the geographic incongruities that surface as Delano slides back to the Atlantic to rationalize his anxiety in the Pacific. Belying the simplicity of Delano's transatlantic racialism and racist stereotypes, the cubby room where Babo shaves Cereno is filled with objects that suggest the global extent of the Spanish empire's routes from Lima to Manila and through the archipelagoes of what today are Indonesia, Malaysia, and the Philippines. The narrator describes the cubby as presenting a "picturesque array of odd appurtenances."[75] Key among them are "two long, sharp-ribbed settees of Malacca cane, black with age, and uncomfortable to look at as inquisitors' racks, with a large, misshapen arm-chair."[76] Today, Malacca is part of Malaysia, but in Delano's time it was under control of the Dutch, who, in the seventeenth century, had wrested it from Portugal, who, in the early sixteen century, had conquered the rajah who had ruled it as a sultanate. It is easy to overlook this Malaccan furniture as being among the colorful details that fill out in realistic fashion the chilling scene without thematic consequence. But the furniture emphasizes the Pacific zone of the China trade through which Delano was moving, an interregional zone in which he is indeed vulnerable to enslavement.

The terms of Delano's vulnerability in this zone extend to the subsequent scene in which Delano narrowly avoids being poisoned during lunch. The trial depositions later explain that Francesco, "one of the first band of revolters" and "the creature and tool of Babo," was plotting to lace Delano's food.[77] The narrator describes Francesco as "a tall, rajah-looking mulatto, orientally set off with a pagoda turban formed by three or four madras handkerchiefs wound about his head, tier on tier," who announces lunch in the cabin with "a saalam."[78] However, Delano's description of Francesco falls back on transatlantic racial stereotypes when, sensing a lingering animosity between Babo and Francesco, he trivializes Babo's cold attitude toward Francesco as "jealous watchfulness" motivated by "that peculiar feeling which the full-blooded African entertains for the adulterated one."[79]

Fixing on Francesco's appearance, Delano observes "with interest that while the complexion of the mulatto was hybrid, his physiognomy was European—classically so."[80] He whispers to Cereno: "I am glad to see this usher-of-the-golden-rod of yours; the sight refutes an ugly remark made once by a Barbadoes planter; that when a mulatto has a regular European face, look out for him; he is a devil. But see, your steward here has features more regular than King George's of England; and yet there he nods, and bows, and smiles; a king, indeed—the king of kind hearts and polite fellows. What a pleasant voice he has, too?" Delano's assessment overlooks the "madras handkerchiefs" wound up on his head in the form of a "pagoda turban" in a fashion that makes him "rajah-looking" and his speaking of Arabic ("a saalam"), not to mention his murderous intent. By focusing on faces, Delano reassures himself as he categorizes Francesco as a transatlantic "mulatto," connecting Barbados to London in King George III's reassuring profile, which began appearing on the obverse of gold British sovereigns in 1817. With Babo listening in, Cereno can only signal the irrelevance of Delano's associative rhapsody with the curt reply: "Francesco is a good man."[81] Delano takes this as a direct affirmation of his judgment and as further evidence of Cereno's Spanish unsociability, replying: "Ah, I thought so. For it were strange, indeed, and not very creditable to us white-skins, if a little of our blood mixed with African's, should, far from improving the latter's quality, have the sad effect of pouring vitriolic acid into black broth; improving the hue, perhaps, but not the wholesomeness."[82] Cereno again demurs, saying that he has heard similar opinions about the "Spanish and Indian intermixtures, in our provinces" but knows little about it.[83]

The narrative presents scenes that puzzle Delano as the story's dramatic irony calls on the reader to figure out not only what is happening (i.e., the disguising of a slave revolt) but also what it means for Delano to conjure transatlantic racial stereotypes in allaying concerns that, if expressed, would doom him. The story's final conversation pushes the irony even further. What does it mean that, in the aftermath of realizing what he has unwittingly survived, Delano is able to maintain his enthusiasm for commerce as he seeks compensation for salvaging the *San Dominick* and its cargo of slaves? This chapter continues by considering how the China trade lends additional insight into Melville's critique of Delano's indefatigable national optimism for trade, and it concludes by tracing the story's "mythical or symbolic devices" of the Spanish empire to the silver dollars that moved commodities through the interwoven geographies of the world economy that connected Canton to Lima to Boston.[84]

Yankee Benevolence, Transatlantic Imperial Histories, and the China Trade

The geographic incongruity of Delano's Procrustean transatlantic racial formulas has yet to attract much attention from literary scholars. Influential readings interpret "Benito Cereno" as Melville's criticism of the political compromises by which northerners tolerated slavery to maintain the Union; others have opened the geographic and historical context of such compromise to align the United States with transatlantic imperial histories.[85]

By way of influential example, Eric Sundquist extends Jean Fagan Yellin's characterization of Delano as the "stock Yankee traveler of plantation fiction" by reading the story's symbols as reference to the Haitian Revolution.[86] Sundquist contends that Melville's depiction of Delano renders "perversely ironic the entire virtue of 'benevolence,' the central sentiment of abolitionist rhetoric and action since the mid-eighteenth century."[87] Although Delano is not a slave trader and pities the enslaved Africans, he does not hesitate to re-enslave them for the compensation of salvage. Reflecting similar hypocrisy, the stock character of the benevolent Yankee sympathized with those enslaved in the South while accepting compromises over slavery that held the Union together—a Union that had supposedly turned the page on European imperialism in championing revolutionary forms of liberty. Sundquist then broadens the historical and geographic context of Delano's morally flexible benevolence to align it with centuries of imperial history in the so-called New World. Accordingly, Melville resets events from 1805 to 1799 in order to "accentuate the fact that ["Benito Cereno"] belonged to the age of democratic revolution, in particular the period of violent struggle leading to Haitian independence," and renames the Spanish ship the *San Dominick* in order to reference

Haiti's capitol.[88] In having Babo replace the *San Dominick*'s figurehead of Columbus with the skeleton of the Spanish slaver (Don Aranda), Melville most dramatically references Spanish imperialism in the Americas.

Through such symbols, Sundquist sees Melville pointedly aligning the United States with Spain in a shared legacy of New World imperialism and satirizing an optimistic pride in the United States as a new nation born of revolution against imperial tyranny. The American ship captain reads bold signs of Spanish imperialism ironically as emblems of Old World decline and degeneration, and yet he is unable to identify with the enslaved as fellow revolutionaries. As for the Haitian Revolution, Delano would not recognize its relevance to the events aboard the *San Dominick* because for him the revolution stands outside of history as a sublimely retributive spectacle of rebellion, a "timeless [image] of terror and damnation" in which racial victims unleash savage violence against France."[89] Sundquist concludes that the "masquerade staged by Babo and Benito Cereno to beguile the benevolent Delano probes the limits of the American's contrived innocence at the same time it eloquently enacts the haltingly realized potential for slave rebellion in the New World."[90]

In a different tack that generates a similarly compelling interpretation while overlooking the China trade, Jeannine Marie DeLombard highlights the tactics through which Babo holds Cereno captive for evoking the profound vacuity at the heart of republican definitions of a citizenship premised on contractual relations.[91] After the revolt, Babo demands that Cereno consent to a new contract: sail the ship to Africa to prevent more killing. Given the coercive premise of Babo's contract, Cereno finds himself in a position similar to that of an enslaved person in the antebellum South—his putative consent is premised on the coercive context of his captivity.[92] This experience has lingering and unshakable consequences for Cereno. Having lived in the shadow of capitulation to Babo's contractual demands, he is unable to reassume presuming the ontology of his own free will, realizing that a "'selective endorsement' of subjectivity" pervades all "contractual processes" predicated on an adversarial grammar of rights discourse in which selfhood is conceptualized as "as something owned in defiance of others and to the exclusion of others."[93] According to DeLombard, when Cereno answers Delano's question, "What has cast such a shadow upon you?" with the cryptic reply of "the negro," he is not referring to "the black race" or even "to the larger problem of slavery" but incanting a term that serves as "a temporal figure for the virtual impossibility of asserting independence after one has occupied a state of unfreedom."[94] Cereno's traumatic experience "blurs the temporal boundaries between captivity and legal personhood, subordination and autonomy, incompetence and authority," and prevents him from feeling restored as an "autonomous legal person."[95] Cereno cannot forget the past. He is stranded in a troubled sense of time that resists sequential relevance. In contrast Melville's ambitious but "blunt-thinking" American is not troubled, having never realized in the moment that he was captive while on the *San Dominick* and oblivious to any lingering significance as he looks back on events with an eye to future opportunity. The story ends with him urging his counterpart to forget the past, offering what DeLombard calls "hackneyed Romantic" odes to winds that "waft the history of the slave trade itself."[96]

In both Sundquist's and DeLombard's interpretations, the Pacific setting of the story is of secondary concern. However, aligning Delano's views on slavery with his ambition as a China trader specifies Melville's criticism of patriotically American free-trade enthusiasm. Delano's hackneyed hyperboles call to mind Ralph Waldo Emerson's aforementioned lecture "The Young American" (1849). Recall that the essay presents Columbus as the first hero of a grand commercial romance in which U.S. traders are opening the North American continent to the world market. Emerson characterizes "trade" as "the principle of Liberty" that "planted America and destroyed Feudalism," "[making] peace and [keeping] peace"; he even predicts that trade will eventually "abolish slavery."[97] Invoking an invisible hand that aligns commerce with an unfolding national destiny, Emerson writes:

> Trade is an instrument in the hands of that friendly Power which works for us in our own despite. We design it thus and thus; it turns out otherwise and far better. The beneficent tendency, omnipotent without violence, exists and works. Every line of history inspires a confidence that we shall not go far wrong; that things mend. . . . Our part is plainly not to throw ourselves across the track, to block improvement, and sit till we are stone, but to watch the uprise of successive mornings, and to conspire with the new work of new days. . . . Trade is also for a time, and must give way to something broader and better whose signs are already dawning in the sky.[98]

The source of the "beneficent" Power that Emerson conjures is unclear. In its patriotic blend of Unitarian divinity and classic economic liberalism, the Power coordinates the merchants' ambition to a greater good, and Emerson advises aspiring merchants to trust the supranational network or system of commerce in which a "beneficent tendency" weaves the "lines of history" into progress.

The target of Melville's refashioned Delano was probably not Emerson but members of the wealthy merchant class, such as Colonel Thomas H. Perkins, who funded Boston's Mercantile Library Association to whose members Emerson was speaking. In Delano's three voyages from 1790 to 1807 he was striving to be one of the great China merchants alongside his contemporaries Perkins, John Jacob Astor, and Stephen Girard. As argued in the previous chapter's consideration of *Israel Potter*, Melville did not look to them as virtuous models of national character.

When the narrator of "Bartleby, the Scrivener: A Story of Wall Street" (1853)—included with "Benito Cereno" in *The Piazza Tales* (1856)— declares that "John Jacob Astor" is "a name which, I admit, I love to repeat; for it had a rounded and orbicular sound to it, and rings like unto bullion," Melville is not enthusing over the beneficially aggregating dynamics of free trade and the power of the Spanish dollar and British pound.[99] Rather, he is setting the narrating protagonist up to face Bartleby's confounding preference *not* to engage the circuitries of power that ring in the name Astor "unto bullion." But the apathies of Bartleby and Don Cereno are neither equivalent nor existential, which is to say that Delano's determinedly optimistic benevolence has important historical implications in the context of the China trade.

The story calls readers to consider how Delano's benevolent toleration of slavery tracks into networks of transpacific trade centering on Canton. Although U.S. merchants did not trade slaves in Canton, slave traffic through the West Indies was integral to the entrepreneurial portfolios upon which they relied as they expanded into the China trade. For example, at fifteen years of age Colonel Thomas Perkins took an apprenticeship in a Boston countinghouse and soon after, in 1785, joined his older brother James, who ran a trading house in Saint-Domingue. They were very successful in generating commissions on transactions that included slaves. In the biography *Merchant Prince of Boston*, Carl Seaburg and Stanley Paterson struggle to set an appropriate tone in speculating on what a young and ambitious Thomas Perkins might have felt upon arriving in a Cape Francis, which "was two weeks away from Puritan Boston by ship if the wind and weather were right."[100] They continue:

> It seemed as if everybody came to the Cape, among them a vicious rabble of adventurers out to make money in a hurry and not particularly caring how they made it or who sweated for it as long as it was not they themselves. Underneath the surface gaiety festered this mass of crooks, criminals, and fortune hunters. The whole voluptuous, shimmering pyramid was carried on the bent back of the black slaves. Forty thousand of them were shipped into Santo Domingo every year. Two thirds of the half-million slaves in the country were African-born, and unlike the domesticated Creole slaves. This fact was soon to have fearful significance.[101]

In their biographical approach, Seaburg and Paterson are perhaps trying to avoid projecting contemporary condemnation of slavery back to the 1790s, but they go on to describe the revolution's "fearful significance" by echoing racist stereotypes as "domesticated Creole slaves" are overrun by the "African-born." Remarkably, they cite T. Lothrop Stoddard's *The French Revolution in San Domingo* (1914) as one of two sources of "general information" and continue by shielding their "merchant prince" Perkins from readers' moral censor by characterizing the brothers' involve-ment in the slave trade as relatively detached.[102] They continue, citing Perkins in parentheses:

> Commission merchants did not get their hands too greatly soiled in the business [of slavery]. Their job was to visit the "Guinea" [West African] ships coming to the Cape, select the prime slaves whom they would purchase either on customers' orders or their own speculation, holding them briefly until they could be sold. They were mid-dlemen and their share of the obvious brutality could be minimal, indeed almost nonexistent. Their transactions were strictly businesslike: getting unsold goods off the shelf ("Your negroes are unsold, we have signified the necessity of finishing this business, and will see it done"); getting all the traffic would bear ("Your negroes were sold at Auction, our W.B. attended and trumped Bob up to 2300 and odd livres, the other went for 1600, he was lame"); coping with special problems ("Almost impos-sible to get rid of an infant negro").[103]

It could go without saying that the Perkins brothers' trading activities were at the heart of brutally commodifying human beings like "unsold goods [on] the shelf." Furthermore, Colonel Perkins was well aware of how slavery worked on Southern U.S. plantations supplied by the Perkinses' West Indian operations. Recuperating from an illness in the 1780s he headed to Charleston, South Carolina, with a letter of introduction from the Revolutionary War hero Major General Henry Knox (for whom Shaw had served as aide-de-camp from June 1782 to November 1782) and paid an extended visit to Mr. Thomas Ferguson's plantation Pon Pon, which "had several rice plantations, upon which he numbered upwards of eight hundred slaves."[104] It was not the Perkinses' consciences that stifled their enterprises in the West Indies.[105] When in 1786–87 the state of Massachusetts outlawed slavery, it became more difficult to insure the human cargo. However, the commission rates on slaving ventures increased and the Perkins brothers outfitted the ship *Katy* for a slaving voyage to Africa in 1792. The ship sank on its return, along with all of those on board.[106]

After the Haitian uprising the Perkins brothers looked to China, diversifying their trade enterprises, along "a pattern of three types of ventures": "Short-term speculations in the West Indian markets; medium-term investments in the Euro-pean market; and long-term adventures in the China trade, which involved an ex-tended journey and a stay on the Northwest Coast to secure skins to trade with in Canton."[107] Perkins and his brothers were also involved in the sealskin trade until it faltered.[108] If it were not for the wealth that Perkins generated in the China trade, he would not have warranted biographies by authors who were intent on rational-izing the Perkinses' investments in slavery. In contrast, Melville depicts the U.S.

China trader in antiheroic terms. Delano is not turning a page on imperial history by turning East to China but rather perpetuating imperial violence in speculative ventures that connect Boston, Saint-Domingue, Lima, and Canton.

Furthermore, Delano and Perkins calibrated strategies of benevolence as they reoriented themselves and their investments in moving through the Pacific. On early voyages to Canton in the 1780s, Perkins pities the enslaved Malay and New Guinea people in Dutch-controlled Batavia. In his journal he notices that "private" or "company slaves" "travers[ed] the city morning and evening, chained two by two," and sprinkled the streets with water to mitigate dust.[109] He rues that the convenience of clean streets comes at the great "expense of human feeling."[110] Nevertheless, he admits his "astonish[ment] at the low price [of the Malaysian slaves]" "in comparison to the Guinea [West African] slaves in America and the colonies."[111] Noticing that Malaysians were being bought and sold for their musical talents, he reacts by balancing sympathy for them against his assessment of opportunity to profit, distinguishing "those bands [of enslaved Malaysian performers] which are brought to some degree of perfection" and "bring a large price" from those "without any particular recommendation" who are "taken from the vessels which import them" and "sold for about one hundred paper-dollars a head."[112]

To extend Sundquist's geohistorical purview, benevolence enabled northern Yankees to balance commercial ambition against moral concerns as they encountered different forms of slavery when pivoting from the West Indies to China after the Haitian Revolution. For example, in *Narrative of Voyages* Delano reflects on his first voyage by urging readers to have faith in a general system of commerce in order to accept economic opportunity that comes from slavery. He reasons that whereas "national prejudices" are "to a certain extent" "very useful, and possibly necessary," they are "always attended by considerable evils in the narrow and intolerant spirit which they perpetuate."[113] He continues:

> The more enlarged a mind becomes in its views of men and the world, the less it will be disposed to denounce the varieties of opinion and pursuit, and more it will enjoy the benevolent results to which wisdom and philosophy point. A narrow mind chafes itself by its own prejudices; but a man, who is accustomed to generalize his observations, principles, and feelings, and to subdue his prejudices by a practical philanthropy, acquires an habitual superiority to the inequalities and provocations of society, and has learned the divine art of extracting good from evil.[114]

As Delano speculates on the benefits of avoiding "national prejudice," counseling readers to appreciate "varieties of opinion and pursuit," he warns against taking a hard stance against slavery, especially as it surfaces in Southeast Asia and the Pacific.

The "benevolent results" of such "practical philanthropy" resonate in his description of recapturing the *Tryal* on his final voyage in 1805. After his crew has put the Africans back into "hand-cuffs, leg-irons, and shackled bolts," Delano reports that the "sight which presented itself to our view was truly horrid."[115] Delano takes pride in protecting the enslaved from the brutal retaliation of the Spanish, "prevent[ing] them from cutting to pieces and killing these poor unfortunate beings"— one Spanish sailor manages to find a razor in the pocket of a jacket of one of the slaves and makes a "cut upon the negro's head," which "bleed[s] shockingly."[116] Delano emphasizes to his reader that he was "obliged to be continually vigilant, to prevent [the Spanish] from using violence toward these wretched creatures."[117] Directing "practical philanthropy" toward the Africans in the specific circumstance of their re-enslavement, Delano plots his course to the Spanish courts in Chile and Peru rather than Africa. By saving their lives and protecting them from the horrid retaliation of the Spanish crew, Delano thus turns a profit. Accordingly, the wise merchant faces the "inequalities and provocations of society" by working through them to a bigger economic payoff. Delano's sense of "practical philanthropy" is so elastic as to caution against a *national prejudice against slavery*. He does not agree with the practice of slavery in principle—whether in the United States, Haiti, or Batavia—and thinks it morally corrupt. But slavery is an evil from which an enlarged mind, dedicated to the opportunities of commerce, can derive economic benefit through the application of a practical philosophy and strategic sympathy.

Silver and Slavery from Peru to Canton

The historical Delano's morally compromised strategic benevolence resonates in his fixation on the Spanish dollars that elude him throughout his first and third voyages and the absence of which motivated him to write *Narrative of Voyages*. Reflecting on his success hunting seals on the second voyage, he does not warn against a potential tragedy of the commons. Instead, he advises potential traders to incentivize the crew with a 1 percent share of potential profits.[118] In capturing the *Tryal* he incentivizes his crew by promising a share of the "one hundred thousand dollars" that her salvage promised.[119] But the historical Delano was not a model of commercial success and was left holding a gold medal of Spain's King Charles IV by which to remember the empty promise of a silver-dollar reward. In Melville's version, there is no eventual disappointment as the American merchant anticipates a small fortune on top of the one he has taken away from Canton.

The "mythical or symbolic devices" of the Spanish empire that emblazon the *San Dominick* also pervade the story's narrative descriptions but not merely to counter Delano's exercise of benevolence with the "hard facts" of imperialistic for-

tune making in the West Indies.[120] These signs are richly suggestive of how commodities moved globally from Canton to Boston as a result of Spanish colonial
dollars and of the geopolitical tensions bound up in attempts to control this movement. Broadening the geographic and historical context to China extends Michael
Paul Rogin's influential interpretation in *Subversive Genealogy* in which he contends that the symbols in "Benito Cereno" reflect Melville's profound disillusionment over the lack of revolutionary potential in the United States following 1848,
a momentous year of revolution across Europe.[121] For Rogin the story's isolated
images and "visual symbols" "crowd out the dynamic human relations of a novel-
istic plot" as "self-conscious forms replace the exuberance of proliferated detail"
and "personal inventiveness and discovery."[122] Thus, the story's allusions to the
sixteenth-century Spanish monarch Charles V register Melville's despondency over
American slavery as it continued amid waves of revolution breaking against the
vestiges of feudal Europe. Echoing Hegel's lament that "when philosophy paints
its grey on grey . . . then it has a shape of life grown old," Rogin concludes that
for Melville "even revolution paints gray on gray."[123] Accordingly, the story's gray
shadows—"Shadows present, foreshadowing deeper shadows to come"—figure
the impossibility of revolution in a liberal marketplace predicated on the signifying
logic of perpetual substitution that turns everything—even slave rebellions—into
masks and masquerade.[124]

Rogin is correct that Melville is critical of Delano but his reading of the story
obscures Melville's allusions to the China trade, earlier revolutions in Spanish
America that disrupted world silver supply, and the merchant princes who used
opium to become the first millionaires of the United States. It is important that
Delano remains oblivious to the gray of Hegel's philosophical crisis that Rogin
highlights. From the beginning, when Delano stares into literal and figurative
shadows, he sees opportunity foreshadowing more opportunity to come. To highlight this optimism, the story begins with him in a miasma or phantasmagoria of
gray in which he struggles to establish his field of vision. Early in the morning the
first mate knocks on Delano's cabin door and reports the sighting of a ship drifting
without an identifying flag. Delano comes on deck to gaze into a "gray" that is more
than a color or a play of light. The gray of this opening scene blurs fore-, middle-,
and backgrounds to warp the description of a horizon, denying Delano or the
reader a visual prospect. This gray also works metonymically to blur layers of ele-
mental composition and to erode classificatory distinctions of kind and class between things. The swell of the gray sea suggests the slow undulations of molten
lead, and the gray of the sky materializes into a gray surtout (or outer coat). The
associative power of gray also blurs frames of geographic reference and the physical materiality of the earth as troubled gray birds seemed "kith and kin" to "troubled

gray vapors," skimming their way over the waters "low and fitfully" like "swallows over meadows before storms."[125] Our blunt-thinking and benevolent American hero nevertheless approaches the strange ship with a wary optimism, sensing opportunity to capture dollars that promise him a power of purchase and brokerage in the global marketplace—a power based on money's ostensible materialization of an exchange value that blurs distinctions between people and places and things.

In the context of *Narrative of Voyages*, the obsession with Spanish dollars of Melville's protagonist made practical sense. As outlined in chapter 1, China's Canton System was designed to pull silver specie into Canton and then to Peking. It worked. The historical Delano describes China as "the richest country in the world for gold, silver, and copper."[126] Most of this was from the Spanish mines of South and Central America that were the world economy's primary source of gold and silver.[127] Of the "world silver economy," James Fichter provides a brief description: "Between Columbus's first voyage and the American Revolution [of 1776], 85 percent of the world's silver came from Latin America. Potosí, the main mine in Peru, was nearly three miles high and a two-and-a-half-month donkey trek to Lima, and yet so great was the demand for silver that Potosí was exploited as the greatest silver lode in the world. . . . Europeans tried to find other commodities to sell, but they found that Indian and Chinese merchants wanted little they could offer, save silver."[128] From the 1790s to 1820s when Delano was trading in China, silver dollars supported up to 70 to 80 percent of the commerce in Canton.[129] By 1817, when Delano's *Narrative of Voyages* appeared in print, silver dollars still accounted for as much as "half of the commodities which Americans used for the purchase of Chinese goods."[130] A decade later, in the 1830s, Spanish dollars were still circulating by the millions as opium traffic rose to rebalance the silver flows between China and the Western traders at Canton. William C. Hunter, who directed the firm Russell & Company from 1837 to 1842, recalls in his 1882 memoir *The "Fan Kwae" at Canton Before Treaty Days, 1825–1844* that in 1831 "three [U.S.] vessels alone brought $1,100,000" in Spanish dollars to Canton.[131]

In China silver was especially important because the government used it to stabilize a bimetallic system of currency in which copper *cash* facilitated most daily transactions throughout the country. As Man-houng Lin explains, China's "private sector [such as the Cohong merchants in Canton] supplied" the government with "silver ingots or silver dollars" as "tax payments and large-scale or interprovincial transactions," whereas "the state provided copper coins, which for the most part were exchanged in local retail trade."[132] The Chinese government issued copper coins, but stored and shipped silver by weight in ingot units of very pure silver called *sycee*. Foreign silver coins circulated for trade in coastal Chinese cities where they wore down and were broken into pieces or "broken dollars" to serve as fractions of dollars. What mattered to the Chinese was their silver content. Whole dollars were monitored carefully for purity and for weight in order to ensure that the coins had not been shaved or perforated. Eventually, as the dollars found their way to Peking, they were melted down and forged into the *sycee* ingots. The general stability of China's monetary system depended on maintaining a reliable correlation between supplies of copper and silver. As long as silver came into China and to Peking in adequate amounts, the imperial authorities were able to sustain parallel currencies of silver and copper. Shortfalls of silver disrupted correlation of silver and copper and the prices of salt, rice, tea, and other commodities. The missionary printer Samuel Wells Williams later described the devastating impact of opium on China's monetary system, characterizing the drug as a foreign "manufacture" originating "beyond the country [of China], so that every cent paid for the drug is carried abroad and misery in every shape of poverty, disease, and dementation left in its stead, attended with mere pleasure while the pipe is in the mouth."[133] Estimating the impact of opium, he speculated that from 1800 to 1848 "fully one hundred millions of dollars [had] 'oozed' out of China" and the country's "productive capital decreased fully twice the sum."[134]

In the commercial contest for silver between China and foreign traders, specific Spanish dollars played a central role as a guarantee of high-quality silver. The signs stamped on their heads and tails authenticated them for exchange, and the ridges around their edges prevented shaving or clipping. The symbols on these dollars convey the mythic scope of the Spanish empire. Given the importance of these signs in the Canton trade and the pervasive symbols that Melville weaves into his adaptation, it is worth reviewing them as historical references. In the late fifteenth century, the marriage of Queen Isabella and King Ferdinand II unified imperial Spain as Columbus set off on his voyage. The obverse of these coins is stamped with Isabella and Ferdinand's coat of arms—Castile and León—framed by the Pillars of Hercules, which in classical terms marked the limit of the known world and, later, of the Christian Empire, beyond which there was nothing more ("Non plus vltra"). The banner weaving its way through the pillars and behind the coat of arms amends this limit with the phrase "Plus Vltra," the "more beyond" of the Indies that Columbus had claimed for Spain in 1492. A small pomegranate commemorates Spain's defeat of King Boabdil, Muhammad XII of Granada, at the Alhambra Palace, where Columbus met with Isabella and Ferdinand to seek patronage for his westward voyage.

This image of the Spanish coat of arms did not appear on Spanish silver dollars or gold doubloons until the reign of the Spanish king Charles I (1500–1558), who was the grandson of Isabella and Ferdinand. He later consolidated his authority across Europe in the title of Holy Roman Emperor Charles V. His reign ran from

A Carolus IIII Spanish dollar from 1805 (*top left*) and a Ferdinand VII from 1812 (*top right*) with their corresponding reverses directly below. From the author's collection.

1519 until 1556 when he abdicated the throne, amid speculation that he was going mad, in favor of his brother Ferdinand I (as Melville alludes to in the story when Delano first gazes at the drifting *San Dominick*). The phrases running around the edge of the Spanish dollar read: "Dei Gratia" (By the grace of God), "Hispan et Ind Rex" (abbreviation of the phrase "King of Spain and the Indies"), followed by "ME" (the mint Limae), the denomination "8R," (i.e., real de a ocho, pesos, or piece of eight), and the assayer's initials "J. P." (for Juan Martinez de Roxas and Pablo Cano Melgarejo).[135] The reverse of the Spanish dollar remained relatively consistent throughout the eighteenth century.

The "old" and "new" heads of Charles (1805) and Ferdinand (1812) on the dollars also reference the historical period when Spain lost control over the mines and mints of the Americas after Napoleon's invasion of Spain. In 1808 there was another abdication of the Spanish throne. This time King Charles IV gave it up under duress in favor his son Ferdinand VII during Napoleon's occupation of Spain. Ferdinand VII tried to placate Napoleon but lasted only a few months before Napoleon installed his brother Joseph Bonaparte as King Joseph I of Spain. After Napoleon's demise, Ferdinand VII reclaimed the throne in 1813, but he could not quell the revolutions breaking out across the Americas. These revolutions provoked a dramatic contraction in the supply of available silver—a contraction that affected Delano's personal fortunes and the world system of the Canton trade in which he had failed to win a fortune.

During and after these revolutions, the specific "old head" (Charles) and "new head" (Ferdinand) dollars maintained their status as the most powerful currency in the China trade. The China trader William C. Hunter explained in his memoir that the most numerous and trusted Spanish dollar circulating in China before 1825 was the Carolus IIII (Charles IV):

> These [dollars] kept the preference above all others, and were currently known as "Old Heads." So accustomed were the Chinese to this dollar, that when Carolus III. or Ferdinand VII. were offered, they were taken with reluctance, while the "Old Head" commanded a premium, and it thus became an exception to the general rule of "breaking up." For a long time they had been taken by dealers in raw silk from the middle provinces, in whole dollars, and finally so much prejudice existed in their favour that they would take no others except as cut money. This caused them to advance in value to 10 and even 15 per cent.; finally, during one season, we sold to the senior Hong merchant $60,000 at a premium of 30 per cent., receiving in exchange $78,000 in cut money. Ferdinand VII.'s dollars became "New Heads," and next came into favour, there being a diminishing supply of the "Old," but they were never at more than 1 to 2 per cent. premium.[136]

Hunter's description outlines the considerable profitability of arbitrage in regard to silver. As the contemporary historian of the China trade Jacques M. Downs confirms, with the abdication of King Charles IV in 1808, Ferdinand VII's head replaced his father's on the Spanish dollar, and both moved through Canton as a premium currency until broken and chopped into valuable lumps of silver.[137] In the 1830s "Spanish and South American dollars [were still] employed as a commercial medium along the coast, and their value [was] understood in most parts of the empire," with the old head Carolus IIII still transacting at a 5 percent premium.[138]

Narrative of Voyages punctuates the power of the dollar and highlights how slavery was embedded in the currency of the China trade. Perhaps because Delano never received what he felt to be his just reward for salvaging the *Tryal*, he offers a fascinatingly detailed account of dollar production at the Spanish mint in Lima,

Peru, where he spent months waiting as authorities considered his claim of salvage. The following paraphrase of Delano's description maintains his use of the passive voice as he overlooks the labor necessary in manufacturing dollars, which he fetishizes for their power of exchange in global markets. In 1805 he toured the Lima mint with the "master or conductor" and watched the minting of "old head" Carolus IIII dollars.[139] He notes that the silver came to the mint having already been separated and was then "cast into pigs that weigh from eighty to one hundred and sixty pound each."[140] Delano is impressed by the massive wealth concentrated in the "many tons of these bars" "piled up like cord wood."[141]

Delano describes "negroes" "refining and separating the ore" and "melting and casting gold and silver in iron moulds."[142] With their feet they knead the metals like dough, adding "some liquid" and quicksilver to the gold, "which separates the ore from the other metals that are mixed with it."[143] The molten metals of gold and silver run "as red as blood" into molds shaped like bars that then move through a "grand water works" that cools them as they pass through "ten pairs of rollers arranged very much like those that sugar cane is run through in the West Indies, made horizontal, and gradually decreasing in space."[144] These rollers flatten the silver "until they are laminated to near thickness of a dollar, and the gold to that of a doubloon."[145] In the next room these resulting thin hoops of silver and gold "run through a plate which brings them to an exact thickness, at which time they are wide enough to cut out the dollar."[146] A "sharp steel trepan" in the shape of a circle carves out the silver dollar or the gold doubloon from the flat, narrow strip of specie. Workers then set the blanks in a mill that turns the coin to etch ridges into its edge. The dollar blanks then get weighed and all that are underweight get pierced and supplemented with the insertion of a silver pin. The potential dollars are next immersed in lime juice as "a man, supplied with strong leather gloves to prevent hurting his hands, rubs and scours until they become bright as silver can possibly be made."[147] The blanks then receive their obverse and reverse impressions from "two pieces of steel, about the size of a blacksmith's hammer . . . the impressions being cut on the face of each" steel piece.[148] One steel piece is fixed with its impression to the ceiling in a frame of wood and iron anchored to the ground. The other steel piece hammerhead hangs directly above on the "lower end of a large screw" with the "impression side down."[149] The screw is fitted into a heavily weighted iron bar, twelve feet in length and attached to a tiller-like handle. A team of men works the striking machine. One man places the coin between the hammerheads; another man "throws back [the tiller] and raises the screw," heaving it back so that it comes back down to strike the coin with great force.[150]

The impressed dollar is brushed away and a new blank set for its turn. Delano reports the striking of one coin every four seconds, for fifteen a minute. The master of the mint answered Delano's questions "with frankness" and was "seemingly pleased to inform [him] of anything" Delano wished to know.[151] Delano reports that the Lima mint usually "coined from six to eight millions of dollars value in gold and silver, and also the mint in Mexico coined from fifteen to twenty millions, and St. Jago, in Chili, from one and half to three millions, which was all the money that was coined in these three kingdoms."[152]

In describing the manufacture of dollars, Delano overlooks the human labor that melted, molded, and stamped the dollars. He thereby maintains the aura of the dollar as a fundamental holder of value and a super signifier of commercial potential in the China trade. Delano's description ignores the mines and blunts the effects of mercury (quicksilver) on the working "negroes" by invoking organic and agricultural commodities, as when noting that the bullion was stacked like wood and carried "in the same manner as corn is carried to a mill to be ground, and that as fast as it was coined it was taken away by the respective owners."[153] He claims that in the mint "almost all the heavy work was done by water," as there "seemed to be as many wheels and bands going in it as in one of our cotton factories."[154] Delano's Lima mint seems to be more of a garden than a factory, a modern marvel of "water works," that combines the ingenuity of engineering with the aesthetics of landscape contouring.[155]

By way of contrast, Adam Smith held a very different view on the worth of hard money, attributing its fundamental value to the labor expended in making it. Questioning why precious metals held such importance in world networks of trade, he dedicated pages to it in book ii of *Wealth of Nations*, which includes the section "Digression concerning the Variations in the Value of Silver during the Course of the Four last Centuries." Smith reaches back as far as 1262 to establish a point of reference for understanding the subsequent increasing flow of silver from "the silver mines of America" to the "East Indies" centuries later after Columbus.[156] Smith is much less impressed than Delano by Spanish dollars or doubloons, the value of which is not intrinsic to the metal (silver or gold) but derived from its relation to other commodities, as well as from the labor necessary to extract and refine it. He reminds the reader that "labour . . . and not any particular commodity or set of commodities, is the real measure of the value of both silver and all other commodities."[157] Furthermore, silver, gold, and other precious metals command value for the concentration of their labor only in markets that have adequate supply of food and water required to sustain life. Accordingly, corn is intrinsically more valuable than silver or gold because "when we are in want of necessaries we must part with all superfluities, of which the value, as it rises in times of opulence and prosperity, so it sinks in times of poverty and distress. It is otherwise with necessaries. . . . Corn is necessary, silver is only superfluity."[158] Smith's labor theory of value debunks neither China's reliance on silver nor Delano's fascination with it but rather highlights the human exploitation behind its coinage and the power of the symbols that appeared on Spanish dollars to sustain exchange between China and the Western traders. As both *Narrative of Voyages* and "Benito Cereno" attest, slavery was embedded in the very medium of silver coinage through which the China trade trade took place. It is quite possible that some of slaves aboard the *Tryal* (Melville's *San Dominick*) would have ended up working to make dollars in some way.[159]

In his rebellion, Babo locks onto the "symbolic devices" of empire to terrorize the Spanish crew by reversing the power relations that they imply in a world economy of Spanish silver. Beyond the visceral intimidation of showcasing his former owner's skeleton, Babo's replacement of Columbus with his owner's white skeleton establishes a micro-economy on the *San Dominick*, where the old and new heads of Spanish currency does not support his exchange as a slave commodity. Focusing on Spanish colonial America, Greg Grandin describes the various roles that the enslaved people such as Babo (and his son Mure in Delano's *Narrative*) played in its expanding economies. As sources of labor, slaves were necessary for Spanish masters to profit in the production of leather goods on the plains of Río de Plata and of silver dollars mined and minted in Chile and Peru. In the "free trade of blacks," slaves were speculative opportunities even as they were holders of value that could serve as collateral in securing loans for investors who coordinated parallel investments across ports worldwide.[160] Slaves were also the premise on which profitable financial services insured owners of slaves against their death.[161]

By revolting, Babo defies the power of dollars and doubloons to measure his value, to facilitate his transfer as another's property, or to speculate on his death. Melville emphasizes this when Delano follows up his compliment of Cereno for "possessing such" an excellent "servant" with a boastful offer to purchase Babo for "fifty [gold] doubloons."[162] Babo replies by murmuring: "Master wouldn't part with Babo for a thousand," implying that on the *San Dominick* no amount of money would enable Delano to purchase him.[163] Babo's revolutionary wit reaches an apex of theatricality in the famous shaving scene as he seats Delano in the Malaccan settee, wraps the Spanish captain with a Spanish flag, and holds his head in his hands, with a razor to his throat, as Delano looks on. Melville refashioned Delano into a character who is fascinated by "the mythological or symbolic devices" of Spanish empire but who sees Babo only as a commodity that moves from port to port because of them.[164] Melville's Delano reads signs of Spanish empire ironically—as symbols of degeneration that bring into relief the vigorous manhood of American commerce—and looks ahead to the purchase power that he will wield in the dollars that he accumulates.

With Delano's retaking of the *San Dominick*, Babo's restricted economy folds back into the more general economy of global trade in which Delano will litigate the salvage claim. Babo's execution takes him out of circulation as his "head" gets "fixed on a pole in the Plaza" of Lima.[165] Cereno soon after follows into death Babo and Don Aranda, whose bones lie encrypted in St. Bartholomew's Church upon which Babo's skull looks down. Delano survives, reveling in the chase of old and new silver heads to and from Canton, entrusting his personal and national prosperity to the benevolent winds and the blue sea and sky of free trade.

CHAPTER THREE

The Troubled Romance in Harriett Low's
Picturesque Macao

Transnational Family Fortunes and the Rise
of Russell & Company

The opium dealer was born and reared in a Christian land, and he justifies his course by adopting the argument of the rumseller, that "if *he* don't supply the poison, some one else will."

HENRIETTA HALL SHUCK, *Scenes in China; or, Sketches
of the Country, Religion, and Customs of the Chinese* (1851), 151

Far fewer women than men voyaged to Canton from the United States. Their existing accounts offer fascinating insight on the gender roles that structured the China trade and the corresponding evocations of the national family that rationalized breaking laws to smuggle opium.[1] One of the first two American women to live in China was a nineteen-year-old woman from Salem, Massachusetts, named Harriett Low. In late September 1829 she arrived in the Portuguese-controlled port enclave of Macao, where she lived for four years with her aunt while her uncle worked up the Pearl River in the counting factories of Canton as the managing director of the new and powerful firm Russell & Company. Throughout her residence, Harriett kept a journal and mailed it back to her older sister in Brooklyn. In her epistolary journal she documented what she read, whom she met, and what she witnessed.[2]

Harriett and her aunt lived in Macao because China's regulations of the Canton System barred all foreign women from visiting Canton in order to prevent residential footholds leading to a permanent settlement. Macao was an exception, leased to Portugal by the Chinese government. At the beginning of the nineteenth century, British traders and missionaries secured terms of residence for their families from the Portuguese governor as they spent longer periods in South China. These expatriates cultivated a microcosm of high society that Nan Hodges characterizes as a "hothouse of gossip and jealousy."[3] They hosted tea parties, dinners, and dances and adhered to the manners of civilized life: leaving calling cards and taking evening strolls as Chinese servants tended to their households. Arriving to this complicated social scene, Harriett and her aunt faced curiosity over what it meant to be an American woman.

Low's journal is particularly fascinating for several reasons. She describes key merchants from Britain and the United States who were positioning themselves for more trade volume with the 1834 expiration of the British East India Company (EIC). In regard to U.S. firms, she offers a firsthand view of the Perkins & Company merger with Russell & Company, which then expanded operations in opium smuggling. She socialized with young compatriot men (John Perkins Cushing, Robert Bennet Forbes, John Murray Forbes, and Warren Delano Jr., among others) who were following in the footsteps of Colonel Thomas H. Perkins to become rich and influential back in the United States, and who figure in the following chapters' account of the First (1839–42) and Second (1856–60) Opium Wars. She also describes the first Western printers in China, including newly arrived American missionaries who became powerful preachers, editors, translators, and interpreters in the subsequent decades. Finally, Harriett describes places important to the China trade, including Macao, with its historical sites commemorating the Portuguese empire; Canton, where she and her aunt were able to live for more than a month; and Lintin Island, the hub of Russell & Company's opium-smuggling operations.

Harriett's written impressions also fascinate as a record of her struggles to find her social footing and realize international class respectability. She registers the aspirations of the expatriated U.S. merchant community, whose goal was to win fortunes comparable to those of British merchants. She details the more personal challenges of dealing with prejudices toward American women as she negotiates the religious conventions and class proprieties structuring American femininity. Plotting her return to the United States, she imagined becoming a cosmopolitan American wife, sister, daughter, and mother whose sense of home would span the metropolitan centers of Boston, Philadelphia, New York, and London. Her writing thus bears similarities to British women who lived for spells in colonial India during roughly the same period. Simon Gikandi describes them as caught up in a "'complicity / resistance' dialectic" in which they "saw empire as an opportunity for freedom and advancement but found it impossible, given their own subordinate positions in the domestic economy, to unconditionally valorize the imperial voice" of their husbands, fathers, and country.[4] Following Ann Laura Stoler's contention that "colonial authority rested on educating the proper distribution of sentiments and desires," Harriett's writings reflect the growing influence of American commercial power as merchants established cultural foundations on the East Coast while speculating and traversing a world network.[5] Writing from the culturally complicated intersection of Macao, Low suggests a global geography of early American intimacies that shaped social distinctions related to culture, religion, language, and

race—distinctions that bear on her developing sense of national identity as it co-
hered in relation to imperial influences of Britain, Spain, and Portugal.[6]

This chapter unfolds in a sequence of sections that describe Low's social circle
in Macao, her modes of socializing through her reading, and her representation of
this socialization to her sister back in the United States. By outlining the reading
practices of her expatriate life, the goal is to adumbrate the layers of cultural, national, racial, and religious sensitivity underlying her self-composure as an American woman. The chapter then turns to her employment of aesthetic rhetoric—the
beautiful, sublime, and picturesque—in her verbal descriptions of the Chinese
landscape. The verve with which she pursued these pictorial conventions is particularly interesting for being fanned by a secret engagement to William W. Wood,
who was at the center of controversies over opium dealing and print publication
in South China. Harriett's landscape scenes convey her privilege, prejudice, and
vulnerability as a niece of an American merchant engaged in opium smuggling.[7]
Ultimately her narrative deflects criticism of the opium trade from her uncle to the
Chinese people whom his company employed to transport it and to the Chinese
users who consumed it.

Of course, Low is an individual, and her representative potential is fairly narrow
in relation to American women. To put her writing in broader cultural perspective,
the chapter concludes by contrasting her experience with that of two American
women missionaries who strove to educate Chinese girls while fulfilling their duties as the wives of prominent ministers. The young Henrietta Hall Shuck was the
first woman missionary to China, and Eliza Gillet Bridgman worked for more than
two decades in Macao, Hong Kong, and Shanghai. Unlike Low, Shuck and Bridgman developed qualitative connections with Chinese people and leveled substantial criticism at those profiting from the opium trade. Although both died and were
buried in China, they also illustrate the prejudices that underpinned Protestant
American evangelism into which the next two chapters delve in detail.

Harriett Low and the Founding of Russell & Company

Low's journals offer a firsthand look into the familial networks and terms of intimacy that sustained the opium traffic in China to build fortunes in Boston, New
York, and Philadelphia. She arrived with her aunt and uncle in China just as two
major American firms were merging to form the more powerful Russell & Company, as the first steamship arrived in South China, and as the amount of opium
smuggled into China increased substantially with private traders anticipating the
dechartering and demise of the British EIC.

Sea voyages were generally homosocial affairs in which men financed and plied the trade as each other's mentors, employers, competitors, partners, friends, and lovers.[8] Harriett accompanied her uncle on such a voyage. Raised in a Unitarian household in Salem, Massachusetts, she had traveled very little before embarking. Her father Seth Low was a successful medicinal drug merchant whose younger brother William Low had taken up a position in Canton with the trading firm of Russell & Company, founded as a commission house by Samuel Russell in 1824.[9] The initial plan was for Low to replace Samuel Russell as the firm's directing co-partner. However, to Russell's chagrin, his partner Philip Ammidon Sr. decided to retire first while on sabbatical in New York. He sent his less-than-competent son to replace him. This set the table for the merging of Russell & Company (1824–91) and Perkins Company (1803–30) under William Low's direction.

For decades before the merger, Perkins & Company had prospered in Canton under the direction of Colonel Thomas H. Perkins and his talented young nephew John Perkins Cushing. In 1803 Cushing arrived in Canton at just sixteen years of age and proved very capable in learning to manage the company's affairs. Under his leadership the company forged an enduring and mutually beneficial relationship with the powerful Cohong merchant Howqua that endured in the decades to come.[10] Cushing weathered the credit crunch brought on by the War of 1812 and the curtailing of silver supply in the wake of revolutions throughout South and Central America after the Napoleonic Wars. As the lines of international credit reconfigured, he made the firm millions on commission trading and beaver furs from the northwest, fending off competition from John Jacob Astor and Stephen Girard. By the 1820s, Perkins & Company had cornered the market on opium sourced from Turkey.[11] In the process Cushing built up an immense fortune estimated at 2 million Spanish dollars. Before returning to the United States, he groomed as his replacement his younger cousin Thomas Tunno Forbes and authorized Samuel Russell to act as a proxy on behalf of Perkins & Company in case of an emergency. His contingency planning was prescient. After returning to Boston, Cushing was shaken out of retirement with the news that Tunno had drowned in a typhoon, leaving Perkins & Company without a director.

Meanwhile Harriett, her Aunt Abigail, and Uncle William had already embarked from Salem. From May to September of 1828 they crossed the Atlantic and Indian Oceans, moving north through the Gaspar Straits (Selat Gelasa) of contemporary Indonesia, past Malaysia and Singapore, and into the South China Sea. She reports learning of Tunno Forbes's death upon landing in Manila, where her uncle conferred with the Philippine-based Russell, Sturgis & Company, a U.S. firm founded by Nathaniel Russell Sturgis to focus on commercial flows between Lima, Peru, and the Philippines.[12] Later while living in Macao, Harriett met several more sons of Sturgis, including Russell Sturgis Jr. who went on to direct the bank of Baring

Brothers in London. Throughout the nineteenth century, "Russell & Co. was Barings' favorite correspondent in Canton," sustaining lines of credit during times of crisis.[13] After two weeks of rest in Manila, the Lows were headed to Macao, where they arrived in late September 1829.

The death of Tunno scuttled Cushing's retirement. Receiving word in Boston of his cousin's death, he rushed back to Canton, arriving in August 1830 on a ship loaded with one thousand cases of opium that provided capital with which to jump start Perkins & Company.[14] (Harriett mentions Cushing's arrival in an entry on 25 August.)[15] Cushing stayed on for two trading seasons, overseeing the merger of Perkins & Company into the new and improved Russell & Company.[16] As Cushing and Samuel Russell again plotted their retirements, Harriett's uncle William took the reins of Russell & Company. The firm welcomed another new copartner, the respected Captain Augustine Heard, who arrived in November 1830 on the *Lintin*, named after the island that served as the headquarters for opium smuggling not far from Macao.[17]

Captain Heard also brought reinforcements: the drowned Tunno's two younger brothers, nephews of Colonel Perkins. The older was named "Captain" Robert Bennet Forbes and the younger was the seventeen-year-old John Murray Forbes. Robert soon oversaw the very lucrative opium station at Linton Island, while John Murray worked in the factory house at Canton under William Low. Over the next decade Robert and John Murray would each take the helm as the directing partner of Russell & Company and, after the U.S. Civil War, both published autobiographical accounts in which they reminisced on their decades in the China trade. With the new and improved Russell & Company established, Cushing again returned to the United States where he enjoyed a more permanent retirement as his cousins moved up the managerial ranks.[18]

Harriett was on the scene as the American torch of the China trade was being passed from one generation to the next. She describes Samuel Russell and the traffic of opium upon which his collaboration with Perkins depended. She recounts that on a Monday morning in late April 1831, three weeks before Russell departed, he called her to the window to watch the first steam-powered ship arrive to South China. She writes to her sister:

> Now you must know this [steamship] is a very odd thing in this part of the great world and now I know you will say where from and where bound. In the first place you must recollect that opium is a great article in these parts and then you must know that the one who gets the new [opium] here first makes the most money. You do not know or hear so much as I do about this *stuff*. I could give you the state of the markets if you *wish*. But to go on with my story of this Steam Boat. The *Forbes* by name, sailed with

the *Jamisina* for the purpose of *towing* her from Calcutta to China being loaded with the precious drug. There had been much privacy going on with this vessel and those concerned in Canton, which if I were to give you in detail would not interest, therefore I shall keep it to myself. This vessel brings news from those parts, among it the failure of an immense house in Calcutta, Palmer & Co., for over 13,000,000 [dollars]. Only think what ruining, I suppose thousands. Very distressing.[19]

Chatting with Harriett, Samuel Russell was sizing up the competition; the British country-trading Mackintosh & Company had built the *Forbes* for the opium trade.[20] In the following decades steamships would become a powerful means of navigating the Pearl River, rendering Chinese pilots less necessary. Steamships also could brave the sea routes of Southeast Asia during the monsoon season.[21] They were also faster. Yet coal was so expensive that opium was "the only merchandise" that could justify its use.[22] Harriett mentions feeling distressed over the "ruining" of thousands who had invested in the opium trade, rather than with the trade's deleterious effects on China. This seems to sum up the sympathies of her general reaction.

Two more Russell & Company clerks figure prominently in her journals: William C. Hunter and William Wightman Wood, both of whom worked under the supervision of her uncle. Harriett characterizes the first as "young Hunter," although they were about the same age.[23] Born in Kentucky, he arrived in Canton in 1825 at the young age of thirteen and spent a year studying Chinese in Malacca at the Anglo-Chinese College.[24] In 1827 Hunter joined Russell & Company as a bookkeeper and clerk. A little more than a year into Harriett's residence in late December 1831, he got sick and took a leave to New York. He later returned and worked with Harriett's brother Abiel Abbot Low, eventually taking a turn as a partner with the firm during a turbulent period from 1837 to 1842.[25] In the decades after the U.S. Civil War, during which he supported the Confederacy, Hunter wrote two memoirs filled with anecdotes. He died in Nice, France, in June 1891, "a few days after the failure of the firm Russell & Co."[26]

William Wightman Wood was especially important to Harriett Low. They fell in love. From Philadelphia, he was the son of the well-known actors William B. Wood and Julia Westray Wood, who counted as friends the famous British actress Fanny Kemble and her father.[27] Wood first arrived in China in 1825 at the age of twenty-five. It is unclear exactly why he came, but the Philadelphia-based China trader and opium broker Benjamin Chew Wilcocks was a benefactor to his father.[28] In his memoirs, William Hunter describes Wood as "a person of great versatility, mentally and materially" who "abounded in wit, was well read," and yet was "of no fixed purpose."[29] He had "remarkable talent" as a sketch artist and composer of verse and struck up a friendship with the colorful British painter George Chinnery, who lived for many years in Macao. What Wood had in wit, he lacked in looks. Hunter fondly describes Wood's face as so "awfully pock-marked" that it "resembled a pine cone," and Chinnery teased him for having wrestled from him the distinction of being Macao's ugliest person.[30]

Wood also was the first American to edit and print an English–language newspaper in China. His publications included the first Western newspaper printed in China, the *Canton Register* (beginning 1827), and his own creation, the *Chinese Courier and Canton Gazette* (1831–33).[31] His provocative opinions regarding British diplomacy with China, the opium trade, and the debate over dechartering the British East India Company got him fired from his first editing job. Wood also published in Philadelphia a book on China called *Sketches of China: with Illustrations from Original Drawings* (1830), an ethnographic overview of life in South China in which he demonstrated his eye as a sketch artist.

Wood never made a fortune and never married Harriett, although he tried. A year and a half into her residence in March 1831, she describes him as "a very clever," "pleasant young man," and "an immense talker."[32] Wood initially bonded with her as he tutored her in sketching. Harriett eventually accepted his marriage proposal, which they agreed to keep secret. However, she had second thoughts, divulged the engagement to her aunt and uncle, and followed their advice in breaking it off. In 1833 Wood relocated to the Philippines where he tried to manage a sugar plantation before settling into work with Russell, Sturgis & Company.[33]

In addition to the Americans, Harriett met people of other nations. Within a day of arriving to Macao, there was a "steady stream" of British residents curious "to meet the first American women to reside in China."[34] Prominent members of the British community greeted them, beginning with the accomplished missionary translator and EIC chaplain Dr. Rev. Robert Morrison and his wife. She enjoyed conversations with presidents of the EIC Select Committee in Canton, including William Henry Chicheley Ploweden, Charles Marjoribanks, and his successor, the future author and governor of Hong Kong, Sir John Francis Davis, with whose wife, Emily, Harriett took long walks. During her residence, she also met the wealthy British private merchants Thomas Dent, William Jardine, James Matheson, and others who would become even more powerful after the EIC devolved. There were other potential suitors, including an assistant surgeon with the EIC named Dr. Thomas Richardson Colledge, who helped start the first Ophthalmic Hospital in Macao in 1827 and the Medical Missionary Society in China in 1838.[35] He eventually married Harriett's friend Caroline Shillaber. Harriett seems to have been a breath of fresh air for the Anglo-American community, and George Chinnery painted her portrait during a six-week period in Macao, from April to May 1833. As

Portrait of Harriett Low by George Chinnery (1833), with detail of hands. Oil on canvas, 24.765 × 21.769 cm. Photo by Mark Sexton. Peabody Essex Museum, Salem, Massachusetts, purchased with partial funds donated by the Lee and Juliet Folger Fund and Joan Vaughan Ingraham, 2001; M18709.

for Portuguese residents, they controlled Macao but figured marginally in the Anglo-American social scene. The very wealthy Mr. Antonio Pereira rented out the famous Casa Gardens to British traders who could afford it, and Harriett enjoyed walking these grounds and describing them to her sister. Substantial social connections across the Catholic-Protestant divide were rare in Macao.[36]

In regard to Chinese people, Harriett mentions servants or workers who maintained her residence, but she neither reports their conversations nor develops friendships with them.[37] She bristles at the more direct curiosity of those beyond her social clique, reporting early in her residence that when walking through Macao she met "no one but Portuguese and Chinese men," who "annoyed" her "very much by their intent gaze."[38] As this chapter goes on to show, Harriett generally notices Chinese people as a group or type with whom she struggles to feel a connection, characterizing them for their simplicity and inscrutability, their poverty, greed, dirtiness, and lack of manners. An exception was her uncle's servant Ayok, who accompanied the Low trio on their ill-fated return voyage back to the United States via Cape Town and London. Another exception to this prejudice is the respect she pays to the very powerful Cohong merchants, upon whom her uncle's business relied. She reports meeting and having small conversations with Old Tinqua, Gouqua, and Kingqua and attended the wedding of Mouqua's son.[39] In a general sense, Harriett's tone infers a hierarchy of respect for Macao's relatively distinct social groups: American and British, French-Dutch-Spanish, Portuguese, and then the Chinese, with special respect for the powerful Cohong merchants and a handful of servants whose trustworthy attention she appreciated.

In regard to China's restrictions on trade, Harriett discovered how disruptive her mere presence could be when she and her aunt snuck into Canton via the opium station at Lintin Island. In November 1830, after a year in Macao and around the time that Cushing returned to China, she managed to stay for a few weeks in the Russell & Company factory at Canton.[40] Two British women had preceded them into the forbidden zone by the permission of Chinese authorities in order to tend to a sick EIC trader. Harriett and her aunt received no special dispensation. When the Canton authorities became aware of their presence, they issued an ultimatum: "If one [William] Low [does] not immediately remove his family to Macao," then all trade would halt.[41] Returning to Macao, Harriett remarked to her sister that "all the Chinese outside say that Chow Tuck (or Governor Le) had 'lost face' very much by letting the English ladies remain and sending the Americans down."[42] With pride she mentions that "a message has gone to the Emperor," but she doubts that he will hear of the incident due to "an insurrection in the upper provinces."[43] As for having to leave Canton, Harriett puts it in her own terms, stating that "she did not wish to stay longer" but "could not bear to let the Chinese know that they could do anything [they wanted] with the Americans."[44] This incident is the most adventurous in Harriett's accounts, and she tells her sister that, upon her return, Macao "seemed more enchanting than ever."[45]

After more than four years in Macao, Uncle William's serious illness brought Harriett's residence to a sad conclusion. Her younger brother Abiel Abbot Low arrived to meet them in September 1833, but it was a bittersweet reunion as their uncle fought to survive consumption. He died in March on the voyage home near Cape Town, South Africa, where he was buried in an Episcopal burying ground. While in Cape Town with her widowed aunt after his death, Harriett writes fondly of their Chinese servant Ayok (the son of Dr. Colledge's servant Afun). She is especially touched after he visits her uncle's grave during the tomb-sweeping festival of Ching Ming in April 1834 (despite being away from China). Ayok accompanied

Harriett and her aunt on tours of sites in London, where they attracted curious onlookers.[46] Her final journal entry is dated 21 September 1834 about ninety miles from Sandy Hook. Moving through bad weather, she anxiously anticipated reunion with her sister; her journal ends: "I cannot explain how I feel. It is a sort of all *overness* [sic] and yet it appears to me that I am going to a strange place as I have been to so many before."[47]

Harriett never returned to Macao but remained connected to Russell & Company for the rest of her life. Two years after returning to the United States, she married a banker and moved to London. By 1848, she and her family were back in Brooklyn as her husband struggled financially before dying in 1859. Meanwhile, Harriett's brother Abiel Abbot had become a partner in Russell & Company in 1837 and helped support her eight children.[48] He went on to partner with three brothers to start the New York–based trading house of "A. A. Low & Brothers" that was on the forefront of commercial expansion into Yokohama, Japan, in 1867.[49] After returning to the United States, A. A. Low invested in railroads, including the lucrative New York Central & Hudson River Railroad.[50] When Abiel passed away in 1893, the *New York Times* obituary "Abiel Abbot Low Is Dead: A Merchant Prince of the City Passes Away" eulogized him by recalling his heralded fleet of clipper ships that included Donald McKay's *Great Republic*.[51] A biographer speculated in the mid-1880s that, with the increasing competition for trade in China, Low's trading house would dissolve to reappear "among the financiers of Wall street."[52] His son Seth Low—Harriet's nephew—served as president of Columbia University and mayor of New York City.

Reading for Romance in Macao

Low's journals are exceptional for their duration and the detail with which it shows her shaping an image of herself as a young American woman. She documents *what* a young American woman from the merchant class of Salem read in the 1830s—a mix of novel, histories, periodicals, world geographies, and sermons—and *how* she would have been reading, with an eye to presenting herself in the world as an educated, engaging, and principled young American. She embraced the adventure of her situation, adapting literary styles to reflect on her own sense of identity—"a young Lady" and, in jest, "a Spinster"—in a global commercial network stretching from Salem to Manila, Canton to Cape Town, and New York to London.

An avid reader, Harriett writes of her voyage as an educational opportunity and commits herself to a disciplined curriculum. Embarking from Salem in May 1829, she seems to have had a small library selected with great care. The books would occupy her on a six-month voyage. She characterizes some as instructively "good for her" and others as entertaining romances of love and adventure that would distract her from the tedium of life at sea. Each book would likely have evoked association with family members or friends who had recommended or given it to her. When living in Macao, Harriett is specific about authors and topics and about the languages in which she is reading. Within two weeks of arrival in Macao, she was thrilled to peruse a catalog of the EIC library where she enjoyed borrowing privileges. She alternates between novels, travel accounts, histories, and sermons—maintaining a balance in developing a method of reading. To cope with the hot and humid summer, the stormy days of bellowing typhoons, and the persistently nettlesome mosquitos, she read books that arrived on ships moving through Macao.

Reading folded consistently into writing. The journal begins on 24 May 1829 aboard the *Sumatra* in the Atlantic Ocean one week outside of Salem, a few days after her twentieth birthday. She confides to Molly that, as the horizon of her home and family receded from sight, and seasickness set in: "I behaved like a *heroine*, as I had resolved to be."[53] Over the following four years, Harriett writes about herself as if she were a character in the unfolding story of her own life adventure and reading instructs her on how to talk about the world and present herself in it. In George Chinnery's portrait, the book in her lap is more than a clever device to hide her hands that demanded more time and attention to paint. The book is an important symbol to Harriett. Commenting on Chinnery's portrait she writes to her older sister Mary Ann: "[Chinnery] has made a little alternation, put a book in the hand, and I like it much better."[54] Perhaps it was *Childe Harold* or *The Bride of Abydos* by Byron, whom she quotes throughout her journals. Mrs. Emily Davis nicknamed her "Byrona."[55]

Harriett's correspondent and specific audience was her sister Mary Ann (nicknamed Molly), who looked ahead to a new marriage and the challenges of domestic motherhood after moving from Salem to Brooklyn. It is poignant to read these sisters' attempt to communicate across the world's oceans as they faced very different paths in their relatively privileged lives. "But remember," Harriett implores, "this is written for you and me—that when I feel like it I can sit down and *open my heart*."[56] In writing to her sister, Harriett also wrote for herself. Margin notations indicate that Harriett frequently reread her own journals, qualifying her opinions and responding to the letters she had received from Molly. Did Harriett imagine a broader audience? Family members often passed journals and letters among themselves and highlighted passages to read out to friends. After settling in at Macao, Harriett introduces volume 2 with the descriptive title "Eight Months in Macao by a young lady in the year 1830 by the author of a Journal at Sea published in 1829," suggesting the other family members with whom she might have been indirectly communicating.[57] As her relationship with Wood deteriorated, she entitles volume 4 of her journal packets "Lights & Shadows of a Spinsters [sic] Life."[58] Years later in 1837, she wrote from London to her parents of Harriet Martineau encouraging her to publish her diaries. She laughs off the suggestion but perhaps contemplated a broader audience in some of her other journal entries as she mentioned the British travel writers and cultural commentators Fanny Wright, Fanny Kemble, and Fanny Trollope. In any case, it was not until the late nineteenth century that her daughter Katherine Hilliard published a heavily edited version. In 2002 Nan Hodges and Arthur Hummel edited the complete and definitive edition, supplementing missing passages in Harriett's diary with other letters.

Harriett describes romance novels as entertaining, but she was careful not to overindulge. Having settled into Macao, she writes: "I don't want novels. I hate to see them come into my house, for they are bewitching," although "one must read them for small talk."[59] At another point, she found a happy medium in "Historical novels," with Sir Walter Scott being a particular favorite among the ex-patriot Americans, because reading them "induces you to search out the real history of the parties concerned, and I always do it with double interest after reading a novel."[60] On the voyage out she read historical biographies, following the lives of Queen Elizabeth, Mary Queen of Scotts, Anne Boleyn, and Napoleon. The day after her fellow American friend and walking partner Lucy Cleveland departed and left Harriett in Macao, she picked up Washington Irving's biography *A History of the Life and Voyages of Christopher Columbus* (1828). In her final summer in Macao, she reports reading Jared Spark's *Life of Gouverneur Morris with Selections from his Correspondence, and Miscellaneous Papers* (1832) in six days.[61] Harriett read about U.S. history in Dr. Dionysius Lardner's *The Western World*, vol. 1, *The United States* (1830) and Abiel Holmes's *The Annals of America, from the Discovery by Columbus in the Year 1492, to the year 1826* (1826). (Holmes was the congregational minister of First Church in Cambridge, Massachusetts, and the father of Dr. Oliver Holmes Sr.) She read books on natural history such as John Mason Good's *The Book of Nature* (1826) and Oliver Goldsmith's *An History of the Earth, and Animated Nature* (1774), which Major Samuel Shaw had taken with him on his first voyage in 1784. In addition to Walter Scott and Maria Edgeworth, she mentions novels and nonfiction by James Fenimore Cooper, James Kirk Paulding, and others. She also read William Wood's *Sketches of China* (1830), Thomas De Quincey's *Confessions of an English Opium-eater* (1821), and much more. As for periodicals, she mentions the Boston-based *North American Review* and the London-based *Quarterly Review* and the newspapers published in Canton, including the *Canton Register*, the *Chinese Courier* (edited by Wood), and a new American missionary periodical named the *Chinese Repository*, to which she refers her sister for information about the manners and customs of Macao's Chinese—information that she admits being too impatient to relate.[62]

On a spiritual level, her reading reinforced a solid American Congregational faith grounded in the Episcopal denomination and leaning toward the energies of Unitarian revival. Sermons by Ellery Channing evoked her father's spiritual advice, and those by Dr. John Prince and Charles Wentworth Upham evoked the particular congregation of First Church Salem. She reacted skeptically to Portuguese Catholicism for the bells and smells of its rituals but appreciated its exotic aura of faded imperialism. Friction between Protestant denominations was compounded by British and American cultural affiliation. She stood her ground in argument with the EIC's chaplain, a British Episcopalian who criticized the minor Christology of American Unitarianism. Harriett reports another anecdote of a "long *tete a tete*" with "a British Lieutenant" who "declared to her that 'he would turn Mahometan rather than be a *Unitarian*'"; Harriett remarks to her sister: "He had not an idea that I considered myself one."[63] After letting the lieutenant continue, Harriett identified herself. She writes that he "was quite non-plussed and begged ten thousand pardons."[64]

Harriett denigrated the Chinese language but strove to be multilingual in European languages. Throughout her residence, she practiced reading and speaking French and Spanish. After a couple of years in Macao, she writes to Mary Ann:

> You may think I spend a great deal of time learning languages (Spanish and French) and so I do, but I do not feel that I waste the time, for independently of the pleasure and benefit of learning the language, or rather of knowing it, I think it is of advantage of having some fixed occupation. It fixes attention too. I might spend a great deal of time in reading but in the warm weather one is apt to fall into a *dreamy* state over a book. You become weary of constant reading and require some stimulus to make any exertion. So I think it far better to divide the time as I do, and I always feel that I have not a moment to waste.[65]

She judged Cervantes's *Don Quixote* the most witty and ingenious thing," whose "beauty" she especially appreciated for "reading it in Spanish."[66] Being multilingual in European languages was a marker of status among the expatriate community, but Chinese was unworthy of her concerted effort in learning to speak or to read it. Early in her residence (Monday morning, 2 November 1829), she writes: "The China men are jabbering below. I should admire to have you hear their jargon. There is no words to be made of it to my ears, it seems to consist of low guttural sounds. They are a stupid set of people. They spend most of their time in sleeping. That is the servants."[67] The categorical prejudice of her observations is obvious, even as she clarifies that by "stupid set of people" she means these particular sleeping servants rather than all "China men." Her prejudice also suggests a frustration born out of a sense of alienation: *Why* does Chinese—in this case Cantonese—sound like to her like "jabbering"?

Harriett's phrasing of "China men" also suggests the broader racial prejudices that were implicit in her sense of cultural hierarchy and aspiration for social recognition. Socializing with fellow Americans, she at times showcases what Reginald Horsman has called the era's developing "American racial Anglo-Saxonism."[68] For example, on a morning in June 1830 two fellow Americans, Oliver H. Gordon (Thomas H. Smith & Sons) and William Hunter (Russell & Company), visited her; she writes: "[Gordon] brought us some capital caricatures of *life in Philadelphia*, taking off the *negroes*."[69] An early work by E. W. Clay, who became a political satirist in New York after beginning his career in Philadelphia, is *Life in Philadelphia* (1828).[70] This collection of caricatures making fun of African Americans was published at the beginning of a tense decade when the "Quaker City" of Philadelphia was a center of abolitionist agitation, even as the Pennsylvania legislature amended the state constitution in 1837 to disenfranchise black people. One of Clay's cartoon features an African American woman shopping for silk stockings, as her friend waits in the doorway. The caption presents her question: "Have you any flesh coloured silk stockings, young man?" to which the man behind the counter (who does not look very young) replies, "Oui Madame! here is von pair of de first qualité!" The customer's oversized garden of a hat suggests that her pretension to style can only be ludicrous. The racist punch of the caricature's lines is that her request for flesh-colored stockings is answered with the presentation of a black pair. By featuring African American women as literally black consumers attended to by a foppish and pale Frenchman with rouged cheeks, Clay's scene of interracial commerce implies that gender categories are eroding along with normative senses of beauty in a mixed-up Philadelphia.

Such crudely racist exercise of wit enabled an American trio from Kentucky (Hunter), New York (Gordon), and Massachusetts (Harriett) to share a sense of being white Americans in Macao. Perhaps Harriett's willingness to laugh with her fellow Americans at the "negroes" also belies her own insecurity. She spent much of her time repairing clothes as she fretted over her appearance in anticipation of being inspected by British matriarchs and potential suitors. She was also making judgments about who would be a good match. As for her personal impression of Gordon, she found him "interesting" and wrote that: "If he was not so ugly, [she] should certainly try to *bewitch* him. He has *lots* of *cash*."[71] With so much attention directed her way, Harriett was sensitive to stereotypes of Americans as single-mindedly practical and unrefined, crude and vulgar in manner, naïve and shallow

Madame (customer): "Have you any flesh coloured silk stockings, young man?" *Young man (shop keeper):* "Oui Madame! Here is von pair of de first qualité!" Aquatint cartoon, drawn and etched by E. W. Clay. From *Life in Philadelphia* (Philadelphia: Published by Wm. Simpson, 1829), pl. XI. The Library Company, Philadelphia.

in intellectual experience. Captain Basil Hall's *Travels in North America, in the Years 1827 and 1828* (1829) particularly nettled her; on a "cloudy foggy unpleasant morning" of Saturday in early March 1830, she finds herself reading it and reflects:

> I do not think [Hall] does the Americans justice, nor do I believe any Englishman ever will. He professes not to be prejudiced, but I think every page shows it. He is constantly drawing comparisons. I feel quite enraged with him at times and would fain throw his book by, but I am constantly in hope to find some thing to redeem it. He seems to think himself a *mighty body*, and I am sure he may be justly called an egotist. He in some places makes the Americans appear quite ridiculous. I hope I shall have patience to finish it, but it requires a great deal.[72]

In her daily conversations, she was pressed to rebut the observations of Hall and Fanny Trollope, whose *Domestic Manners of the Americans* (1832) reached Macao soon after its publication. On the brink of rejecting a marriage proposal from fellow American William Wood and as the late-summer heat made it difficult to sleep well, she writes of feeling especially irritated and depressed after reading *Refugee in America: A Novel* (1832), and she charges Trollope with being ungenerous and simplistic in depicting "the foibles of our countrymen"; Trollope "*caricatures* all she touches."[73] At a party in late June 1833 thrown by the Dents, a powerful name in British opium trafficking, everyone was again talking about Trollope's book, which made Low feel especially lonely. Looking out to sea offered little comfort or inspiration: "After dinner we were sitting in the verandah and saw 4 ships come round the point one after the other in rapid succession, all from Bombay, with opium. How I wished one might be an American."[74]

Did the reading practices of Harriett's male counterparts similarly reflect their anxieties of class standing and cultural respectability? There were many similarities in regard to the importance of books. When in the early 1800s Colonel Thomas H. Perkins endorsed his young nephew J. P. Cushing as the primary contact for Perkins & Company in Canton, he sent him a small collection and advised that "Shakespeare is a library in itself, the Spectator, Rambler, etc. contain much information, and may be read once a year to advantage."[75] Two decades later on his return voyage, J. P. Cushing's younger cousin Robert Bennet Forbes focused on Sir Walter Scott, the complete works of whom his mother had given him.[76] As mentioned, Robert Bennet first arrived in 1830 at age twenty-six. Two years later he returned to the United States with a small fortune, prompting Harriett to write: "Happy man! Would that he would put me in his pocket."[77] In a final note to Harriett, he confided feeling that while "his horizon was so cloudless," "there must be a dark day in store."[78] This dark day came during the Depression of 1837 when he lost his fortune in disastrous investments relating to the manufacture of nails and railway construction. At thirty-three he headed back to China as a husband and father, and he kept an epistolary journal in the form of a running correspondence with his wife Rose, mailing back installments via passing ships or opportune ports of call.

Unlike Harriett, Robert Bennet returned to China to remake a fortune. He writes of opium as a crucial component of his strategy, declaring to his wife: "Whenever I am inclined to murmur at my present lot I look back to 1837—during which my only comfort was in disburthening my troubles to you—I have now come a great distance & made a great sacrifice to get a Competency & *I must have it.*"[79] As the First Opium War loomed, Robert Bennet amplified his determination: "I did not come here for my health; neither to effect a reform, moral or political, but to get the needful where with all to be useful & happy at home & I shall stay as long as I can carry on my business in safety & I consider myself as safe in China as in any place of the world."[80]

Sketching American Life in China

Harriett was circumspect about opium dealing but did not criticize it. To do so would have meant impugning her uncle and all those with whom he worked. Nevertheless, her avoidance of opium as a topic of moral consideration pervades her descriptions of Macao where she struggled to sustain a personal sense of romantic potential as an unmarried American woman. William Wood was smitten with Harriett upon meeting her, visited her frequently, and instructed her in drawing as he amused her with his caricatures.[81] In the summer of 1832 he proposed marriage, even though her uncle was his boss and did not approve of him. She accepted, and they plotted to keep the engagement a secret until she was about to return to the United States. But as the summer wore on Harriett worried about her future. By December 1832, she had broken with Wood. To her sister she explained her initial acceptance: "He is not handsome, though he has a most intellectual face—high and noble forehead, blue eye and brown hair, a turn up nose and sweet smile. Full face he is tall and a good figure. His manners are those of a perfect gentleman. He talks a good deal, but always sensibly, wise, witty or grave as suits his hearers. His talents are first rate, and various. He can do anything with a pen or pencil. He understands business too. So that whatever he applies himself to he can do. His morals are excellent."[82] Harriett's uncle disagreed and criticized Wood's skills in business. William Hunter offers an illustrative anecdote of Wood incorrectly filling in a bill so as to request Baring Brothers in London to pay the bearer "one hundred lacquered ware boxes" instead of silver dollars.[83] After breaking off with Wood, Harriett lamented to her sister "Our dearest and fondest hopes are dashed for the want of the *filthy lucre*."[84] But she also criticized Wood for being too boldly determined and having a short and hot temper—qualities apparent in his controversial editorship of two Canton-based newspapers, considered briefly in chapter 4.

Wood's talents in the visual arts seem to have most charmed Harriett, and landscape description became her tool for reflecting on her experiences in Macao. Describing Wood's initial advances, she writes, "He draws very well; and he immediately took me under his protection and became my *teacher*. I received many little *billet doux* upon *fine arts*."[85] Harriett also read his book *Sketches of China: with Illustrations from Original Drawings* (1830), published in Philadelphia during his hiatus from China.[86] The table of contents encompasses a diverse array of topics, including "Gardens at Fa-Tee," "The Execution Ground," "Streets of a Chinese City," "Pagodas," "Barbers," "Literature—History—Fiction," "The Art of Printing," "Money—Bullion—Rate of Interest," "Snake Catchers," "The Opium Trade," and "Food." Wood admits to having developed a general prejudice against the Chinese, but he takes a capacious view of China's social energies as he embraces illustration to appeal to his Philadelphia reader's curiosity.[87] Wood was well read and refers in the introduction to the "ponderous volumes" on China written or compiled by the French Jesuit Jean-Baptiste Du Halde and the seventeenth-century French sinologist Joseph de Guignes and to contemporary works, such as Rev. Morrison's Chinese dictionaries, and works by Jean-Baptiste Grosier, Sir George Thomas Staunton, and Sir John Barrow.[88] Wood hoped to write something more engaging—and, most importantly, attractively illustrated.

In *Sketches of China*, Wood's narrator conveys impressions of China as an artist versed in the literary grammar of scenic composition. His prose appeals to a reader's imagination through the literary exercise of ekphrasis—the verbal description of visual scenes. Wood did not strive to mirror what he saw, and many art historians over the past few decades have considered the economic and political ideologies of landscape painting and description.[89] Wood's grammar and vocabulary of scenic composition echo eighteenth-century aesthetic debates regarding beauty, sublimity, and the picturesque—debates in Britain among estate improvers such as Lancelot "Capability" Brown and Humphrey Repton and aesthetic philosophers such as William Gilpin, Uvedale Price, and Richard Payne Knight over standards of taste reflected in the art of gardening and related landscape aesthetics.[90] The point here is not to trace any direct influence of particular theorists on Wood but to relate his sketching of China to a legacy of landscape description in which the visual mode was a multilayered semiotic field of personal and cultural signification.

To summarize, eighteenth-century "beauty" conveys symmetry and order that reassures and settles the viewer in appreciative recognition of inherited classical standards. The risk of such beauty is that it can be uninteresting and insipid. Conversely, "sublimity" leaves the viewer disoriented, without a sense of measure or boundary or perspective upon which to establish a point of view. Edmund Burke's treatise *Philosophical Inquiry into the Origin of our Ideas of the Sublime and the Beautiful* (1757) registers the sublime in physiological effects of having our senses overloaded to produce a moment of terror. After the senses adjust, the witness recovers his or her footing and can realize a scene that represents the extremes that had shaken his or her perception—a scene that allows for appreciation of the sublime without its terrifying effects.[91] In *Critique of Judgment* (1790), Immanuel Kant theorizes sublimity in realizing the mind's ability to reflect on the experience of facing what initially seems sublime. In contemplating the perceptive experience of mathematical sublimity (the seeming boundlessness of time and space), the subject senses the profound dynamism of cognitive abilities, registering self-apprehension of thought in the setting of new frames of reference that reorient the perceiving self.

As for the picturesque, Coleridge summarized its effect in *Biographia Literaria*: whereby "parts by their harmony produce an effect of a while, but where there is no seen form of a whole producing or explaining the parts of it, where the parts are seen and distinguished, but the whole is felt."[92] The picturesque has specific connections to the China trade because of the eighteenth-century architect and China trader Sir William Chambers, who embraced the term in reporting on what he saw in China. The son of a successful Scottish trader, Chambers was born in Sweden, and twice sailed with the Swedish East India Company to Canton in the 1740s. During his residence in Canton, he made sketches that informed his subsequent influential publications, including *Designs of Chinese Buildings, Furniture, Dresses Machines and Utensils, Engraved by the Best Hands, From the Originals Drawn in China by Mr. Chambers, Architect, member of the Imperial Academy of Arts at Florence, To Which is Annexed, A Description of their Temples, Houses, Gardens, &c.* (1757), and *Dissertation on Oriental Gardening* (1772).[93] Chamber's 1757 essay exhibits a few key themes that would develop in the debates between Repton, Brown, Gilpin, Price, and Knight. Chambers proposes that assessments of any particular landscape scene ought to include consideration of geographic propriety and the potential for acclimatization of the foreign specimens to the home soil. Using his visits to Canton as a foundation of experiential authority, Chambers advocated to the British Imperial Academy of Arts the harmonizing principles of Chinese garden arrangements and highlighted the connection between China and England in the British context of debates about how to prepare English gardens in representing the global reach of British Empire.

Wood shared Chamber's appreciation of aesthetic verve in scenic composition, fascination with China, and situated experience in Canton, but neither Chamber's positive opinion of the Chinese nor his critique of the British Empire. Wood's verbal scenes in *Sketches of China* of 1830 are a commercial exercise of the "picturesque" that balances beauty and sublimity to promote delight and curiosity in the face of intense social activity. For his American audience he strives to capture a "genius of place," but the result tells us more about his impressions and prejudices than any actual China. The allegorical energies that suffuse his sketches convey China's commercial opportunity and the challenge of navigating Canton's waters to profitable end. The details that he selects and the way he layers them in the exposition are implicit commentary on the viewer's unfolding relationship to the scene. There is a dramatic tension to the verbal descriptions, and the reader must work to compose the elements, generating a scene that implies a narrative.[94] There are potentially many threads of symbolism, but the resulting visual allegory suggests the superiority of Western civilization in a contact zone of commerce where principles of free trade are being testing by the adversary of pagan Chinese.

Exemplifying the political implications of picturesque composition, the following passage, "Approach to Canton," challenges the reader to see with the eye of a sketch artist in picturing commercial opportunity implied in the charivari of pagan life. With its long train of adjectival clauses, the passage unleashes a slew of visual elements that readers must work to compose or be overwhelmed by detail. Wood puts the reader in China as "a stranger," escaping the confines of the ship to witness novelty and variety "beyond measure":

In coming up the [Pearl] river, a stranger is completely absorbed in contemplating a scene without a parallel in any other country. When he has just escaped from the confinement of the ship, the beautiful scenery and luxuriant appearance of vegetation, is delightful beyond measure; added to this, the extraordinary sight of the multitudes of boats, vessels, and craft of every description, swarming with the water population, contributes to amuse and astonish him. Myriads of boats moored in long, regular streets, no one interfering with the other, and fleets of them moving in every direction, and yet without confusion, the bustle of business visible every where, the salt junks discharging their cargoes into the canal boats, the vessels from the interior of the country laden with wood, and immense rafts of timber and of bamboos floating down with the tide, managed by a few miserable little wretches, who dwell in huts built upon the raft or in small boats attached to them. Revenue cruizers rowing in every direction, painted with the brightest colours, the men protected from the sun and wind by a kind of moveable thatched roof, and the large triangular white flag with vermilion characters inscribed upon it floating over the stern, while a cannon, with a red sash tied round its muzzle projects over the bow. Thousands of small ferry boats cover the river, laden with passengers of every age and rank; in one a dozen coolies or day labourers, in another a brace of Chinese beaux, luxuriating on the clean mats with which the cabin floors are covered, their heads resting on bamboo pillows, pipe in mouth, regarding with a lazy eye the active scene without, or possibly contemplating the portrait of some celebrated belle, with finger nails six inches long, dependant [literally, hanging down] from the screen-work of the cabin. Immense junks of four or five hundred tons, and even larger, moored in the stream, and gorgeously embellished with the fascinations of dragons, paint, gold-leaf, and ginger-bread-work, with huge eyes painted on either side of the bow, to enable the vessel to see her way, as the lower classes term it! In the evening, when the actual bustle begins to decrease, the tremendous din of a thousand gongs, and the glare of flaming papers, which are set on fire in the boat, and thrown blazing into the stream, as an evening sacrifice, keep up the excitement of the scene, and the night until a large hour, is disturbed by the shouts of the boatmen, and the discordant music from the flower boats, in which the women of the town reside. The number, variety, and arrangement of the boats, is the most surprising matter to an American or European, and it is long after arriving in China, that a foreign eye learns to observe uninterested the gay and active scene perpetually passing on the river.[95]

A *sketch* presumes attempted representation of elements coordinated in a whole of what might initially seem an overwhelming variety of color, shadow, tone, and shifting perspective. Looking at the harbor of Canton, how does one capture on the canvas or pad the disparate elements of vegetation, a multitude of vessels and craft of every description, and people of various occupation, gender, and social statuses? The first challenge of composing a scene (or reading Wood's descriptive passage) is to establish internal points of self-reference as each sentence follows in sequence. The reader is of course not *there* to *see* what is happening, and the act of reading these phrases heightens the dramatic tension of composing a scene. In gathering impressions, the reader moves from words to images and (with patience) configures a scene that approximates the experience of Wood's hypothetical commerce-seeking stranger, who, emerging from the confinement of a ship and months of monotonous seascape, *sees* China. The lazy eyes of the smoking "Chinese beaux" will not suffice. The description privileges the eye, but the stranger hears "gay and active" life in the river's "perpetual passing" and the "swarming water population" of port traffic. "Approach to Canton" challenges the reader to be a stranger who realizes a picturesque configuration in the sensory overload, senses the potential for profitability in the swarming energy of Canton, and organizes commercial activity in the face of potentially perpetual distractions.

In contrast to this scene of arrival in Canton, Wood introduces Macao's melancholically picturesque memorial bowers that afford American readers the chance to appreciate the grand scale in which empires fall. He selects and carefully describes ruins in ways meant to inspire his readers to claim influence over the future. Whereas Canton is the destination of the national merchant's commercial quest, Macao is a gothic landscape of a fading Portuguese empire that had once colonized India and China, from Goa to Canton. In describing the Catholic college of St. Joseph, Wood notes its role as a "public institution for the cultivation of learning," but he is more interested in the antiquarian treasures waiting to be uncovered in its library—documentary treasures on par with those found by "Mr. Washington Irving in the old Spanish libraries" to generate his Spanish histories, Columbian biographies, and *Tales of the Alhambra* (1832).[96] For Wood, former seats of imperial power have not been simply eclipsed by the sublime westward course of empire; rather they stand in ruin as opportunities to exercise a participatory mode of historically sensitive rumination that realizes in literary and visual sketching a sense of national futurity.

Harriett described herself as Wood's pupil but she took control of representing visual experiences in communicating with her sister in Brooklyn. Her verbally rendered scenes of Macao reflect a struggle to remain connected to her family's expectations and the national ideal of American womanhood. Like Wood's, Harriett's descriptions derive from experiential familiarity. For example, she writes of Casa Garden of Macao in late summer 1832 when she was having second thoughts about her secret engagement and was reading Fanny Trollope's dispiriting depictions of Americans:

> Casa Garden, Macao: "8th [September 1832] Read til 12 this morning, then dressed and spent the rest of the morning with Mrs. Mac[dondray]. Met [Charles Sidney] Bradford, [Philip] Dumaresq and [John Murray] Forbes there. After dinner went to Mrs. Fearon's, or rather "the Casa Garden." You cannot fancy anything more romantic. It is a most lovely place. It is now quite in a dilapidated state, the walls were thrown down in the Typhoon, trees torn up by the roots, temples and summer houses demolished. The moon was shining beautifully through the trees and reflecting itself upon the waters *a la distance*. Oh if I could transport you out here for two days, and then set you down again in your own happy home I would. For you cannot fancy how romantic it was, it only needed Mr. D. to be my *adorer* and it would have been a scene for romance. Seated upon a rock at the edge of a precipice, a thick wood above and below, up-turned trees, and twining shrubs around us, the moon shining brightly above us, *our faithful dog Dash* in the *foreground*. Oh how lovely. Felt tired when I got near home, went into Mrs. Macondray's, Bradford and Dumaresq took tea there, went home, found Wilkinson, Blight, Forbes, and Petit there. Now love I am going to bed so good night."[97]

In this sketch, Harriett objectifies herself as the human element sitting in a literal garden space that she renders by mixing elements of the beautiful, sublime, and picturesque. Harriett strives to do more than describe Casa Garden to her sister, she yearns to transport her there in a flight of fancy so that they both occupy the same moment and place and share her excited experience. Such a unity of feeling would mean relocating Mary Ann from the geographic situation of her American family and to a seat beside a man, who is not a family member, on a rock's edge that is bathed in Macao's moonlight. In suggesting and dispelling this flight of fancy, Harriett takes care to respect her sister's life, depositing her back to a "happy home" in Brooklyn just as she takes herself to bed in Macao and says "good night."

Harriet's reveries in "Casa Garden" take on deeper social significance because

William Heine, "Camoens' Cave, Macao." Woodcut. Hawks, *Narrative of the Expedition of an American Squadron to the China Seas and Japan*, 1:142.

she knows and mentions that the site memorializes the great Portuguese poet Camoes. In *Sketches of China*, Wood explains that "this celebrated little spot is situated in the large garden grounds of the house called the *Casa*, at the northern extremity of the town, and forms one of the interesting sights of Macao, from the historical recollections connected with it, and the intrinsic beauty of the locality."[98] In Casa Garden, Luís Vaz de Camões is said to have written the epic *Os Lusíadas* (1572) celebrating the voyages of Vasco da Gama. Wood notes that a "beautiful sketch of Camoens' Cave" by George Chinnery was exhibited at the Philadelphia Academy of Fine Arts.[99] Woodcuts by William Heine from the narrative of Commodore Matthew C. Perry's expedition to Japan in the 1850s illustrate the site.

Harriett imagines herself perched on the edge of a precipice in this garden. She signals irony in calling this a *potential* (rather than a realized) "scene of romance."

William Heine, "Camoens' Cave, Macao—Rear View." Woodcut. Hawks, *Narrative of the Expedition of an American Squadron to the China Seas and Japan*, 1:143.

On a personal and familial level, this is because she sits with Captain Philip Dumaresq whom she describes as "a most gentlemanly quiet youth, *small*, good looking however, smart, spirited, and honourable [in] feelings."[100] Dumaresq started with Russell & Company in the 1820s, earned an excellent reputation as a ship captain, and married Miss Magaretta DeBlois in Boston in 1836. But Dumaresq would not have then been Harriett's appropriate adorer, a role occupied by her fiancé William Wood, about whom she was having serious reservations. Precariously seated at the edge of a precipice, she chats with Dumaresq. Dare she look down? Will she fall into a marriage that disappoints her family? If she breaks her promise to Wood will she fall into a future of spinsterhood? The "Typhoon" she mentions reasonably reflects the storm of her emotional state. It could also denote the typhoon of 1829 that took the young life of Tunno Forbes and severely damaged the grounds of the Casa Garden. Life was precarious, and her uncle was already sick. Affairs of the heart involved more than the feelings of the two people. Marriage implied relationships between extended family members who shared a name and claims on fortunes that extended across generations.

In hindsight, Harriett's Casa Garden scene of "would-be" romance potentially registers her experiential struggle to find footing as a young American woman in her sense of world-historical time. The garden commemorating the Portuguese poet in Portuguese-controlled Macao was part of China. The garden was also attached to the estate of the wealthy Portuguese trader named Manuel Pereira, who had built a mansion in 1770. By the time Harriett arrived, the Pereira descendants were renting out the estate to British families with the stipulation that the Casa Garden would remain accessible to the public. At the time of Harriett's visit with Dumaresq, the British couple Mr. Christopher Fearon and his wife Elizabeth were the tenants of Antonio Pereira.[101] Over the years, British renters had reworked the garden space around the Camoes memorial. The Typhoon of 1829 upturned these improvements, blending the garden elements into a hybrid overlay of Chinese, Portuguese, and British styles. From our historical perspective, Harriett places herself not just in the Casa Garden or in China but also in the history implied by these layers of British improvement and Portuguese memorialization.[102] As Sara Suleri comments about contemporaneous British women writers in India, Harriett seems to be "entering the political domain in order to aestheticize rather than to analyze," producing a "picturesque" that "provides a densely detailed documentation of the imaginative strains engendered by" the "pragmatics" of maintaining a national romance of the Canton trade in which she can find position.[103] Taking a seat on the precipice that is well outside of the territory of the United States, she reorients herself, vis-à-vis a landscape shaped by forces of nature and cultural contest, to the promise of a return home and into an American family. Accordingly, this moonlit scene of Harriett and her "adorer" is embedded in a daily entry that begins with her waking up to anticipate a routine of reading and visiting friends. The moonlit visit to this garden breaks the routine, but the diary entry provides an envelope for Harriett to fold herself back into the routine of a typical evening: she feels tired, rejoins the social circle, and soon after retires for bed, closing the entry with direct address of her sister: "good night."

Soon after her moonlit conversation with Dumaresq, she revealed the engagement to Wood to her uncle. As predicted, he opposed it, and soon after she broke it off. Curiously, William Low tried to cheer up his niece with a family outing to Lintin Island where Russell & Company headquartered its smuggling operations. Guided by Dumaresq and others, she stayed aboard the *Lintin,* the same ship that had carried Augustine Heard and the Forbes brothers two years before.[104] In an entry she writes of passing these evenings by reading aloud Scott's *Waverly*.[105] However, her impressions of Lintin Island imply that the romance of residence in China had been nearly exhausted. Consider that even though Lintin Island "deriv[ed] its celebrity entirely from the circumstance of being the station of the opium fleet," Wood describes it in *Sketches of China* in a dramatic style as "masses of granite which form a mountain of considerable altitude" and that are complemented by a quaint fishing village of a "few houses."[106] Ascending to the island's peak in 1827, he reveled in the magnificent view. On the contrary, Harriett failed to find a view when she visited its peak in the autumn of 1832. After touring the island, she describes it as barren with the exception of a few pretty spots. Its village disgusts her. She describes the "women, *pigs*, and children" "all eating together and inhabiting the same place" and concludes that the scene presented "perfect pictures of filth and all uncleanness."[107] One morning in November, she gets a close view of a "smuggling boat" from the deck of the warehouse ship *Lintin*. Here is what she sees:

13th [November 1832] A lovely morning. Went on deck. A smuggling boat alongside. Such a sight you never saw. They contain generally about 100 men, when *alongside* they generally take this opportunity to eat or "*catchy chow chow*" and they form in little groups of 4 or 5 each round 5 or 6 little messes of fish and oyster cooked in divers ways. Each has his bowl of rice in his hand chopsticks in the other which each one dips into the *public* bowl and from these into their mouths. Having none of the delicate ideas of more refined people, they then *shovel* as much rice into their mouths as they can possibly *crowd* in. They appear to eat with *glorious appetites* I assure you. They sit on their feet, and are *dirty* and *ugly*. They are generally the lowest class of people and as to morals, I will not say. If they have a moment's leisure, they commence *gambling* and I see them generally as soon as they have crammed down their food either have cards or dominos, each playing with all the interest possible. It is a curious sight to watch the expressions of their faces and if by chance they have any expression at all, it is an expression of avarice and love of gain. You see one laying on the side of the boat smoking his long pipe with apparent indifference to every thing in this world and the next. I often wish to ask what they *do think*, or if they think at all.[108]

From the deck of the *Lintin*, Harriett literally looks down on these "100 men" who are dirty and ugly to her eye and incomprehensible to her ear; smoking their pipes and gambling, they seem inaccessible to her not only across the space separating the ships' decks but also through any mode of communication; they seem possibly incapable of thought, not unlike the pigs that she notices mixing with the people in the village. There is no broad composition into which they fit as the human

"Russell & Co.'s 'Levant' and 'Milo' off Lintin Station, Whampoa, China, Twelve Miles Below Canton." Walton Advertising and Printing Company, *Old Shipping Days in Boston* (Boston: State Street Trust Company, 1918), p. 19.

element. There is no culminating delight in the description as there is in Wood's scene "Approach to Canton." Harriett's Chinese are in themselves expressions of "avarice and love of gain." Her prejudice seems ordered by the very lines of perspective that structure her gaze. There is little room for irony as she stands on the deck of Russell & Company's opium ship and looks down on those in the transport.

Fully aware of the opium business in the last year of her residence, Low struggled to understand the gap between how she *ought* to feel and how she actually felt. She notes examples of opium's deleterious effect on Chinese people; for example, she explains the behavior of a young man who is caught hiding in her aunt's room behind a dressing screen at night by speculating that he must have been "under the influence of horrid opium."[109] But she defers careful consideration of how opium is available and mulls over why she *lacks* sympathy for Chinese people. As her residence wore on to its conclusion, she sank into a deeper malaise. Three months before departing, during a particularly rainy period in August 1833, she describes a Sunday afternoon after church when "everyone [was] stretching their vision to Cabarita point [figuratively speaking, a very long way south, all the way to Australia]"; she continues: "Lots of Ships expected and a fine breeze today for them. Two arrived from Bombay, but they bring nothing but *opium*, which is the most interesting article to merchants and speculators. IT is amusing to see how many of their thoughts they give to it. It seems to be a never failing source of conversation."[110] Her assertion of amusement rings hollow with irony.

During these months Low began to hypothesize something that disconcerted her: that Chinese people did not warrant her sympathy because they were essentially a different type of being. She understood that such a severe conclusion contradicted the core beliefs of her Christian upbringing. Her ambivalence registers in a description of a conversation with her uncle. On an evening stroll in February 1833, he recounted to her the rescue of Chinese fishermen whose boat had capsized in the waters near Canton, killing five of the crew. Writing to Mary Ann, Harriett muses over the meaning of their felt "indifference" toward "these creatures"; she continues, "We hear of their being killed and drowned and misfortunes of divers kinds occurring but not with the feelings that we have in parallel cases in our own country or Europe."[111] Her comments seem to echo the first part of Adam Smith's famous anecdote in *Theory of Moral Sentiments* (1759) about a "man of humanity in Europe" who is more disturbed by knowing he will lose his finger tomorrow than by learning that far away on the other side of the world the whole of China has been "suddenly swallowed up in an earthquake."[112] However, Smith continues by noting the absurdity of gauging moral judgment on feelings calibrated by the proximity of threats to the self. He marvels at the extent to which "reason, principle," and "conscience" motivate a true "man of humanity" to realize that "we are but one of the multitude, in no respect better than any other in it."[113] Smith points out that the proposition of saving one's finger (or one's life) at the expense of millions of others seems so ghastly because of a moral imperative to sympathize with others that exceeds our anxiety over self-preservation. Conversely, Low's commentary mulls over her failure to build sympathy with Chinese people proximate to her in the context of the opium trade. Instead of considering why she enjoys an elevated social position in China and how opium trading might limit her ability to sympathize with Chinese people, she hypothesizes that Chinese people lie beyond the pale of her sympathetic recognition as fellow humans of Smith's multitude. She continues by suggesting that the lack of feeling elicited from hearing of the death of Chinese people "must be" because:

> we have no sympathy with them, [who] appear to me to be a connecting link between man and beast, but certainly not equal with civilized man. And you see the different grade and links in all the rest of nature's of men? [The Chinese] certainly do not possess the sensibility and feelings of other nations. And when we hear of these accidents, our imaginations never picture distressed and bereaved families, and happy families destroyed—for knowing their brutal customs we cannot think such distress

exists. "More is given us, and more of us will be required." Therefore how anxious we should be to be able to give a good account of our stewardship.[114]

The concluding quotation from of the Gospel of Luke seems an afterthought of lingering guilt. At other moments in her journals she seems more willing to work through her prejudice, for example, when railing against Chinese women's endurance of foot-binding or appreciating Dr. Colledge's work at the eye hospital. But the drift of her opinions seems summed up in her chance meeting of the "famous *Phrenologist*" Dr. George Bennet, who stopped in Macao on his return journey to England from New South Wales.[115] Their conversation is reassuring as she begins to justify her sympathetic disassociation from Chinese people with a (pseudo) scientific rationale. She specifically notes meeting Dr. Bennet a year after her heartbroken visit to the smuggling depot of Lintin. She describes him to her sister as an "exceedingly agreeable" and a "very scientific man," who touts his ability to read a person's character from the shape of his or her skull.[116] Harriett is intrigued and wonders to her sister "what a phrenologist might say to my hypotheses."[117] She also reports that in their conversation Dr. Colledge offered to give her the " '*Skull*' of a Chinaman," which Dr. Bennet offers to mark up.[118] She declines this macabre keepsake, but admits her preference for "a *cast*" of a skull that would be an aid to "a very useful study if one could have sufficient *faith* to educate children upon the strength of it—that is if it [phrenology] was *proved*."[119] Harriett may be writing to let off steam and trying to shock her sister and herself out of intensifying doldrums rather than stating a definitive opinion, but it is difficult to infer irony about the potential reassurance of proving the inferiority of the Chinese through the measurement of skulls. One wonders how her views changed over the subsequent decades. In her four years of residence in Macao, her dialectic of complicity and resistance maintains the gendered propriety of an American woman anticipating wifely duties with a merchant prince. Qualitative connections with Chinese people might have pushed her to reassess the terms of such marital commitments. After witnessing opium traffic, she dehumanizes Chinese people and does not consider the implications of her uncle and brothers building fortunes on it.

The Missionary Romances of Henrietta Shuck and Eliza Bridgman

Although missionaries and merchants both lived in Macao, the structure of family feelings pervading their expatriation tended to be quite different. Merchants and the occasional wives (or nieces) who accompanied them were on a quest to win a competency with which to establish, enhance, or maintain a family back in the

United States. Missionary husbands and wives hoped to convert the heathen through investments of faith that promised little in terms of material reward.[120] They set their sights on bringing light to fellow human beings stranded in pagan darkness, inspiring to similar action the members of congregational communities in which they had been raised, and contributing to the broader international network of Protestant evangelism.

At one level, American women missionaries were expected to adhere to the same gender script as Low, especially if they accompanied husbands and had the responsibility of caring for their children. But in marked contrast to Harriett Low, American women missionaries in Macao were adamantly critical of opium traffic. They were also more open than she to enduring relationships with Chinese people. Missionary openness exemplified belief that Christian faith transcended national allegiances of the secular world and that the capacity to believe was not predetermined by the shape of skulls. In the "work of converting," as the missionary Mrs. Eliza Jane Gillett Bridgman professed, "the world is one large community."[121] Dedicating one's life to service in China meant reconceiving senses of family, stretching bonds of affiliation not only across the globe but to the people who lived there. Keeping an eye to heaven in spiritual matters, missionaries were nevertheless nostalgic in regard to the friends and family whom they had left behind back home. For the sake of illustrative contrast to Harriett Low, consider briefly the missionary efforts of Mrs. Henrietta Shuck and Mrs. Eliza J. Bridgman.

Born and raised in northern Virginia, Henrietta Shuck became the first American woman missionary to China, sent under the aegis of the American Baptist Board of Foreign Missions (ABBFM). In the summer of 1836, the eighteen-year-old Henrietta and her husband the Rev. J. Lewis Shuck arrived to Macao after an extended voyage that took them to the British colony of Kedgeree (near Kolkata, India) and Penang and then to Singapore, where she spent a few months studying Malaysian and Chinese as her husband readied himself to begin preaching and distributing evangelical tracts. During her eight years in China Henrietta had four children for whom she cared with help from servants as she ran a small school for Chinese boys and girls. At twenty-eight she died in Hong Kong while expecting her fifth child and was buried there.[122]

Shuck was an avid reader, as signaled by the book that she holds in the frontispiece to her memoir. She does not mention reading any bewitching novels. In her journal she mentions the aforementioned Sir John Davis's *The Chinese: A General Description of the Empire and Its Inhabitants* (1836), and periodicals that included the *Chinese Repository* and the *Indo-Chinese Gleaner*. She read Andrew Combe's *Principles of Physiology*, perhaps due to her concern with the health of her children and her own chronic illness, and made her way through Charles Rollin's multi-

Frontispiece to Jeter, *A Memoir of Mrs. Henrietta Shuck.*

volume *Ancient History of the Egyptians, Carthaginians, Assyrians, Babylonians, Medes and Persians, Macedonians, and Grecians.* In letters home to her father, stepmother, younger sisters, and pastor, Henrietta assured her family that she was profoundly satisfied to risk her life by serving China. As a Baptist, she was particularly concerned with those loved ones back home who had not been baptized and risked eternal damnation. Imploring her younger sisters to find the Lord, she shudders at the prospect of an eternal separation that is too terrible to contemplate.

Remarkably Shuck found time to write a substantial book entitled *Scenes in China; or, Sketches of the Country, Religion, and Customs of the Chinese* (1851). It is less pictorial than Wood's *Sketches of China* as it presents topics on China. It includes a remarkable chapter entitled "Opium" in which Shuck declares that its "trade is doubtless one of the most enormous national sins known upon the earth."[123] She blamed China's state of social distress on the British and American merchant class who trafficked opium. She likened them to rum sellers who had plied Native communities with liquor on the Western frontier. Whereas Low writes to her sister of feeling distressed over the loss of British fortunes in India, Shuck laments the social impact of opium on the Chinese people, noting that an addicted man could smoke a dollar's worth of opium a day and estimating that China had lost $15 million from its illegal importation. Her understanding of its trade is systematic. She describes the cultivation of opium in India and its impact in China, concluding that "this unholy traffic, with which the treasury of a professedly Christian government is replenished, is fast ruining China, and destroying the souls and bodies of the people."[124] As for the First Opium War (1839–42), she deemed it "disastrous and revolting."[125]

The Episcopal missionary Eliza Jane Gillett offers an insightful contrast to both Low and Shuck because she never conceived children. Born in Derby, Connecticut, she taught boarding school before turning to missionary work later in life. In the spring of 1845 at forty years of age, she arrived in Hong Kong and soon after married Rev. Elijah Bridgman, the influential editor of the *Chinese Repository* (who features prominently in the following chapters). Working alongside him, she dedicated herself to speaking Chinese in various dialects, including Cantonese, Mandarin, and Shanghainese, explaining that the best way to do so was to "*mingle with the people; hear them talk; and learn as the little child does.*"[126] She traveled with her husband in distributing missionary tracts to people in the countryside, to the Tanka boat people on the Pearl River, and to the wealthy wives of Cohong merchants and salt merchants. Such excursions in tract distribution could be dangerous, and she reports a harrowing episode in which a crowd of angry villagers pummeled her boat with large stones, nearly sinking it and almost killing members of the crew by whose effort they narrowly escaped. Nevertheless, she resists condemning Chinese people whose animosity she explains as a reaction to the opium wars and the stultifying influence of the Qing government. In regard to Chinese peoples' forward curiosity about her appearance—particularly her hair, clothing, and fair complexion—she reports the lighthearted nature of conversations resulting from their questions and desire to touch her.

In regard to printing and education, she and her husband were at the forefront of promoting intercultural communication after the First Opium War. They collaborated with the printer and preacher Liang A-fa or "Leang-afa" (1789–1855; 梁發, A-fá, Liáng Fā; Leung4 Faat3), the first convert of the British missionaries Rev. Robert Morrison and Rev. William Milne.[127] For decades Liang A-fa had printed and preached with the American and British missionaries at great risk to himself and his family. When Elijah Bridgman arrived in 1830, Liang A-fa asked him to take his ten-year-old son Liang A-teh under his wing and teach him English. A-teh became an influential interpreter and translator and a lifelong friend of the Bridgmans.[128]

Eliza and Elijah never had any children, although they taught and cared for many who attended their schools in Macao and in Shanghai. Among Eliza's first students were a young boy named Kwei-lum and his younger sister Ah-yee whose father was a fortune-teller. Another girl named A-lan was the daughter of Liang A-fa's wife's sister. In 1847 Ah-yee and A-lan accompanied the Bridgmans to Shanghai, where Eliza started a school for girls that grew to forty students. Interestingly, she prioritized Chinese literacy alongside instruction in Christianity, so it was imperative to find reliable Chinese students such as Ah-yee, and A-lan who, young as they were, could pick up the Shanghai dialect easily, enabling them to serve as mentors for new students and as reassuring emissaries to skeptical parents who made the Bridgmans promise that they would not take their children away to foreign lands. As for the curriculum, Eliza explains that it began with flash-card recognition of Chinese characters and progressed to San Tsz-king's *Three Chinese Classics*. To instill Christian faith, they taught the children short rhymes, had them memorize the Ten Commandments and the Lord's Prayer, and then continued to instruct them in the reading of the New Testament.

The school's methods also suggest the missionaries' prejudices. In her accounts Eliza characterizes poverty as a symptom of paganism that only Christianity can cure. The frontispiece to *Daughter in China; or, Sketches of Domestic Life in the Celestial Empire* (1853) pictures a model pupil from Shanghai named King-meh (Jīn-mèi; 金妹; literally "golden sister"), a girl from a poor family in Shanghai whose parents agreed to allow her to board at the school with the Bridgmans. She became an important student and nurse, eventually accompanying the Bridgmans to San Francisco, New York, and other cities in 1853. In the posthumous biographical memoir of her husband, Eliza recalls that King-meh impressed "the friends of missions in the United States by her gentle and winning manners."[129] The frontispiece, engraved from a photograph of her, resembles contemporaneous pictures of Native American children, putatively civilized by boarding school life into portrait-ready propriety by federal boarding schools. Eliza's description of the school philosophy reinforces this resemblance in describing how she strove to transform what she characterizes as "dirty" and often orphaned Chinese children into tidy young boys and girls who would grow capable of striving after a Christian household; or, as she put it more colorfully, the children were "flowers that under gospel-culture are watered in heathen soil, and then transplanted to the paradise of God."[130] However, the Bridgmans were not trying to assimilate Chinese children into property-holding U.S. society. Chinese literacy was set alongside Christian ministry and the learning of English. Furthermore, Eliza reports the care that she took to gain the trust of King-meh's parents and to ensure that her students were happy.

"King-meh." Bridgman, *Daughters of China.*

In a portrait King-meh is depicted wearing Chinese clothing. The Bridgman school experience enabled King-meh to become literate in Chinese and English, to travel to the United States, and to return home.

Eliza never presented herself in a frontispiece portrait with a book in hand, but she was an avid reader and writer. Furthermore, she dared to publish in ways that challenged highly regarded literary authors such as Thomas De Quincey whose representation of opium and of China she undoubtedly resented. The literary sophistication of her reading registers in her choice of a quotation from De Quincey's essay "Suspiria de Profundis" as the epigraph of *Daughters of China*: "Woman is sitting in darkness, without love to shelter her head, or hope to illumine her solitude, because the heaven born instincts kindling in her nature germs of holy affections, which God implanted in her womanly bosom, having been stifled by social necessities, now burn sullenly to waste, like sepulchral lamps amongst the ancients."[131] The quotation marks appear in the original to signal Bridgman's unattributed borrowing of this passage that traces back to "Suspiria de Profundis: Being a Sequel to the Confessions of an English Opium-Eater," a fantastically neurotic, densely literary reverie on the glorious perils of addiction to laudanum that appeared in *Blackwood's Edinburgh Magazine* in June 1845.[132] De Quincey's earlier book *Confessions of an English Opium-eater* (1821) had circulated widely in the decades after publication; Harriett Low mentions reading it in September 1832.[133] And in the spring of 1840 during the First Opium War, De Quincey contributed three essays to *Blackwood's* in which he celebrated the war as an overdue defense of British honor. In choosing an epigraph, Eliza Bridgman could have directly cited the Gospel of Matthew (4:16). Instead she quotes De Quincey's allusion to it in "Suspiria de Profundis," thereby refuting the literarily allusive terms of his interpretation. She turns his reflections on the exhilarating perils of upper-class British opium addiction to the oppression of Chinese women who are "sitting in the darkness" of pagan life, enduring abuse and neglect at the hands of their fathers, brothers, and husbands as Chinese society continues to rattle from the aftershocks of the opium war.

As the book's title *Daughters of China* indicates, Bridgman is primarily concerned with Chinese women across social class hierarchies, from the wives of wealthy merchants to humble villagers and the deeply impoverished. Meeting the wives of the Cohong merchants, she contemplates their lives of isolated privilege and the double standard permitting wealthy husbands to amuse themselves with multiple wives.[134] She objects to foot binding as cruel deformation that severely curtailed women's physical and social mobility, and she inveighed against the beating of women. In regard to the humbler classes, she lamented the chilling practice of infanticide to which baby girls were especially vulnerable and the intentional maiming of children, who were then put to work begging in the streets. After her husband's death in 1861, Eliza stayed in China to run the school in Shanghai and established Bridgman Academy in Peking. She passed away in 1871, and she was buried next to her husband in Shanghai.

The efforts of Shuck and Bridgman lend perspective on Low's four-year residence in Macao. Striving to convert the heathen Chinese, they broke the conventions of intimacy to which Low adhered. Although they were more receptive to Chinese people, their ministry was laced with prejudicial assumptions related to the civilizing function of Christianity—prejudicial assumptions that the following chapters consider more carefully through the print endeavors of the American missionary husbands who embraced the concept of free trade.

CHAPTER FOUR

The Sacred Fount of the ABCFM

Free Press, Free Trade, and Extraterritorial Printing in China

A punch is the foundation of perpetuity.

British missionary REV. SAMUEL DYER, quoted in "Literary Notices,"
Chinese Repository (February 1833), 417

American missionaries followed their merchant compatriots to Canton and dedicated themselves to extraterritorial printing, which is the operation of a printing press outside the territorial jurisdiction of their own nation. Sponsored by the Boston-based American Board of Commissions of Foreign Missions (ABCFM), Rev. Elijah Coleman Bridgman arrived in China in 1830, and three years later the young missionary printer Mr. Samuel Wells Williams joined him. For the next two decades they oversaw the publication of hundreds of thousands of pages. Striving to reach readers in both English and Chinese languages, they learned not only to speak, read, and write Chinese but also to adapt their system of print publication to accommodate Chinese characters. Extraterritorial printing was a massive investment of time requiring technological improvisation and significant capital streams to fund manufacture and transport of print equipment.

Over the decades Bridgman and Williams printed a diverse array of texts, including commercial guides, dictionaries, treaties, and the monthly periodical the *Chinese Repository* (1832–51), an incredibly rich resource that conveys the global scope and intellectual range of their printing efforts.[1] Generically, it was like a magazine or review in organizing sundry topics for timely reading reference.[2] Whereas the terms *magazine, courier, times,* or *register* all suggest timely news reportage, the *Chinese Repository* projected a longer range of relevance. Like a bank vault, its volumes stored and protected the intellectual capital about China and the Far East that Bridgman, its main editor, deposited every month. The *Chinese Repository* also documented the print efforts of the missionaries themselves as they collaborated with members of the London Missionary Society who had preceded them to Bengal and Canton and established printing stations in Penang, Malacca, and Singapore.

Aligning evangelism and commerce in a global network of print production, Bridgman and Williams coordinated readers in many "publics" as they modeled the operation of a free press, offering China an example of modern civility in action. There were multiple layers of imagined audiences. The most immediate was the multinational merchants and sailors moving through China, South Asian, Southeast Asia, and Bengal. The initial monthly print run of four hundred in 1832 grew to six hundred in 1836 and eventually to one thousand. These numbers might seem relatively low, but the well-established, Boston-based *North American Review* and *Westminster Review* averaged three thousand monthly subscriptions.[3] Furthermore, the *Chinese Repository* was referenced and excerpts reprinted by other publications, including Britain's *Blackwood's Edinburgh Review*, the *Westminster Review*, and the *North American Review*, further boosting readership. Bridgman estimated in August 1836 that of the 600 issues printed, 200 copies circulated in China, 154 in the United States, 40 in England, 5 in Hamburg, 51 throughout the Straits Settlements (21 in Batavia, 6 in Malacca, 6 in Penang, 18 in Singapore), 15 in Manila, 11 in Bombay, 7 in Bengal, 2 in Ceylon, 3 in Burma, 4 in Siam, 13 in the Sandwich Islands, 4 in Cape Town, and 6 in Sydney.[4]

From the trading hub of Canton, the *Chinese Repository* documented a particularly volatile twenty-year period. Each month concluded with a section entitled "Journal of Occurrences" that synthesized information from the imperial court's *Peking Gazette* and other Western periodicals. The missionaries reported on the escalating opium imports and ensuing confrontations between Britain and China after the British East Indian Company (EIC) ceased operations in 1834. With China's defeat in the First Opium War, the Treaty of Nanking (1842) essentially dismantled the Canton System by opening four new treaty ports and claiming Hong Kong as a British possession. As Hong Kong and Shanghai began superseding Canton and Macao as centers of trade and print publication, Bridgman headed north to Shanghai with his wife, Eliza J. G. Bridgman, leaving Williams to edit and supervise the presswork. To close out the *Chinese Repository* in 1851, Williams compiled a comprehensive index of its twenty volumes, characterizing the journal as a "permanent record relating to, and illustrating, China" for "posterity."[5] As for the Canton-based Mission Press, in 1856 residents of Guangzhou destroyed the press equipment and the inventory of printed texts at the start of the Second Opium War (1856–60).

The final issues of the *Chinese Repository* also noticed the beginnings of the Taiping Rebellion (Tàipíngtiānguó yùndòng, 太平天國運動; 1850–64), whose main leader Hong Xiuquan (Hóng Xiùquán; 洪秀全; 1814–1864) had been influenced by the American missionaries' publications. Hong became a believer after repeatedly failing the national examination that would have qualified him for a government job and surviving cycles of debilitating illness and depression during which he read missionary tracts. Deeply inspired by the sense of millennial urgency that these tracts conveyed, he sought the counsel of U.S. missionaries before concluding that he had experienced something more profound than a typical conversion. He announced that he was in fact divine, the Son of God, the younger brother of Jesus Christ, whose mission was to overthrow China's corrupt emperor in Peking.[6] The resulting civil war lasted fourteen years, and it is estimated that by 1864 20 million Chinese lost their lives because of it.[7]

The U.S. missionaries did not know what to make of Hong. It is important to stipulate that they regarded their print operations as extraterritorial in a literal but not a legal sense. For more than a century, China's imperial edicts banned Chinese subjects from teaching foreigners to speak Chinese, let alone advising them on how to manufacture typefaces of Chinese characters or disseminating tracts; nevertheless, a handful of Chinese converts, most importantly the printer and preacher Liang A-fa, discussed in chapter 3, risked the consequences.[8] Bridgman and Williams did not dismiss Chinese regulations as irrelevant. As Presbyterian evangelists, they took pride in risking the Chinese emperor's punishment to adapt New England's "Protestant vernacular tradition" and save pagan Chinese souls.[9] Inspired by the millennial urgency of a Calvinist legacy, they regarded any secular law as a potential challenge to overcome through courageous adherence to convictions of faith. Nevertheless, while the goals of their print evangelism ostensibly transcended national affiliation, they paradoxically sustained pride in being Americans. Williams especially regarded his print career as a vocation, grounded in a New England heritage. The challenge would be to align faith with printing in the commercial hub of Canton.

As for China, they hoped to reanimate its literary and political culture by modeling a free press in at least two related senses: as a tool that civilized the print workers who participated in material publication and as a print forum for controversial topics such as the opium question. In holy defiance of the Canton System, they asserted the freedom of the press as a universal human right, born out of Enlightenment principles, realized in the Protestant Reformation, and enshrined after the American Revolution in the Constitution's First Amendment guarantee that the federal government would not infringe on "the freedom of the press." A civic mantra thus served evangelical ends as the *Chinese Repository* presented a forum in which contributors of various and opposed opinions engaged in a rational debate about the meaning of free trade. As editors, Bridgman and Williams coordinated diverse perspectives, juxtaposing articles by merchants who profited from the opium business and others who decried it. They printed missionary exhortations against the traffic, firsthand accounts of the miserable toll that the drug was taking on addicts, letters of British politicians, memorials of Chinese administrators, edicts from the emperor, commentaries by provincial governors, and letters from the Cohong merchants. In the process they became the first documentarian historians of the Opium Wars.[10]

Today it is easy to dismiss characterizations of the *Chinese Repository* as a free press by questioning its extraterritorial premise, prejudicial vilification of pagan China, and accommodation of opium smuggling under the guise of arguing over free trade. It is harder to dismiss the missionaries' claim to have a fundamental right to print, publish, and disseminate. Since 1948, the United Nations' "Universal Declaration of Human Rights" has enshrined such rights in Article 19 that states "everyone has the right . . . to seek, receive and impart information and ideas through any media and regardless of frontiers."[11] Putting aside conceptual quandaries over the political assumptions necessary in universalizing rights of free expression, it is unsettling to see how "freedom" served rhetorical purposes for merchants and missionaries who attempted to coordinate Christianity, commerce, and print publication as Britain, France, and the United States broached Chinese territorial sovereignty and justified broader military aggression.

This chapter adumbrates the global context of Bridgman and Williams's pursuit of extraterritorial printing in South China and eventual disappointments related to the opium trade and the wars related to it. It begins by charting the international circuitries of American faith upon which they relied for support as they straddled the sacred and secular divide. The chapter continues by analyzing their attempts to publish on China as they covered opium in the *Chinese Repository* and concludes by charting their intensifying frustration over their inability to control the interpretation of the Gospel in the aftermath of the First Opium War as the Taiping movement justified revolutionary violence through millennial interpretation of the translated Bible.

Global Geography of American Evangelism and the Mission of Extraterritorial Printing

In 1810 a small circle of believers at Williams College founded the ABCFM that would send Bridgman and Williams to China in 1830. The cofounder Rev. Jedidiah Morse was a member of the standing order of conservative ministers who matched Calvinist conviction to federalist ambition.[12] When Harvard College selected a Unitarian for the Hollis Professorship of Divinity in 1805, Morse and his fellow ministers were devastated. Inspired by the example of David Brainerd, Jonathan Edwards, and Samuel Hopkins and by the London Missionary Society (founded in 1795),

Morse reacted in a first wave of sacred rage by founding a periodical called *The Panoplist; or, The Christian Armory* in 1805, the Andover Theological Seminary in 1808, and the ABCFM in 1810.

For the ABCFM, the field of ministry was the world. American missionaries made their first forays to Marathi (India) in 1813 and Ceylon in 1817 to join British missionaries who had preceded them. In the same period ABCFM members sojourned to the territories of the Chickasaw, Choctaw, Dakota, and Cherokee peoples in North America. Missionaries arrived in the Sandwich Islands (Hawai'i) in 1820, Sumatra and Borneo in 1834, and Micronesia (the Marshall and Caroline Islands) in 1843. Meanwhile, the Foreign Mission School in Cornwall, Connecticut, educated the young Hawai'ian student Henry Obookiah, Elias Boudinot from Cherokee Country, and several students from Malaysia and China.[13]

This international scope from the Far East to the Far West makes sense given Rev. Morse's notoriety as the preeminent American geographer of his time. In the late eighteenth century, he influenced generations of students with *Geography Made Easy: Being an Abridgement of the American University Geography For the Use of Schools and Academies in the United States of America* (1784) and his more scholarly tomes. These geographies helped shape not only the geographic imagination of early Americans but also their reading practices. As Hsuan L. Hsu explains, a global scale of reference underpinned conceptions of locality so that the "formal, thematic, and intertexual aspects of nineteenth-century literature reflected—and helped to produce—readers' identifications with domestic, urban, regional, national and global spaces."[14] By folding geography into literacy training, Morse influenced generations of early American students who were orienting themselves spatially and culturally in the world. The cultural geographer Martin Brückner explains that after the Revolutionary War new citizens were concerned with the legal feasibility of their claims to property that had originated in a royal charter.[15] In this context Morse linked faith and literacy to the imaginative resources of surveying and measuring literal tracts of land, thereby naturalizing a "homosocial landscape governed by codes of male proprietorship."[16] Morse's mode of instruction extended the conventional "visual pedagogy of the picture primer" by linking these maps of specific tracts to states and regions, encouraging readers to imagine relationships between different parts of their nation.[17] As Brückner quotes Morse, "Geography is a speceies [*sic*] of composition" such that the geographic imaginary promoted a federalist sense of local affiliation, a federative logic that set *the local* in an individual state that, in turn, hung together with other states in a united national configuration.[18] Historian Richard Moss goes as far as to describe Morse's *Geography* as "a jeremiad surveying the state of the nation and calling Americans back to a vision of moral perfection and simplicity, a vision rooted in an image of New England and most specifically of Connecticut."[19]

The geographic imaginary of Morse's faith also stretched beyond the nation's inchoate territorial boundaries, inviting readers to see the world as a context for investments of faith and capital.[20] His *Geography* explicitly registers Canton's world-historical centrality in networks of nineteenth-century commerce. Whereas China's center of political authority was the capital of Peking (Beijing), Morse prioritizes the trading port. In *Geography Made Easy*, which by 1814 had gone through seventeen editions, he describes Canton as containing "2,000,000 inhabitants, and often see[ing] 5000 trading vessels at a time, waiting to receive its rich commodities."[21] According to these figures, there were more people in Canton than in all the major cities of the United States combined. Also notice the absence of latitudinal and longitudinal coordinates. Morse's *Geography* situates Canton as a primary destination in the global trading network. The same could not yet be said of Boston, New York, or Philadelphia.

The nineteenth-century biographies of Bridgman and Williams reflect the global awareness of early national faith. The Bridgman family traced its ancestors back to "the Pilgrim Fathers."[22] Elijah grew up in Belchertown, Massachusetts, and attended a strict congregation that held to New Divinity conventions of a self-consciously revived Puritan tradition.[23] Leaving his family's farm, he made his way to Amherst College and on to Andover Theological Seminary. Bridgman was deeply moved by missionary accounts that he read in the *Panoplist*, which in the 1820s would morph into the ABCFM's *Missionary Herald*, and eventually report on the efforts of Bridgman and Williams. Arriving to Canton, Bridgman was inspired by the *Oriental Christian Spectator* (1831–63; Bombay) and sent copies back to the oversight committee in Boston.[24] Talking with the EIC's Rev. Robert Morrison, Bridgman committed to starting an ABCFM periodical in China.

In order to print in Canton, Bridgman needed to foster relationships with generous U.S. congregations. Helping make the case was the anti-opium New York merchant David Washington Cincinnatus Olyphant, who appealed to his congregation of the Bleecker Street Presbyterian Church. The church members raised money to purchase and transport a lightweight Washington press, manufactured in New York and designed for ease of transport and reassembly.[25] They named it the Bruen Press in honor of their recently deceased pastor, Rev. Matthias Bruen.[26] This press printed the first issue of the *Chinese Repository* in May 1832. Five years later it was still running after a total estimated output of 1,478,400 octavo pages.[27]

Editorial and print experiences lead to other opportunities, and as Bridgman improved his abilities in Chinese, he became very useful in diplomatic affairs.

"Elijah C. Bridgman." Frontispiece to Eliza J. Gillett Bridgman, ed., *The Life and Labors of Elijah Coleman Bridgman* (New York: Anson D. F. Randolph, 1864).

Before the First Opium War, he was in direct conversation with Commissioner Lin Zexu (Lín Zéxú, 林則徐), the Chinese official tasked with ending opium smuggling. Bridgman stood as a witness when Lin destroyed opium confiscated from the British traders.[28] In 1842 he accompanied the U.S. commodore Lawrence Kearny of the East India Squadron up the Pearl River to Canton to signal protection for the Americans who continued to trade there and to arrest those who continued to smuggle opium.[29] Two years later Bridgman served as a translator for Caleb Cushing, the U.S. "Envoy Extraordinary and Minister Plenipotentiary of the United States" negotiating the Treaty of Wanghia (1844).[30] Bridgman contributed accounts of all of this activity to the *Chinese Repository*. When in 1847 Bridgman and his wife Eliza relocated to Shanghai, they ran a school as he worked on a new translation of the Bible. He grew frustrated arguing with prominent British Sinologists Rev. Walter Medhurst and Rev. James Legge over how best to translate the Word of God

"S. Wells Williams." Frontispiece to F. Williams, *The Life and Letters of Samuel Wells Williams, LL.D.*

(and the actual word *God*) into Chinese. In 1854 Bridgman served as the translator on U.S. commodore Robert McLane's embassy to the Taiping leaders in Nanking. There he distributed his "Meilige hesheng guo zhilüe" or a *Brief Geographical History of the United States* (美理哥合省國志略), first written in Chinese during his years in Canton.[31] Initially hopeful that the Taiping would revolutionize China, he grew deeply disappointed with the uprising. He died of illness in 1861.

Samuel Wells Williams headed to China as a missionary printer in the 1830s, became a crucial diplomat in the 1850s and 1860s, and held a professorship at Yale University in the late 1870s. He was never ordained. Resigning from the ABCFM in 1857, he reminded it of "the fact that I am not a minister" and had always held a "secular" post, "identified with the press."[32] Williams's first and only major biographer is his son Frederick Wells Williams, who developed a vocational account of his father's printing career in *The Life and Letters of Samuel Wells Williams, LL.D.*:

Missionary, Diplomatist, Sinologue (1889), weaving his father's letters into a chrono-logical narrative of faith dedicated to developing a global influence to hereditary print craft steeped in Puritan cultural foundation.[33]

Williams traced the inspiration for printing back to his roots in New York State, where he attended the First Presbyterian Church in Utica, graduated from the Rensselaer Institute in Troy, and underwent an accelerated apprenticeship at his father's print shop in anticipation of his missionary work. Frederick echoes his father's characterization of this intensive preparatory training as "dry and irksome drudgery," the preliminary test of his resolve:[34] "The end of April [1833] found [Sam-uel] ready for the long journey. Continuous industry and a mind quickened by the exceptional interest and importance of his task had enabled him within six months to serve a hasty apprenticeship in every department of book-making. From the compositor's room he had followed the types to the press, thence with the printed sheets to the proof-reader, then to the folder, the sewing frame, and the process of binding; it was possible in his father's establishment to finish his training in these departments very thoroughly."[35] Frederick imbues his father Samuel's subsequent extraterritorial printing career with a ritualistic aura that stretches the horizontal geographic associations of Congregational faith from New England to Canton while maintaining the vertical intergenerational legacy of colonial printing. Williams's father would shut the doors of his print shop in 1836. Meanwhile his son was just getting started, systematizing the printing of Chinese language in movable type to evangelical ends.

Upon arrival to Canton in 1833 Williams took charge of printing operations. In 1844 after twelve years of printing in China, he returned to the United States, lec-turing widely to raise money for German-made steel punches that would complete a Chinese fount of movable type. His lectures and the *Chinese Repository* became the first drafts of his two-volume magnum opus, *The New Middle Kingdom: A Survey of the Geography, Government, Literature, Social Life, Arts, Religion, &c., of the Chinese Empire and Its Inhabitants*, first published in 1848 and revised into the final ex-panded edition of 1883. On his visit to the United States he also married the mis-sionary Sarah Walworth. Upon return to Canton in 1847, Williams took over the editorship of the *Chinese Repository*, which in 1851 he brought to a close, compiling its comprehensive index. His duties as a "diplomatist" eventually pulled him north after a fire destroyed the Mission Press in 1856.

This chapter focuses on Williams and Bridgman, but the *Chinese Repository* documented the missionary work of various denominations and nationalities.[36] Rev. David Abeel accompanied Bridgman in 1830. He was a member of the Dutch Reformed Church and a graduate of New Brunswick Seminary in New Jersey. He left Canton to embark on voyages throughout the Straits Settlements, and into

Borneo, Java, and Siam. Abeel's immediate replacement at Canton was Rev. Edwin Stevens who arrived from Yale Divinity in late October 1832.[37] He was more active as an extraterritorial preacher than as an editor or printer, distributing thousands of tracts in China and preaching to crowds who gathered. He also advised Hong Xiuquan before and during the Taiping Rebellion. Rev. Dr. Peter Parker was a very influential medical doctor and diplomat who arrived to Canton in 1834.[38] A Yale graduate of both the medical and divinity schools, he started a hospital in November 1835, where he performed surgeries that saved the lives and eyesight of many. The *Chinese Repository* included summaries of Parker's impressive medical practice. His conversations with Secretary of State Daniel Webster helped shape U.S. diplomacy that led to the Treaty of Wanghia (1844).[39]

Bridgman and Williams's printing endeavors also reflect the broader denominational tensions and collaborations of the early republic. Outside the pale of the ABCFM coalition stood the Baptists, who were more interested in preaching than printing. The American Baptist Board of Foreign Missions sent missionaries worldwide including the aforementioned Henrietta Hall Shuck and her husband Rev. J. Lewis Shuck, who moved to Shanghai after Henrietta's death and eventually returned to the United States to minister in San Francisco.[40] While living in Macao, the Shucks shared a house with Rev. Issachar Jacox Roberts. Born in Tennessee, Roberts affiliated with the Southern Baptist Convention and studied for a few months at Furman Academy and Theological Institute in South Carolina. After the official Baptist Board rejected his application, he mortgaged his farm in Mississippi and founded his own organization, the China Mission Society. In the 1840s Roberts mentored Hong Xiuquan on spiritual matters and visited him in Nanking.[41] Roberts had been inspired by the dynamic Karl Friedrich August Gützlaff, a Lutheran from Prussia who in 1826 went to Java for the Netherlands Missionary Society.[42] His seemingly inexhaustible efforts included helping to found the Canton branch of the Society for the Diffusion of Useful Knowledge and editing its magazine.[43] There is space here only to sketch the interdenominational coalitions of which Bridgman and Williams were mindful as they operated the Bruen Press. Most important were the British missionaries who had preceded them.

Global Circuitries of Faith and the Quest for Metallic Fonts

Bridgman and Williams's goal of converting the pagan Chinese suffused their material and social practices of printing texts in English and Chinese. In *The Printing Press as an Agent of Change* (1979), Elizabeth Eisenstein writes: "When ideas are detached from the media used to transmit them, they are also cut off from the historical circumstances that shape them, and it becomes difficult to perceive the changing context within which they must be viewed."[44] The Bruen Press operated at the intersection of "ideas" and "media" on the levels of editorial strategy, acquisition of printing equipment, and management of print workers, who, despite not sharing a common language, produced millions of printed pages in the form of dictionaries, commercial guides, treaties, and pamphlets. From the very start there was an instructive aspect to the missionaries' print project. It was not just a matter of producing Chinese texts.

Early in their Canton residence, Bridgman and Williams committed to metallic types as the preferred mode of production. In 1834 Bridgman weighs the opinions of preceding British missionary printers in describing the state of Chinese print culture as it relates to the evangelical ambition of his printing endeavor: "We [editors of the *Chinese Repository*] are inclined to think, judging from what we have seen, that *metal types* will prove to be (in some instances at least) as much superior to the common *block printing* of the Chinese, as a fine European merchantman is superior to a common Chinese junk. We do not expect that the Chinese will at once see, or rather *acknowledge*, this superiority. They have long seen the superiority of the European ship, but they are slow to acknowledge that superiority, and do not avail themselves of the improvement."[45] This analogy of a Western merchant ship outpacing a Chinese junk ship to movable metal type improving woodblock xylography conveys succinctly the ideological confluence of commerce, Christianity, and print culture. It echoes ubiquitous characterizations of China as an isolated Middle Kingdom, out of step with Western advances in print and maritime technologies, and out of sync with the rising Western phase of empire that such technologies heralded. Bridgman continues, extending his analogies to diplomacy, by asserting that "the Chinese mode of printing is, like their national policy, very *unsociable*; it is ill-suited to sort with that used in other languages."[46] Bridgman's metal frame of the Western print production would not only re-sort and combine literal fonts of English letters and Chinese characters on the same galley but also reframe the Chinese language in a socially transformative mode of printing that revolutionizes China into a "sociable" neighbor of the free-trading world community.

In advocating metal types, Bridgman was also aligning himself with the precedent set by British missionary collaborators.[47] The ABCFM printers stood on the shoulders of William Carey, Joshua Marshman, Robert Morrison, William Milne, Samuel Dyer, and others. They had traced a global pattern for international print production, working in West Bengal, in China, and on the periphery of Chinese influence in Southeast Asia. They had immersed themselves in learning to speak, read, write, and print in Chinese, striving to develop the necessary print technology. In 1799 the British Baptist missionary Joshua Marshman arrived in the former Danish colony of Serampore in West Bengal, joining Rev. William Carey, the founder of the Baptist Missionary Society and translator of the Bible into Bengali and San-skrit.[48] Meanwhile, Rev. Robert Morrison arrived in Canton in 1807 and managed to learn how to read, write, and print in Chinese. When an 1812 imperial edict threatened capital punishment for printing books—a threat to which collaborating Chinese converts such as Liang A-fa were especially vulnerable—Morrison and fellow British missionaries established printing stations throughout the Straits Settlements in Malacca and Penang, Batavia, and Singapore.[49] William Milne's *China Monthly Magazine* (察世俗每月統記傳; Chá shìsú měi yuè tǒng jì chuán; 1815–22) first appeared in August 1815, printed in Malacca by "traditional Chinese woodblock."[50] It ran for seven years with a monthly run of five hundred, "circu-lat[ing] through the Chinese communities in Southeast Asia and some parts of China."[51] Milne and Morrison also oversaw an English-language periodical, the *Indo-Chinese Gleaner* (1817–22), and started the Anglo-Chinese College in Malacca. Bridgman and Williams hoped to help support the regional network of metallic-font printing stations throughout Asia.[52] At practical and conceptual levels of print ambition, Rev. Samuel Dyer of the London Missionary Society was a key figure for Bridgman and Williams, linking their efforts with these larger networks. Dyer arrived to Penang with his wife in 1827, the same year that William Wood began editing the *Canton Register*, the first Western newspaper in Canton. Dyer would move to Malacca, Singapore, and finally Macau where he died. His modest grave-stone is in the Protestant Cemetery of Macao.

Articles throughout the two-decade run of the *Chinese Repository* reflect the Americans' sustained practical interest in the varieties of print production—from woodblock and wax-tablet xylography, to stereotype, lithography, early electrotype, and various models of hand-presses that utilized movable type, forged and cut in interrelated projects of typeface production spanning South and Southeast Asia from India to China. Chinese xylography or "wood-block" printing had certain ad-vantages. For centuries it had been the primary mode of printing throughout the Chinese provinces, each with many skilled artisans who knew best how to optimize local wood resources for printing plates.[53] Carved wood rendered a more pleasing typography, an important consideration in attracting Chinese readers. Bridgman's article (February 1833) cites Milne to describe the method: printers took a wood-block or plate half an inch thick, planed its surface until it was very smooth, and then rubbed it with a paste made of boiled rice to soften the surface for the engrav-ing tools. Next, the printer placed the paper sheet of manuscript text face down on the block and rubbed it to leave an inverted, mirrored impression of the characters. The printer then cut away the area around these reversed characters to render the text in relief. The block would then be inked and pressed onto a single side of thin, blank paper.[54] Bridgman estimates that each wood block could produce twenty thousand to thirty thousand impressions before wearing out. Another advantage to xylography was its mobility; Bridgman acknowledged this in recommending xylography for missionaries who planned to pursue *"itinerant printing"* throughout China.[55] He notes that the traveling preacher would need to carry only a small toolkit—not a heavy hand press, lead fonts, tin type cases, steel punches, and sorting cabinets. An itinerant preacher could divide a day into proselytizing and carving. And, "if persecuted in one place" he or she could, "in the silence of the night," retreat elsewhere and "be at work again early the next morning."[56]

Nevertheless, "Cutting of Punches and Casting Metal Type" was the Holy Grail of print production, and Bridgman quotes Dyer's proclamation that "a punch is the foundation of perpetuity."[57] In the grand scale of print production that the missionaries imagined, steel punches ensured the capacity to reproduce the molds or matrices for many fonts (character sets) of durable metallic type. Bridgman and Williams set their sights on acquiring steel punches (the face of which was a three-dimensional character in reverse) that could punch a character into a slug of softer metal such as copper, thus forming a matrix (or mold). Into these matrices printers poured molten lead that hardened into a discrete font block with the character protruding in relief. These fonts or types are what compositors placed and lined-up in a print galley, framed by a metal brace that would tighten to secure the resulting forme or print plate, which print workers ultimately inked and pressed on a sheet of paper with a press apparatus such as the Bruen Press. Dyer estimates that each character set could last at least twenty years. Steel punches were a "fount of perpetuity" because they could punch out many, many matrices that, in turn, could mold many, many font pieces.

In addition to the great expense of manufacturing steel punches, there were other challenges that the Chinese language presented for the "metal" and "movable" attributes of Western type. In Chinese, each character is itself a word or logotype. There is no alphabet. To print a book with movable type requires an individual font for each word that appears on a page. Dyer estimated the Chinese language to have forty thousand different words, so manufacturing a comprehensive set would have tested the endurance of anyone's faith. But working in Malacca to print Morrison's "Holy Scriptures" and the New Testament, Dryer used only around thirty-six hundred characters. With this in mind he surveyed a set of fourteen classics in Chinese literature to determine the five thousand characters sufficient for missionary publication and the additional eighteen hundred that would round out a character set for almost any "literary purpose whatever."[58]

The broader ideological implications of metallic types are apparent in the descriptions of the printing headquarters where presswork served grander evangelical designs of civilizing the print workers. Consider a letter that Williams writes in January 1839 to his retired and increasingly ill father in New York. Having just relocated to Macao in the months before the First Opium War, Williams describes his printing office:

> I have one of the oddest printing offices you can possibly imagine; 't is quite unique, I am sure, in its way. In the first place there are the Chinese types, which are arranged on frames on the side of the room, so as to expose their faces, for they must all be seen to be found. There are sixty cases of large type—which is about the size of four-line pica—and there are upwards of 25,000 types, hardly any two of which are alike. The small type stands on frames, one case above the other, and justifies with the Gt. Primer [a description of size], being contained in twenty cases, all so arranged that the type stands on the base, exposing all the faces. So much for the Chinese type, which fills up half the room. There is one clumsy, English press of iron, and three compos-ing stands. But my workmen are really the most singular part of the office furniture. There is a Portuguese compositor, who knows not a word of English and hardly a Chinese character, yet sets up a book containing both; I speak to him in Portuguese, after a fashion, tho' imperfectly. A Chinese lad, who knows neither Portuguese nor English, sets Chinese types, and does his part pretty well. Lastly a Japanese, who knows nothing of English, Portuguese, or Chinese (hardly), picks out the various characters, and makes plenty of errors. When all hands are employed I must talk to each in his own tongue, and direct them all to print a book, the contents of which not a single person engaged on it knows any thing of; yet I think it will be printed tolera-bly accurately notwithstanding. I am sometimes amused at the mutual endeavors of my motley group to hold intercourse; but conversation is so tedious, and withal so imperfect, that my office is much stiller than No. 60, 3d story, used to be whilom.[59]

Setting the scene with the arrangement of stands, tables, the press, and other items, Williams establishes continuity between his printing work in China and his fa-ther's in New York ("No. 60, 3d story"). In distinguishing his Macao printing office as the "oddest" and quite "unique," he signals the expanded terms brought on by the missionary endeavor. With the diplomatic standoff between Britain and China escalating in Canton on the eve of war, Williams focuses on lining up Chinese and English fonts in the same frame. The conventional "English press of iron" (maybe the Bruen Press) very reasonably seemed "clumsy," and yet there is a sense of familiarity and order that Williams creates in describing this scene of printing for his father. With the phrase "office furniture," Williams figures the human print workers as components in a system of production that he oversees. His character-ization echoes standard tropes that figure all missionaries as tools of God.[60] But in this scene each worker seems isolated in a particular language—of Chinese, Japa-nese, or Portuguese—as he performs tasks that Williams supervises. Of course, in logistical terms, compositors did not need to be literate. The font letters appear backward in their cases (as a mirror image of the printed character) so the task of lining up individual fonts on the galley in a frame was an exercise in serial pattern recognition. Nevertheless, Williams's assertion of the workers' illiteracy or functional nonliteracy highlights his fantasized control over the social process and consequence of metallic-font print production. He distinguishes himself as the only one who understands comprehensively—at logistical and spiritual levels—a system of textual production that conveys facts and spiritual truths. Williams has grown into the role of his father, training pagan sons into Western print culture through the printing of evangelical texts, commercial guides, and articles for the *Chinese Repository*.

Taking command of the material process of print, Williams of course kept his eye on the evangelical effect of circulating his publications. In *The Middle Kingdom* (1848), he characterized magazines as "aids and precursors" for the "introduction of the Gospel," opining that the "influence of newspapers and periodical literature will probably be very great among the Chinese, when they begin to think for themselves on the great truths and principles which are now being introduced among them."[61] While acknowledging that some may not consider it the "business of a missionary to edit the newspaper or publish a penny magazine," he contends "those who are acquainted with the debased heart of the heathen mind know that any means, which will convey the truth and arouse the people, tends to advance religion, since it stirs up their powers."[62] Such presumptive optimism regarding the free press presumed the reinforcing progressive effects of commerce, liberalism, and Christianity.

Civic Lessons of the Chinese Repository

As the ABCFM missionaries began operating their press, they took a long view of history to imagine revolutionary consequences for China. The ancient Middle Kingdom had invented printing, but centuries of pagan tyranny had ossified its practice into dutifully sycophantic copying. Imperial decrees had shut down communication among Chinese people and between China and the world's nations. The Mission Press would revolutionize China by supporting the free flow of ideas. In the first article of the first issue of the *Chinese Repository* (May 1832), Bridgman writes without attribution as the editor to interweave the strands of Christian faith, commerce, Enlightenment curiosity, and Christian piety in describing a civilizing braid of sustained print production. Lamenting that, despite "the long intercourse which has existed between nations of Christendom and eastern Asia," "there has been so little commerce in intellectual and moral commodities," he pledges to supplement centuries of lost knowledge.[63] Faced with a vast "Middle Kingdom" in which "foreigners can by no means be permitted to enter and reside," except for the "very narrow place at Canton and Macao," the editor of the *Chinese Repository* will "review foreign books on China" to derive a historical view of the empire, relating to the categories of "natural history," "commerce," "social relations," "moral character," "literary character," and "religious character."[64] In his pledge of encyclopedic coverage resonate his evangelical hopes of motivating more Americans to become missionaries. He also is showcasing for potential Chinese readers the powers of the press to produce and distribute knowledge "so richly enjoyed by the nations of the West" and, thereby, hoping to "elevate" the "nations of the East."[65]

The general headings in Williams's 1851 index to the *Chinese Repository* suggest the broad scholastic scope of its project. The first eleven headings echo the eighteenth-century encyclopedic endeavors overseen by the Jesuit editor Jean-Baptiste Du Halde and others whose landmarks of sinology the *Chinese Repository* reviewed in the articles listed under the heading "8-Travels." Topics 10 through 18 register the political events of the era, and the topics 19 through 30 take a broader view of the region:

1- Geography	16- War with England
2- Chinese Government and Politics	17- Hongkong
3- Revenue, Army, and Navy	18- Relations with America
4- Chinese People	19- Japan, Corea, & etc.
5- Chinese History	20- Siam and Cochinchin
6- Natural History	21- Other Asiatic Nations
7- Arts, Science, and Manufactures	22- Indian Archipelago
8- Travels	23- Paganism
9- Language, Literature, & etc.	24- Missions
10- Trade and Commerce	25- Medical Missions
11- Shipping	26- Revision of the Bible
12- Opium	27- Education Societies
13- Canton, Foreign Factories, etc.	28- Religious
14- Foreign Relations	29- Biographical Notices
15- Relations with Great Britain	30- Miscellaneous

The articles grouped under the first category of "Geography" move from the generally regional to the more locally specific in describing the distinct topographies of China's provinces, departments, districts, cities, and towns where people had lived for thousands of years. This fold of geography into topography implies the deeper environmental logic by which Bridgman and Williams understood the distinct development of China's social mores. In the same decades in which Samuel

George Morton, Josiah C. Nott, and Harvard University's Professor Louis Agassiz were theorizing multiple origins to color-coded races thereby fragmenting humanity into separate species, Bridgman and Williams held to the monogenetic orthodoxy of biblical Genesis. However, they maintained a hierarchy to the world's savages, barbarians, and ancient pagan civilizations, privileging Europe as the most advanced and modern civilization of humankind's diverse developmental pathways. Thus their sense of "geography" not only plots China on a horizontal scale of the contemporary world map but also suggests a historically significant vertical rootedness in specific environments that have produced China's unique cultural attributes over a span of time that renders them ancient.

In Bridgman and Williams's natural historical presentation of China, "Language, Literature, & etc." (heading 9) indicated China's relatively subordinate status in a hierarchy of civilizations. Bridgman's article "Periodical Literature: Chinese Almanacs; imperial Court Calendar; the provincial Court Circular of Canton; the Peking Gazette; with remarks of the condition of the press in China" (May 1836) characterizes the "medium of the press" as an index of a people's political and social status: "Through the medium of the press, when its freedom is sufficiently guaranteed, errors and abuses are disclosed; improvements and reforms, suggested; and multitudes, stimulated to noble enterprises. And thus the condition of the press and the character of its productions in any country, form a criterion by which we may very safely estimate its rank in the scale of nations."[66] Alas, the state of China's press was not free and its ranking among world-historical civilizations suffered accordingly. The ancient civilization of China had invented printing, but the West had taken the technique to the next level as a revolutionary instrument, liberating faith and reason from Catholic dominion and establishing for individuals a direct relationship with God. In the 1834 article on "The Chinese language," Bridgman explained that "since the sun of the Reformation arose," "freedom of thought" had been "agitat[ing] and shak[ing]" Europe "to her very centre," inspiring "men" "to feel that each had a right, and that each was bound, to think for himself."[67] From a European core, this agitating energy of free thought had then expanded to the non-Christian periphery of the world. Through the operations of the Canton Press, Bridgman and Williams hoped to expose the Chinese to a way of printing and reading that continued this print revolution of faith, commerce, and political organization.

There was a problem. China's despotic emperors had long restricted print production. It was as if Chinese "Thought" had been "stereotyped"—frozen in a literal printing plate—as "all the ideas which the Chinese wish to cherish or inculcate are contained in [the] records which have come down to them from venerable sages of antiquity."[68] Here Bridgman cleverly turns the tool of print production into a metaphor of textual literalism to highlight the dynamism of Western print culture.[69] Elsewhere he cites the *Indo-Chinese Gleaner* (April 1819) to assert that China had always been "subject to an absolute monarchy."[70] Thus, China's "press has not been free" but merely "*tolerated*, and that under a surveillance which paralizes the soul."[71] The emperor of China monopolizes operation of the press to threaten and intimidate; "to guard the morals of their subjects," he and his "officers of government send forth annual proclamations, admonishing all people to be good, and threatening transgressors with condign punishment."[72] Chinese print publication shows that, "indeed, so far as we know, freedom and liberty, as understood by the people of Christendom, are ideas for which the language of this country has no appropriate terms."[73]

The Chinese press was deficient not only in *what* but in *how* it published. A specific example of the emperor's soul-paralyzing surveillance is the *Peking Gazette*. Known in Chinese as "*King Chaou*" (京報; jīng bào)" or "transcripts from the Capitol," it was the major vehicle for transmitting the memorials and imperial edicts throughout the provinces of China.[74] Bridgman sets the scene for its production: each morning the emperor receives obsequious attendants who present him with memorials that they have read and answered in different ways, hoping to anticipate the emperor's opinion. The emperor reviews the options, selecting and marking "in red ink, with a heavy stroke of the pencil" his choice.[75] If unsatisfied with the options, he dictates a fresh answer, which his attendants dutifully record in the red ink of autocratic dictum. Bridgman also mentions separate papers called "*shang yu*" (Shèngzhǐ; 聖旨), or supreme (imperial) edicts, issued by the emperor through his Inner Council or members of the Imperial Academy. All imperial decrees close with "the words *kin tsze*, 'respect this,' which none except the one man may use."[76] After the imperial session, the court attendants issue the official transcripts. Imperial and private couriers distribute these throughout the provinces to booksellers, who wait to transcribe the edicts and carve away the empty space on woodblocks for printing.[77] The resulting print publications appear in various forms: "In their best style they form a daily manuscript in small octavo of about forty pages; but in an inferior style, they appear only once in two days, and then do not contain more than twenty pages, and often not so many."[78] Through these means, a few copies of the *Peking Gazette* reached Canton every other day. Bridgman also notes the popularity of almanacs and the six-volume Court Calendar, which is a directory of imperial army officers and general accounting of "revenue, granaries, schools, etc."[79] From observations in Canton he describes the rough-and-ready publication of the "provincial Court Circular" (*yuen mun paou*) or "report from the gates" by the "chief provincial officers"; imprinted from "waxen block and only on one side," the report communicates activities of the magistrates and governor, and administrative promotions throughout the province.[80] The process of printing was thus fairly open, but great care needed to be taken not to "offend the government."[81] Alas, this was not the operation of a free press.

Despite this print cultural stagnation, the ABCFM missionaries regarded Chinese literature and print traditions as an encouraging premise for their evangelism. In the *Chinese Repository* article "Promulgation of the Gospel in China" (1835), Rev. Edwin Stevens celebrated the strong "taste for reading" among the Chinese, estimating that "nearly nine-tenths of adult males are able to read ordinary books, though not one-tenth of the female populations."[82] He predicted that as a "trait of national character," the general respect for books "will help to secure a willing reception and perusal for Christian books when distributed."[83] Bridgman had put it more emphatically the year before: "Whether we regard the subject in a commercial, political, literary, or religious point of view, there is, we think, no foreign language, which holds out to the people of the West so many considerations for studying it as the Chinese."[84] The challenge was to use Chinese to convey the evangelical message of Christian salvation and civilized life.

Exposing a passively literate Chinese people to the Word of God would revolutionize Chinese society at a time when broader crises were breaking out to destabilize the emperor. Bridgman predicted in several articles that China was on the verge of a great upheaval that would afford missionaries a prime opportunity to penetrate and convert millions of Chinese people. In the article "The Chinese Language" (May 1834), he considers how best to intervene, through military power or softer power of print cultural influence:

> If we mistake not the signs of the times, a crisis is rapidly approaching in the affairs of this nation [China]; a revolution, though it may be long delayed, seems inevitable; and it must be effected by a military force or by the means of the press. . . . A military conquest would cause the destruction of thousands of human lives and millions of property; but a conquest of principles, the triumph of right reason, the victory of truth, will cost a far less expenditure of men and means, will be glorious in the results, and carry the blessings of peace and bright hopes of immortality to the multitudes of this nation.[85]

Bridgman's phrase "signs of the times" refers specifically to developments in secular history but his abiding concern is with the signs that foretell imminent final judgment. There is urgency to converting and saving as many pagan souls as possible. His comparison of the press and military force implies the great degree and scope of intervention that he imagined for his printing efforts.[86] It also underscores the rationalization of opium smuggling as historical activity that could serve grander evangelical purposes.

With printing technology that enabled publication of Chinese characters, the missionary printers imagined taking control of the social media and labor relations by which Chinese language and literature conveyed meaning through textual production. Bridgman continues in "The Chinese Language" by reflecting on the stagnant sense of communal political consciousness that he sees in the form of Chinese literature: "The inhabitants of this land will never be effectually waked up from their long, deep slumbers, until a new era is formed in their literature, and they are excited to think for themselves, and to exchange their galling tyranny and their abominable idolatry for just notions of individual and national rights, and the holy religion of the living God."[87] Assuming the universality of "individual and national rights" born out of the one true religious experience, Bridgman works to control the figurative capacity of the Chinese language. In the status quo, Chinese literature is stuck in the rut of literalism as "tyranny" stifles freethinking people of China from questioning the "abominable idolatry" of inherited literature. By printing in China and, with Williams's help, in the Chinese language, Bridgman hopes to activate the capacity of Chinese readers to see beyond the literal, to think and interpret for themselves as individuals. However, Bridgman holds the potential Chinese convert on a very short leash in the field of figuration, exercising his skills in interpretative thinking to very specific ends. He counters imperial China's literalism with a capacity for free thought that necessarily leads to the transcendent truth of Christianity, the embrace of individual and national rights, and the free-trade ideals of commerce. Opposing one literalism with another, Bridgman invests the act of printing with deep spiritual consequence that leaves no room for interpretation. He continues by reasoning that evangelical treatises need to use the "idioms" of the Chinese or they will "find very few readers"; conversely, "if new and interesting thoughts, pure and elevated sentiments, and above all the sublime truths of divine revelation are rightly exhibited in a native costume, then they may have a charm and power which will rouse the mind, sway the passion, correct the judgment, and eventually work a mental and moral revolution throughout the empire."[88] If Chinese language is a "native costume," Bridgman's printing press will weave a textual dress that exhibits to Chinese people the true potential of their Chinese language as it adorns the divine truths of Christian revelation. In the missionaries' big picture, the *Chinese Repository* would realign the history of national commerce in converting the Chinese to Christianity.

Bridgman's reflections on the Chinese language exceeded China and promised reorganization of the South and Southeast Asia. In another article, "European Periodicals Beyond the Ganges" (August 1836), Bridgman highlights the "great responsibilities" of editing periodicals "beyond the Ganges" by likening their editors to "sentinels" standing "on high ground. On every side wide fields for observation are spread around them. The whole world of nature and all the handyworks of the Almighty, are open to their inspection."[89] It is interesting to notice that such geographic scope of evangelical ambition overlapped with the routes of opium commerce. It might have been better if Bridgman's sentinels had raised the alarm over opium shipments instead of projecting Christian responsibility for pagans.

Covering Opium in the Chinese Repository

Running the Bruen Press meant having to accommodate, at least to some extent, the merchant power brokers of the region. By framing debates about opium as a *question*, ABCFM printers succeeded where their predecessor William Wood—Harriett Low's discouraged suitor—had failed. Wood's editorship of the *Canton Register* reflected the balancing act of covering a drug whose traffic was as lucrative as it was controversial.[90] The *Canton Register*, which began in November 1827, was owned and financed by the Scottish country traders James and Alexander Matheson, who moved goods under the British flag between Canton and Bombay and Calcutta through their private house of Magniac & Co. (After the Opium War they partnered with William Jardine to found Jardine, Matheson, & Co, one of the most profitable and lucrative companies in history.)[91] The Mathesons fired Wood in February 1828 after he had edited six issues.

From the perspective of the Mathesons, the primary purpose of the *Canton Register* was to publish a table of current prices ("Price Current") for imports, exports, stores, and exchanges. This table was meant to serve as a tool for negotiating the sale and transfer of everything from "Alum" and "Borax" to "Taffeta" and "Velvet," and in deciding what ships to send where and when on their tacks to and from Bombay and Canton. The Price Current listed "Opium" under its own separate heading and accounted for deliveries into Canton, tallying the remaining stock at Lintin Island in storehouse ships holding thousands of chests of different types, including Patna, Benares, and Malwa. The Price Current also listed the value and amount of EIC "Bills on Bengal" and other bills of exchange through which private traders moved the drug from Bengal to Canton with a promise of payment in London.

From the start of his editorship, Wood held grander designs than updating a Price Current alongside a breezy social register. The first issue laid out an ambitiously wide field of international reportage and reflection on the "peculiarities of the Chinese" and "translations from their standard works."[92] The second issue of 24 November 1827 "compressed" the "Price Current," and a letter-to-the-editor (signed "Amicus") encouraged publication of "more extended views of trade, than simple details of the value of mercantile commodities."[93] By the fourth issue, Wood was leading with a historical overview of the "Portuguese Trade with China" from the perspective of a "Philosophical Historian" who reviewed the "causes which have operated in accelerating the rise and fall of nations."[94] Appreciating Portugal's early reach to India and China, the article asserts the "general decay of the Portuguese nation" and its "tame submission to the impositions of the Chinese."[95] This would not have pleased the Mathesons, the EIC, and the other traders from Britain or the United States, who did not want to ruffle any feathers. In Wood's sixth and final issue (4 February 1828), he ruffled even more by protesting Spain's special trading privileges at Amoy.[96] Waxing nostalgic, the article recalls that Britain once "had a Factory at *Amoy* in 1676, which was destroyed during the civil wars by the Tartars" and "re-established in the year 1686" until "trade was by an Imperial Edict removed to Canton."[97] Reflecting on the "tombs " of the murdered British merchants at Amoy, Wood implies that their sacrifice for king and country had been ignored.[98] Wood never worked on another issue. The next one reported the former "Editor's" resignation and promised not to overreach by covering India, for although "we are not opposed to the freedom of the Press or of liberal discussion," it is nevertheless not "within our limits, and publishing so unfrequently justice [can] not be done to any subject of importance."[99] There was a final dig at Wood: "A *free* press we admire, but a *licentious* one, either on morals or politics, we abhor."[100]

Unlike Wood, Bridgman and Williams enjoyed the financial support of the U.S. anti-opium merchants David Olyphant and his partner Charles King. They regarded opium as the fly in the ointment of an ideal commerce working synergistically with the press to open China, breaking down the barriers separating it from the "most enlightened and peaceful states of Christendom."[101] Of course, Bridgman did not want to alienate rich and powerful representatives of the U.S. firm Russell & Company, including the brothers Robert Bennet and John Murray Forbes. The consequences could have reverberated to New England and potentially jeopardized the general missionary operations of the ABCFM. Furthermore, opium merchants substantially supported some missionary endeavors. For decades Rev. Robert Morrison had been chaplain of the EIC, and the private traders Jardine, Matheson, and Lancelot Dent contributed substantially to the Morrison Education Fund. They also supported Karl Friedrich August Gützlaff's extensive travels throughout South Asia and China.[102]

Bridgman and Williams managed to cover opium in their magazine by conflating freedoms of the press with freedoms of commerce under a big tent of Christianity that stretched back to the Catholic missionaries' scholastic endeavors. In a long view on Chinese history, opium was not in itself the problem. The article entitled "Cultivation of the poppy, in Europe, China, and India; extent and quality of land so occupied; time and mode of culture; and the amount of population capital engaged therein" (February 1837) introduces "Papaver somnifernum" as a specimen of natural history with a long history in China, Europe, and India as a medicine for pain relief and recreation, tracking descriptions back to Homer and Ovid.[103] Nevertheless news about opium eventually frustrated their scholarly ambition. Topics in Williams's 1851 index move from: "9- Language, Literature, & etc." to "10- Trade and Commerce" to "11- Shipping," and then to "12- Opium," after which follow the headings related to the Canton System, "16- War with England," diplomatic relations with England and the United States, and finally "17- Hongkong," control over which China relinquished to England in the Treaty of Nanking (1842).

The *Chinese Repository* managed a systematic view, outlining Britain's country trade. Articles such as "Opium smoking in Penang" highlighted the wide network of traffic through the Straits Settlements and the advantages of warehousing opium throughout the trade network to modulate its availability from season to season in relation to the basket of commodities moving through the commercial zones of Southeast Asia.[104] They also noted the smuggling stations on islands outside the Pearl River. They delved into the international dynamics of diplomatic courtesy that changed when the EIC monopoly expired and Britain's foreign secretary Lord Palmerston appointed Lord William Napier as the chief superintendent of trade and to represent His Majesty King William IV in overseeing the British subjects' relationship with China. Lord Napier expected to be treated with the respect due to a British king's representative. He arrived in June 1834 and insisted on direct communication with the governor of Canton in delivering a letter that announced his presence. As the *Chinese Repository* described it, Napier's "great object [was] to open and maintain a direct and personal communication with the viceroy."[105] When rebuffed, he ordered two British war ships to proceed up the Pearl River without the customary permits. China responded by halting all trade—much to the dismay of the British traders. Tensions eased after Napier became very ill and retreated to Macao where he died.

In 1836 Lord Palmerston appointed Charles Elliot as the new superintendent and instructed him not to offend the Chinese authorities or to "assume a greater degree of authority over British subjects than you in reality possess."[106] Nevertheless, Elliot referred to himself as the "chief English authority in China" and pressed for the diplomatic recognition that had eluded Napier.[107] Superintendent Elliot disapproved of the opium trade and had a tense relationship with the British traders who conducted it—particularly the heads of the two most powerful British firms of James Matheson and Lancelot Dent. In reports back to Palmerston, Elliot criticized "opium traffic" as "mischievous to every branch of trade," even sympathizing with the Chinese attempts to crack down on those smuggling the drug.[108] However, throughout Elliot's superintendence, he took great offense at China's poor treatment of him as a representative of the British Crown. Harkening back to the thwarted embassies of Macartney (1792) and Amherst (1816), Napier's death became Elliot's rallying cry in pushing for diplomatic recognition as an equal.

In the months leading up to the war, Bridgman took a strong stand against opium smuggling in the *Chinese Repository*. He ascribes the causes of the "remarkable crisis in commercial intercourse with China" to the "low state of morality, among western nations" in regard to "their political and commercial relations with the east" and criticizes the EIC for ignoring the baneful "effects of the drug on the Chinese people."[109] Under the guise of "free trade," the EIC had extended the cultivation of opium, shipping it to China to generate increasing rates of revenue that in 1837 totaled $12 million, "drawn off to India, in exchange for its 'flowing poison'" and threatening China's rank as "an independent empire."[110] Thus "distinguished merchants" had put profits before moral consideration of social consequences, "enag[ing] freely in the traffic" while winning over public opinion in England. Bridgman also blames the emperor for losing credibility among local Chinese officials who dared to circumvent his edicts of prohibition. Finally, he chastises the Western governments for tacitly accepting the opium trade by not offering clear direction to consuls; "western governments" had brought "odium on themselves," leaving "our national character" "in the dust, prostrated by our own folly and negligence."[111]

When war broke out, Bridgman continued to put his free press to work as Charles W. King and Robert Bennet Forbes argued for and against opium in the *Chinese Repository*. Under the pseudonym "CR," King contributed a thirty-two-page article entitled "Review of the difficulties between the English and Chinese authorities."[112] It so riled Robert Bennet that he retorted the following month (February 1840), under the pseudonym "Non Sine Causa" (Not without cause), taking a page out of William Wood's playbook to mock "CR" for suffering the insults of China's terms of quarantining foreigners. Forbes also ridiculed Olyphant and King for being self-righteous in asserting clear lines of commercial virtue while ignoring the complex fog of commercial transactions in which commodities folded one into another. As an alternative to silver, opium worked to the benefit of all interested merchants—even King—by stabilizing prices across whole inventories of trade. For Forbes, the real problem was the Canton System and China's attempt to restrict trade through the monopolies of the Cohongs. Opium was a red herring that China used to justify its unreasonable behavior. Bridgman prefaced Forbes's reply with the following editorial clarification: "Our pages are designed for a Repository of facts, rather than forensic debate. Yet when great and difficult questions are pending, it is desirable they should be freely and fairly discussed."[113]

Did China not have the right as a sovereign kingdom to set laws against the importation of opium? The former president John Quincy Adams did not think so. In a speech he delivered to the Massachusetts Historical Society during the war, he cast China as beyond the pale of international law for rejecting the fundamental premise of Christianity: love your neighbor as yourself. Bridgman and Williams reprinted Adam's speech in the *Chinese Repository* in May 1842.[114] In a qualifying footnote they explain their decision to print it, first acknowledging the former president's "extensive experience in public life" and his "lucid manner" of reasoning that "the Chinese government has not the right to shut themselves out from the rest of mankind, founded on deductions drawn from the rights of men as members of one great social system."[115] They did correct Adams's dismissive characterization of opium traffic, pointing to it as "the great proximate cause" of a war that "could not have risen, had not the opium trade been a smuggling trade."[116]

Chinese Perspectives on Opium in the Chinese Repository

In the run-up to the war, Bridgman tried to include Chinese perspectives in the debate. In framing a "diversity of opinion" over legalization, Bridgman clearly imagined readership extending back to the United States as he remarks in an editorial aside that the translated memorials will clarify for "distant readers" the "introduction of opium" and "its present position."[117] However, the translation and publication of these documents had unintended effects on the diplomatic scene. Reading the *Chinese Repository* in Canton, it seemed as though the imperial court was reconsidering its policy restricting opium and inviting debate on it.

The Chinese perspectives in the *Chinese Repository* included officials advocating for legalization and taxation of opium and those arguing against legalization, insisting that the emperor ought to hold the line and punish severely those who sold or used opium. Rev. Robert Morrison's son John R. Morrison translated memorials to the imperial court of Emperor Daoguang (Dàoguāng Dì, 道光帝, 1783–1850), including "Hü Náitsí's memorial to legalize opium, 1838," in which the former judicial commissioner drew from his experience overseeing Canton's salt agency to assess the state of "trade carried on at Lintin," that is, the smuggling of opium.[118] Observing that the costal islands were difficult to monitor and that chasing down fast crab boats had proved impractical, Hü Náitsí suggests reverting to the previous policies of emperors Yung-ching [Yōngzhèng Dì, 雍正帝; 1722–35] and Keënlung [Qiánlóng Dì, 乾隆帝; 1735–96], who had taxed the importation of opium and regulated its sale like a medicine.[119] Hü Náitsí reasoned that legalization would lead to lucrative import duties that the government could regulate in order to stem the export flow of silver.

Two memorials rebutted these arguments for legalization, including "Memorial of Choo Tsun on Opium: character of the trade in it: impolicy of sanctioning it; its baneful effects on the property and on the physical and moral character, of the people. Dated October, 1836."[120] As a "member of the council and the Board of Rites," Choo Tsun was deeply troubled by the foreign traders' disrespect of the imperial law: "Our government, having received from heaven, the gift of peace, has transmitted it for two centuries; . . . For governing the central nation, and for holding in submission all the surrounding barbarians, rules exist perfect in their nature, and well-fitted to attain their end."[121] Citing the ineffectiveness of the 1796 imperial prohibitions on opium set forth at the beginning of the reign of Emperor Keaking, he lamented that the laws that forbid Chinese subjects "to do wrong may be likened to the dykes which prevent the overflowing of water. If any one, then, urging that the dykes are very old, and therefore useless, we should have them thrown down, what words could express the consequences of the impetuous rush and all-destroying overflow!"[122] Bridgman followed this memorial with a translated edict in which Emperor Daoguang announced that he was weighing the "diversity of opinion" and considering the "subject [of legalization] carefully in all its bearings, surveying at once the whole field of action."[123]

In translating and republishing these memorials, Bridgman recontextualized them in ways that changed their very meaning within the jurisdiction of China. The emperor's edicts were not invitations for debate or speculative publication among Chinese subjects or readers about what might happen. In the process of decision making that was unfolding in Peking, only mandarin officials would participate. In their style, the memorials carefully maintained deference to the emperor. Williams put it this way in *The Middle Kingdom*: "History, so far as we know, does not record a similar mode of an arbitrary, despotic, *pagan* government, taking the public sentiment of its own people before adopting a doubtful line of conduct."[124] Most importantly, the emperor was not recognizing foreigners such as Bridgman as potential contributors to a relevant "diversity of opinion." And yet, reading the pages of the *Chinese Repository*, the emperor seemed to be on the verge of recognizing Western nations as peers rather than tributaries in changing policies to regulate opium importation. As Williams later wrote, Hü Náitsí's memorial created "the impression general at Canton that the trade would be legalized, and increased preparations were accordingly made in India to extend the cultivation of opium."[125] When the emperor ended up reinforcing the ban on opium, his decision seemed all the more arbitrary, unreasonable, and expensive.

In 1839 the Chinese emperor decided on enforcing long-standing prohibitions on opium. The culprits included Chinese users of opium, the inland merchants who brokered the drug, the Cohong merchants at Canton, and the foreign traders who insisted on bringing it to and smuggling it into China. The emperor appointed

Commissioner Lin Zexu (林則徐, Lín Zéxú; 1785–1850) to enforce the law. As Lin made his way south, provincial mandarin administrators began enforcing the imperial edicts. In late February 1839, Chinese authorities publicly executed a Chinese trafficker, staging the strangulation inside the foreign factory area at Canton to scare the foreign traders. Elliot framed the execution as an escalation of Chinese disrespect toward Britain.

When Commissioner Lin arrived in March, he amplified the message by arresting the Cohongs, putting them in chains, and demanding under threat of execution that they persuade the foreigner traders to comply with the law and surrender any illegal stores of opium. Lin also summoned the British merchant Lancelot Dent to the city gates of Canton. Dent refused, suspecting that he would be held hostage for the delivery of his company's opium stores. A standoff ensued as the British traders holed up in their factory. Superintendent Elliot came to the rescue on warships, arriving in Canton dressed in his naval uniform. He hoisted the British flag and took Dent in under his protection. In reports back to Palmerston, Elliot characterized Commissioner Lin as "this intemperate man" who was responsible for "dark proceedings": the "life, liberty, property of British subjects" were now "under attack."[126] To secure their evacuation from Canton, Elliot persuaded the British merchants to surrender their opium stores, guaranteeing their losses with the queen's money. Strategically, this turned confiscation of the private British merchants' contraband into a debt that China owed the British Crown.[127] On 21 May 1839 Lin received 20,283 chests of opium and destroyed it; Bridgman witnessed and reported on the event.[128] Lin pushed his efforts of enforcement, demanding that all foreign traders sign bonds promising, under penalty of death, "not to deal in opium, nor to attempt to introduce it into the Chinese empire."[129] U.S. merchants signed it, including members of Russell & Company. Elliot was angry at what he saw as defection from a united Western front. However, during the ensuing war, Americans moved merchandise as a neutral party, and this helped keep British merchants afloat.

Commissioner Lin knew of the missionaries' print work. Bridgman describes the four Chinese translators who had "made some progress in the English tongue" and had helped him.[130] The first was "a young man, educated [from 1825 to 1826] at Penang and Malacca" at Rev. Milne's Anglo-Chinese College (Malacca) and "for several years employed by the Chinese government at Peking"; the cultural historian Lydia Liu identifies him as Yuan Dehui.[131] The second was "an old man, educated at Serampore" under the British missionary Joshua Marshman; this would have been Ya Meng.[132] The third was a "young man who was once at Cornwall, Conn., U.S.A" in 1822; this would have been Liang Tsintih, also known by the names Ya Lin, Liaou Ahsee, and William Botelho.[133] The fourth was well known to

Bridgman: "a young lad, educated in China, who is able to read and translate papers on common subjects, with much ease, correctness, and facility."[134] His name was "Liang Ateh—the son of Liang Afah [Liang A-fa or Liang Fa] and Bridgman's favored pupil."[135]

During the months after the confiscation and destruction of opium, Commissioner Lin and his translators teamed up with Governor Tang and Lieutenant Governor Yi to write a letter to Queen Victoria. They consulted with the missionaries. The first question was how to frame the correspondence. As Lydia Liu explains, "Lin treated international law not as the universal truth but as a mode of persuasion that would enable him to argue against the harmful effects of the opium trade in a language he thought the British could understand."[136] He was adapting the "official genre" of communication called *xi*, "a dignified statement and official declaration to the enemy in the times of military conflict."[137] In July 1839 he visited Dr. Peter Parker as a patient and then asked him to translate sections from Emer de Vattel's *Law of Nations*.[138] The incident is recorded in the tenth annual report of the Ophthalmic Hospital for the year 1839—published in the *Chinese Repository*—in which Parker identifies patient "No. 6565" as "Lin Tsihseu, the imperial commissioner, late governor of the two lake provinces (i.e. Hookwang), now of the two wide provinces Kwangtung, and Kwangse."[139] Lin seemed not to need "medical relief" and instead requested a "translation of some quotations from Vattel's Law of Nations, with which he had been furnished: these were sent through the senior Cohong-merchant; they related to war, and its accompanying hostile measures, as blockades, embargoes, &c.; they were written out with a Chinese pencil."[140] Lin also wanted an "exposé of views in regard to opium" and "a general prescription for the cure of those who had become victims to its use."[141]

The *Chinese Repository* published two versions of Commissioner Lin's letter to the queen of England, the first in May 1839 and the second in February 1840.[142] Twentieth-century historians have gone back to the original Chinese version to translate it anew, but it is insightful to consider the British interpreter R. Thom's and Bridgman's versions that circulated at the time.[143] A parenthetical editorial note in May 1839 of the *Chinese Repository* vouches for the first draft's authenticity, noting that it had first circulated for a couple of months "among the people, in the same manner as many official documents commonly do."[144] Published as "Letter to the Queen of England, from the high imperial commissioner and the provincial authorities requiring interdiction of opium," Lin's first draft employs a tone of reasonable address as it appeals to a common moral law above the authorities of either government: "That in the ways of heaven no partiality exists, and no sanction is allowed to the injuring of others for the advantage of one's self,—that in men's natural desires there is not any great diversity (for where is he who does not abhor death and seek life?)—these are universally acknowledged principles. And your honorable nation, though beyond the wide ocean, at a distance of twenty thousand miles, acknowledges the same ways of heaven, the same human nature, and has the like perception of the distinctions between life and death, benefit and injury."[145] Ssu-yü Teng and John K. Fairbank describe the "phraseology" as "courteous within the limits of traditional tributary language."[146] Lin's arguments for mutual neighborly respect challenge former President Adams's characterization of China as bad neighbors; clearly Lin was appealing to a sense of respectfully mutual coexistence as he tried to convince the queen to prevent her subjects from violating Chinese laws on Chinese territory. Given that war was breaking out, it is rather remarkable to contemplate that Bridgman seems to have published this letter without the explicit consent of Lin and before it had any official legitimacy as a diplomatic correspondence. This was the free press in action. But to what end? According to Peter Ward Fay, Queen Victoria never saw the letter.[147] Furthermore, Bridgman seemed to overlook the merits of Lin's arguments in trying to stay on a side of political events that enabled his printing to continue as war began.

Meanwhile, over the summer of 1839 Commissioner Lin continued to rework the letter with Yuan Dehui and his small team of translators. Russell & Company's William C. Hunter had studied with Yuan Dehui at Milne's Anglo-Chinese College in Malacca and Commissioner Lin asked Hunter to translate a new English version of the letter back "into Chinese, as a test of the proper reading of the original."[148] Commissioner Lin issued his official letter to Queen Victoria in August 1839, and by February 1840 the *Chinese Repository* had published this revised version as "Letter to the Queen of England, from the high imperial commissioner Lin, and his colleagues. From the Canton Press." It was the lead article in the same issue as Forbes's article rebutting Charles King. Lin's letter also found its way into the *Times* (London), although it is not known whether the queen or Lord Palmerston ever read it.[149] Lydia Liu notes that Commissioner Lin "did not trust the English mail carriers and made multiple copies of the letter for captains of other European ships to take to England."[150] In any case, the *Chinese Repository* seems to have been the major vehicle of distribution, and Lydia Liu has recently juxtaposed the Chinese original of 1840, the English translation of 1840 from the *Chinese Repository*, and the English translation of 1954 by Teng and Fairbank.[151]

There are significant differences between Lin's draft and the official letter that deserve closer consideration than is here possible. Both versions maintain the central authority of the Chinese emperor, addressing the queen as a sovereign who warrants respectful address despite being much less powerful. Both letters, signed by Lin and his colleagues, put the emperor on a higher plane than the queen. Both letters assert that the long legacy of trade between China and England had been conducted by permission of the emperor and to the great benefit of Britain. Both emphasize the devastating effect of opium on China's population. As for differences, the second official letter is more severe in its tone, alerting the queen that foreigners who continue to import opium will hereafter receive the same punitive sentence as Chinese people: death by decapitation. The second letter is also filled with effusive exclamations such as, "Our celestial empire rules over ten thousand kingdoms! Most surely do we possess a measure of godlike majesty which ye cannot fathom!"[152] The official letter also criticizes the systematic nature of opium production, reminding the queen that "in sundry parts of your colonial kingdom of Hindostan, such as Bengal, Madras, Bombay, Patna, Malwa, Benares, Malacca, and other places where the very hills are covered with the opium plant, where tanks are made for preparing the drug."[153] It ends: "Let your highness immediately, upon the receipt of this communication, inform us promptly of the state of matters, and of measures you are pursuing utterly to put a stop to the opium evil. Please let your reply be speedy. Do not on any account make excuses or procrastinate. A most important communication."[154]

The letter mattered very little to Elliot, who had solidified a political standoff over the confiscation of property and renewed diplomatic insult to the British Crown. British steamships and artillery decimated China's ships and forts. After losing several battles along the Pearl River, Lin was recalled to the capital and sent into exile. (In 1850 he would be recalled at the start of the Taiping Rebellion.) Elliot's forces, backed by troops from colonial India, pressed the conflict all over China, opening fronts in Ningbo, Pei Ho, Tientsin, and Amoy. After a year of success, Elliot secured concessions from China, but Lord Palmerston deemed these to be too little and too late. He replaced Elliot with Sir Henry Pottinger, who pressed further Britain's advantage, occupying Shanghai in June 1842 and Nanking in August.

To end the conflict, the emperor appointed Kíying (耆英; also Keying and Qíyīng) as the "imperial commissioner to negotiate peace."[155] The war ended with the Treaty of Nanking, which the *Chinese Repository* printed in Chinese and English.[156] The treaty's thirteen articles opened up four more treaty ports at Amoy (Xiàmén, 厦门), Foochow (Fúzhōu, 福州), Ningpo (Níngbō, 宁波) and Shanghai (Shànghǎi, 上海) and annexed Hong Kong (Xiānggǎng, 香港). It abolished the exclusivity of Cohong merchants and permitted the British "to carry on their mercantile transactions with whatever persons they please"; obligated China to pay $21 million to England to reimburse the private traders for the destruction of their opium and for outstanding balances owed to them by the Cohong merchants; and ceded "the Island of Hong-Kong, to be possessed in perpetuity by Her Britannic Majesty, her heirs and successors, and to be governed by such laws and regulations as Her Majesty the Queen of Great Britain, &c., shall see fit to direct." This treaty was followed with the Supplementary Treaty at the Bogue (8 October 1843), the Treaty of Wanghia with the United States, and the Treaty of Whampoa with France.[157] They effectively ended the Canton System.

After the Opium War ended, Bridgman revised his firsthand accounts of the "Crisis in Opium Traffic" into a series of twelve articles in the *Chinese Repository* running from January to December 1842. Entitled "Retrospection, or a review of public occurrences in China during the last ten years, from January 1st, 1832, to December 31st, 1841," these articles offer a revisionary account of the opium conflict so that "errors may be corrected; and from the past, useful lessons derived for the guidance of future conduct."[158] Closing the "chronological list of events," he directly addresses "our readers, who have followed us in this retrospect" and "will be able to draw their own conclusions regarding the merits of the dispute which has arisen in the past ten years."[159] In the end, he fell back on statements of faith. Bridgman concludes his final "retrospect" in December 1842, writing: "The agency, in these great movements, is human: the directing power, divine. The high Governor of the nations has employed England to chastise and humble China: He may also soon employ her to introduce blessings of Christian civilization and free intercourse among her millions."[160]

Williams also tried to square his missionary printing with opium traffic and the war. On 20 August 1840, as British troops amassed for an assault on Canton, he wrote to his father back in Utica, New York: "It is well that one cannot pry into futurity; if we could, it appears to me, that the vista which would open through this land would so fill us with horror, doubt, and grief, that all our energies would be unnerved, our hope go out in gloom, and our faith wellnigh be lost."[161] Like Bridgman, Williams fell back on asserting faith in a divine plan that mystified him. He acknowledged that "the bonds of social intercourse among the Chinese are strong for a healthy nation, and God's hand should be seen in thus forming their social polity"; however, this social polity was "not based on the knowledge of His truth, His designs to a world through His son, nor on His overruling Providence."[162] Williams continued to pray and to print, claiming "it is better to leave all cases in His hands; we are quite willing to do so when they look favorable, but we think we must help Him a little in caring, when we think the prospect is gloomy and results troublesome to ourselves."[163] Nevertheless, eight months later (26 April 1841) Williams condemned Britain in a letter to his father, judging the "whole expedition" of the war

> an unjust one in my mind on account of the intimate connection its sending here had with the opium trade, but we shall find very few expeditions that have not had a good deal to find fault with in them. There is a way some have of saying that "it will all work

well, and that good will come out of evil," which is only a sheer excuse for leaving themselves in indolence. For my part, I am far from being sure that this turn up is going to advance the cause of the Gospel half so much as we think it is. England has taken the opium trade upon herself nationally, and can that be a cause to bless? [F]or the success of her arms here would extend that wicked traffic ten thousand times more than the Church is ready to extend her stakes here. The 50,000 chests annually brought to China would rise to hundreds of thousands shortly, and only think of the destruction of it.[164]

He was quite correct. The importation of opium increased dramatically in the decade between the First and Second Opium War. In October 1844, the "Journal of Occurrences" reported that "the growth of opium advances steadily" and that at Malwa and Bengal were 48,000 chests, each priced at $700, promising a total return of $33,600,000.[165]

Closing the *Chinese Repository*

Heading back to the United States in 1844, Williams hoped to raise funds to complete Dyer's set of "steel punches for a font of Chinese types."[166] After the economic depression in 1837, the main ABCFM Prudential Committee had withdrawn financial support of the Canton Mission Press.[167] Despite losing funding from the ABCFM, Bridgman and Williams kept printing the *Chinese Repository* throughout the First Opium War and for eight years after.[168] Upon returning to Canton, Williams resumed editing but felt that the *Chinese Repository* had outrun its usefulness. By 1849 he was contemplating "stopping the *Repository* and turning [his] attention to a Chinese magazine" [i.e., a magazine printed in the Chinese language] because the "class of merchants here now take very much less interest in the condition of China than they used to do."[169] Also, the *Chinese Repository* was running "an annual deficit of 300 to 400 dollars."[170] In its final year, subscriptions (three dollars annually) had dwindled to three hundred and there was barely enough revenue to cover wages.

In 1850, reflecting these disappointments, Williams described his print shop in terms much less positive than in the January 1839 letter to his father. The press had moved back to Canton in the mid-1840s after a wartime hiatus in Macao and brief period in Hong Kong. But upon its return it never had the same influence. To his longtime friend and correspondent, the geologist and Yale professor James D. Dana, Williams describes a day in the life of his editing and printing:

I am writing in such a furnace—I had had almost termed it [hell]—that I can hardly put any ideas straight upon paper. The thermometer at 88 [degrees] is not the true index of heat, for I am sweltering as if in a steam bath, and the feelings induced by such a constant perspiration are not the most favorable to collectedness of ideas. Then, instead of having a quiet, pleasant room for writing, where only those who have business might come, I am scribbling within ten feet of my printing press which is going all the time and close to the printers—all of them Chinese and as loquacious as ducks—every few minutes asking for proof, copy, or instruction; then, in runs the nurse with the baby crying at her bent for something to eat or to be attended to, and I have hardly minded them when a visitor is announced, or a note must be answered. I am well satisfied with my position, but earnestly desire more purity of motive and singleness of heart in God's service, more love to the Chinese, and more humility. It is much easier loving the souls of the heathen in the abstract in America then it is here in the concrete, encompassed as they are with such dirty bodies, speaking forth their foul language and vile natures, and exhibiting every evidence of their depravity. My printers call for much patience, and I have not so large a supply of this as I thought I had; they steal my type, my books, my tools, selling them for a mere song of course, but spoiling a whole font or set of books for the sake of a few pennies. I am soon to be released from my editorial position, for the *Repository* is to cease in a few months, the demand for it by no means recompensing the strain upon its manufactors.[171]

In contrast to the earlier description of 1839, this passage conveys Williams's sense of having failed in his evangelical quest of extraterritorial printing. The intergenerational pride in printing has dissipated, and the innovatively effective divisions of labor have been scrambled. He no longer boasts of controlling the material production across his workers' several languages. Instead, his crying son, the intruding nurse, and the banter of Chinese workers distract him to a point of infuriation. As Williams stews in frustration over the piecemeal erosion of his publishing equipment, he is uncharacteristically vicious in describing the Chinese workers, who seem beyond the reach of any redemptive training in presswork. As Williams pleads with God to grant him "more purity of motive and singleness of heart," he materializes their untrustworthiness and dishonesty in a dirtiness of their body that permeates their language and even their nature. Writing to his longtime friend Professor Dana, who was ensconced at Yale, Williams is perhaps exaggerating his animosity for humorous effect. Nevertheless, the diligent editing and printing of the *Chinese Repository* had not brought about the results for which he and Bridgman had prayed. On the contrary, the efforts seem to have unleashed Williams's prejudices as he evokes categorical differences of culture and even race. In some ways his disillusionment was just beginning. In the broader historical frame, his description anticipates the even deeper senses of alienation that he would experience in facing the profound social consequences of the Taiping Rebellion.

The troubles ahead further challenged Bridgman and William's assumptions that printing in China would convert and civilize the heathen Chinese. In September 1850 Williams received word of his father's death more than three months earlier. The following year, in June 1851, the Canton press's major benefactor David W. Olyphant died in Cairo. Williams looked to close out the *Chinese Repository* and compiled the index, with a prefatory "Editorial Notice" signed "Elijah Coleman Bridgman and S. Wells Williams" and dated "Canton, December 31st, 1851." There is a melancholy tone to the preface as the editors admit that the "typographical appearance" of the *Chinese Repository* had "never met the wishes of the Proprietor" as "the work has been printed from the first by natives of the East, who were almost wholly ignorant of the language in which their copy was written, and set up the types by the merest imitation of the manuscript before them."[172] Looking ahead, Williams hopes that something bigger than the *Chinese Repository*'s sixty pages will provide "discussion of important questions, the description of interesting places, the reception of valuable translations, and the preservation of facts." In any case, the twenty complete volumes would stand as a "permanent record relating to, and illustrating, China" for a "posterity" that would assign it its "proper place."[173]

After closing the *Chinese Repository*, Williams did not dwell on the deteriorating social stability in South China as the Taiping Rebellion gathered force. Instead, he went to Japan with Commodore Matthew C. Perry as the "Chief Interpreter of the Mission to Japan" on both phases (1853, 1854).[174] Meanwhile, Britain and the United States were pressing China to open more treaty ports, to allow foreigners to live in the city of Canton, and to extend diplomatic access to Peking. The British royal governor of Hong Kong John Bowring found an excuse to escalate hostilities and begin another opium war after Chinese authorities arrested a crew aboard the opium-laden ship *Arrow* that was illegally flying a British flag to cover smuggling operations.[175] On 14 December 1856 as the Second Opium War began, the Mission Press and all the back issues of the *Chinese Repository* were destroyed in a fire set by Chinese residents to the quarters of the foreign traders. Williams wrote to his brother that he had not believed that "the Chinese would set the Factories on fire" and had left "only two days before" "to see how [his wife] Sarah was situated in her newly rented house in Macao."[176] He continued:

> My printing-office and household gear perished with the rest, and all the books I had on hand, excepting the "Dictionary" and "Commercial Guide." The type and materials are all valued at some $20,000, most of which belongs to the mission; whether we shall ever receive any compensation is a matter of doubt, for the United States is not often in a hurry to collect such claims. . . . The remaining copies of the *Repository* were burned in boxes ready to move, and had I been there most of *them* could have

been saved, though not the printing-office. The loss is one I much regret, for 't was in good working order, and I was in hopes of doing something with it.[177]

For Williams the fire marked the definitive end to the Mission Press in Canton. He had already accepted a position as the secretary of the United States Legation to China and would phase out his Canton-based labors. In *The Life of Letters of Samuel Wells Williams*, Frederick summarizes the extraordinary output of "The Mission Press at Canton and Macao, during its twenty-five years' existence":

> 1832–51. *The Chinese Repository*, 20 vols. 8° In all 23,000 copies, including reprints of vols. i to iv.
>
> 1837. Medhurst's "Hok-këen Dictionary." 4°. 300 complete copies.
>
> 1841. Bridgman & Williams. 'Chinese Chrestomathy. 4°. 800 copies.
>
> 1842. Williams. "Easy Lessons in Chinese." 8°. 700 copies.
>
> 1844. Williams. "Topography of China." 8°. 200 copies.
>
> 1844. Williams. "English and Chinese Vocabulary." 8°. 800 copies.
>
> 1844. Williams. "Commercial Guide." 2ᵈ edition. 8°. 800 copies.
>
> 1845. "Treaties between China, Great Britain, the United States and France." 8°. 100 copies.
>
> 1847. Bridgman. "Translation of Premare's Notitia Linguae Sinicae." 8°. 600 copies.
>
> 1848. Williams. "Commercial Guide." 3d edition. 8°. 800 copies.
>
> 1849–56. Williams "Anglo-Chinese Calendar." 8°. 8 issues; in all about 2,000 copies.
>
> 1849. Meadows. "Translations from the Manchu" (text printed from blocks). 8°
>
> 1854. Bonney. "Vocabulary, with Colloquial Phrases in Canton Dialect." 8°. 800 copies.
>
> 1856. Rutter. "Calculations of Exchanges between England, India, and China." 8°. 300 copies.
>
> 1856. Williams. "Tonic Dictionary." 8°. 800 copies.
>
> 1856. Williams. "Commercial Guide." 4ᵗʰ edition. 8°. 1000 copies.[178]

This added up to around thirty-eight thousand separate volumes without counting all the pamphlets that the press produced.[179] Notably absent from this list are any missionary tracts that one associates with itinerant proselytizing or the apocalyptically sublime Book of Revelation. The leaders of the Taiping Rebellion would do more than steal fonts, or destroy the Mission Press. They would appropriate the entire mode and method of evangelical print production and use biblical interpretation to unleash and justify forces of violent rebellion, with which Williams never came to terms.

Books of Revelation and the Taiping Rebellion

Writing to his brother in 1850, Williams lamented that the "unsettled political time" was bad for "missionary operations" and summed up his frustration: "Our preaching is listened to by few, laughed at by many and disregarded by most."[180] The ABCFM missionaries never won many converts. Taiping leader Hong Xiuquan was a particularly troubling exception. The final words of the final issue of the *Chinese Repository* ominously report violent discontent spreading through South China—discontent that became the massive civil war of the Taiping Rebellion.

The missionaries' project of extraterritorial printing had played an inadvertent part in sowing the textual seeds of civil war. As a young man, Hong Xiuquan had grown profoundly frustrated by China's national examination system, failing over and over again at Guangzhou. In 1836 someone outside the entrance to the examination hall passed to him Liang A-fa's tract "Good Words for Exhorting the Age" (Quànshì liángyán; 勸世良言).[181] Liang A-fa's book includes an account of his own conversion, "ten homiletic essays by himself," and passages of "Genesis, Psalms, Ecclesiastes, Isaiah, Jeremiah, Matthew, John, Acts, Romans, 1 Corinthians, Ephesians, Colossians, 1 Thessalonians, 2 Thessalonians, 1 Timothy, Hebrew, James, 1 Peter, 2 Peter, 1 John, and Revelation" from Milne and Morrison's Bible, with scriptural commentary by Liang A-fa.[182] Hong Xiuquan put it aside and went on to endure severe illnesses that brought about dramatic dreams and visions. In 1843 Liang A-fa's text featured in his recovery. Reading it with a relative, Li Jingfang, in the wake of the First Opium War, Hong locked on to passages featuring the prophet Isaiah exhorting of the Israelites. After first conferring with the ABCFM missionary Rev. Edwin Stevens, Hong turned to an American Baptist missionary, Rev. Issachar Jacox Roberts, whom Jonathan Spence describes as a "self-educated preacher, raised in the passionate religious world of tent revivals and covered-wagon services, independent-minded, free of supervision and bored with rules."[183] Mere baptism and conversion could not contain the inspiration that Hong felt in reading the word of God. He was convinced that he was the brother of Jesus and had come to earth in preparation of the Apocalypse as foretold in Revelation. Working with his relatives Hong Rengan and Feng Yunshan, Hong built a fanatical religious base dedicated to overthrowing the Chinese emperor in Peking.

Hong Xiuquan declared the establishment of the Taiping Heavenly Kingdom in January 1851 from "Jintian (金田) Village, Guiping County (桂平縣), in the present-day Guangxi Zhuang Autonomous Region (廣西壯族自治區)."[184] The code of conduct was derived from multiple sources, an amalgamation of Liang A-fa's translated Ten Commandments, Leviticus, and Deuteronomy.[185] It also synthesized "Christian ideas and native Chinese practices," including adaptations of "Confucianism, Buddhism, Taoism" and local beliefs.[186] Hong demanded "rigid discipline" and "forbade the use of opium and spirits, introduced the observance of the Sabbath, and regulated the worship of God."[187] The Taiping segregated its followers by gender and prohibited sexual relations.[188] Over the next twenty-four months, his army headed northwest, conquering city after city. Two years later, it entered the city of Nanking and declared it the Heavenly Capital (天京; Heavenly Capital). The Taiping established the "Taiping printing and publishing program" and issued all of four gospels, with the Book of Matthew in its entirety.[189] In *The Middle Kingdom* (1883), Williams acknowledges Hong's "skill in turning the doctrines and requirements of the Bible" into "the ground and proofs of his own authority," which indicated "original genius, since the results were far beyond the reach of cunning imposter"; Williams continues, "From first to last, beginning with poverty, obscurity, and weakness in [the province of] Hwa, continuing with distinction, power, and royalty at Nanking and throughout its five adjacent provinces, [Hong] never wavered or abated one jot of his claim to supreme rule on earth."[190]

As immensely destructive events threatened the stability of the Qing emperor in Peking, the missionaries pondered from their new treaty port stations whether extraterritorial printing was serving evangelical goals. How could they control the revolutionary energies of millennial urgency once they had been unleashed? After alarming potential converts with the proposition of an imminently ending world, how could they reorient them in Chinese society as practicing Christians? As a professor at Yale in the last years of his life, Williams remained haunted by Hong Xiuquan. In the first edition of *The Middle Kingdom* (1848), he had sounded optimistic in asserting that "nothing but the Gospel" would be able to embolden Chinese people to "resist official tyranny in preserving their own liberties." He continues optimistically:

> And the leaven of Christian principles will, it is to be hoped, diffuse itself through the mass when once the people perceive their tendency. Chinese society is like a stagnant pool fermenting in its own feculence, whose torpor is disturbed by monstrous things its own heat brings forth, and becoming more and more polluted, casting up mire and dirt, by its own internal commotions: and until the river, whose streams maketh glad the city of God shall flow through this rotting marsh, there is no hope of any permanent improvement,— the clear waters of peace, good order, purity, and liberty, flow from no other fountain than the Gospel.[191]

In the 1883 revision, Williams struck out this passage. He also edited out another passage that claimed that missionaries could "show [the Chinese] the secrets of another world, and teach them their obligations to obey the commands of their

Maker, and accept the proffered grace of their Redeemer."[192] His concern had shifted to maintaining a balance between paying "regard to the authority of their rulers which is necessary for the maintenance of good order" in China and resisting the specter of the imperial order's "official tyranny."[193] When revising his account of the Taiping Rebellion for the final edition of *The Middle Kingdom*, Williams reflected in his diary: "The more I learn about that terrible visitation, the more perplexed am I to understand what was God's purpose in permitting it."[194] In the *Middle Kingdom* he put it this way: "As a revolution involving a reorganization of the Chinese nation on Christian principles," it "failed entirely within a year after the possession of Nanking," concluding: "Their presence was an unmitigated scourge, attended by nothing but disaster from beginning to end."[195]

As Williams's diplomatic duties intensified in the 1860s and 1870s, he continued editing, but his major project was *A Syllabic Dictionary of the Chinese Language: Arranged According to the Wu-fang Yuen Yin, with the Pronunciation of the Characters as Heard in Peking, Canton, Amoy, and Shanghai* (1874). He began overseeing its print production in the Shanghai-based printing offices of the American Presbyterian Board in November 1871. It was tedious work. The dictionary's title registers the opening of the five treaty ports in noting the regional variations of spoken Chinese. The 1874 edition was 1,356 pages long and included definitions of 12,527 Chinese characters.[196] Writing to his wife, he seems reassured by the anonymity and supervisory routine of his print labors, addressing her as a beloved audience of one who shares with him a parental interest in the developing toddler of a text. He writes "You can see by the proof-sheet enclosed how the dictionary crawls on; it is not as thrilling as a page of Dickens' 'Little Dorrit,' and yet I think that you for one take as much interest in these sheets which I send you one after another."[197] He still battled Chinese printer workers, who, "notwithstanding all my oversight and proof-reading," "show their spite against my repeated alternations by changing the types after I have dismissed the page as correct."[198] As his faith was tested, he remained committed to the missionary project, claiming to "see in every page the hope that it is likely to help in the good work of evangelizing China."[199] But he was no longer effusively optimistic that exposure to the Word of God would herald China's redemption. His extraterritorial printing had also become a practically focused endeavor. The only pamphlet he ever printed in Chinese is "Words to Startle Those Who are Selling Their Bodies [to go] Abroad" (1859). He estimated printing six thousand copies of it to protest the Coolie trade that exploited thousands of Chinese in Macao with false promises and labor contracts that doomed them to brutal sea voyages.[200]

CHAPTER FIVE

Caleb Cushing's Print Trail of Legal Extraterritoriality

A Confederated Christendom of Commerce, from the Far East to the Far West

[If Napoleon Bonaparte] will consent to our receiving Cuba into our union to prevent our aid to Mexico & the other provinces, . . . I would immediately erect a column on the Southernmost limit of Cuba & inscribe on it a *Ne plus ultra* as to us in that direction. We should then have only to include the North in our confederacy . . . and we should have such an empire for liberty as she has never surveyed since the creation: & I am persuaded no constitution was ever before so well calculated as ours for extensive empire & self government.

THOMAS JEFFERSON to President James Madison, 27 April 1809

The Treaty of Wanghia (1844) is the first treaty between China and the United States.[1] After negotiating it, the U.S. minister Caleb Cushing (1800–1879) claimed its Articles 21 and 25 established extraterritoriality for U.S. citizens in China that was "absolute and unqualified," meaning that U.S. citizens in China would be tried exclusively according to U.S. law.[2] Whereas Britain had exacted the territorial concession of Hong Kong from China in the Treaty of Nanking (1842) and set the stage for extraterritorial consideration in the supplementary Treaty of the Bogue (1843), Cushing made no territorial claim as he projected exclusive U.S. jurisdiction over all U.S. citizens in China.[3] Such categorical severity disregarded China's centuries-long legacy of readjusting terms of legal authority as empires consolidated internal rule and negotiated relations with tributary kingdoms and varieties of foreign peoples.[4]

In making the claim that China had conceded *absolute and unqualified* extraterritoriality, Cushing was as clever as he was incorrect.[5] Nevertheless, his bravado cast a long shadow, and his confrontational style of gunboat negotiation provided the template for Commodore Matthew C. Perry in confronting Tokugawa Japan in 1854.[6] The cultural and legal scholar Teemu Ruskola characterizes the treaty as a "turning point in American relations with Asia more generally."[7] Reviewing the imperialist implications of absolute and unqualified extraterritoriality, Ruskola highlights the irony that the "recently emancipated" United States—the "world's leading anticolonial power"—tried to "reconcile its extraterritorial jurisdiction in China" with the cornerstone assumption that "the jurisdiction of a nation within its own territory is necessarily exclusive and absolute."[8]

Cushing's bold assertion of absolute and unqualified extraterritoriality in China highlights how the Far East figured in the young nation's commercial ambition during a precarious era of westward continental expansion two decades before Civil War. Pär Kristoffer Cassel admonishes that reducing history to discrete encounters between "the 'East' and 'West'" obscures the "complex and triangular relationship between China, Japan, and the Western powers."[9] Accordingly, this chapter complicates a singular sense of "Western powers" by opening the Treaty of Wanghia to the multinational dynamics of U.S. Manifest Destiny. To understand how Cushing aligned gunboat diplomacy in China with the pursuit of free trade, this chapter considers the Treaty of Wanghia in relation to the anticolonial imperialism of the Monroe Doctrine (1823), a presidential address authored by Secretary of State John Quincy Adams. As the historian Jay Sexton writes, the Monroe Doctrine was a "great paradox" for avowing principles of republican self-government, anticolonialism, and an "open world economy," on the one hand, while justifying an "imperialist role" for the United States in "international affairs," on the other.[10] This chapter extends Sexton's characterization to the Treaty of Wanghia as it manifested principles conveyed in the Tyler Doctrine (1842), a presidential address authored by Secretary of State Daniel Webster that modified the assumptions of the Monroe Doctrine, linking American pursuit of the China trade to contestation of the Pacific Northwest in North America.

Within the general diplomatic context of the Monroe and Tyler doctrines, the legacy of the Treaty Wanghia is particularly paradoxical because its actual language does not in fact secure extraterritoriality that is "absolute and unqualified." Most strikingly, Article 33 explicitly disqualifies from U.S. legal protection any U.S. citizen who smuggles opium or other contraband, or who trades outside the designated five coastal treaty ports in China. Furthermore, Article 24 advises that the adjudication of claims between citizens of the United States and subjects of China be considered by a committee of officers from the two nations. Other ambiguities pertaining to the shared nature of jurisdiction surface after comparing the version ratified by the U.S. Senate to the Chinese version, and to alternative English translations by U.S. missionaries of the Chinese version.

The Treaty of Wanghia packed its influential punch in large part because of Cushing's administrative and legal skills. The son of a Massachusetts merchant, he became an influential lawyer, politician, and U.S. attorney general in the mid-1850s during the administration of President Franklin Pierce. To formulate his claim of "absolute and unqualified" extraterritoriality through the treaty, Cushing did a couple things. First, he wrote diplomatic dispatches in China that framed the treaty's reception and ratification in Washington, DC.[11] In the dispatches he explained his philosophical premise of negotiation: that China was a pagan nation and unfit to be recognized as a peer. He also summarized the treaty articles in ways that simplified them and reinforced his categorical prejudice. Second, in 1855 he revisited the treaty after he had become the U.S. attorney general. He wrote an opinion that cited his own diplomatic dispatch of September 1844 in restating a bold assertion: the treaty had "obtained the concession of absolute and unqualified" U.S. extraterritoriality from China; in the words of Cushing, "the laws of the Union follow its citizens, and its banner protects them, even within the domain of the Chinese empire."[12] It is worth pondering the audacity of Cushing in leveraging interpretative influence. Faced with a vacuum of diplomatic authority, he seized opportunities in relaying the treaty documents to issue statements that framed the treaty's interpretation back in Washington and then later reinforced these statements as attorney general to influence diplomatic policies.

To explain Cushing's legal rationale and administrative methods, this chapter reviews decades of his writing from the 1820s and 1830s when he was a new lawyer and upcoming politician.[13] After graduating from Harvard College, he contributed at least thirty-six articles to the *North American Review* on a diverse range of topics ranging from botany and the Pennsylvania coal trade to Boccaccio's *Decameron* and revolutions in Haiti and the Americas. Cushing continued writing at an amazing pace through the 1830s, producing two multivolume histories of Spain and of France. During the summer of 1844 as Cushing negotiated the treaty, he even managed to place two articles in the *Chinese Repository*. In regard to his legal theorizations of China's relationship to international law, an 1835 review article "Modern Law of Nations" that considered Emer de Vattel's landmark legal writings and his writing on the U.S.-British dispute over Oregon Territory are particularly significant.

Cushing's articles in the *North American Review* were a testing ground for ideas that he would later deploy to justify China's concessionary extraterritoriality as a defense of free trade. In Cushing's mission to protect the extension of national commerce, pagan China was one adversary among others. From Peking, China's despotic emperor had attempted to monopolize commerce through the Canton System and insultingly refused to receive diplomats from foreign nations. However, pagan China was not the only threat. In going to China, Cushing was protecting free trade from assaults of the fellow civilized nations that composed a confederation of what he called Christendom. In Cushing's national romance of commerce, Revolutionary forefathers had broken the shackles of British mercantilism to establish the United States as a rising democratic republic dedicated to free-trade expansion. The U.S. struggle against colonial subordination had not ended in 1783 or 1817. It was still unfolding on battlegrounds of the Oregon Territory, Canton, and Mexico. In order to achieve Manifest Destiny, it was imperative that the United States maintain trade with China at a level comparable to Britain. Capital from the China trade was crucial to developing the western frontiers and spanning the continent to yield a Golden Gate of commerce on the Pacific Coast. In summary, Cushing wrote of his China mission as supporting a U.S. commercial revolution that drove pioneers into the Far West.

In waging this defense of revolutionary commerce in the Far East and Far West, Cushing championed U.S. principles of political confederation as an innovative technology of free-trading Christendom. The U.S. Constitution had ordered the states into a national Union, offering a model for the world's emerging republics. Looking to expand the nation's Pacific horizons of influence, Cushing was proud to extend the protections promised by the Monroe Doctrine to fellow postcolonial nations in the Americas by putting the Truman Doctrine into action. Cushing thus tested the supranational boundaries of the nation's confederative principle in imagining a world of rising republics networked into a commonwealth dedicated to free trade—a network overseen by the United States. After returning from China, his rationale for promoting confederated international commerce became explicitly racialist and racist as he justified the U.S. war on Mexico by differentiating Mexicans from Anglo Saxons according to a fundamentalist racial logic that had underpinned his earlier exclusions of pagans from the nations of Christendom.[14]

This chapter begins with a brief overview of Cushing's life to provide a national context for understanding his assertion of absolute and unqualified extraterritoriality in China. It then turns to his diplomatic dispatches in order to consider how he asserted that the Treaty of Wanghia spelled out China's concession of unqualified and absolute extraterritoriality. To explain the relevance of China to Cushing's views on continental development, the chapter delves into his early review articles, cultural histories, and congressional speeches in which he celebrates the United States for its confederative principles of revolutionary commerce. These principles of commercial confederation justify not only China's concession of absolute and unqualified extraterritoriality but also the federal removal of Native peoples and the war on Mexico. The chapter then returns to the *Chinese Repository* to highlight ambiguities at the heart of the Treaty of Wanghia's references to protocols of intercultural law—ambiguities that contradict Cushing's assertions and suggest alternative ways of understanding extraterritoriality. It concludes by registering Samuel Wells Williams's objections in the final edition of *The Middle Kingdom* (1883) to

Cushing's diplomatic legacy through Williams's memorialization of Cushing's Chinese counterpart in the negotiations, the imperial commissioner Kíying (1787–1858; 耆英, Qíyīng).

The Diplomatic Adventures of Caleb Cushing

Born in Newburyport, Massachusetts, Caleb Cushing led a seemingly tireless public life that left him stranded between political parties before the U.S. Civil War. His father was John Newmarch Cushing, a successful shipbuilder and sea merchant with a fleet in the lucrative West Indies trade that made him the "fifth richest man in Newburyport" by 1840, with an impressive net worth of $60,000. Caleb's older cousin John Perkins Cushing (cousin of the brothers John Murray and Robert Bennet Forbes) retired from Perkins & Company much wealthier after working for decades in Canton for his uncles James and Colonel Thomas H. Perkins.[15] Caleb eschewed the merchant's path, but he followed his father's advice in recognizing "the intimate relationship of the Northwest Territory and the Far East" and the "potential riches" that were "threatened by British dominance in the region."[16]

Cushing entered Harvard College at thirteen and began a long association with Edward Everett, a renowned professor of Greek literature who went on to serve in the House of Representatives, as governor of Massachusetts, as ambassador to England during the administration of President John Tyler (1841–45), as president of Harvard College (between the terms of Josiah Quincy and Jared Sparks), and as secretary of state under President Millard Fillmore (1850–53).[17] In the early 1820s Everett also served as the editor of the *North American Review* that published Cushing's first significant book reviews.[18] Having graduated Harvard with a degree in law, Cushing was keen to publish. His review articles clustered titles that addressed topics of particular political relevance and often worked across languages of English, French, and Spanish. When Jared Sparks replaced Everett as editor, he tried to rein Cushing in, responding to Cushing's proposal to write on Cervantes by cautioning, "An article merely for entertainment should be on a minor topic. Nothing is gained by making a show and carrying away the multitude, all solid reputations arise out of the approbation of the wise and well informed."[19] Cushing was undeterred and his articles also appeared in other major American periodicals, including the *American Quarterly Review*, the *Annual Register*, and the *U.S. Literary Gazette*.

In 1826 Cushing ran for the U.S. House of Representatives, inspired by the 1824 elections of former secretary of state John Quincy Adams to U.S. president and Professor Everett to the U.S House of Representatives. Cushing was defeated.

Caleb Cushing. Negative from Matthew Brady photographic portrait, Library of Congress, cwpbh 04453 http://hdl.loc.gov/loc.pnp/cwpbh.04453.

He immersed himself in his law practice while planning a European tour with his new wife. In July 1829 the Cushings embarked for Rotterdam and traveled through Holland, Belgium, France, and Spain, spending ten weeks in Paris, five months in Madrid, and two months in London, before returning to the United States in September 1830. The tour inspired Cushing to publish the two-volume *Review, Historical and Political, of the Late Revolution in France, and the Consequent Events in Belgium, Poland, Great Britain, and other parts of Europe* (1833) and another two volumes on Spain.[20] In 1832 he made another unsuccessful run for Congress. Later that year his wife passed away. Cushing never remarried. He threw himself into public life, protesting in print President Andrew Jackson's attempt to abolish the Second Bank and rebutting James Fenimore Cooper's pro-Jacksonian *Letter to His Countrymen* (1834) that had criticized the Senate for manipulating federal bank deposits to oppose Jackson's policies.[21]

On his third try in 1834, Cushing won a seat in the U.S. House of Representatives. He served eight years alongside former president John Quincy Adams. During this period the field of national politics was realigning into the two opposing parties: the Jackson Democrats and the Whigs, led by Henry Clay and Daniel Webster. A highly regarded orator, Cushing wrote and delivered hundreds of speeches throughout his life, teaming up with Adams in May 1838 to exhort the House of Representatives that the future of the United States depended on annexing Oregon in order to hold the line against Britain's imperial monopolies. In 1841 he supported the successful Whig presidential candidacy of William Henry Harrison by writing the political biography *Outline of the Life and Public Services, Civil and Military, of William Henry Harrison* (1840). Harrison won the election but died just weeks into his term. The lines of party alliance became even more tangled with the presidential ascendance of Vice President John Tyler, a southern Democrat from Virginia. Secretary of State Daniel Webster (Whig) stayed on in Tyler's cabinet and wrote the Tyler Doctrine.

In 1843 Webster also appointed Cushing to be the U.S. envoy extraordinary and minister plenipotentiary. (Webster's first choice had been Cushing's mentor Professor Everett, but he opted to remain in London as the U.S. ambassador.) In the aftermath of the Treaty of Nanking (1842), Webster was concerned that China had opened to "English commerce" four more ports "belong[ing] to some of the richest, most productive, and most populous provinces of the empire"—ports likely to become very important marts of commerce.[22] Cushing's mission was to "secure the entry of American ships and cargoes into these ports on terms as favorable as those which are enjoyed by the English."[23] In pursuit of this objective, Webster directed him to convey peaceful intentions. Cushing's "constant aim must be to produce a full conviction on the minds of the Government and the people [of China], that the mission is entirely pacific" and that the U.S. government "will not encourage, any violation of the commercial regulations of China."[24] Webster also penned a letter (12 July 1843) from President John Tyler to the emperor and tasked Cushing with delivering it to Peking. The letter's condescending cordiality conveys presumptions of cautious free-trade imperialism. Acknowledging the far greater population of China, Webster aligns the two countries along similar latitudes and, without mentioning opium, asserts, "The Chinese love to trade with our people, and to sell them tea and silk, for which our people pay silver, and sometimes other articles."[25] It concludes with President Tyler's reassurance to the emperor that "we shall not uphold them that break your laws," before signing off: "Your good friend, John Tyler."[26]

Cushing embraced the opportunity to go to China, studying books recommended by the American missionary Dr. Rev. Peter Parker and trying to learn Manchu, the prestigious language of the Qing Empire. He was elected to the American

Oriental Society.[27] Cushing left for Canton on 31 July 1843 in a four-ship fleet includ-ing two frigates, a sloop, and a brig. John R. Haddad describes Cushing's quixotic voyage out. Arriving in Gibraltar on 26 August 1843, a fire destroyed the steam-powered flagship *Missouri*, along with the ceremonial uniform Cushing had de-signed.[28] The remaining three wind-reliant ships of the squadron continued around the Cape of Good Hope as Cushing "boarded the British steam packet Oriental bound for Egypt" and then "trekked overland from the Port Said on the Mediterra-nean to Suez on the Red Sea to await a mail steamer to Bombay," where he rejoined his mission secretary Fletcher Webster (the son of Daniel Webster) on the new flagship the *Brandywine*.[29] On 27 February 1844 they anchored outside Macao on the frigate *Brandywine* with the sloop *St. Louis* and the brig *Perry*.[30]

In the letter that Webster wrote for President Tyler, Webster reduced China to the function of an ideal trading partner, but he also reassured the emperor that Americans would not "break your laws" in conducting trade.[31] Cushing pursued a different course, pushing beyond his official remit in attempting to render China's laws irrelevant to Americans in China. Upon arriving to Macao, he learned that China had already granted the U.S. access to the four additional treaty ports. In the spirit of Webster's directions, his mission to China had been made redundant. Nevertheless, Cushing still had President Tyler's letter in hand. Cushing used its delivery as a pretense to insist that China negotiate a separate treaty with the United States. Enlisting the U.S. missionaries Dr. Rev. Peter Parker, Rev. Elijah Bridgman, and Samuel Wells Williams, he spent two months exchanging commu-niqués with the acting governor and imperial commissioner to whom he repeat-edly declared his intention of proceeding to Peking with his squadron.[32] His per-sistence paid off with word in May that Imperial Commissioner Kíying was traveling south from Peking to meet him. Kíying had negotiated the Treaty of Nan-king (1842) with Britain's Sir Henry Pottinger. Unlike his predecessor, Commis-sioner Lin Zexu, who had confronted British opium dealers to enforce the impe-rial prohibitions, Kíying attempted to "[mollify] the invaders," "keeping them from further warlike acts."[33] The losses of the First Opium War had been considerable, and Peking had to worry about concurrent uprisings in the Southwest, West, and Northeast.[34] Kíying's tried to stave off further Western extension into the mainland, but it was a high-wire balancing act to appease the United States and France while reassuring the Emperor Daoguang (道光帝, Dàoguāng Dì).

On 3 July 1844 in a village temple outside of Macao, Cushing and Kíying signed the Treaty of Wanghia, including four originals in English and four in Chinese.[35] Cushing sent two copies in English and two copies in Chinese back to Washington on the *Sappho* with Augustine Heard, who had directed Russell & Company in Canton from 1831 to1836 before starting his own company in 1840.[36] After negotiating the Treaty of Wanghia, Cushing proposed pressing on to Japan but did not get the necessary permission and support. He stayed on for a few more weeks and then returned home by crossing the Pacific Ocean and traversing Mexico. Upon receiving the treaty, the newly appointed secretary of state John Calhoun transmitted it to President Tyler and then on to the Senate. Ratification was unanimous. U.S. commodore James Biddle then embarked to China with the ratified treaties. The *Chinese Repository* reported an exchange ceremony on Wednesday, 31 December 1845, outside Canton at the estate of the Chinese negotiator and former Cohong merchant Pan Shicheng.[37] Kíying and his team of negotiators (Hwáng Ngantun, Chau Chángling, and Pwán Sz'shing) represented China. Commodore Biddle, Consul Paul S. Forbes (of Russell & Company, and cousin of John Murray and Robert Bennet), Parker, and Bridgman represented the United States.[38] Alexander Hill Everett, the older brother of Cushing's mentor Edward Everett, succeeded Cushing as minister to China, but illness prevented him from delivering the ratified treaty. He arrived a year late and died soon after in Canton.[39]

Meanwhile, back in the United States Cushing lectured widely on China. He then turned his attention to supporting the war on Mexico (1846–48). In Massachusetts he raised a volunteer corps and headed down to Mexico, attaining the rank of brigadier general in the reserve corps. His increasing toleration of slavery and willingness to compromise over its expansion into the West soured his relationships with Adams, Webster, the emerging Republican Party, and his political base in Massachusetts. After serving in Tyler's administration, he seemed "no longer a Whig, not yet a Democrat."[40] He shifted his publication venue from the *North American Review* to the Democratic *United States Magazine and Democratic Review*, where the editor, John O'Sullivan, popularized the phrase "Manifest Destiny."[41] Cushing clung to political life in Massachusetts as the first mayor of Newburyport and then serving by appointment on the Massachusetts Supreme Judicial Court in 1852.

In 1853 President Franklin Pierce (Democrat) appointed Cushing U.S. attorney general, lifting him back into national relevance. During this appointment he reviewed the Treaty of Wanghia. As the Civil War loomed, Cushing reinforced his reputation for being a "doughface," a Northerner with sympathies for the South. As an early biographer explained, "thrown into contact with southern statesmen, [Cushing] became more tolerant of their views on slavery; indeed one of his [judicial] opinions anticipated the doctrine of the Dred Scott decision."[42] In 1854 he pursued speculative ventures in western real estate as railway networks expanded. The Cushing Land Agency was "one of the earliest and most important land agencies in northwest Wisconsin."[43] During the Civil War Cushing supported the Union, but his reputation as a Southern sympathizer endured for decades thereafter. After the war, his diplomatic missions included negotiating at Bogotá, Columbia, for the building of a canal across the isthmus of what today is Panama, negotiating claims with Britain for its wartime sale of battleships to the Confederacy at the Geneva Conference, and diffusing tensions with Spain after the Ten Year's War in Cuba.[44] President Ulysses S. Grant nominated him to be chief justice of the Supreme Court, but he was unsuccessful as Cushing's complicated legacy of political allegiances proved insurmountable. He died in Newburyport in 1879.

Inventing the Chinese Concession of Absolute and Unqualified Extraterritoriality

Extraterritoriality is not necessarily imperialistic. In the nineteenth century, legal scholars looked to the Treaty of Westphalia (1648) to establish the inherent territorial sovereignty of individual nation-states as the basis for recognizing an international law that could arbitrate relations between them.[45] As Eileen P. Scully explains, for centuries before and after Westphalia, *exterritoriality*—or degrees of extraterritorial consideration for ambassadors—resulted from mutual diplomatic courtesy, extended through unfixed agreement between states.[46] Today's foreign embassies and consulates are a legacy of such consideration.

However, Cushing's diplomatic dispatches and ruling as U.S. attorney general emphasized extraterritoriality as a *concession* from China whose pagan status precluded its sovereign territorial jurisdiction and made its laws inapplicable to Americans to an *absolute* and *unqualified* degree.[47] To appreciate Cushing's intervention, it helps to first look at the Treaty of Wanghia in total. For the most part, it echoes Britain and China's Treaty of Nanking but does not annex any land or demand an indemnity or reparation. It also includes a working formulation of extraterritoriality in Article 21: "Subjects of China who may be guilty of any criminal act towards citizens of the United States shall be arrested and punished by the Chinese authorities according to the laws of China. And citizens of the United States who may commit any crime in China, shall be subject to be tried and punished only by the consul or other public functionary of the United States thereto authorized according to the laws of the United States. And in order to the prevention of [*sic*] all controversy and disaffection, justice shall be equitably and impartially administered on both sides."[48]

Article 21 indeed secures an extraterritorial basis for adjudicating crimes and disputes involving U.S. citizens. However, there is no mention of this consideration being "absolute and unqualified." Article 25 further elucidates the extraterritorial reach of U.S. legal coverage in regard to disputes between U.S. citizens or between a U.S. citizen and a foreign national who is not Chinese: "All questions in regard to rights, whether of property or person, arising between citizens of the United States in China, shall be subject to the jurisdiction, and regulated by the authorities of their own government. And controversies occurring in China between citizens of the United States and the subjects of any other government shall be regulated by the treaties existing between the United States and such governments respectively, without interference on the part of China."[49] Again, there is no indication that this legal arrangement is a concession or that the extraterritorial terms are an absolute condition of adjudication. On the contrary, Article 24 explicitly states: "And if controversies arise between citizens of the United States and subjects of China, which cannot be amicably settled otherwise, the same shall be examined and decided comfortably to justice and equity by the public officers of the two nations sitting in conjunction."[50] Other articles in the treaty explicitly qualify the terms of extraterritorial consideration set forth in these three articles.

Most glaringly, Article 33 denies Cushing's claim that extraterritorial exemption of U.S. citizens from Chinese laws is absolute. Echoing the reassurances of President Tyler and Secretary Webster to the emperor in the diplomatic letter, and the official U.S. diplomatic policy then practiced in China, the article stipulates that that any American attempting to trade clandestinely beyond the five open ports or trafficking in opium will lose protection of the United States and will be dealt with by the Chinese government: "Citizens of the United States, who shall attempt to trade clandestinely with such of the ports of China as are not open to foreign commerce, or who shall trade in opium or any other contraband article of merchandise, shall be subject to be dealt with by the Chinese Government, without being entitled to any countenance or protection from the United States; and the United States will take measures to prevent their flag from being abused by subjects of other nations, as a cover for the violation of the laws of the Empire."[51] Contemporary histories acknowledge the discrepancy between Cushing's interpretation and the treaty's actual language, but render the discrepancy insignificant for the impracticality of enforcing Article 33.[52] After all, how would U.S. citizens, who are innocent until proven guilty, lose extraterritorial exemption unless they were first convicted through U.S. legal proceedings? And, if a U.S. citizen were actually convicted of opium smuggling in a U.S. proceeding, would U.S. authorities actually turn her or him over to China for prosecution and sentencing? Article 33 may have been an empty threat, or perhaps Cushing strategized a loophole of de facto extraterritorial protection for U.S. citizens that rendered the article mute. However, the treaty's stipulations of extraterritoriality are important to recognize because standardizing Cushing's claim unwittingly establishes a powerful precedent: China has relinquished territorial jurisdiction to a Western nation.

Cushing was able to invent China's categorical concession and establish its diplomatic precedence by writing up dispatches that summarized the treaty as it was received in Washington in 1844 and then by citing the interpretative summaries a decade later as U.S. attorney general. For an example of Cushing's initial summary, consider the "Abstract of the Treaty" that accompanied the treaty to the president and then to the Senate in December 1844 and January 1845. According to Cushing's summary, Article 21 "provides that subjects of China and citizens of the United States in China, charged with crimes, shall be subject only to the exclusive jurisdiction, each, of the laws and officers of their respective Governments"; and Article 25 "provides that all questions in regard to rights, whether of person or of property, arising between citizens of the United States in China, shall be subject to the jurisdiction and regulated by the authorities of their own Government."[53] Both of these summaries substantially simplify the treaty's language. Finally, Article 33, according to Cushing, "provides that citizens of the United States, engaged in contraband trade or trading clandestinely with such of the ports of China as are not open to foreign commerce, shall not be countenanced or protected by their government."[54] The gloss never mentions opium, and it strips Article 33 of the threat that U.S. citizens would lose all ground for extraterritorial consideration if engaged in contraband trade or other trade beyond the five treaty ports.

Cushing did not speak Chinese, but that mattered little as he summarized the treaty in the tone of a legal scholar laying out a philosophical premise for negotiating with pagan China. Actually, he used the confusion of the negotiation process as an opportunity to reinterpret the treaty in the diplomatic dispatches. There was considerable room for misunderstanding as Cushing communicated with Kíying through a small team of translators, including Parker and Bridgman, who were the "Joint Chinese Secretaries of the American Legation."[55] In his biography of Parker, Edward Gulick sums up Rev. Parker's important role in these scenes of translation that unfolded in Cantonese and Mandarin: "Judged by the perfectionism of the Chinese literati, Parker's linguistic skills were poor and probably laughable. Judged by the appalling Western ignorance and with regard for both the difficulty of the language before the development of adequate teaching aids and the general competence of a job fairly well done, he was quite impressive."[56] Cushing even tried to use Manchu as the official language of negotiation. There are no signs that this was effective, but traces of his attempt appear in his reference to Kíying as "Tsiyeng."[57] Furthermore, the copied English versions of the treaty are riddled with errors: "The writing of the scriveners and their collating (if any) of the various originals, was done with extraordinary carelessness."[58] And, as Cushing explained in his Dispatch 86 of 19 August 1844, the British missionary Rev. Walter Medhurst and the American missionary Bridgman each translated the Chinese version and produced translations that "differ[ed] very materially from the official English counterpart."[59]

In the context of this ambiguity, Cushing's used his dispatches as a vehicle for rendering significant legal claims about the legal competency of pagan China. From Webster's instructions he established the pursuit of commerce as diplomatic common ground. Commerce was the putatively apolitical objective of the entire mission as Cushing writes: "The interests of the United States in China are commercial, not political; and it was the primary purpose of my mission to make satisfactory arrangements for the prosecution of our commerce with this country, under new and more favorable circumstances."[60] Cushing's description of "commerce" here is a conceptual Trojan horse in a legal assault on China's territorial sovereignty. Commerce establishes a common ground for China and the United States as a basis for U.S. citizens to be in China's territory. However, Cushing then takes control of the legal ground of the commercial interaction by defining China as a pagan state that ought not be trusted to exercise jurisdiction over U.S. citizens. Consequently U.S. citizens who occupy China's literal territory are exempt from the Chinese regulation.

According to Cushing, Christendom is an exclusive club of civilized nations that are on the way to learning the beneficial commercial effects of confederating authority. In Dispatch 97 to Secretary of State John Calhoun, which Cushing wrote aboard the brig USS *Perry* on his return voyage, he theorizes a confederacy of Christendom undergirded by international law that supports commerce.[61] Reviewing the legal theorists Emer de Vattel and Johann Ludwig Klüber, he asserts "the all-important fact, that what they denominate the law of nations, as if it were the law of *all* nations, is, in truth, only the international law of *Christendom*."[62] China's willingness to trade with states of Christendom is not enough to earn Christendom's respect of China's legal sovereignty over its territory. Cushing employs the passive voice to assert that in fact "nothing, it would seem, correspondent to our law of nations, is recognized or understood in China."[63] He continues: "How different is the condition of things out of the limits of Christendom! From the greater part of Asia and Africa, individual Christians are utterly excluded, either by sanguinary barbarism of the inhabitants, or by their phrensied bigotry, or by the narrow-minded policy of their governments. To their courts, the ministers of Christian governments have no means of access except by force, and at the head of fleets of armies. As between them and us, there is no community of ideas, no common law of nations, no interchange of good offices."[64]

In Cushing's circular logic, pagan China's refusal to trade with Christian nations on terms dictated by the Christian nations is evidence of its pagan unwillingness to communicate. The military force ("fleet of armies") that Cushing invokes is defensive rather than aggressive, a reaction to China's refusal to communicate like civilized Christians. It is at this point in Dispatch 97 that Cushing remarks on having "entered China with the formed *general* conviction, that the United States ought not to concede to any foreign State, under any circumstances, jurisdiction over the life and liberty of any citizen of the United States, unless that foreign State be of our own family of nations; in a word, a Christian State."[65] He continues by asserting that the treaty is China's "concession" of "absolute and unqualified" extraterritoriality in consequence of which "the laws of the Union follow its citizens, and its banner protects them, even within the domains of the Chinese Empire."[66] Cushing's reasoning in regard to pagan China was not idiosyncratic or innovative. Rather, it had grown out of his decades of imagining the territorial extension of the United States across North America, where free trade faced pagans of a different sort.

Native Savagery and the Civilizing Project of U.S. Territoriality

Considering the implications of Dispatch 97's categorical divide between Christians and pagans, Ruskola describes Cushing's sense of law as "an almost ontological character of American *being*—the glory of the law-loving Anglo-Saxon race, a kind of white lawyer's burden."[67] This cast a shadow over any prospect of international law being universal. But people from "Asia and Africa" are not rejecting Christianity out of ignorance or after informed deliberation. Rather, they are fundamentally incapable of adapting Christian beliefs and civilized habits—at least in time to protect U.S. interests from Britain's imperialistic pursuit of commercial advantage that is playing out in North America. Differing in "degree" and "kind" from the member nations of Christendom, the pagans of China, Africa, and the Americas are a distinct and separate "legal personality."[68]

To appreciate the imperial significance of Cushing's relegation of China to a pagan empire, Ruskola likens Cushing to his contemporary Chief Justice John Marshall, who authored the Supreme Court's Marshall Trilogy: *Johnson v. M'Intosh* (1823; 21 U.S. [8 Wheaton] 543); *Cherokee Nation v. Georgia* (1831; 30 U.S. [5 Peters] 1); and *Worcester v. Georgia* (1832; 31 U.S. [6 Peters] 515).[69] The first two cases of the Marshall Trilogy defined the original inhabitants of North America (specifically the Piankeshaw and the Cherokee peoples) as savages, setting them beyond the civic pale of the federal government's recognition as either U.S. citizens or foreign nationals. Immediately after the American Revolution, the federal government secured treaties of "peace and friendship" with Native peoples as foreign governments.[70] This changed with *Johnson v. M'Intosh* (1823). In the majority opinion, Justice Marshall invoked the Doctrine of Discovery as the basis of Europe's dominion and opined that the United States had inherited from Britain its rights of conquest. According to Marshall, "the title of the United States to the land on which it

was established derives ultimately from the European 'discovery' of the Americas—
an expressly colonial notion that denies legal subjectivity to the indigenous inhabitants of this continent."[71] Marshall admits the ostensible injustice of such aggression but concludes that the discovery doctrine is the necessary premise for U.S.
plenary power. He then justifies the aggression by contrasting the young nation's
productive citizens with indigenous inhabitants who are categorically savage, nomadic hunters, incapable of possessing land as individuals or of improving it in
accordance with civic principles of property.[72] Ruskola characterizes the ensuing
continental "expansion from the Atlantic to the Pacific" as "a landgrab of world
historic proportions, claiming half a continent as the new homeland of overseas
settlers"; he also notes the irony that such a land grab was not "regarded as imperialism at all but only as the young nation's manifest, preordained destiny."[73]

In writing about the Cherokee people who resisted federal removal, Cushing
indeed echoes Marshall's characterization of savage peoples whose community
will vanish as each individual either perishes or assimilates into the white population of the United States through intermarriage and education. Cushing views
are apparent in his review of "An Address to the Whites; delivered in the First
Presbyterian Church of Philadelphia, on 26th of May, 1826. By Elias Boudinot, a
Cherokee Indian" for the *North American Review* in 1826.[74] Boudinot had grown up
as Gallegina Uwati in the land of the Cherokee, which the United States recognized in the Treaty of Hopewell (1785) as a foreign and sovereign nation. He attended the Foreign Mission School in Cornwall, Connecticut, run by the American
Board of Commissioners of Foreign Missions, where he renamed himself in honor
of his mentor Elias Boudinot, the former president of the Continental Congress
and president of the American Bible Society. With the support of ABCFM missionaries, Boudinot went on to edit and print the bilingual *Cherokee Phoenix*, protesting
removal adamantly in the years before passage of the Indian Removal Act (1830).[75]

In his 1826 review, Cushing facilitates the absorption of Cherokee land into the
state of Georgia while ignoring the communal basis of Cherokee identity. He acknowledges that Boudinot is a member of the "Cherokee nation," situated "within
the chartered limits of the states Georgia, Tennessee, and Alabama," but then dismisses Boudinot's contention that the Cherokee people are a civilized group who
deserve recognition as a nation. Using Boudinot's educational accomplishment
as evidence, Cushing argues that only individual Indians "are susceptible of the
attainments necessary to the formation of polished society."[76] Boarding school education can basically turn a savage into a civilized person, but a U.S. citizen is, by
definition, no longer a Cherokee or a savage. Cushing continues: "A community of
civilized Indians is an anomaly that never has existed, nor do we believe it ever will
exist. Bring the Indians up to this mark, and you put them on a level with whites;

they will then intermarry, and the smaller mass will be swallowed up by the larger; the red skin will become white, and the Indian will be remembered only as the tenant of the forests, which have likewise disappeared before the march of civilization."[77] With the category of "Indian," Cushing appreciates the primal energy of Cherokee people while overlooking their legal standing as a community.[78] Cushing uses Indian savagery to segregate Cherokees as a community, but the racial divide is flexible in regard to individual Cherokees who might intermarry and assimilate in white U.S. citizenship.

Extending Ruskola's insightful notice of Cushing's racialist views toward savage American Indians and the pagan Chinese reveals telling differences between the ways in which Cushing excludes them from the states of Christendom. Cushing never imagines absorbing China's territory in the United States. Consequently, he carves out extraterritorial exception for U.S. citizens on Chinese soil without suggesting that the Chinese will ever disappear or assimilate into the community of white Christendom. Furthermore, his exclusions of pagan Chinese and savage Indians from the law of civilized nations imply racial dynamics of world-historical affiliation and antagonism—racial dynamics that would become increasingly categorical and essential as he conjured Manifest Destiny's expansive global significance stretching from the American Far West to the Far Eastern shores of China to redeem Europe's primal savagery and original sins of papal imperialism.

Confederating Christendom, from the Monroe to the Tyler Doctrine

Race is a complicated term in Cushing's writings and his assertion of its categorical implications changed over his career as he broadened the geographic and historical appreciation of how confederative principles harnessed the energies of commercial ambition to the benefit of free-trading nations. It is fascinating to see that in his early writings from the 1820s Cushing was more concerned with asserting alliances between revolutionary movements in the Americas than he was with excluding racial others from Christendom. Race did not yet impede his imagining an international confederation of free-trade republics across the Americas in Columbia, Guatemala, Haiti, Mexico, and Peru. Furthermore, he used race to destabilize the cultural foundation of Europe by excavating its savagery in historicizing the dialectical forces that gave rise to Christendom. He even characterizes the Doctrine of Discovery as a great crime of tyrannical, Papal avarice before asserting that the American Revolution offered Christendom the chance for world-historical redemption.

In the 1820s, Cushing was not yet looking directly to China, but he was already testing the extraterritorial basis on which Americans would continue resisting the lingering tyrannical influences of Europe. Looking across the American hemisphere, he relished revolutions as long as they led to the formation of democratic republics that would rise to fit into a global network of commerce overseen by the United States. Reviewing books on the revolutions in Haiti and South and Central America, Cushing praises revolutionary "black" and "aboriginal" individual men throughout the hemisphere and embraces Spanish and French "creoles" who have valiantly severed colonial connection with rapacious empires of Europe.

In these articles, Cushing echoed the extraterritorial ambitions of the Monroe Doctrine, written primarily by Secretary of State John Quincy Adams and delivered by President Monroe as an address to Congress on 2 December 1823.[79] Concerned that the revolutions in Central and South America would tempt Europe's members of the Holy Alliance to intervene and would embolden Russia to move into Northwest America, Adams and Monroe used a presidential address to proclaim a condition of nonintervention. One of the key characteristics of the Monroe Doctrine was its ambiguity. It was not a treaty, and yet it addressed foreign nations to inform them of U.S. foreign policy in ways that evoked the premise of diplomacy.[80] In the address, Monroe recognizes the revolutions in Columbia, Buenos Aires, Chili, and Mexico by declaring that "the American continents, by the free and independent condition which they have assumed and maintain, are henceforth not to be considered as subjects for future colonization by any European Power."[81] Reasoning that Europe's distance from the American continents makes it difficult to maintain credible control over uncooperative colonists, Monroe asserts that no one could possibly "believe that our Southern brethren, if left to themselves, would adopt [political allegiance to an empire of Europe] of their own accord."[82] He reassures that the United States has no intention of interfering with "existing colonies or dependencies" of "any European Power": "But, with Governments who have declared their independence, and maintained it, and whose independence we have, on great consideration, and on just principles, acknowledged, we [the United States] could not view any interposition for the purpose of oppressing them, or controlling in any other manner, their destiny, by any European Power, in any other light than as the manifestation of an unfriendly disposition towards the United States."[83]

This concern with European colonies in the Americas complemented the young nation's westward aspirations. Monroe had himself helped negotiate the Louisiana Purchase (1803) during the Jefferson administration. New States had since emerged on this territory, broadening the continental territory and balancing power in a wider confederation. Consequently "Consolidation and disunion" had "been rendered equally impracticable," and "each [state] Government, confiding it its own strength, has less to apprehend from the other" to enjoy "a greater freedom of action."[84] Revolutions in the Americas might not widen the United States in a formally territorial sense by adding new states, but the revolutions would yield an informal confederation of sovereign republics overseen by the United States. In declaring the American hemisphere off limits to European colonization, Monroe offered the U.S. Constitution to his postrevolutionary "Southern brethren" as the blueprint for fostering republican stability.

As Thomas Jefferson's playfully imperialistic epigraph to this chapter reflects, imperial power and conquest were not necessarily problems for those who had won independence from tyrannical Britain. In fact, military capability was the basis for protecting the American experiment of republican freedom; the question was how the republic's footprint might expand and contract in relation to the liberty of the people. Peter Onuf describes Jefferson's "empire for liberty" as it extended beyond the thirteen original states. Jefferson imagined "an expanding union of republics held together by ties of interest and affection," "dispens[ing] with concentrated power and metropolitan rule."[85] Whereas Jefferson idealized small republics of citizens rooted virtuously in farmers who worked the soil, he did not see these republics surviving if they stood in isolation. The United States was an experiment that tested the limits of composing and confederating individual states. He "could envision unions of unions, spreading circle upon circle, layer upon layer, until the whole enlightened world was transformed and redeemed."[86] Empire designated a safe zone within which individuals, communities, and states could act independently, free of tyrannical intrusions in pursuing self-interests, assured of the government's "hallowed principle of non-interference."[87] The Monroe Doctrine widened the scope of the U.S. interests and protection beyond the established borders of the United States and the sites of potential statehood in the Far West.[88]

In his 1820s reviews of these American revolutions, Cushing expands the purview of Jefferson's phrase "empire for liberty" as he tasks the United States with the responsibility of protecting various young nations across the hemisphere. According to Cushing, young nations such as Haiti, Peru, Columbia, and Mexico had followed the revolutionary example of the United States. They deserved to be recognized as independent peoples struggling to develop their own republican governments and to claim their rightful positions within a world network of commerce. For example, in two articles on "Hayti" from January 1821 and January 1829 he reaches out to the revolutionaries as "Southern brethren."[89] The first article reviews nine books published in French and "written by descendants of negroes, and by nobles of the late kingdom of Hayti"; the review characterizes the 1791 revolution in Saint Dominque as an extension of the American Revolution.[90] Cushing recognizes the impulse of fellow human beings to resist oppression—and he validates such resistance on the basis of fellow humans' inchoate yearning for a constitutional order that will promote commerce in the way that the U.S. Constitution had. In line with the biographical templates Quincy and Sparks were developing, Cushing personifies historical forces, plotting national development in the struggles of Haiti's representative individual man. Cushing seems to have not yet developed racist prejudices that prevent him from identifying Haitian leaders as heroes of a rising peer nation. It is the prejudiced revolutionaries of France who stand as cruel hypocrites for not upholding in Haiti the democratic principles that had brought down the European monarchy in 1789:

> France, in the madness of the revolution, proclaimed liberty through the colony, and at once conferred political rights on these miserable beings; but shortly repenting of her generosity, she tried to reduce them again to slavery, by force or fraud; and when she found they had not tasted the sweets of freedom in vain, she commenced that series of barbarities, which surpassed even her own reign of terror, and which will never be forgotten as the revolution of Saint Domingo. But the party prevailed, which deserved to prevail; for once poetic justice was done in this grand drama of life; the blacks fought on, through reverses and sufferings unrivalled, till they became independent, and not a single one of their old oppressors remained on the soil of Hayti. What revolution has the world ever beheld, that was comparable to this in credit which it does to the aptitude and perseverance of its leaders?[91]

Cushing continues by celebrating Haiti's quest to develop "a free and republican government."[92] Under Christophe's leadership, Cushing predicts the "regeneration of Hayti" as the designation of English as the official language will suppress French and any French-based patois, and the "confused admixtures of English, Spanish, and the native languages of the slaves of Africa."[93] By 1821, when Cushing's article had appeared in print, Christophe had died and his son had been assassinated. Haiti was again at war. Eight years later in a second review article on Haiti, Cushing does not give up on Haiti. He laments the gunboat diplomacy through which France had intimidated Haitian leaders into signing a treaty exacting debilitating reparations in exchange for carefully worded recognition of Haiti's independence.[94]

Haiti's revolt from France was one of several revolutions that captured Cushing's imagination for portending an age of free-trade confederation. He reviewed books written in Spanish, celebrating more anticolonial American heroes. In "Insurrection of Paez in Columbia" (July 1827), he asserts that "there is no period in the history of man without its memorable vicissitudes, full of instruction,— its marked individual, a Caesar, Washington, Bonaparte, or Bolivar, towering like a beacon above the ever rolling tide of time, and seeming ordained to fulfill an extraordinary destiny."[95] In "Insurrection of Tupac Amaru," Cushing inspires his readers with the story of José Gabriel Túpac Amaru, a Cacique of Tungasuca, "directly descended, by maternal line, from the last of the acknowledged Incas," and named after the sixteenth-century Túpac Amaru who had faced down the Spanish, by whom he was finally executed.[96] Cushing portrays the eighteenth-century Túpac Amaru as rising up heroically against the especially brutal "slavery of the *repartimientos*" through which Spanish magistrates "stripped the poor Indians of their little substance" in exploiting the "inexhaustible silver mines in the bowels of mount Potosi."[97] Cushing closes another article on the Columbian revolution by encouraging his U.S. readers to take a "lively interest in the condition of Spanish America," whose "bravest and wisest and purest patriots" are "guided" by the "leading star" of the United States.[98]

In celebrating these American revolutions and their corresponding heroes, Cushing keeps an eye on the global geography of commerce that the United States will supervise as it connects the Atlantic to the Pacific and Europe to Asia. Considering Guatemala (including contemporary Panama) in the review of "A Statistical and Commercial History of the Kingdom of Guatemala in Spanish America" (January 1828), he takes especial note of its potential as a crossroad.[99] Lacking "abundant mines of gold or silver," Guatemala's hereto hidden value lies in being "comprised most of the isthmus, which unite North and South America, stretching along from Yucatan and Tabasco to Veragua, and with the Atlantic ocean on one side, and the Pacific on the other."[100] The "bare inspection of a map" "show[s] how favorably this region is situated, in a geographical point of view, for cultivating commercial intercourse, either with parts of America, or with nations of both Asia and Europe."[101] This observation about literal geography ("bare inspection") serves figuratively to reinforce criticism of European imperialism for having warped the global network of trade; so, "whilst Guatemala lay buried in the darkness of Spanish colonial administration, the advantages of its position, although known to the world, were held of little account, because it required the intervention of revolution to create the possibility of converting them to any useful purpose."[102] With independence, Cushing hopes Guatemala will be "guided by the principles, and stimulated by the invigorating spirit of liberty" as exemplified by the United States so that "we may, perhaps, hope to see Central America one day become the point of union for the commerce of both oceans."[103]

Savage Europe's Imperial Sin of Colonial Tyranny

In the 1830s Cushing continued to balance pursuit of U.S. commerce on the cultural edge of affiliation and antagonism with the Christian nations of Britain, France, and Spain. He did this by championing principles of confederation ("one confederated republic") as the best means of harnessing the revolutionary energies of commerce and preventing the rise of tyranny. He held out the United States as the world-historical paragon of effective confederation. Consider again Cushing's China Dispatch 97 from 1844 in which he imagines commercial and cultural solidarity among the states of Christendom. His idealization of Christendom in fact papers over the competitive concern motivating the trip: that the United States would be disadvantaged relative to Britain in pursing commerce in China. Here is his hyperbolic description of the "States of Christendom" as a happy confederation in Dispatch 97:

> [They] have a common origin, a common religion, a common intellectuality, associated by which common ties, each permits to the subjects of the other in time of peace ample means of access to its dominion for the purpose of trade, full right to reside therein, to transmit letters by its mails, to travel in its interior at pleasure, using the highways, canals, stage coaches, steamboats, and railroads of the country as freely as the native inhabitants. And they hold a regular and systematic intercourse, as Governments, by means of diplomatic agents of each residing in the Courts of the others, respectively. All these facts impart to the States of Christendom many of the qualities of one confederated republic.[104]

Putting aside the obvious rebuttal that the United States would never on principle have allowed citizens from Europe to conduct trade illegally in the United States, this is a remarkable statement of solidarity. However, the technologies of transportation to which Cushing refers not only brought these States of Christendom together. The stagecoaches, steamboats, and railways were also crucial to U.S. settlement of the West that depended on removing pagan Indian savages from the continent in a competition with the Christian empires of Britain, France, and Spain to control the trade routes through and settlement of North America and the Americas.

Despite Cushing's overarching love of European cultural heritage, focused on Britain, France, and Spain, he did not want to lose the thread of American national distinctiveness as he looked back on the historical development of Christendom. Interestingly, as Cushing writes about the European religion and politics, he evokes race to destabilize the continuity of Christendom. For example, in the article "Modern Law of Nations" (October 1835) published in the *North American Review* he conjures "one great organized Christian Commonwealth of Europe and America" that sustains a "law of nations" to which aggrieved members may appeal when, for example, there are confrontations on the seas between ships of different Christian nations.[105] This "law of nations" was the result of a supranational communal consciousness on territory that became Europe only after centuries of violent conflict. Through "blood and religion," Cushing takes Christendom back to the sacking of Rome by "savage" tribes of Vandals, Goths, and Franks who "swept over the civilized world, like a tropical hurricane" and brought on a "period of universal desolation and misery."[106] In his two-volume *Review, Historical and Political, of the Late Revolution in France, and the Consequent Events in Belgium, Poland, Great Britain, and other parts of Europe* (1833) Cushing similarly takes his reader back to the "crumbing frame of the Roman Empire" to see "in the fusion of the invading Barbarians with the conquered inhabitants of Italy, Gaul, Spain, Britain" the "elements of modern European civilization."[107] For Cushing this "disastrous epoch of our history" marks a point "when rapine and violence ruled the world" in a "fury of human passion," "loosed from the control of reason and religion."[108] But there is a vital creativity to this destruction, and this "tremendous disorder, that shock of classes, races, and opinions," has "impressed upon European society its characteristic features" and given rise to "the combinations of modern society."[109] Cushing relishes this perpetual agitation, an "incessant movement," deriving from the "the combination of the opinions and social forms of the northern Barbarians with those which previously existed among the Romans."[110] Comparing the barbarians of "the Norman and German tribes" to "our own North American Indians," he celebrates their savage defiance as a cultural impetus for emboldening individualistic ambition.[111]

In regard to unbridled savagery, Christianity comes to the rescue in the form of Catholicism that slowly tames and "humaniz[es] the barbarians" during a "long period of transition" lasting throughout centuries of the Crusades and to the death of Charlemagne.[112] Catholic authority regulated barbarians and savages "to combine and cement together the sovereignties of Europe in a great Christian republic" but, alas, the "meddlesome and grasping ambition of the Roman See," in "the ordinary course of human affairs," necessitated waves of reformative revolt.[113] After the establishment of Christendom, the energy of this conflict lived on, inspiring commercial competition between Europe's empires and colonial expansion to the Americas, where Europe's colonies eventually rebelled and became "nations descended" from Europe through "the ties of blood and religion."[114]

As Cushing denigrates Catholicism, he singles out the Doctrine of Discovery as the most "extraordinary" abuse of its concentrated power. Cushing does not excuse the "grasping ambition" of the papacy, but he accepts it for giving rise to the modern and civilized nation-states of Protestant Christendom, whose colonies would eventually rise and redeem the pope's original sin of abusive power: "Without dwelling upon the fact of the conquest of America. Without dwelling upon the fact of the crusades, look at the grant of the East and West Indies, made by Pope Alexander to Spain and Portugal. This concession proceeded on the idea, which obtained in Europe after the preaching of the crusades, that countries, inhabited by a pagan people, were lawfully open to invasion and subjugation by the first Christians, for the purposes of conversion."[115] Cushing does not consider the price that "pagan people" paid for the conquest. Instead he appreciates "Chivalry" and the "Feudal System" for laying the groundwork of mutual recognition and restraint "among princes and barons of separate countries" after the conquest has taken place.[116] When the Reformation finally broke the pope's tyrannical hold on Christianity, the community of Christendom faced the prospect of perpetual war between Protestants and Catholics, each regarding the other as "natural enemies."[117] However, the general influence of Christianity lead the various "nations of Europe" to realize a "distinctly useful respect of the reciprocal relations of sovereignties," marked by the Treaty of Westphalia (1648) that ended the religious Thirty Years' War (1618–48).[118] Cushing analogizes these "federative sovereignties" of Europe to the "organization of the United States," with a key difference being that each of the European sovereignties derived power from a "feudal baron[s]" and not "the vassals in the aggregate."[119]

European colonialism is thus a great crime that can be traced back to the original sin of concentrated power expressed in papal advocacy of conquest. The pope's "grasping ambition" became the foundation of Europe's colonial projects that unleashed commercial energies in the era's "great extension of commerce" to the West Indies, to Africa and to the East.[120] As commerce intensified, Europe's imperial nations strove to stabilize peaceful relations back in Europe by "preserv[ing]" a "balance of power."[121] Terms of international law emerged to govern the territorial sovereignties of European kingdoms, "the art of printing" drew "closer the intellectual associations of the inhabitants of different countries, to multiply their ties, and of course to humanize their general intercourse," and the establishment of "resident embassies, protected in the country where they were accredited" likewise attested to a "unity of the nations of Christendom as one great republic."[122]

The colonial projects of Protestant empires such as United States would eventually lead to the next phase of world-historical development. These new republics could not undo the sin of papal tyranny, but they could redeem it in the future for the sake all humankind. After the American Revolution, Europe's other American colonies followed suit, rebelling to become "nations descended" from Europe through "the ties of blood and religion."[123] There was then a deep ambivalence in the colonial condition: a great spiritual promise sprung from the ground of imperial overreach. But the hope for historical redemption was carried forward not by the Native people but the colonial settlers. As Cushing averred in *Review, Historical and Political of the Late Revolution in France*, "a European Colony in the New World possesses at all times . . . the right of separating from the Metropolis in Europe."[124]

As Cushing brings his article on the "law of nations" to a conclusion, he seeks to redeem European Christendom's imperial crimes through revolutionary American commerce that finds its most progressive expression in national republics based on the principle of confederation. The final pages of the "Modern Law of Nations" celebrate Grotius's "Of the Right of War and Peace," "the great authoritative guide in the public intercourse of Christendom," along with Vattel's work on international law as "the best manual for common reference."[125] This "law of nations" not only enables nations of Christendom to respect each other's sovereignty. It also redeems Europe's acts of conquest and colonization. Living in the shadow of imperial conquest, Cushing sees progressive light in the "great body of law-text"—the "treaties, conventions, deeds, and charters"—that relate to the "international relations of Christendom" and "the positive institute of the public law in Europe and America."[126] This allows Cushing to blame Europe for policies of conquest in the Americas, while defining the United States as a correction of those crimes and a path to subsequent refinements promised by the synergy of Christianity and commerce.

It is interesting to see that Cushing's concern over the legality of conquest motivates him to go so far as to question the basis of United States territorial sovereignty. He notes that the U.S. Constitution had not empowered the president (Thomas Jefferson) to purchase land from the empires of Europe (France and Spain). However, having witnessed the redemptive historical arc of national development, Cushing concludes that congressional ratification established in the president's overreach a functional premise for territorial expansion that would prove virtuous. Cushing settles the legal inconsistency with a tautology, just as Justice Marshall had, by invoking the Doctrine of Discovery in 1823; Cushing recognizes "the great utility of the thing and the acquiescence of the people" to the purchases that have yielded an expanding confederation of United States.[127]

The Tyler Doctrine—of which the Cushing Mission was the most dramatic early expression—was the next stage chronologically and geographically in the development of U.S. power and influence, widening a confederation of republics into the Pacific. The full name of the Tyler Doctrine is the "Message from the President of the United States, on the Subject of the Trade and Commerce of the United States with the Sandwich Islands, and of Diplomatic Intercourse with their Government; also, in Relation to the new Position of Affairs in China, growing out of the Late War between Great Britain and China, and recommending Provision for a Diplomatic Agent, December 31, 1842."[128] Written by Secretary of State Daniel Webster, the doctrine justifies the U.S. oversight of the Sandwich Islands in the Pacific Ocean by noting their relative proximity to the United States—"much nearer to this continent than to the other"—and their importance as a station "for refitment and provisioning of American and European vessels."[129] Acknowledging that U.S. vessels compose most of the traffic moving through Hawai'i, Tyler appeals to a general interest among the world's commercial nations in ensuring independence for an incipient nation "just emerging from a state of barbarism."[130] Tyler pledges to protect Hawai'i "in the midst of a vast expanse of ocean" from the remote "dominions of European powers" seeking to "take possession," "to colonize," or "to subvert the native government."[131] It should be noted that Tyler's pledge to protect Hawai'i was not new. In 1826 the United States had exerted significant extraterritorial influence on the "Sandwich Islands," signing agreements that recognized Hawai'i as an independent nation while obligating them to repay collectively (as a nation) the debts owed to American trading firms, including those of John Jacob Astor and William Sturgis.[132]

In any case, with an eye to China, the Tyler administration put into action the tenets of the doctrine by claiming the same rights as Great Britain to appoint a "commissioner to reside in China."[133] In 1843 Cushing would become the republic's hero who would take up his nation's commercial quest to China. As he pronounced at the dinner commemorating the Battle of Bunker Hill with President Tyler, Secretary of State Webster, and Josiah Quincy in attendance: "I have myself been honored with a commission of *peace*, and am entrusted with the duty of bringing nearer together, if possible, the civilization of the old and new worlds— the Asiatic, European and American continents."[134] Five years earlier, on the floor of the U.S. Congress, Cushing had similarly looked to China as a crucial point of commercial connection when exhorting his countrymen to rededicate themselves to an ongoing revolutionary struggle with Britain that had begun in 1776 and not yet ended.

Northwest Passages, Redemptive American Commerce, and the Road to Canton

Reflecting on the past dialectical struggles that had produced the "law of nations" in Europe, Cushing relished the progressive impact of a clash between the free-trading United States and colonizing European empires. For Cushing, the Revolutionary War had continued long after the Peace of Paris in Britain's ongoing contestation of U.S. westward expansion. Whereas England was a fellow Anglo-Saxon nation in the state of Christendom, it was also an imperial adversary working to frustrate the advance of revolutionary commerce across North America in the extended confederation of the United States. In May 1838, three months before Lieutenant Charles Wilkes embarked on the United States Exploring Expedition (1838– 42) to the Pacific Ocean, Cushing was on the floor of the House of Representatives, exhorting Congress to annex the Oregon Territory and exert outright possession. It was the only hope of saving the nation.[135]

Cushing focused the legal dispute over Oregon on an 1818 treaty agreement between Britain and the United States to jointly occupy the Pacific Northwest. Since 1818 the two countries had wrangled over the Northwest every decade. Cushing raised the alarm over this "joint occupation," pronouncing it a grave threat for exposing the United States to the tyranny of British monopolies. At stake was nothing less than "the whole of our fur trade; our whale fisheries; our intercourse with Asia, giving profitable employment to millions of our capital and to the population of all parts of country."[136] His congressional speech was published as a pamphlet the same year, and two years later he expanded his argument for the *North American Review* (January 1840) in the long review article "Discovery beyond the Rocky Mountains."[137]

To illustrate the nation's vulnerability, Cushing analogized the United States to China and India as potential colonial victims of Britain's devastating corporate imperialism. According to Cushing, Britain had cleverly avoided overt military aggression in the Northwest while waging insidious proxy assaults through its chartered monopoly companies. Cushing declared that, before losing its charter in 1834, the British East India Company had "conquer[ed] millions after millions" in the East Indies, all the while "throwing the blame of the fraud and violence by which the conquests were gained upon the servants" of the Company.[138] Cushing rips away the veil of deniability: "Whatever these great empire-seeking corporations do," they "profess to do, under their charters," amounting to "special authorization of the Government of which they are the creatures."[139] In 1838 Cushing singles out the Hudson's Bay Company as a formidable foe: "rich, strong, and rapacious, with immense territories, and numerous tribes of Indians subject to its rule; rising analogous in all these respects to the East India Company, and second only to that in power."[140] Raising the alarm, he exclaims, "The Hudson's Bay Company, as now organized," is "in itself a great foreign power, most injurious and hostile to [the citizens'] rights and interests. It is to America what the East India Company is to Asia."[141] He builds to a dramatic climax: "If the United States would retain the independence they have achieved, they must look well to the commercial enterprises of Great Britain. Other nations have pursued a course of conquest in the undisguised aim of military ambition: with her, it is commercial ambition supported by associated arts and arms."[142]

Building his case, Cushing marshals treaties, travel narratives, and diplomatic correspondence as evidence of the U.S. right to primary title over Oregon as derived from the Doctrine of Discovery, based on a consensus among "European nations" that "their settlements on this Continent" depended on "priority of discovery, followed in reasonable time by the actual occupation," thus conferring "exclusive jurisdiction and sovereignty."[143] In refuting England's appeal to joint occupancy, Cushing also cites the Adams-Onís Treaty (1819), eliciting testimony from his fellow Massachusetts representative John Quincy Adams, who had negotiated the treaty as the secretary of state under President Monroe. By that treaty, the United States had promised not to intervene in the revolutions unfolding in Mexico and the Central and South Americas. In exchange, Spain "ceded to the United States all her claims on this continent north of the latitude 42 degrees north," including, Cushing argued, the jointly occupied area of the Northwest.[144] (In the treaty, Spain also sold Florida to the United States for $5 million.) An 1824 convention with Russia further corroborates a border at the fifty-fourth parallel. Cushing thus asserts "a right of dominion" for the United States at least up to the forty-ninth parallel—a right "not to be shaken by any European Power."[145] Citing the voyages of Captain Robert Gray in the 1790s, the Louisiana Purchase, the Lewis and Clark expedition, and the Adams-Onís Treaty, Cushing demonstrates "discovery, purchase," and "exploration." Washington Irving provides him the last piece of the evidentiary puzzle for outright possession.

To prove the "formalities of occupation" that secure the nation's "rightful title," Cushing cites Irving's *Astoria; or, Anecdotes of an Enterprise beyond the Rocky Mountains* (1836) as if it were reporting events in the present rather than a retrospective account of twenty years before.[146] In Cushing's words, "The narrative [*Astoria*], by Washington Irving, of that magnificent undertaking, belongs to the classic literature of the world, combining the truth of history with the stirring interest of romance."[147] Washington Irving's *Astoria* is an odd book, mashing up several genres in an attempt to dramatize an entrepreneurial failure of John Jacob Astor, whose fortunes in fur trading, shipbuilding, and opium trading established him as one of the wealthiest men of the early nineteenth-century United States.[148] Astor had first ventured to China in the 1790s, at the same time as his American competitors, the Perkins brothers and Stephen Girard. Astor's construction of Fort Astoria on the Columbia River was an expensive side project that began in 1808 after he chartered the American Fur Company in the state of New York with $1 million of his personal fortune. The Pacific Fur Company followed the next year. Cushing presents Astor's companies as the David to the imperial Goliath of Britain's corrupt corporate monopolies. The quest to build Fort Astoria entailed three simultaneous expeditions, two by sea and one by land. Astor lured four clerks from the British North West Company and planned to establish a "line of trading posts along the Missouri" culminating in a "chief trading house or mart" at the mouth of the Columbia River that would serve as a relay point in Pacific commerce to Canton's "great mart for peltries" and with the Russian Fur Company.[149] Irving's *Astoria* chronicles the arduous establishment and brief history of the resulting trading house that stood with a U.S. flag from June 1810 to December 1813. The venture itself was a fiscal failure, doomed when the partners, whom Astor had lured away to begin with, ultimately double-crossed him in an anticlimactic sale of the three-year-old Astoria at a cut-rate price to the rival North West Company in the middle of the War of 1812. In the first edition of *Astoria*, this "snug commercial arrangement" "forestalls" the grand finale of a battle scene or a national victory for the United States in Astoria.[150] By enlisting Irving to write the book, Astor seemed intent on establishing a national literary commemoration of his fur-trading enterprise. The challenge to Irving and his nephew was to align the potentially errant transnational currents of Astor's enterprise in a narrative promoting national U.S. identity. The genre of national biography gave them the appropriate frame.

In emphasizing the national significance of Astoria, both Irving and Cushing characterize *Astoria* as John Jacob Astor's national biography. His state-chartered and free-trading companies are extensions of Astor himself as Cushing organizes vastly complex, global economic networks of finance capital into a romance of Manifest Destiny. In the book's 1836 introduction, Irving acknowledges the narrative's "somewhat disjointed nature," before assuring his reader that the book's disparate "facts . . . will prove to be linked and banded together by one grand scheme, devised and conducted by a master spirit."[151] In his 1838 House speech, Cushing also equates Astor's "own interests to those of the United States" in the "establishment of Astoria."[152] Thus, Astor becomes "fully aware of the great value of Oregon country" when he "extensively engaged in the fur trade south and west of the Lakes" in "a line of trade to be carried across the continent" and "thence communicating directly with China.[153] With Astor as his national hero and *Astoria* as a "classic literature of the world," Cushing expounds for Congress the "truth of history" in Irving's "stirring interest of romance."[154]

But Cushing was playing fast and loose with the facts in his push for annexation. For example, he conjures a fantastical abundance of beaver pelts waiting to be harvested.[155] Alas, by 1838 the fur trade had for years been in steep decline, as Samuel Wells Williams noted in an article published in the *Chinese Repository* in April 1835.[156] Cushing also downplays the long history of collaboration between U.S. companies and British monopolies. In fact, after Astoria fell, the Boston-based and Massachusetts-incorporated Perkins & Company profited monetarily while strengthening its transpacific network of trade. This is because in order to get furs to Canton, the British Northwest Company needed to work around the monopoly of the British East India Company. By November 1824, "Perkins & Co. had made over $90,000 profit on their business with the Northwest Company, and that figure did not include the 5 percent commissions on sales in China or America."[157]

Facts aside, Cushing's speech showcases the ambivalent status of Britain in his national romance of confederated revolutionary commerce. After ratcheting up the commercial tensions between Britain and the United States—between Britain's imperialistic monopolies and the free-trade companies of the United States as characterized by Astor—he then settles the antagonism in a shared racial heritage of Christianity progressing in the postcolonial form of a democratic republic. Cushing "honor[s] the Anglo-Norman race; its energy perseverance, love of liberty, courage, and civilization; its vigor and steadiness of mind, its masculinities of moral and physical organization," and asserts, "We [English and Americans] are the same stock. Its eminent traits are developed in our growth and prosperity as colonies and as independent States."[158] In light of this, if the United States acquiesced to the imperial aggression of British monopolies, it would hurt the Anglo-Saxon race itself. He draws his speech to a close with this warning: England "*must not encroach*. Whilst our territorial expansion is restricted to this continent, hers must be excluded from it. There can be no other condition of harmony between her and us. We are not suns that may culminate together in the same sky."[159] He concludes:

> The world is wide enough for England and for us. We have much to gain by a cordial
> intercourse, conducted as becomes nations of the same blood and the same tongue,
> each at the head of civilization in its proper hemisphere; much to hazard, by practic-
> ing or suffering encroachments on either side. Off-shoots of that dominant race,
> which starting from the mountains of Caucasus, has proceeded in opposite directions,
> east and west, encircling the globe, if we are to confront each other on the adverse
> shores of Asia and of America, there let us meet in confident good-will, imbued with
> that just consciousness of each other's power, and that mutual respect for each other's
> rights, which are the only sure foundation of stable peace.[160]

In the 1820s, Cushing had embraced the philosophy of the Monroe Doctrine to encourage interracial affiliation with American revolutionaries in promoting free trade that could stand up to Britain and other European empires. But in the 1830s and 1840s, Cushing reformulated his sense of Anglo-American racial affiliation to distinguish the United States from "England" in dramatizing a world-historical contest for commercial influence. Cushing's rallying cry to nationalize territory of the Northwest justified gunboat diplomacy in China and extraterritorial projection of U.S. power to protect rights of free trade.

After returning to Massachusetts from his diplomatic mission to China, Cushing turned his attention to Mexico and sang the praises of the "White man" for civilizing the colored world.[161] His writings became more racialist and racist as he wrote for the *United States Magazine and Democratic Review* to support the U.S. war on Mexico (1846) in the name of Christianity and commerce, crediting revolutionary principles of free trade to an evolving Anglo-Saxonism that had inspirited the historical development of the United States. In the article "Mexico" (June 1846), a review of M. Duflot de Mofras, *Exploration du Territoire de l'Orégon, des Californies, et de la Mer Vermeille* (1833–34), Cushing compares and contrasts Mexico and the United States as two contrasting cases of postcolonial nations adopting a national constitution at the conclusion of a revolutionary war. Cushing first praises the "great virtue of ONE MAN [George Washington] who saved us from the same train of events which have occurred in Mexico."[162] Cushing then pushes his explanation into openly racialist discourse, asserting that "throughout the world, the spectacle is everywhere the same, of the whiter race ruling the less white, through all gradations of color, from the fairest European down to the darkest African. On every throne of Europe, (except Turkey,) there sits a sovereign of Norman or Teutonic lineage."[163] He projects the truism of light over dark into China, and back to "America" where "the aboriginal Red man and the imported Black Man, are everywhere subject to the White man."[164] Looking at Mexico's "population . . . of seven million human beings," he estimates six million as "Indians or half-breeds."[165] With the future of "a free representative Democracy" in doubt, he advocates going to war with Mexico for the benefit of its people.[166] Attaining its Manifest Destiny, the United States would become the crossroad of traffic between Europe and Asia and the supervisor of the world's new confederated states of Christendom.

Rereading Extraterritoriality in the Chinese Repository

Cushing's grand narratives aside, his assertions that China's concession was "absolute and unqualified" supported the U.S. companies such as Russell & Company that were profiting from opium smuggling. However, there are alternative ways of reading the Treaty of Wanghia. In fact, Cushing's interpretation went against the official and prevailing U.S. policy of enforcing Article 33 that banned opium smuggling and the use of the American flag to hide illegal activities.

In 1842 as the war wound down to an end, U.S. commodore Lawrence Kearny of the U.S. East India Squadron cruised up along the Pearl River Delta to take a firm and proactive stand against opium smugglers as he signaled protection of U.S. citizens. In a dispatch to the secretary of the navy, Kearny described "the first object of the present cruise of this squadron" as that of "punish[ing] the smuggling of opium on the coast of China by American citizens or any others should it be attempted under the American flag."[167] In April 1842 Kearny "arrested the opium clipper ship *Ariel*, warning other American vessels against engaging in the traffic."[168] He even reprimanded U.S. consul James P. Sturgis (1791–1851), one of the several Sturgis brothers in the China trade, for ignoring the use of the American flag to camouflage the transport of British opium.[169] Kearny's attempts did not have much impact. Back in Washington, DC, it was an open secret that U.S. consuls prioritized commercial self-interest over diplomatic duty. Secretary of State Hugh Swinton Legaré, Webster's successor to the office, even directed Cushing in a letter (12 June 1843) to reprimand Sturgis's successor as the U.S. consul at Canton, Paul S. Forbes (the younger cousin of John Murray and Robert Bennet Forbes), who is "likely to be associated in business with a firm avowedly engaged in the opium trade."[170]

Article 33 prohibiting opium smuggling appears in the treaty in large part due to the efforts of U.S. missionaries such Dr. Rev. Peter Parker, Rev. Elijah Bridgman, and Samuel Wells Williams, who had helped Cushing communicate with the imperial commissioner Kíying during negotiations and afterward print the treaty. Bridgman had accompanied Commodore Kearny up the Pearl River and reported on it in the *Chinese Repository*.[171] Bridgman and Williams had spent decades registering the social effects and commercial impact of opium, ultimately rationalizing its traffic as part of divine plan that they could not understand for the apparent misery it entailed. Nevertheless, they condemned its smuggling and regarded it as the major reason behind the war.

In an article published in the *Chinese Repository* relating to the Treaty of Wanghia, one can sense skepticism regarding Cushing's interpretation of extraterritoriality and criticism of his inability to understand Chinese. Arriving in China, Cushing tried to take control over the language through which negotiations would transpire. His early writings in the *North American Review* showcase impressive facility with European languages. But faced with Chinese, he opted to learn Manchu. His resulting elementary knowledge was of little practical use. However, he embraced Manchu as a means of controlling China's diplomatic engagement—at least this is the implication of one of his two articles that appeared in the *Chinese Repository*. In "Language of Communication between Chinese and Europeans" (June 1844), he describes Manchu as China's equivalent of classical Greek and Latin, which had molded the "nations of Christendom" into a united linguistic front now facing an un-neighborly China whose "negligence" in not learning "any languages of Europe" (except some Russian), had left them with an uneducated and "corrupt jargon" of business English ("pidgin English") that Cushing deems "utterly useless for the higher objects of public business."[172] He then laments that one year spent studying Chinese is of not much use, while three years of effort yield only a very basic ability. Facing the linguistic summit of Mandarin, Cushing impugns it as a mere dialect. He concludes that Chinese is "the most imperfect, clumsy, and awkward, of all the various instruments ever devised by man for the communication of thought."[173] Manchu is the noble alternative. It has an alphabet, nominal case structures to denote genderless nouns, "tenses, modes and conjugations" for verbs, and prepositions and conjunctions.[174] He notes that it is the hereditary language of both the emperor and Kíying.

In their writings, Cushing, Bridgman, and Williams similarly justified their authority on the basis of having read centuries of scholarship. It is striking then that in the first edition of *The Middle Kingdom* (1848) Williams disagreed with Cushing's estimation of Manchu. Drawing on his experience, Williams judges the Chinese language of Mandarin as "better fitted than any other language for becoming a universal medium of communication," especially for having already "become so to a much greater extent than any other."[175] He allays the fear of difficulty for those who are willing to commit to "much hard study."[176] Chinese was not for dilettantes. Judging by the index of the *Chinese Repository* (1851), Williams did not think very highly of Cushing's reviews. He put his article on Manchu under the fourteenth heading of "Foreign Relations" rather than the more scholarly ninth heading "Language, Literature, &c."

Bridgman worked much more closely with Cushing than Williams but kept the controversies over opium visible in the *Chinese Repository*. From September 1844 through December 1845, as the treaty went back to the United States, moved through Senate ratification, and made its way back to China, Bridgman contributed several articles that edited official documents to narrate Cushing's arrival, introductory address, and subsequent negotiations of the treaty.[177] To compose this "drama of diplomatic intercourse," the editor explains having selected "essential parts of Mr. Cushing's correspondence with the Chinese government" in order to enable "our readers to form their own opinions of the policy adopted."[178] Editorial annotations criticize Cushing's use of Manchu, noting, for example: "We see no good reason for deviating, as Mr. Cushing has done, from the usual orthography of Kíying's name. *Tsiyeng* may possibly represent the Manchu orthography better than the usual form, but it does not conform so nearly to the Chinese."[179] In this editorial "We," one assumes Bridgman is speaking for other collaborators who composed the *Chinese Repository*. He continues by contesting Cushing's term for the "United States," writing, "We may here remark that we do not like the term, *Ho chung kwoh* [合衆國; Hézhòngguó], which his excellency [Cushing] adopted for the United States, nor that he has used for the president [*sic*]. To both there are, in our opinion, strong objections; but we need not, at least for the present, enter on their discussion."[180]

The nature of these "strong objections" is implied in an earlier January 1845 issue of the *Chinese Repository* that includes either Bridgman's or Rev. Walter Medhurst's translation into English of the Chinese version of the treaty. In this version,

Article 33 is subtly but significantly different than the Senate-ratified version cited earlier in this chapter. It reads: "Article 33. All people of the United States who presume to take upon themselves to go to other ports, where no custom-house has been opened, and privately carry on trade, smuggle and evade the duties, or introduce opium and other prohibited articles in China, the Chinese local officers may themselves adjudicate it and punish them. The government or people of the United States must not afford the least protection. If vessels of another country assume the flag of the United States, and carry on illegal trade, the United States must take measures for prohibiting and preventing it."[181] This sounds less like Cushing and much more like Commodore Kearny, who had tried to stop opium smuggling. The "Journal of Occurrences" of the same issue then considers the treaty's clumsy translation of the "United States" into Chinese. The article speaks in an editorial "we" to say:

> The translator [Bridgman or Medhurst] of the second treaty, in a note, has the follow-ing remarks: "in the 34 articles [of the 1844 treaty], the United States are designated as *Hoh Chung Kwoh*, the literal meaning of which characters is either, 'the united all nation,' or 'the union of all nations;' they do not, however, in any sense express the 'United States.' Throughout the English treaty, when wishing to point out other na-tions, the character *kwoh* is used, meaning a nation; which character is also used in the English treaty, when designating England as a nation, being the same as the last character of the national designation of the United States of America. In the 34th article the character *kwoh* is used to express each state." We wish the translator would, at his convenience, give us the proper characters for the "United States of America," which will oblige us very much.[182]

There is ambiguity as to whom the "we" exactly refers and as to the identity of the translator. However, it is clear that Cushing's clumsy attempts to use Manchu led to awkward translations. The writer of this article may be Elijah Bridgman's cousin James R. Bridgman of the ABCFM, who had begun working on the *Chi-nese Repository* earlier in the year and would take the editorial reins when Elijah relocated to Shanghai in May 1847 and before Williams returned from the United States. In effect, James (if it is him) is quoting either his uncle's or Rev. Med-hurst's criticism of Cushing. Bridgman would have probably preferred the phrase 美理哥合省國 (Měi lǐ gē hé shěng guó) that he used in his *Brief Account of the United States* (美理哥合省國志略; 1837). As the article mentions, *Ho chung kwoh* (合省國) would be a confusing abbreviation, meaning literally "a country of joined provinces," and offering little to differentiate "the United States" from "the United Kingdom."

處合得罪事中人有嗣罰有准查該
港眾但等國由後貨影開照商
口國須官例中入射俟該收
聽現存偏兩捉國中官夾出執
其與護得拿罪地訟民帶售船一
船中致其審合方交人情免進面
隻國敗平訊官涉與事其口行
往訂爭秉照國捉事合經重查文
來明端公本民拿件眾海納聽別
貿和斷國人審中國開稅符口
易好結例由訊國民查銷合海
倘五不治領照民人出若即關

and shall also certify the facts to the officers of customs of the other ports; all which being done, on the arrival in port of the vessel in which the goods are laden, and every thing being found on examination there to correspond, she shall be permitted to break bulk and land the said goods, without being subject to the payment of any additional duty thereon.   But if on such examination, the superintendent of customs shall detect any fraud on the revenue in the case, then the goods shall be subject to forfeiture and confiscation to the Chinese government.

ART. XXI.   Subjects of China who may be guilty of any criminal act towards citizens of the United States shall be arrested and punished by the Chinese authorities according to the laws of China.   And citizens of the United States who may commit any crime in China, shall be subject to be tried and punished only by the consul or other public functionary of the United States thereto authorized according to the laws of the United States. And in order to the prevention of all controversy and disaffection, justice shall be equitably and impartially administered on both sides.

ART. XXII.   Relations of peace and amity between the Unied States and China being established by this treaty, and the vessels of the United States being admitted to trade, freely to and from the five ports of China open to fo-

"Article XXI of the Treaty of Wanghia." [Elijah Bridgman], "Treaty between the United States and the Chinese Ta Tsing Empire, . . . by their excellencies Caleb Cushing and Kiying, in Chinese and English," *Chinese Repository* 14.12 (December 1845): 573.

Finally, consider again the language of Article 21. In December 1845 the *Chinese Repository* printed the treaty with the final U.S. Senate version in English underneath the Chinese version. The vertical juxtaposition on the same page highlights the dialogic quality of the text.[183] Rereading the *Chinese Repository* demonstrates that the Chinese version of the treaty does not concede extraterritorial exception of Chinese law by virtue of U.S. citizenship or presume the maintenance of rights guaranteed by the United States to its citizens. The compounded ambiguities of translation highlight the cultural specificity of legal authority rather than the universal legitimacy of "rights" framed in the U.S. Constitution.[184]

As the treaty appears in the *Chinese Repository*, the principle of extraterritoriality is qualified and not absolute. China arguably oversees the application of foreign law on its territory by virtue of it being a sovereign state—an assumption maintained in both the Chinese version and Bridgman's translation of it.[185] As noted, the editorial "we" of the *Chinese Repository* criticized the treaty's awkward naming of the "United States." Further confusion comes with the Chinese phrase "ben guo" (本國; Běnguó) (tenth column of text from the right of the page)—suggesting "this country's" law—an even vaguer phrase than *Ho chung kwoh* (合衆國; Hézhòngguó). Importantly, the Chinese version of Article 21 makes no categorical guarantee of U.S. legal extraterritoriality, and it is arguably ambiguous whose laws (ours or theirs) would be applicable in particular cases that would arise.

Bridgman's (or Medhurst's) January 1845 translation of the Chinese version renders Article 21 like this: "Art. 21. Hereafter should any Chinese have any quarrels, disputes, or get mutually involved with the people of the United States, the Chinese will be seized and examined by the Chinese local officers, and will be punished according to the laws of China.—The people of the United States shall be seized and examined by the consuls and other officers, and will be punished according to the law of their country; but it is requisite that both should in justice and integrity divide the question, and neither side cherish partiality, which would lead to quarrels."[186] This version ties any application of foreign laws in China to pursuit of "justice and integrity" based in cooperation between Chinese and American authorities. There is no categorical guarantee of an individual's rights by virtue of citizenship outside of this shared sense of "justice and integrity." The Chinese version and Bridgman's (or Medhurst's) translation embed adjudication in the jurisdiction of China, where the cross-application of Chinese and U.S. ("the people's" or "this country's") laws happens in a spirit of "justice and integrity." It seems more accurate to read Article 21 as China's pledge to afford courtesies of extraterritorial consideration in ways to which Eileen Scully draws our attention.[187] Such nuance did not merely escape Cushing's attention. He was determined to erase it.

Beyond Cushing's bold interpretation as U.S. attorney general in 1855, his subsequent career holds little insight into the legacy of the treaty he negotiated in China. As he pursued the war on Mexico, he honored his Chinese counterpart "in the best New England tradition, as the newest family vessel was christened the *Ke ying*."[188] Nevertheless, Cushing's formulation of "absolute and unqualified" extraterritoriality would endure as Bridgman and Williams stayed on in China to document the increase in opium traffic that led to a Second Opium War (1856–60).

Coda: Memorializing Kíying in The Middle Kingdom

When Dr. Rev. Parker returned to the United States in 1856, Williams replaced him as the secretary of the U.S. Legation. He went on to serve many ministers who followed Cushing, including those responsible for the Treaty of Tianjin (1858), the Peking Convention (1860), and the Burlingame Treaty (1868), which chapter 7 considers in more detail. Over these decades, Williams dealt with the issue of extraterritoriality many times.

Williams rejected both the racial exclusivity of Cushing's Christendom and his presumptive use of Manchu to relegate China as a barbaric nation beyond the law of nations. As a diplomat in the service of the U.S. Department of State, Williams accepted the characterization of China conceding extraterritoriality so as to use it as a strategic point of reference in negotiations. He repeatedly asserted that China had only itself to blame as its imperial administrators had misjudged the capabilities of Britain. However, Williams saw great danger in dismissing China's ruling government as Cushing had in asserting that extraterritoriality in China was absolute and unqualified. As a missionary, Williams hoped to foster trust between China and the United States—trust that depended on respecting China as a peer nation and working through issues regarding international adjudication in ways that depended on mutually constructive qualifications and courtesies.

Williams also understood that in exacting these concessions, Western nations had contributed to eroding imperial authority at Peking. In the revised *Middle Kingdom* (1883), he linked invasive assertions of extraterritoriality by Western powers to the Taiping Rebellion and uprisings elsewhere in China, noting that after the First Opium War the Chinese, "much against their will," had "been forced into political relations with Europe and America, and in a measure deprived of their independence under the guise of treaties which erected an *imperium in imperio* in their borders."[189] While criticizing China for its ignorance "of the real meaning of these principles of ex-territoriality," he also laments a Western diplomatic legacy in which China's rulers "were tied down to observe [principles of extraterritoriality], and found themselves within a few years humbled before those of their own subjects who had begun to look to foreigners for protection."[190]

Williams wrestled with how best to interrelate the jurisdictions of China and Western nations. His pursuit of extraterritorial printing never questioned China's territorial sovereignty. Most importantly, Williams never validated Cushing's assertion that China's concession was absolute and unqualified.[191] In the first edition of the *Middle Kingdom* (1848), he stiffly credits Cushing with having effectively negotiated the Treaty of Wanghia but does not mention extraterritoriality when summarizing it.[192] Reflecting on the general effect of the British, American, and French treaties in the *Middle Kingdom* (1848), he offers a bleak description: "The opium trade, for this dark feature everywhere forces itself into the prospect, was also extending, and opium schooners plying up and down the coast, and lying on the outside limits of every port to deliver the drug."[193] He predicts that intensifying opium traffic and the marshaling of British troops in Hong Kong are "more likely than anything else to give rise to collision," lamenting that "there are so many motives operating to start another war with China."[194] Williams was correct.

The Second Opium War started in 1856 after Chinese authorities seized a ship called the *Arrow* that was illegally flying the British flag to cloak its transport of contraband on the Pearl River. British authorities in Hong Kong used the occasion to press for access to the city of Guangzhou as promised in the 1842 treaty. Hostilities intensified as city residents set fire to the foreign factories in Canton. In 1883 Williams recalls the events that led to the war with the allied powers of Britain and France (Russia and the United States initially maintained neutrality). The Treaty of Tianjin and the Peking Convention ended this second war, but Williams decried the legalization of opium that followed from tariff agreements appended to the treaty, describing them as exemplifying "the inherent wrong of the principle of ex-territoriality."[195] The treaty also intensified gunboat diplomacy as China's "every infraction" of trade agreements became a potential "*casus belli*" and effective diplomacy depended on the difficult and unlikely precondition of bringing the treaty powers back together for negotiations.[196] He rues extraterritoriality for enabling "a systematic violation of the Chinese laws against opium" that "cannot be excused."[197]

Williams's disagreements with Cushing register poignantly in the changing terms by which Williams portrays Kíying in the first and final editions of *The Middle Kingdom* (1848; 1883). After Cushing's departure, Kíying negotiated a treaty with the French. He then became the governor of Kwangtung and Kwangsi and faced discontent from Guangzhou's residents who were dispirited by the increasing opium traffic and angry that foreigners would now be allowed to enter the city.[198] In the 1848 edition, Williams overlooks any social unrest in praising Kíying as a rational and friendly intercultural negotiator who, despite the opium problem, promised to continue opening China for printing and preaching Christianity. Williams honored him by featuring his portrait as the frontispiece to volume 1; the complementary frontispiece of volume 2 was the portrait of Rev. David Abeel, who had arrived with Bridgman as one of the first two U.S. missionaries to China.

Williams's hopeful gesture was based on a misunderstanding of Kíying's difficult position as a negotiator. Williams explains that Kíying's portrait was "engraved from a native painting" owned by J. R. Peters Jr., the young civil engineer who served as an attaché to Cushing and gathered a collection for a Chinese museum that he exhibited in Boston, Philadelphia, and New York City, before P. T. Barnum

"Kíying, Imperial Commissioner." His signature in Manchu. Frontispiece to S. Williams, *The Middle Kingdom* (1848).

purchased it in 1850.[199] Over Kíying's right shoulder are five Chinese characters 詩書結靜緣 (Shīshū jié jìng yuán) that conclude the well-known short poem 山水畫 (shān shuǐ huà)—literally, "mountain," "water," "painting," or, "landscape painting"—by the renowned poet, scholar, and painter Táng Yín (唐寅; or 唐伯虎, Tángbóhǔ; 1470–1524), active during the Ming Dynasty. In sequence the characters can literally mean a few things, such as: "poem," "book," "to form" (verb), "quiet," "connection" (a complicated word regarding the relational dimensions of one's identity as it changes over time). Translating the five characters as a phrase out of the context of Tang Yin's complete poem is doomed to fail. Nevertheless, using the

"Portrait of Rev. D. Abeel." His signature underneath. Frontispiece
to S. Williams, *The Middle Kingdom* (1848).

portrait as a frontispiece, Williams seems to be appropriating the phrase to characterize Kíying as an exemplary scholar whose contemplative engagement of literary
works has prepared him to forge enduring cross-cultural bonds with like-minded
missionaries such as Abeel, Bridgman, and Williams.[200]

Williams's homage to Kíying aside, Kíying's policy of pacification ultimately
failed. Initial compromises with Britain, the United States, France, and Russia led
to more demands and a second more devastating war. When in 1858 the Imperial
Court sent Kíying to the northern port city of Tianjin, it expected him to use the
rapport that he had established with Britain in the 1840s. However, Thomas Francis Wade, the British mission secretary and translator to Lord Elgin, embarrassed
Kíying and discredited him by confronting him with his memorial "Ch'i-ying's
Method for Handling the Barbarians, 1844" retrieved from the Canton archives. In

the memorial to the emperor, Kíying had outlined a strategy of feigning friendship with his Western counterparts in order to manipulate and placate them.[201] In Wade's translation, Kíying explains to the emperor that the "barbarians" insist on exchanging small gifts and that "on the application of the Italians, English, Americans, and French, your slave has presented them with a copy of his insignificant portrait."[202] The British negotiators confronted Kíying with the document, disavowed their trust in him, and thus discredited him among the other Chinese negotiators. When Kíying returned to Peking, he was sentenced to death.

The 1883 edition of *The Middle Kingdom* suggests Williams's deep disappointment in Kíying's execution. Williams recalls his reunion with the elderly Kíying in Tianjin in the spring of 1858, describing him as having "grown old and infirm and deaf," while retaining "the lineaments as given in the portrait in the 'Middle Kingdom'" of 1848.[203] Over the course of their few days' conversation, Williams informed Kíying that he had "published a portrait of him in the 'Middle Kingdom' from the daguerreotype taken by [George R.] West," the official artist of the Cushing embassy.[204] Kíying "expressed no little anxiety to see it," and Williams promises "to try and get him a copy."[205] Kíying first thought that the book to which Williams referred was in Chinese and, according to Williams, "showed much pleasure in hearing" otherwise, no doubt excited "that his name and features were known in America." Next, "he made us each take a mouthful from his chop-sticks, and then let us go in peace, evidently gratified with the visit."[206] This was their last meeting. Williams records in his diary that Kíying suddenly "left for the capital" one morning, "having been ordered by the court to return there immediately," adding ominously "but no one tells us the reason."[207] Williams later learned that upon his return to Peking, Kíying received "the silken cord" "from the emperor's hand" and was "tenderly allowed to strangle himself in lieu of going out to meet the executioner."[208]

In pursuing a policy of appeasement with Pottinger, Cushing, and the French legation in the 1840s, Kíying made compromises that cost him his life in 1858. His tactic of appeasing the foreigners while reassuring the emperor that he was in fact manipulating these foreigners stranded Kíying between imperial authorities in Peking and Western negotiators. In Tianjin the walls closed in on him as he faced evidence of having broken sacrosanct rules of diplomatic protocol and portraiture. The scholar of fine arts Yeewan Koon explains that only the emperor was deemed worthy of having his likeness taken. Kíying, in his capacity as an imperial commissioner, had crossed a line by gifting his own portrait to Pottinger and Cushing.[209] Reading Williams's account with this in mind, it makes sense that Kíying was extremely "anxious" to learn from Williams that his portrait was circulating so prominently and widely in *The Middle Kingdom*. He may have been feigning friendship as he fed Williams with his chopsticks, quietly resigned that it was only a matter of time before copies reached the Imperial Court.

In the final edition of *The Middle Kingdom*, published two decades after Kíying's death, Williams replaced the two volumes' frontispieces. Volume 1 begins with a Chinese painting of the "Worship of the Emperor at the Temple of Heaven" and volume 2 with a Chinese drawing of the "Signing of the Treaty of Peking" (1860). Kíying's portrait appears in the body of the text near the end of volume 2. It seems a melancholic memorial as Williams concludes that Kíying's "prominence abroad, arising from his connection with the Nanking treaty, was no criterion of his influence at home or of the loss to the government by his death."[210] Noticeably absent is mention of Cushing, the Treaty of Wanghia, or the boast of having won concession of absolute and unqualified extraterritoriality from China after the First Opium War.

Extraterritorial Burial and the Visual Aesthetics of Free-Trade Imperialism in Commodore Matthew Perry's *Narrative of the Expedition of an American Squadron to the China Seas and Japan* (1856)

There was a time when the ancient laws of your imperial majesty's government were first made. . . . About the same time America, which is sometimes called the New World, was first discovered and settled by the Europeans. For a long time there were a few people, and they were poor. They have now become quite numerous; their commerce is very extensive; and they think that if your imperial majesty were so far to change the ancient laws as to allow a free trade between the two countries it would be extremely beneficial to both.

PRESIDENT MILLARD FILLMORE in a Letter to His Imperial Majesty, the Emperor of Japan, written by Secretary of State Edward Everett in 1853, and delivered by Commodore Matthew C. Perry in 1854

In the age of the sail when a sailor died at sea, his fellow shipmates sewed his body into a weighted canvas hammock and dropped him into the ocean. For those who mourned, this watery grave seemed cold comfort as the visual monotony of seemingly limitless sea horizons matched unfathomable oceanic depths.[1] A headstone at least fixed a point of reference for those who grieved. Land burial was also loaded with political implications that are apparent in the textual representation of extraterritorial burial and the subsequent opportunity for national memorialization it afforded. Adapting what Hester Blum calls the "imaginative geography of burial," this chapter considers the national ideology of free-trade imperialism that pervades burial scenes situated in China and Japan in the small marvel of print publication, the multivolume *Narrative of the Expedition of an American Squadron to the China Seas and Japan, performed in the years 1852, 1853, and 1854, under the Command of Commodore M. C. Perry, United States Navy by the Order of the Government of the United States, Compiled from the original notes and journals of the Commodore Perry and his officers, at his request and under his supervision* (1856).[2]

As the title implies, *Narrative of the Expedition* portrays the voyage to Japan as an adventure of national commercial development, establishing influence in the

Pacific and inspiring further frontier development in North America. Commodore Matthew C. Perry (1794–1858) made two trips to Japan. The first lasted eight days in July 1853 when he established diplomatic contact by delivering a letter of peace and friendship to the emperor of Japan from the U.S. president Millard Fillmore. The letter—written by Secretary of State Edward Everett—outlined the continental breadth of the United States with much more accuracy than President Tyler had in his letter to the emperor of China a decade earlier. As a result of the war on Mexico (1846–48), "the United States of America" did indeed reach "from ocean to ocean" and, with the acquisition of the "Territory of Oregon and State of California," U.S. steamships could "go from California to Japan in eighteen days."[3]

Perry also issued an ultimatum. In one year's time he would return. Japan could then negotiate peacefully or defend against a steam-powered U.S. naval squadron. Perry spent the intervening months in Macao organizing a massive amount of data that would become the *Narrative*. He returned in February 1854 with a larger squadron and a team of translators led by Samuel Wells Williams. They negotiated for four months to produce the Convention of Kanagawa and its additional regula-tions. By the year's end, Perry was in New York City working with Rev. Francis L. Hawks to write and compile the congressionally funded *Narrative*.[4] Relishing the imperial implications of connecting the Far East and Far West and realigning com-mercial geography, Perry gushed: "With our territory spreading from ocean to ocean, and placed midway between Europe and Asia, it seemed that we might with propriety apply to ourselves the name by which China had loved to designate her-self, and deem that we were, in truth, 'the Middle Kingdom.' "[5]

In the course of the three-year expedition, dozens of American sailors died from illness and accidents. According to the *Narrative*, it seems that by the 1850s steam technologies had made land burial easier if not always convenient.[6] Steam-powered ships were less reliant on wind in moving through tricky straits and navigating treacherous coastlines. Steamers could tow wind-dependent clippers and move peo-ple and goods more rapidly, agilely, and with greater reliability. Steam also made it easier to outrun pirates.[7] The improved reliability of shipping networks meant that those who became critically ill on a voyage could be dropped off at major ports to receive medical care or to convalesce. Those who died could be more easily buried on the land. For the family and friends of the departed, it became more feasible to visit the gravesite and even to disinter the body for reburial back home. Take, for example, the naval officer Lieutenant Henry George Preble, who voyaged to Can-ton in the spring of 1853 to join Perry. He writes to his wife of attempting to visit her uncle's grave on the island of Madeira. He could not find it but reassured her that "the stranger's grave yard is a pretty place and is planted with cypress trees," although it had "few monuments or headstones" to "tell the brief history of its tenants."[8] A month later in June 1853, Preble reported that the sixteen-year-old son of his ship captain had died in the Atlantic Ocean off the coast of Africa, a few hours from Prince's Island (part of contemporary São Tomé and Príncipe). Preble finds a measure of reassurance that the boy was buried amid "beautiful and picturesque" surroundings that presented a "picture of living tropical luxuriance."[9] They encased his body in lead so that "it [could] at some future time be removed to the U.S."[10]

Perry and Hawk's *Narrative* similarly memorializes the dead with sentimentally evocative woodcut tailpieces and several grand landscape scenes, but the memorials are for a national audience rather than members of any specific family. The point of illustrating these graves is not to facilitate the eventual repatriation of those buried. Rather, the descriptions enjoin readers to appreciate the enduring sacrifice of American dead on foreign shores. This chapter focuses on the gravesites in Macao (China) and the Japanese sites of Yoku-hama (Yokohama), Simoda (Shimoda), and Hakodadi (Hakodate) where the crew of the East Asia Squadron performed "the melancholy duty" of burying a few Americans and erecting gravestones.[11] For example the *Narrative*'s last illustration, appearing on the final page after the printed text and before the volume's index, depicts two sailors standing together in casual but somber contemplation of two large cenotaphs. A man with crossed arms looks directly at a grave, while his companion, with pocketed hands, looks at his friend, their posture suggesting a quiet, reflective intimacy.

In the context of Perry's gunboat diplomacy, there is undoubtedly a political significance to the ways that the *Narrative*'s gravesites pull readers' interwoven sense of national identity and sacrifice beyond the shores of the United States. Such depictions recall the melancholic sentiments with which Benedict Anderson begins *Imagined Communities* and suggest that all American readers (whether in Salem or Philadelphia, New Orleans or Baltimore) could contemplate with the two soldiers the supreme sacrifice on behalf of the nation. The lack of any overt Christian symbols—no crosses or prayer books, for example—suggests that readers would register this loss as fellow citizens of an enduring national American community, "moving calendrically through homogeneous empty time."[12] However, this is not a tomb for an unknown soldier in Washington, DC, but in a treaty port of Japan. We can only conjecture what the sailors are thinking, but *where* they are thinking is especially significant. Literally they are in Hakadadi (Hakodate), one of the three ports that Perry opened. For centuries previous, Japan had barred all foreigners from Japan, with the exception of the Dutch who were quarantined in the small island enclave of Dejima offshore from the southern port city of Nagasaki, on the southern tip of the island Kyushu. The American graves defy this prohibition through the disarmingly poignant appeal for respectful treatment of the dead in a Christian burial. Other images in the *Narrative* are more complicated

ROBERTS.S.

W. Heine, "Graves of American Dead in Japan." Because there are two graves, this is probably at Hakodate. Woodcut tailpiece. Hawks, *Narrative of the Expedition of an American Squadron to the China Seas and Japan*, p. 513.

than this vignette. In them American graves appear in larger landscape configurations that are specifically American in their grammar of composition as they allegorize a national romance of free trade.

These illustrations complement the *Narrative*'s grand narrative that boldly trum-
pets the broad historical significance of the mission. The book's introduction is a
prime exercise in the epic vault of empire's westward course—*translatio imperii et
studii*—and the absorptive force of dialectical progression that assimilates or con-
stellates cultural difference into imperial order. As the reader, we are assumed to
partake in the "curiosity of Christendom" regarding the "self-isolated Kingdom"
(Tokugawa) of Japan.[13] The narrator calibrates this curiosity in relation to physical
geography, commerce, navigation, ethnology, and commerce, thus setting up the
expedition as a foray into *terra incognita*. There is definite pride in being "the first"
nation to effect a treaty with Japan in regard to commerce.[14] As with Caleb Cushing

in 1844, this linkage of Christianity and commerce was the civilizationist premise of appreciating the rising United States by distinguishing it from Asia's ancient empires. Hawks and Perry present a long cyclical history of Western empire beginning in 1295 with Marco Polo's return to Venice from *Zipangu*. Polo's "written story and maps" then migrate to Genoa where they inspire Christopher Columbus to conduct his westward voyage to the Grand Khan. Columbus may have failed to find and to open Japan, but "in the order of Providence" he discovered instead the continent where "a nation" would grow to complete the work by becoming "the instrument of bring[ing] [Zipangu] into full and free communication with the rest of the world."[15] Thus, the "ball of destiny" rolls westward with the United States as the new vehicle of imperial accomplishment. The narrative relishes the irony that the "youngest of nations" would "break down at last the barriers with which this singular people had surrounded themselves" and be the first "to establish with [the Japanese] a treaty of friendship and trade," the "initiatory step in the introduction of Japan into the circle of commercial nations."[16]

The *Narrative* focuses appreciation of American power not on the U.S. Navy but rather on the ambition of U.S. trading companies such as the Russell & Company to build and control systems of transportation. This is most explicit in volume 2 of the *Narrative* that includes two of Perry's essays that first appeared in the newspaper the *New York Courier and Enquirer*. In "Remarks of Commodore Perry upon the expediency for extending further encouragement to American commerce in the East," he urges U.S. merchants to continue their pursuits of wealth not only by linking up to Japan but also by taking advantage of the turmoil in China resulting from the Taping Rebellion (1850–64), a civil war that reflects the "weakness of the reigning dynasty" and "the insurrectionary spirit of the people," and that has led to the "derange[ment] of [China's] outward trade."[17] Perry exclaims that a commercial solution to social catastrophe "requires the talents and energies of the strong-minded men (and such are *most* of the American and English merchants resident in China) to comprehend the mysteries and overcome the obstacles which stand in the way of all mercantile transactions with people well enough inclined, but so stultified by national forms and prejudices as to make them, in many essentials, obstinate and impracticable."[18]

This chapter begins with an overview of Perry's mission before turning back to the *Narrative*'s visual and verbal aesthetics of extraterritorial burial. As these images memorialize dead Americans, they inspire readers to imagine systematic connection of the Far East and the Far West, transposing national and foreign landscapes to promote the spanning of the globe through steam technologies of ship and railroad forged by the merchant princes. The memorials refract Christian epiphanies of redemptive sacrifice to inspirit national ambition of independent companies such as Russell & Company and A. A. Low & Bros. Gunboat diplomacy thus opens spaces on foreign soil for mourning that promotes U.S. corporate investments, aligning companies' profitability with the national interest of freeing trade to move through East and Southeast Asia, from Japan and Lew Chew (Okinawa), across Formosa, to the Philippines, Macao and Hong Kong, and beyond. In this grand narrative of human progress, such civilizing effects exceed U.S. national interest by pulling pagans out of their incommunicative superstition and into Christendom.

The East Indian Adventures of Commodore Matthew C. Perry

Commodore Perry was born and raised in Newport, Rhode Island, and began his naval career as a teenager during the War of 1812. His older brother Admiral Oliver Hazard Perry became a national hero after winning an underdog victory over the British navy in the Battle of Lake Erie (1813). Matthew claimed Key West Island for the United States in the 1820s and oversaw the modernization of the U.S. Navy by integrating steam power. In the war on Mexico (1846–48) he won key battles as captain of the steam-powered war frigate *Mississippi* that would become part of the East India Squadron.

Japan was Commodore Perry's next frontier. In November 1852 he embarked for Macao from Chesapeake Bay on the *Mississippi*. He proceeded to Madeira and St. Helena, rounded the Cape to Goa, and passed through the Straits of Malacca to the South China Sea. In early April 1853 he arrived outside the Pearl River Delta, signaled his arrival at the Macao Roads (small islands), and continued to Hong Kong, expecting to meet the rest of his squadron.[19] He was underwhelmed by the reception. To protect American interests against the spreading Taiping Rebellion, the U.S. commissioner Mr. Humphrey Marshall had redirected the steam-powered *Susquehanna* to Shanghai with the U.S. legation secretary Dr. Rev. Peter Parker and U.S. consul at Canton Mr. Paul S. Forbes, a nephew of John Murray and Robert Bennet Forbes and the Canton head of Russell & Company.[20] Perry steamed up the Pearl River to Canton where he enjoyed the hospitality of Russell & Company. He eventually headquartered his mission in Macao, enjoying a "magnificent residence" that belonged to Russell & Company near the Camoes Gardens that Harriett Low had described twenty years before (see chapter 3).

From Macao, Perry organized the first phase of the Japan expedition, enlisting the missionary Samuel Wells Williams as his chief interpreter. Williams had been part of the thwarted *Morrison* mission in 1837 to repatriate Japanese sailors, who thereafter worked in his print office. Initially reluctant, Williams found someone to take temporary charge of the Canton Printing Station and purchased a $120 lithographic printing press "in order to assist in promulgating the wishes of the American people and let the people know what we had come for."[21] Perry also rendezvoused with his fourth son, the twenty-eight-year-old Oliver H. Perry II (1825–79), who joined the mission as the flagship secretary. Some months after the Japan expedition, in February 1855, Oliver became the U.S. consul at Canton, replacing Paul S. Forbes, who returned to the United States with a fortune that Lieutenant Preble estimates at $700,000.[22]

Commodore Perry's next stop was Shanghai. He headed up the Chinese coast on the *Mississippi* in May 1853 and down the Yang-tse-Keang (Yangtse River) to rendezvous with the *Susquehanna*, which would become the squadron flagship. He again enjoyed the hospitality of Russell & Company "in whose splendid establishment, as at Macao, every want was satisfied."[23] He was particularly impressed when served the specific Saratoga Springs mineral water that he had requested. Russell & Company made money supplying coal for the squadron's steamers, maintaining supply lines to the Islands of Lew Chew (the Ryukyu Islands, the largest of which is contemporary Okinawa), where the *Susquehanna, Mississippi, Plymouth*, and *Saratoga* assembled with 967 sailors and sixty-one guns.[24] After initiating talks with the inhabitants of Lew Chew to establish a U.S. coal station, Perry sailed on to the Bonin Islands (Ogasawara Island Group) and then on to what he considered the territorial empire of Japan.

Perry's gunboat approach to Japan echoed Caleb Cushing's to China in the previous decade.[25] There were similarities between China's and Japan's restrictive policies of regulating foreign trade. In the sixteenth century, Portugal, Spain, and the Dutch East India Company had established substantial commercial and missionary activity in Japan. However, as these three powers, two Catholic and one Protestant, went to war across the globe, resentments spilled over into Japan as they vied for influence. Japan's "ruling warrior government" grew increasingly wary of Christianity for its challenge to traditional political authority of the Shogun.[26] The Sakoku Edict (1635) was a bold countermeasure. It closed Japan to foreigners and expelled all except the Dutch on Dejima, who received limited commercial privileges.[27] The Sakoku policy also banned Christianity, making its practice punishable by death, and forbid all Japanese people from leaving Japan. Equating this to China's Canton System, Perry demanded that Japan respectfully receive him as the diplomatic embassy of the United States.

The U.S. East India Squadron bypassed the quarantine island of Dejima and went directly to Edo Bay's largest home island of Honsu. The *Narrative* describes the arrival of the squadron's two coal-power steam frigates, what the Japanese called kurofune (黒船) or "black ships"; on a hazy morning in early July, "the steamer, in spite of the wind, moved on with all sails furled, at the rate of eight or nine knots, much to the astonishment of the crews of the Japanese fishing junks gathered along the shore or scattered over the surface of the mouth of the bay, who stood up in their boats, and were evidently expressing the liveliest surprise at the sight of the first steamer beheld in Japanese waters."[28] Anchoring the war ships within artillery range of the shore village of Uraga, his men lowered boats and proceeded to sound the water's depths and chart its navigability. Perry kept aloof from the first Japanese emissaries. Through his representatives he conveyed his intention of proceeding to the city of Edo, where he expected to meet the emperor and deliver the letter from the U.S. president. After days of negotiations with the governor of Uraga, Perry relented. He handed over three letters for delivery that outlined the squadron's requests and presented a timeline for further negotiation. Williams writes that "Perry told the officials he would come next year with a larger force to get their answer to the points mentioned, which are good treatment of all Americans visiting or wrecked on the shores of Japan, a port at which to get coal for our steamers and provisions for the vessels coming after coal."[29] Perry also made it clear that refusal to negotiate would be taken as expressions of hostility. "To drive the point home," Perry included with the president's greeting "two white flags" and a letter explaining "how to use them": "[hoist] the flags" when "ready to surrender, whereupon American fire [will] immediately cease."[30]

Perry justified his tactics by appealing to the mutual benefits of commercial intercourse. For example, the *Narrative* mobilizes a national "we" in preempting criticism of the expedition's aggressive approach and asserts the systematic benefits of national selfishness for a world of commerce:

> Of the selfishness of our motives we readily admit that we sought commercial intercourse with Japan, because we supposed it would be advantageous. Such, we suppose, is the motive of all intelligent nations in establishing friendly relations with others. We can only smile at the simplicity of those who expect to deceive the world by professions of pure, disinterested friendship from one nation toward another, irrespective of all considerations of national benefit. We think that every nation which has sought intercourse with Japan has supposed that such intercourse would prove advantageous to the seeker; nor are we aware that there is anything very criminal or selfish in the desire that advantage may result from the communication. But it is quite possible to believe that benefit to *both* nations may result from the intercourse we would establish, and such benefit may be honestly desired, even while we seek our own interest. This is not selfishness.[31]

According to Hawks, the Creator had deposited valuable resources in Japan, and the Japanese should learn to share, loving their neighbors as they love themselves. As for "communication"—How could anyone oppose it? And after the conversation starts, it would become clear that Japan must open itself up to U.S. commerce. This was an offer not to be refused. The premise of the conversation blends Christianity and commerce into the virtuously competitive ambitions of national characters. The *Narrative* continues: "But we knew, too, that [Japan] possessed valuable production, and ought to be brought into communication with the rest of the world. By some, indeed, the proposition was boldly avowed that Japan had no right thus to cut herself off from the community of nations; and that what she would not yield to national comity should be wrested from her by force."[32] In Perry's imagined community of nations, Japan has no right to refuse communication that leads to extraction and distribution of her resources in return for resources that the other nations have to offer. She—and the gendering is significant—must learn to be a good neighbor by opening her door to this mutually beneficial exchange. Putting aside the pretense of common moral sense, Japan faces a commercial imperative couched in the vague euphemism of a "comity." In order to gain recognition as a sovereign state with rights that the United States will in turn respect, she needs to submit to the conditions that Perry demands. To refuse to trade prevents establishing peaceful relations and is a step toward armed conflict.

There were major differences between China's Canton System and the Sakoku policy. President Fillmore's letter (13 November 1852) of "peace and friendship" was addressed in English "To His Imperial Majesty, the Emperor of Japan." But when Perry showed up, the "hereditary imperial house in Kyoto was virtually powerless," "having ceded de facto authority some seven centuries before to warriors headed by a Shogun, or Supreme Commander."[33] Japan's political structure was complex in ways that Perry did not try very hard to understand. Shogun clans oversaw regional networks of Daimyo lords and vied for control over the major islands of what constitutes contemporary Japan. The general administrative body of the reigning Shogun Tokugawa Ieyoshi of the Tokugawa clan was (in transliterated Japanese) the Bakufu, headquartered at a fortress in Edo and directed by a powerful privy council called the Roju. The governing Daimyo negotiated with Perry and relayed the communication up to Edo. Perry referred to these interlocutors as the "Imperial Commissioners." In Edo, the head of the Roju Shuseki, who was tasked with figuring out a response to the Americans' arrival, was a "youthful" man named Abe Masahiro. He worked as a sort of prime minister managing the opinions of other Roju members, including Tokugawa Nariaki, who pushed for a direct and violent response to Perry's ultimatum.[34] Perry never met the Japanese emperor.

After the first leg of the expedition, Perry returned to Macao as the Taiping Rebellion continued to gather momentum. Over the intervening months until January 1854, he organized the pictures and charts that had been collected, enjoying the quarters provided and maintained by Russell & Company. Meanwhile, his squadron was anchored off the islands of Whampoa, Hong Kong, and at the "great opium depot" of Cum-sing Moon—"a port lying between Hong Kong and Macao" that was a nexus of opium traffic.[35] The opium trade into China was booming. When in September 1853 Lieutenant Preble arrived on the *Macedonia* to "Cum-sing Moon," he noted "five receiving ships" for storing opium, including four "under the English flag and one under the American flag."[36] He later describes as "incredible" "the quantity and value of the opium used by the Chinese," with the Cum-sing Moon harbor storing "2 to 3 million dollars" worth throughout the year.[37] In these intervening months, a major outbreak of a deadly fever took its toll on the squadron, and the "hospital soon had a good number of inmates sent from the different ships. Scarcely an officer or man escaped an attack of fever of more or less severity, and some few deaths occurred," including Lieutenant Joseph Harrod Adams, whose substantial gravesite appears, albeit without designation, in the *Narrative*.[38]

Perry returned early to Edo Bay in February 1854 with a squadron twice as large, including the steam-powered *Powhatan* (his new flagship); the *Alleghany, Susquehanna,* and *Vermont 74*; the war sloops *Plymouth, Macedonia, Saratoga,* and *Vandalia*; and the store ships *Lexington, Southampton,* and *Supply*. Matters of governance in Japan had become more complicated since the previous summer with the death of Shogun Tokugawa Ieyoshi. In the end, Abe adopted a policy of strategic appeasement in the face of Perry's potentially overwhelming force, hoping to bide time in order to strengthen Japanese defenses in expectation of similar demands from the Russians, British, and French.

Like his diplomatic predecessor Caleb Cushing, Perry pushed his demands beyond the remit of the Secretary of State Everett and President Fillmore. Tasked with helping to facilitate the negotiations, Williams grew frustrated, writing to his wife from the Bay of Edo on 11 March 1854: "I've been busy translating Perry's answer to the Emperor's reply. The President's letter asked for one port, now Perry wants five; that [letter] desired simply an assurance of good treatment, now the Commodore demands a treaty, and suggests, in no obscure terms, 'a larger force and more stringent terms and instructions,' if they don't comply."[39]

The burial of Americans on Japanese soil became Perry's leading point of contention. Early in this second round of negotiations, an American sailor named Robert Williams died of injuries previously sustained in China. Perry insisted that he receive a proper Christian land burial in Japan, as "undisturbed resting places were granted by all nations"; as a site he proposed Webster Island (Natsushima Island).[40] His journal reveals that he was "anxious for special reasons to acquire an interest in this island to subserve some ulterior objects."[41] The Japanese negotiators refused, explaining that Nagasaki was the only option. Perry pushed the matter to a compromise: Robert Williams was buried in a "temple yard near Yokohama."[42]

W. Heine, woodcut tailpiece of "Japanese grave-yard at Yoku-hama—Grave of the Marine on the right." Hawks, *Narrative of the Expedition of an American Squadron to the China Seas and Japan*, p. 366.

We can only speculate what Perry meant by "ulterior objects," but Webster Island was positioned very favorably for overseeing traffic through Edo Bay and would have made a very convenient coal depot. The *Narrative* uses the occasion of describing the burial to emphasize its historical importance, citing Reverend George Jones, who, in officiating the funeral service, could not help but mention that, "more than two hundred years before, it had been written in Japan, 'so long as the sun shall warm the earth, let no Christian be so bold as to come to Japan; and let all know that the king of Spain himself, or the Christian's God, or the great God of all, if he violate this command, shall pay for it with his head.' "[43] So, in the pages of the *Narrative*, the burial of the dead American sailor heralded the end of the Sakoku policy.

Perry won more substantial concessions from Japan with the 31 March 1854 signing of the American Japan Treaty of Amity and Friendship (日米和親条約, Nichibei Washin Jōyaku), also known as the Kanagawa Treaty (神奈川条約, Kanagawa Jōyaku), for the village where it was signed on the coast of Edo Bay near Yokohama. Williams summarized the treaty as "opening to American trade the ports of Simoda and Hakodaki, permitting consuls to reside at these places, and granting free access to the country surrounding them; good treatment and safe-conduct to either of these two ports was also guaranteed to Americans shipwrecked upon any coast of Japan."[44] In the treaty's Article 9, Williams secured "most favored nation" status for the United States, thus ensuring that no other nation would gain competitive advantages in ensuing treaties.

After celebrating the treaty in an extravagant banquet with the Japanese dignitaries, Perry wasted no time in testing and expanding the agreements. He sent ships from his squadron to the ports of Shimoda and Hakodate where he renegotiated with the local governors, who relayed the amendments back to Edo, resulting in twelve "Additional Regulations" (June 1854).[45] During these negotiations, three more U.S. sailors lost their lives and were buried, one in Simoda, and two in Hakodate. Article 5 of the "Additional Regulations" obligates Japan to the "setting apart" of an area "near the temple of Yokushen, at Kakizaki" outside Hakodate as "a burial-ground . . . for Americans, where their graves and tombs shall not be molested."[46] In late June 1854 Perry left Japan for Lew Chew, where he signed another treaty on 11 July 1854 and buried more American sailors. Perry continued on to Formosa, scouting out its potential as a transit station for American ships, and then made his way back to Hong Kong and Macao, and eventually to United States by way of continental Europe and London.

Perry's Kanagawa Convention paved the way for U.S. commissioner Townsend Harris, who arrived in Shimoda in 1856. Two years later Townsend managed to negotiate a second treaty called "The United States–Japan Treaty of Amity and Commerce," signed aboard the *Powhatan* on 29 July 1858.[47] This treaty pushed the concessions to something comparable to the Treaty of Wanghia (1844) that Cushing had negotiated with Kíying outside Macao. Article 3 opened up four more treaty ports (Kanagawa, Nagasaki, Niigata, and Hyogo) and allowed Americans residence in the imperial city of Osaka and in Edo (Tokyo). Article 4 prohibited the importation of opium and prevented placing higher duties on American vessels than those of the Japanese. Article 6 established the extraterritorial jurisdiction of the United States in Japan through "American Consular courts," which would try those Americans committing offenses against the Japanese and punish "according to American law." Article 8 guaranteed to Americans in Japan the "free exercise of their religion."

Monumental Print Production

Perry did everything in his power to make sure that the story of his expedition would be remembered. Before embarking he planned publishing something more readable than Charles Wilkes's *Narrative of the United States Exploring Expedition, during the years 1838, 1840, 1841, 1842* (1852).[48] To this end, from the start of the mission Perry tried to control reportage of the events. He discouraged his crew from writing about the expedition and collected his officers' writings at the journey's end. Lieutenant Preble defied Perry in the form of letters to his wife in which he bristled at Perry's restriction, writing in September 1853 "My letters to you are the only journal I shall keep this cruise . . . principally because Commodore Perry has

issued his vermillion edict, that all journals and diaries are to be sealed and delivered up to him on and at a certain date an infringement of our private rights we
are not disposed to tolerate."[49] Preble's metaphor of the "vermillion edict" signals
that he was an old hand in China, having served on the *St. Louis* during Caleb
Cushing's mission in 1844.

Congress funded Perry's publication with $400,000 to print thirty-four thou-
sand copies.[50] The *Narrative* appeared in two final editions, one printed by the
House of Representatives and another by the Senate. More-affordable editions
appeared in New York (Appleton & Company) and London (Trubner & Company).
All the versions include hundreds of woodcut and lithograph illustrations by the
twenty-five-year-old artist William Heine, the main illustrator of the expedition. A
Dresden-born sketch artist and watercolorist, Heine had migrated to New York to
escape the crackdowns following the 1848 May Uprisings. He later became a U.S.
citizen and served in the Union army during the Civil War.[51] The expedition pho-
tographer Eliphalet Brown Jr. took hundreds of photographs that did not survive
the voyage.[52] Today, the digital humanities projects at MIT and Brown University
draw on these images to introduce Perry's imperial adventure to contemporary
audiences.[53]

In addition to pictures, Perry needed a writer who could properly monumental-
ize his expedition and settled on Rev. Francis L. Hawks, D.D., L.L.D., and rector of
Episcopal Calvary Church. Perry had first approached Nathaniel Hawthorne, who
was then serving as a U.S. consul in Liverpool. Hawthorne declined and recommended Melville, who was probably revising "Benito Cereno" (1855) into final form
for its run in *Putnam's*.[54] Perry wrote to Williams in Canton asking him to write a
Japanese vocabulary and a historical sketch; Williams avoided any contributions,
focusing instead on his Chinese dictionary.[55] Hawks seems the perfect writer to
work up Perry's expedition into a national adventure. He was known for the biographical series "A Library for My Young Countrymen," including *The Adventures
of Henry Hudson* (1842), *The Adventures of Captain John Smith, the Founder of the
Colony of Virginia* (1842), *The Adventures of Hernan Cortez, the Conqueror of Mexico*
(1842), and *The Adventures of Daniel Boone, the Kentucky Rifleman* (1844). Robert
Tomes, Esq. M.C., a "competent literary gentleman" who had accompanied Perry
on the expedition provided further assistance in the process of editorial "compila-
tion," particularly in sketching the "descriptions of scenery."[56]

Over a period of twelve months in the Manhattan office of the American Bible
Society, Perry, Hawks, and Tomes worked the account up from Perry's three-folio
manuscript notes and personal reminiscences. Perry's short statement "Authenti-
cation of the Narrative" prefaces the account, and the *Narrative* refers to Hawks as
a "compiler merely" who is organizing "*facts* only," with the commodore's journal

being the primary source. The preface repeatedly assures the reader that the narrative is a *"verbatim* copy," and the long title again reassures: *Compiled from the original notes and journals of Commodore Perry and his Officers, at his request, and under his supervision.*[57] And yet the preface lists a battery of source materials, including official correspondences, diaries of the fleet captain and flag lieutenants, reports of special duties officers, and public documents, as well as natural histories of the German Engelbert Kaempfer (1651–1716), the Swedish naturalist Carl Peter Thunberg (1743–1828), and the German physician Philipp Franz von Siebold (1796–1866) and several travel accounts.

The National Aesthetics of Extraterritorial Memorialization

The road to Japan went through China. The scene "Protestant Grave Yard—Macao" offers a specific setting for readers to respect the American dead—a setting that connects U.S. commerce in China to the goal of opening Japan to trade and that simultaneously differentiates the United States from European imperial projects of the previous centuries. Although the scene is an actual place in Macao that one can visit today, Heine's primary concern was not accuracy or mimetic reproduction. He was composing this scene with an eye trained as an artist, pulling from various templates and effects of landscape painting.[58] Furthermore, whatever Heine sketched "by Nature" (as the attributions read), his renderings went through several layers of editorial selection, revision, and engraving before appearing in the *Narrative*. Chapter 3 outlined the concept of "genius loci" (or spirit of place) and the principles of beauty, sublimity, and the picturesque when considering how Harriett Low and William Wood sketched and described Macao in the 1830s. Working in the 1850s, Heine, Perry, and Hawks show how these visual dynamics could change to allegorize national commercial configuration of free trade in different parts of Asia.

The history of the site is fascinating. Today the "Protestant Grave Yard" is attached to the ecumenical Macau Protestant Chapel, also known as the Morrison Chapel.[59] The graveyard dates back to 1821, before which the British East India Company housed its printing operations there. At that time there was no place in Catholic Macao for the bodies of dead Protestants. In the 1780s Major Samuel Shaw, the first American consul to Canton, criticized Portuguese policy, explaining that "if a heretic [i.e., Protestant] happens to die [in Macao], he cannot obtain burial in the Catholic city; and a bargain must be made with the Chinese, who own all without the walls, before he can be conveyed to his long home."[60] This changed with the death of Mrs. Mary Morrison, the wife of the eminent British missionary, translator, and linguist Rev. Robert Morrison. The painter George Chinnery (who

Wilhelm Heine, "Protestant Grave Yard—Macao." Woodcut. Hawks, *Narrative of the Expedition of an American Squadron to the China Seas and Japan*, p. 298.

is himself buried in the graveyard) was instrumental in winning an exception to the Portuguese prohibition. The obituary for Mrs. Morrison in the *Chinese Repository* outlines the parallel struggle to find a burial plot for Protestants in China:

> The Chinese having refused a place of burial where it was desired, and where an infant of Mrs. Morrison's was before interred; and those Christians who inhabit Macao, not allowing other Christians any place of internment but within the limits of the Fosse, outside the city wall; and the Managing Committee of the English factory in China, with a humane and liberal feeling assisted by some worthy Portuguese gentlemen, to overcome legal impediments, purchased a piece of ground, to be a Cemetery for the English, and we doubt not for other Protestant Christians, who in future choose to avail themselves of it. This arrangement enabled Dr. Morrison to lay the remains of his lamented wife in a place decently appropriated to sepulture.[61]

A later article by Reverend Elijah Bridgman describes the situation of the "The English burial ground," "situated just beyond the church of St. Antonio, eastward from the entrance to the Casa."[62] It is a "spot . . . rendered sacred by the remains

of many who were very dear and much loved by those who yet live, was well cho-
sen, being sequestered, and so surrounded by a high wall as to be screened from
public view. . . . These are chiefly graves of seamen, who have died in the hospitals.
But the care of friends and relatives has here and there erected mementoes, with
inscriptions to perpetuate the memory of those for whom they mourn."[63] Bridgman
and the *Chinese Repository* highlight the friction between Catholics and Protestants,
but Heine's "Protestant Grave Yard—Macao" removes all Christian iconography
from the scene—no crosses and no chapel—leaving the national monuments to
the extraterritorial dead. In reorganizing the lines of perspective, the image omits
many gravestones, including those of other prominent early Americans and British.[64] The most significant omissions are the graves of Mary and Rev. Robert Morrison, which should appear in the obscuring shade at the top left corner. The image
also narrows the yard into a sort of alley with the effect of stretching the perspectival line of sight into the distance beyond what one actually sees when standing
where Heine has placed the viewer. (Today apartments block this line of sight almost completely.)

In the scene, four anonymous cenotaphs receive particular emphasis. Two on
the left in the foreground are conspicuously large. They memorialize British officers killed during the First Opium War (1839–42).[65] The other two prominent
graves, attended by visitors, memorialize Americans. A kneeling woman and a
man standing behind her appear smaller in the middle ground before the fourth
large grave (center-left), that of "John F. Brooke M.D. Fleet Surgeon to the United
States East India Squadron, Fleet Surgeon of the U.S. Navy (died on 17 October
1849)."[66] Two officers and a sailor visit the large one to the far right. This is a new
monument to the aforementioned Lieutenant Joseph H. Adams, the grandson of
former president John Adams and a nephew of former president John Quincy
Adams. The inscription on the north side of the monument reads: "Died on Board
U.S. Steam Frigate Powhatan / October 4 1853 Aged 36 Years"; and the inscription
on the east side: "Erected to his Memory / by his brother officers / of the East India
and / Japan Squadron."[67]

When Lieutenant Preble arrived in China in 1853, his ship, as mentioned, anchored off the opium station of Cum-sing Moon. On 4 September he described
Lieutenant "Joe Adams" to his wife as looking "fresh and hearty" but complaining
that he had "seen quite enough of China and the East."[68] A month later, Adams had
died. Preble continues his letter from the Victoria Harbor, Hong Kong (Sunday,
9 October 1853):

> Leaving Cum-sing Moon on the 3d we anchored here on the 6th, and were greeted
> with the melancholy news that Mrs. Boyd's cousin Lt. Jos. Adams of the Powhatan

Gravesite of Joseph H. Adams, Protestant Cemetery, Macao. Photograph by the author.

was both dead and buried; his death having occurred within 24 hours of our departure from Cum-sing Moon though we left him, as it was supposed, convalescing from a sudden but slotic [*sic*] illness. It is difficult to realize that one we saw only a few days since, so full of life and enjoyment of this world's pleasures, should now be tenanting a cold and silent grave. He was buried at Macao, and the officers propose to raise by subscription a monument over his remains.[69]

Preble later recalls being "on board the *Powhatan*" as Adam's shipmates packed up "his wardrobe to send home by a merchant ship," and he notes that "officers of the squadron have already subscribed $175 for a monument over his remains," and that "Mr. Heine is to make a drawing of it and the cemetery at Macao to send to his sister."[70]

In the scene of the graveyard, Heine's selection of these graves has the effect of dividing the burial grounds between Britain and the United States in the foreground and middle ground of the populated present. The lines of perspective that reach over the graveyard wall highlight the historical diminution of the Portuguese empire into the past. As the kneeling woman hides her face in her hands, her standing companion looks up and away, beyond the back wall of the yard, toward the Portuguese Guia Fortress (Fortaleza da Guia) in the upper left, and the ruins of St. Paul's Cathedral (Ruínas de São Paulo) in the center. When Heine sketched the image, the once majestic cathedral had been reduced to this mere façade by a typhoon and fire in 1835. Both sites are open today, preserved in China's Special Administrative Region (SAR) of Macao and designated by UNESCO as a World Heritage Site.

The constellation of four tombs and the layout of the graveyard turn the memorialization of Lieutenant Adams into an allegory of the rising power of the United States in East Asia. The standing man's line of perspective continues that of the Chinese vendor (left of center) who sits on one of two baskets, with the shoulder pole leaning against the other. Whatever he or she might be selling, this person denotes the setting as China. So the vendor's line of sight runs to the fourth grave, aligning with that of the standing man, forming a vector reaching up and beyond the wall. In connecting fore-, mid- and background layers, the perspectival vector implicitly juxtaposes the life cycles of people (in the graveyard) and of empires (in the elevated fort and ruin). Individual graves in the middle- and foregrounds stand in the shadow of the ruins of Portuguese Macao on ground carved out as an exception to Portuguese law. Compared to the centuries-long cycles of history in which dynasties rise and fall, an individual human life seems particularly evanescent. The scene not only honors the American dead but also invites the reader to contemplate human mortality in relation to long periods of historical time. The brevity of these sailors' lives challenges readers to seize the day as citizens of a young nation rising to surpass the former glory of Portugal.

In other places the *Narrative* similarly teases out an American vigor by placing figures in melancholic scenes of Portuguese memorialization and ruin. For example, the *Narrative* singles out the famous bust of the Portuguese poet Camoens in Casa Garden (see chapter 3), where Harriett Low had her moonlit "scene of romance" when sitting on a precipice with Captain Dumaresq. In the verbal description of this scene, Hawks notes that the site is "picturesquely situated at the summit of a small hill" and then describes the scene in the ways that challenge the reader to create images from his words. Again, as with the scene of Adam's grave in Macao, the *Narrative*'s version of Casa Garden registers the fading afterlife of the Portuguese empire, and the narrator remarks, Macao was "at one time . . . one of the most flourishing marts of the East," but now "there is not much at present to interest the visitor at Macao, as it is but a ghost of its former self. There is almost a complete absence of trade or commerce."[71] Despite the general rubric of "genius loci," these images have little to do with China or Macao per se. They offer American readers an extraterritorial setting from which to contemplate the past glories of Portugal in appreciating the sacrifice of fellow U.S. citizens.

American Scenes of Burial in Japan

The *Narrative*'s memorial scenes in Japan work a bit differently. Whereas Heine's Protestant Cemetery in Macao directs our gaze inland and into the past, the *Narrative*'s gravesites in Japan orient the viewer's gaze outward into stylized, expansive sea horizons of future commercial opportunity. For example, when two American sailors died in Hakodate, Japanese authorities designated for their burial a place outside the village that Hawks describes as "exceedingly picturesque," for "command[ing] a fine view of the harbor, the Straits of Sangar, and the adjacent coasts."[72] There is not a big picture depicting these American graves in Hakodate, only the tailpiece that ends the *Narrative*, depicted earlier. However, there is a full-page landscape illustration of Simoda (Shimoda), where another sailor fell to his death aboard the *Powhatan*. He was buried outside the village of "Kaki-zaki, or Persimmon point" in the graveyard near the monastery "Guku-zhen-zhi."[73]

The illustration appears in the *Narrative* as Perry visits the treaty ports and pushes for more concessions. Notice that in this view of Shimoda, American graves line up with the steamships in the harbor. The cloud-filled sea horizon appears beyond them. As the implied viewer, we stand a bit back from the funeral ceremony in progress, looking down on it and into the bay. In the spirit of picturesque landscape description, we realize a scenic composition by balancing various fore-, middle- and backgrounds. In the left foreground, the burial ceremony is underway. The trees offer a protective bower as an audience of both American sailors and Japanese onlookers encircle the sacred center of a Christian ritual that will deposit the American body into the Japanese ground. As in the scene of Macao's graveyard, there is no cross or comparable Christian iconography, only the figure of the minister, Rev. George Jones, to the right of whom Commodore Perry stands in uniform. Perhaps in Jones's posture, the overhanging tree, and the arrangement of the American and Japanese audience, Heine is echoing Benjamin West's famous painting "The Treaty of Penn with the Indians" (1771–72). Further to the right, in a separate burial area, trees bend to form a bower that shelters the sacred monuments to the Japanese dead. There is clear division between the two burial sites, but between them is a pathway leading down to the harbor where two steamers (nearer) and two sailing sloops (farther) are anchored. The clouds and the reflections of sky on water create an effect of chiaroscuro that heightens the spiritual aura of this burial ceremony as the eye stretches out to the horizon from the point

"Simoda from the American Grave Yard." "From Nature by Heine" (*lower left corner*). Litho-graph. Hawks, *Narrative of the Expedition of an American Squadron to the China Seas and Japan*, opposite p. 425.

where the Americans and Japanese are gathered. One could read this horizon as the Heaven of Christian redemption, but it seems more appropriate as the firma-ment of commercial potential, meant to inspire readers to develop the pathways of prosperity that reach to and establish national communication with this inter-nationally sacred ground of Shimoda, a newly opened treaty port.

Aesthetically speaking, Heine's scene of Shimoda has little to do with its unique-ness of place. Rather, the image echoes with connotations that are specific to the United States, appealing to readers who would have recognized a safe, quiet, and cultivated landscape that encourages spiritual contemplation of mortality in terms that are more national than religious and more secular than spiritual. There is a democratic aura to these scenes of national sacrifice to free trade. In the eighteenth-century British Empire, such honorific landscapes would have been reserved for the landed nobility with a prestigious family name. The bodies and lives of com-moners would not have warranted such attention. Heine's landscapes are not darkly ominous plots of land, overgrown with weeds, in the shadow of a church or, even worse, a field of common graves in cart-carry distance from dense population centers. He is not depicting the desolate grounds of common burial in Daniel Defoe's *Journal of a Plague Year* (1722) or the ill-kept field of stones across which Pip scampers in the first chapter of Charles Dickens's *Great Expectations* (1861).

Heine might have been influenced by design of nineteenth-century American suburban cemeteries (from the Greek, meaning "sleeping place"). John Conron's *American Picturesque* explains that the "rural cemetery movement" transformed how Americans honored the dead, creating public parklike spaces where visitors could walk the grounds, have a picnic, and socialize in the open air. In this movement, the American landscape designer Andrew Jackson Downing (1815–52) was very influential. For example, his lead article in the July 1849 issue of the *Horticulturalist, and Journal of Rural Art and Rural Taste*, which he edited, aligns aesthetic principles and civic lessons.[74] Marveling at the "great attraction" of Greenwood Cemetery in New York City and Mount Auburn in Boston and Philadelphia's Laurel Hills, he sees cemeteries as vital substitutes for public parks, which the young nation lacked, and as a precursor to public works projects such as New York's Central Park. In 1849 Downing describes cemeteries as more than "solemn places of meditation for the friends of the deceased" or "striking exhibitions of monumental structure."[75] They offer opportunities to cultivate "natural beauty" through "the tasteful and harmonious embellishments of these sites by art" that would "civilize and refine the national character, foster[ing] a love of rural beauty" and an appreciation of public endeavors.[76]

Picturesque terminology pervaded the design of distinctively American cemetery spaces and was in turn redefined by its designers and painters. Downing's major work was the influential *A Treatise on the Theory and Practice of Landscape Gardening, Adapted to North America* (1841; 1857; 1859), dedicated to former president John Quincy Adams and republished in several additions over the next two decades.[77] Advising his young nation on the development of taste, Downing strives to adapt British conventions of "Landscape Gardening" grounded in "the Beautiful, Sublime, and Picturesque." He reviews "ancient" forms of Greek, Babylonian, and Roman beauty, as well as French, Dutch, and British styles of landscape composition, and then the work of William Gilpin, Uvedale Price, Richard Payne Knight, Thomas Whately, and Humphrey Repton, whom he regards as the "most distinguished" of "English Landscape Gardeners."[78] He alludes to the eighteenth-century China trader William Chambers when noting that a "Chinese taste in gardening" inspired the "modern style" of English gardening. He then diminishes the influence, asserting that "the harmonious system which the taste of the English has evolved in the modern style, is at the present day, too far beyond the manner to admit any comparison."[79]

After sketching this genealogy of British landscape theory, Downing highlights the potential for U.S. innovation, declaring that "North America" is a blank canvas upon which citizens who believe that "the rights of man are held to be equal" will fashion new democratic designs.[80] Downing presents his American aesthetic as a break from cultural sensibilities that derive from aristocratic wealth, but landscape improvement generally required a well-capitalized estate and money to maintain it. Downing points to an increasing number of merchants who have earned enough to own land and refine it, thereby showcasing the meritocratic basis of American fortune-building. As examples of such monumental accomplishment, he points to William H. Aspinwall's cottage residence on Staten Island; John Perkins Cushing's gardens at the Belmont estate in Watertown, Massachusetts; Colonel T. H. Perkins's estates at Brookline and Pine Bank; Nathan Dunn's Mount Holly outside of Camden in New Jersey; and John R. Latimer's "country seat" in Delaware.[81] He also mentions Warren Delano's estate of Algonac" in Newburgh, New York, and the Newport, Rhode Island, mansions of William Henry King (Kingscote) and William S. Wetmore (Chateau-sur-Mer).[82]

Without the China trade, none of these monuments to earned wealth would have materialized. But did it take great wealth to contribute to the general project of transforming landscape aesthetics? Absent great personal fortunes, funding for cemetery spaces required public funding, and Downing outlines the benefits of modest citizens' forays into groundskeeping. Without digressing much farther into the theoretical shades of national landscape aesthetics, consider that Downing presents landscape gardening as a civic exercise that mobilizes local taste and public intellect in rendering a unique sense of American place that gets realized in the unity of its complementary regional varieties. In his view, the rising merchant class ought to set an example for all homeowners who can develop their smaller plots in the broader national mosaic. The creative essence of improving a landscape, painting a scene, or strolling the grounds of an estate, cemetery, or public park boils down in Downing's estimation to "an expressive, harmonious, and refined imitation" of the European tradition, epitomized by the genius of Claude Lorraine and Salvator Rosa.[83]

The challenge in the United States is to "[arrange] materials" of the physical ground and of visual attribute (e.g., color, light, shade, tone, dimension, surface) "so as to awaken emotions of grace, elegance, or picturesqueness, joined with unity, harmony, and variety, more distinct and forcible, than are suggested by natural scenery."[84] The national excitement lies in seeing "North America" as a "new starting ground" on which citizens have the "liberty to define, and clear up, the confused and cloudy views of the end or aim of imitation, pervading most European authors on this subject."[85] As Downing looks at trees, vines, climbing plants, and architectural design, from diverse states and geographic regions as different as Michigan, New Jersey, Virginia, Florida, the Ohio and Mississippi Rivers, and the Gulf of Mexico, we can see the national harmonization of various scenes in the "production of the whole" that depends on the "proper connection of the parts."[86] Different regions sit like colors on a painter's pallet for future artists to blend, combine, and compose in creating general national scenery. Downing exemplifies how national appreciation of distinctively regional and local senses of American place was implicitly related to the capital of Far Eastern trade and to the commercial ambition of young Americans looking to establish a family name in the antebellum republic. Heine, Hawks, and Perry may or may not have read Downing, but they pursued principles of "unity, harmony, and variety" in representing "exceedingly picturesque" American gravesites in China and Japan; *Narrative* thus balances the melancholic scene of Macao against the aspirational scene of Shimoda—balances a temporally vertical abyss of the imperial past's degenerative ruins against a spatially horizontal expanse of the democratic future's commercial oceanic horizon.[87]

It could go without saying that the deep traditions of visual art in China and Japan offer very different philosophies that structure the relation of place to people in history. Heine's projection of American visual aesthetics begs a question: What was the role of landscape in Chinese and Japanese memorialization of the dead? Interestingly, the very U.S. sources on which these chapters have relied suggest the power of Chinese and Japanese burial practices in generating lived reverence for land. For example, in 1785 Major Samuel Shaw described the deep spiritual importance among wealthy Chinese people of respectfully memorializing the dead by selecting a burial site:

> The great concern of a rich Chinese is to procure a pleasant spot for a tomb, for which, provided it be to his mind, he thinks no price too great. It must be airy, shaded by trees, watered by a running stream, and situated on an eminence commanding an extensive land and water prospect. So great is their attention to these circumstances, that a Chinese, on meeting with any extraordinary misfortune, is sometimes lead to suppose that it is because his father's bones do not rest comfortably. In this case, a new situation is taken and consecrated by the priests, and a tomb prepared, wherein the relics of his father, removed from their former abode, are deposited with much ceremony and expense.[88]

In Shaw's description, wealth enables Chinese sons to honor their departed fathers by establishing memorial sites that command "an extensive land and water prospect." Heine's depiction of the Japanese burial site at Shimoda evinces similar concern in Japan with the location of burial sites. Even though Heine projects American cemetery aesthetics onto Japan, his image might be read against the nationalist grain to suggest memorialization rituals that exceed Perry's American romance of free trade.[89]

Stretching the Horizon of Free-Trade Imperialism from the Far East to the Far West

Standing from the American grave at Kaki-zaki, looking into the sea horizon from the treaty port of Shimoda, what does Perry's ideal reader see? Perry's essays in volume 2 give us a sense of what he envisioned beyond the vanishing point: a network of world commerce that echoed the sphere of protective oversight promised by the Monroe and Tyler doctrines (1823; 1843). His essay "The Expediency of Extending Further Encouragement to American Commerce in the East" is a concise exercise in an imperialistic ambivalence or double-speak of peace, friendship, and free trade.[90] Perry asserts that humankind's common goal is to increase "the commerce of the world" through application of the "constantly accumulating capital," such as that then being extracted from the mines of "California and Australia."[91] Recognizing British, Dutch, Spanish, and Portuguese spheres of influence in the world, Perry directs his reader to the "extensive areas of cultivated and populous lands, which have so far escaped the grasping policy of those powers."[92] Since the United States has negotiated treaties of friendship with Japan, Lew Chew, and Siam, Perry encourages the nation "to extend the advantages of our national friendship and protection" to "Siam, Cambodia, Cochin China (Vietnam), parts of Borneo and Sumatra, and many of the islands of the eastern archipelago, and more especially the island of Formosa."[93]

Perry outlines the great responsibility of such oversight. He urges Americans to set a high standard of "national probity" and chastises all Western nations, including the United States, for not having lived up to Christian principles in violating treaty promises and inciting local disturbances in order to "inculcate reciprocity of rights, and recognize contracting parties as equals."[94] However, such episodic lapses in Western probity have ironically, in the long run, yielded beneficial results. For example, Perry acknowledges that the first "opium war" was "brought about by causes not to be commended" but it was, nevertheless, "greatly to the benefit of China and the whole commercial world."[95] Thus, he sees Britain's true mistake in having ended the conflict too soon: "If the occasion and opportunity had been seized upon," then Britain could have "establish[ed] throughout the empire [of China] a more liberal form of government" and "insist[ed] upon the unconditional recognition of those reciprocal interchanges of just and friendly intercourse which subsist between all civilized nations in time of peace."[96] Perry's pledge of "national friendship and protection" implies the positive results of regime change through-out Asia in fostering "liberal form[s] of government."[97]

Perry's essay echoed contemporaneous justifications of the Second Opium War (1856–60). Alluding to the Taiping Rebellion, he laments the "terrible state of an-archy" that "distracts the whole land," but he also sees an opportunity for the "ul-timate reorganization of the political condition of the empire"; he continues that "it would be the undoubted policy of all to unite in bringing about a revolution, civil and military, (and it might be a bloodless one,) which would place China upon a footing with the most favored nations."[98] With the fall of the Chinese emperor, Perry predicts a domino effect of falling Asian despots in "Japan, Lew Chew, and other countries already mentioned in this paper" who "would enter of necessity into this new family of commercial, or at least, trading nations; and the commerce of the East would be improved ten-fold by the impulse thus given to the advance of civilizations and the industrial arts."[99] The consequent commercial interaction promotes "religious, moral, and political" benefits that exceed Perry's ability to estimate. "The end would therefore unquestionably justify the means" as "the empires of China and Japan" joined "the family of nations, upon the basis of equal international *duties* as well as rights."[100]

To promote expansion of free trade among liberal governments, Perry advocates colonization of Formosa (contemporary Taiwan), a land rich with coal and well-situated to supply U.S. steamships. He asserts that Formosa is only "nominally a province of China" and "practically independent," speculating that China would welcome "American settlement at Kelung" (Keelung City, 基隆市; on the northern tip of Taiwan) for the protection it would afford from pirates and nefarious coloniz-ing agents whose presence would threaten commercial development. Owing to its prime "geographical position," Formosa would offer the United States what En-gland has in Hong Kong and Singapore—"an entrepôt for American trade, from which communications might be established with China, Japan, Lew Chew, Cochin China, Cambodia, the Philippines, and all islands situated in the adjacent seas."[101]

Perry realizes that U.S. colonization of Formosa sounds more like imperialism than the reassuring neutrality of mere communication. Anticipating objections, Perry does not deny it. In fact, he embraces the irony of an America empire, con-tending that "colonies are almost as necessary to a commercial nation as are the ships which transport from one country to another the commodities."[102] He is optimistic that "small and distant settlements established [by the United States] for purposes of trade or some religious or moral object" throughout the Pacific would indeed fit within "our federative organization."[103] In another essay, "Probable Fu-ture Commercial Relations with Japan and Lew Chew," he urges the U.S. govern-ment to "protect defenceless communities, in remote parts of the world, from the acts of injustice and outrage not unfrequently committed by the crews of ships navigating distant seas."[104] As the lines between friendship, regime change, and colonization blur, the moral and ethical justification of his proposals hinge on the eventual humanitarian benefits of trade pursued by American companies in a world system overseen by the United States.

The Love of System from the Far East to the Far West

Behind Perry's ideas were the material technologies that enabled him and his readers to traverse the long horizons of geography, connecting Japan's treaty ports to ports throughout the world. In this spirit, the demonstration of technological innovations related to steam power, railways, and telegraphy featured prominently in Perry's negotiation tactics. In March 1854 at Kanagawa, Perry presented the Japanese with gifts, including specimens of firearms, multiple volumes of Audubon's *Birds of America* and *Quadrapeds*, more than a hundred gallons of whiskey, and a telescope. The Americans also set up participatory demonstrations. The *Narrative* lists gifts in the footnoted inventory, such as "1 locomotive and tender, passenger car, and rails complete" and "2 telegraphic instruments," along with "4 bundles telegraph wires."[105] Hawks reports that, as the Americans set up the demonstrations, "Japanese authorities offered every facility" and looked on "with an innocence and delight."[106] Samuel Wells Williams and Mr. Draper assembled the telegraph, extending the wire nearly a mile from the treaty house in Yokohama. "When communication was opened up between the operators at either extremity," Japanese people looked on with "intense curiosity" and "were greatly amazed to find that in an instant of time messages were conveyed in English, Dutch, and Japanese languages from building to building."[107] For days thereafter, "dignitaries and many of the people would gather, and, eagerly beseeching the operators to work the telegraph, watch with unabated interest the sending and receiving of messages."[108] As for the "Lilliputian locomotive car," two engineers set up the small-scale model and "the Japanese . . . were not to be cheated out of a ride."[109] The *Narrative* reports "a spectacle not a little ludicrous to behold" of "a dignified mandarin whirling around the circular road at the rate of twenty miles an hour, with his loose robes flying in the wind."[110] It is very likely that these technologies elicited fascination from the Japanese spectators, but in characterizing their interest as innocent, the *Narrative* underscores the expressions of power implicit in the demonstrations. In the following decades, profitable construction and maintenance of these technologies went hand in hand with controlling the flows of communication and transport that they enabled.

With this in mind, turn back and reconsider the horizon view from Kaki-zaki, or Persimmon point, looking down at Shimoda. The outward reach of vision into the sea finds commercial analogy in what Perry calls the "federative organization" of the United States, developed through the steamships, railroads, and telegraphs that were spanning North America and that Perry and U.S. merchants envisioned setting up in China, Japan, and East Asia, not only to speed up communication and travel but also to reconfigure the flows of international commerce so they passed through the United States. In "Probable Future Commercial Relations with Japan and Lew Chew," Perry acknowledges that the expedition's treaties at Kanagawa and Napha (Okinawa) amount to "nothing more than a compact, establishing between the United States and that empire certain obligations of friendly intercourse."[111] The next step is for the U.S. government to "develop American trade" and establish explicitly "*commercial* treaties, which will embrace, in their details, all the stipulations of reciprocal trade."[112] He puts his faith in the "enterprise of our own merchants, who are rarely wanting in this element of success."[113] Recall that Russell & Company had provided Perry with his accommodations in Canton, Macao, and Shanghai and supplied his squadron with coal on the voyage to Japan. As mentioned, in 1856 Perry's son Oliver Perry replaced Paul S. Forbes of Russell & Company as the U.S. consul to Canton. Other companies, such as A. A. Low & Bros., similarly developed networks connecting Shanghai and Yokohama.[114]

Perry's optimism regarding Russell & Company was based in part on the company's significant expansion in China after the First Opium War. By 1846 Russell & Company had established a branch in Shanghai that in 1848 became the company's "head establishment" with the arrival there of Mr. John N. A. Griswold, who performed double duty as the American consul in Shanghai.[115] As a port city at the mouth of the Yangtse River, "Shanghai provided foreign merchants with access to China's largest artery of inland commerce" and between 1850 and 1860 became the "principle port for foreign trade."[116] Canton's importance continued to fade. Opium remained lucrative as more treaty ports opened after the Second Opium War but Russell & Company profited most by overseeing commissions-based trade operations and a new company dedicated to steamship transport.[117] The commissions services included providing timely market information, reliable and safe modes of "transfer[ing] capital from New York to Shanghai," and dependable extensions of credit.[118] In the midst of economic slowdowns and depressions, Russell & Company enjoyed an advantage in having had its former partner Russell Sturgis Jr. (1805–7) join Baring Brothers Bank in London. With a secure line of international credit, the firm survived economic downturns, outlasting rivals whom it bought out to consolidate power.

Steam technology enabled Russell & Company to penetrate further into the Chinese mainland. As noted in the introduction, the frontispiece to F. O. Matthiessen's

The American Renaissance is of Donald McKay, the master builder of clipper sailing ships that raced across the world's oceans in the 1850s. But in 1850, when Edward Cunningham joined Russell & Company in Shanghai, he envisioned moving goods up and down the Yangtse River on steamboats like those plying the Mississippi River. In 1862, as the Civil War raged in the United States, he lobbied his colleague Walter Delano in Hong Kong to finance a new shipping venture between China's treaty ports. Delano was skeptical, as were Paul S. Forbes and John Murray Forbes back in the United States. Looking to maintain their investments in the North American West as the war continued, the Forbes cousins appreciated the steady income from treaty-port commissions and the now legal opium traffic into China. Cunningham persisted, putting up his own money and gathering Chinese and British investors to form a joint-stock company with ownership transferable through stock certificate.[119] The resulting Shanghai Steam and Navigation Company (SSNC) operated as a subsidiary of Russell & Company to which it paid 5 percent of all receipts for overseeing the operations. SSNC's great success over the next decade depended on coordinating a fleet of boats, not enthusing about the clipper masterworks that McKay had crafted.[120] Systematizing traffic meant establishing a timetable, ensuring regularity and dependability of transport. Cunningham also developed a series of warehouses along the six-hundred-mile Yangtse River, from the cities of Shanghai to Hankow, thus enabling the SSNC to control the movement of goods into China and from port to port on the China coast. By 1872, the SSNC line had grown from five to nineteen steamers by subsuming its major competitors.[121]

Meanwhile, back in North America money from the China trade continued to finance western railway development. In 1870 Robert Bennet Forbes rode the Pullman railcar from Boston to San Francisco, where he delivered a lecture describing the transformative effect of steam, rail, and telegraphic technologies on modern life. Forty-five years earlier in 1825, he had visited San Francisco by sea. Recalling the primitive state of the city, he marveled at the efficiency with which steamships now ferried tens of thousands of people around the vicinity of San Francisco and to Sausalito. Whereas in 1825 it had taken five months for a handwritten letter to reach Boston, in 1870, it was possible to get a "reply in 'less than no time'" by "touch[ing] the electric wire."[122] And in 1825 the sailing voyage from Boston to San Francisco had taken five months; in 1870 Forbes merely stepped "into a miniature palace on wheels" and was "whisked home" "in *seven days or less*."[123] He predicts that "steam lines to Australia, China, the Pacific Islands, Japan, Alaska, and the West Coast" would transform California into "the richest, the most respectable, and the most influential State in the Union."[124]

Robert Bennet knew what he was talking about. His uncle Colonel Thomas

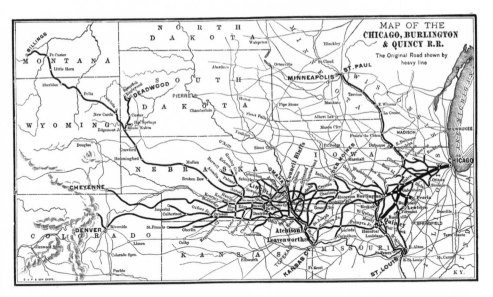

"Forty years' growth of the Chicago, Burlington and Quincy Railroad." Forbes, *Letters and Recollections of John Murray Forbes*, p. 212.

Perkins had financed one of the first railroads to move granite in building a monument to the Battle of Bunker Hill. Robert Bennet's younger brother John Murray Forbes had put his China trade fortune to work in acquiring western lands and securing rights for railway construction. Today, John Murray Forbes is usually known in terms that Henry Greenleaf Pearson invokes in his biography *An American Railroad Builder: John Murray Forbes* (1911). Pearson introduces Forbes as the "president of the Michigan Central Railroad from 1846 to 1855; of the Chicago, Burlington, and Quincy Railroad he was director from 1857 to 1898, and Quincy Railroad he was director from 1857 to 1898, and president from 1878 to 1881."[125] The first ten pages summarize Forbes's youth, including his voyages to China, before focusing on his speculation in real estate, steamships, his Civil War activities and investments, and his oversight of the railways. During these decades as a railway developer, Forbes remained "the guiding spirit of Russell & Company" and arbitrated various matters of dispute as Russell & Company developed operations from Shanghai into the Chinese mainland.[126]

Robert Bennet and John Murray Forbes epitomize the type of systematic vision on which Perry was counting when he imagined the commercial development of East Asia in the wake of opening Japan to free trade. Turning to railway ventures, John Murray saw opportunity in how interlocking railway lines extending west of the Mississippi River composed a system, a general configuration, that controlled the spatial and temporal flow of people, goods, and information across North America. Accounting for Forbes's skill in coordinating complex systems, John R. Haddad counts his China experience as prerequisite. After years of brokering international trade and coordinating layers of schedules, he found himself "in the 1850s . . . overseeing something that had never previously entered his imagination" but which he had been trained to understand, "a *system* of interlocking [railroad] lines."[127] The Chicago, Burlington and Quincy Company grew from a " 'feeder of the Michigan Central' of one hundred and fifty miles into the great organization" of "seven thousand miles of rail."[128] Such configurations, mirroring what Russell & Company had done to succeed in the China trade, transposed to land the shipping lanes that spanned the oceans.

Perry embraced such systematic frames in imagining the United States as a New Middle Kingdom. Land and sea would merge as railways across the North American continent connected the Far East and Far West through shipping lands across the Pacific. The Shimoda horizon of his *Narrative* highlights the to-and-fro movement underpinning the ideological mapping of land and sea routes, inviting the reader to brave the ocean horizon, into and across the Pacific Ocean and back to California of the developing Far West. Today the celebratory energy of Perry's *Narrative* seems both prescient and naïve. It is prescient for echoing the benevolent imperialism that equates free trade with civilizing communication and naïve for overlooking the intense fracturing of the United States into the North and South. After the Mexican War, the same westward expansion that spanned the continent made the long-running compromises over slavery impossible to maintain. The Civil War (1861–65) is a stunning contradiction of Perry's optimism. And yet, during the war, U.S. diplomatic efforts in China continued. After it ended, the commercial allure of East Asia continued to inspire merchants from Russell & Company, missionaries such as Samuel Wells Williams, literary figures such as Mark Twain and Walt Whitman, and diplomats such as Anson Burlingame in imagining a reconstructed and reunited United States.

CHAPTER SEVEN

Passages to India from the Newly United States

Revising *The Middle Kingdom* (1883)

Like Franklin, beginning as a printer, Williams was called to stand before kings; but he never forgot his Master in heaven.

REVEREND NOAH PORTER, president of Yale College,
eulogizing Samuel Wells Williams in the *Missionary Herald*

In the final weeks of his second return visit to the United States, Samuel Wells Williams contemplated the moral implications of the U.S. Civil War's first battles. Convinced of their great spiritual significance, he wrote in his diary that "the affliction which has come on our formerly united country" was both "a judgment" and also "a remedy for the awful blights and wrongs of the system of slavery."[1] Four years later, President Abraham Lincoln similarly invoked God's judgment in his Second Inaugural Address of 1865, characterizing the war years of carnage as a shared penance for the sin of slavery—a penance that would lead to peace and national redemption.

Looking back on his decades of extraterritorial printing and diplomatic service in China, Williams wondered whether future decades would similarly redeem the people of China for the great troubles they had suffered. There were specific disappointments in which Williams had played a role. He was not proud of the Treaty of Wanghia (1844) after former U.S. minister Caleb Cushing set it as precedent for claiming China's concession of absolute and unqualified extraterritoriality. Such bravado resonated for years: not only did China find it difficult to negotiate terms of extraterritorial consideration, but Western missionaries also used extraterritoriality to shield their evangelism from the supervision of local administrators and opium smuggling continued to increase.[2] Williams also opposed the tariff agreements appended to the Treaty of Tianjin (1858) that legalized opium trade to end the Second Opium War.

The U.S. Civil War did not shake Williams's resolve to return to China where he would continue to serve as the diplomatic secretary of the American Legation.

His next task upon returning to Hong Kong was to receive the new minister pleni-potentiary Anson Burlingame (1820–70) and to assist him in establishing resi-dence in Peking. With Williams's help, Burlingame used his diplomatic mission to initiate a new cooperative approach that won the guarded trust of the Chinese imperial administrators in Peking. Working with Burlingame offered Williams a way to clarify his diplomatic service, realigning principles of Christian faith with commercial ambition in ways that did not excuse opium smuggling, accept that gunboat diplomacy was necessary, revel in the arbitrary power implied in absolute and unqualified extraterritoriality, or ridicule the Chinese as backward pagans with a barbaric legal system beneath recognition of civilized Western nations.

This redemptive turn reached its apex in 1867 with Burlingame's retirement as minister after a term of six years. He then accepted China's request to lead its diplomatic embassy to Western nations. Leaving Williams in Peking, Burlingame headed east across the Pacific and landed in San Francisco as the impeachment of President Andrew Johnson got underway. He then proceeded to Washington, DC, to negotiate on behalf of China the "Additional Article to the Treaty of Commerce between the United States and China, of June 18, 1858. Signed at Washington, 28 July, 1868," popularly known as the Burlingame Treaty.[3] At ensuing celebratory dinners in New York and Boston, Burlingame relished new horizons of commer-cial cooperation and Christian brotherhood between the peoples. On 23 June 1868 at a Delmonico's steak house in New York, he announced this dawn of a new age to an illustrious audience of former China traders, diplomats, politicians, promi-nent clergy, and publishers; China was ready and willing "to trade with you, to buy of you, to sell to you, to help you strike off the shackles from trade."[4] He reached the peak of hyperbole in enthusing that China "invites your merchants, she invites your missionaries. She tells the latter to plant the shining cross on every hill and in every valley."[5] Mark Twain, who would become a strong critic of U.S. imperial-ism at the end of the century, sang the praises of Burlingame and heralded the civilizing prospects of developing railways and telegraphy in China. The poet Walt Whitman echoed this enthusiasm in revising *Leaves of Grass* to preface his elegy for Lincoln "When Lilacs Last in the Dooryard Bloom'd" with the extended poem "Passage to India" (1871).

Having revived an American romance of free trade with China on putatively cooperative terms, Burlingame headed to Europe. However, he met with a cool re-ception in France and died soon after in St. Petersburg, Russia. Over the next few years in Peking, Williams watched the ark of Burlingame's cooperative covenant flounder, swamped by new international confrontations, Chinese violence against missionaries, and crosscurrents of political infighting at the imperial court. In the 1870s U.S. negotiation of extraterritoriality in China rebounded back on domestic immigration policy as California State spawned racist legislation that violated the spirit and letter of the Burlingame Treaty and that echoed in federal laws restricting Chinese immigration in 1882. In the field of evangelism, events were also dispiriting. Although many more Catholic and Protestant missionaries lived in China, there seemed to be very few shining crosses of cooperation. At the end of the century, Western missionaries and Chinese Christians became the main targets of a wide peasant-based anti-foreign uprising known in the Western press as the Boxer Rebellion (1899–1901). The eventual defeat of the Boxers led to further rounds of concession from China, including indemnity payments to the American Board of Commissions of Foreign Missions (ABCFM) that Mark Twain condemned in the popular press as nakedly opportunistic and imperialistically predatory.

Williams died in 1884 and was not alive to witness these later disappointments. He left China for the last time in 1876, returning to New Haven, Connecticut, where he took up a chair professorship at Yale University in Chinese Language and Literature.[6] In his remaining years he focused on revising his masterwork *The Middle Kingdom* into a final expanded edition, noting in the new preface that his forty-three years of "life in China were coeval with the changes" that "culminated in the opening of the country."[7] Looking back on decades of opium wars and on the Taiping Rebellion, he tried to maintain faith that God had a redemptive plan for China in which he had played a constructive role.

To foreground the shifting terms of free trade by which U.S. merchants, missionaries, and diplomats looked to China after the Civil War, this chapter considers the textual trail of contradictions and blind spots that riddled Williams's romance of evangelical free trade in China. Williams's attempts to frame social catastrophe in renewed statements of faith surface when comparing the first (1848) and final (1883) editions of *The Middle Kingdom*. At key points, the final edition seems oddly detached from the social reality that Williams had witnessed and documented throughout his life. His revisions also suggest that Williams did not anticipate the U.S. imperialist policies that would fold the Spanish-American War (1898) into the Philippine-American War (1899–1902) in an embrace of what Rudyard Kipling called the "white man's burden."[8] His revisions show him pondering the injustice of opium smuggling, the unintended consequences of extraterritorial print evangelism, and his country's racist immigration policies of exclusion and disenfranchisement.

From the Second Opium War to Burlingame's Cooperative Policy

Before Burlingame arrived to the scene, Williams had been active as an interpreter in another cycle of the opium wars that punished China with treaties of peace and friendship. After the First Opium War, he had lamented the Anglo-American merchants' disregard of Chinese laws banning opium.[9] There was little China could do to stop the drug's escalating importation. By 1856, as the Taiping Rebellion continued to wreak havoc, Chinese authorities tried to take a stand. When patrolling the Pearl River, they arrested the ship *Arrow* for smuggling opium while illegally flying a British flag. Britain amplified the ensuing dispute to initiate what became a two-phase Second Opium War.

The war's first phase ended in 1858 with Britain's Lord Elgin negotiating the fifty-six articles of the Treaty of Tientsin (Tiānjīn tiáoyuē; 天津條約) alongside France, Russia, and the United States. As the secretary of the U.S. Legation, Williams helped diplomatic Minister William Bradford Reed obtain the parallel treaty entitled "Treaty between the United States of America and the Chinese Emperor," signed in the English and Chinese languages on 18 June 1858. It begins with the standard reassurance of peace and friendship and then echoes the concessions that Britain had secured from China: Article 5 established the right for ministers and diplomats to visit Peking and reside there while conferring with Chinese authorities; Articles 11 and 27 outlined extraterritoriality by which Chinese subjects would be tried and punished by Chinese authorities, and U.S. citizens tried and punished by U.S. consuls in accordance with U.S. law; Article 12 allowed U.S. citizens living in the treaty ports to maintain houses, hospitals, churches, and cemeteries; Article 14 opened additional treaty ports; Article 29 legalized Protestant and Catholic missionary work in China; and, the final Article 30 invoked most-favored-nation consideration to accrue all the unstated benefits of the British treaty for the United States. Negotiations related to commerce also produced a tariff schedule (18 November 1858) that in effect legalized opium traffic.

The word *opium* never appears in the American or British treaties, but this appended agreement between Britain and China taxed it at thirty taels of silver per one hundred catties.[10] In the 1883 final edition of *The Middle Kingdom*, Williams concludes that "the inherent wrong of the principle of ex-territoriality was never more unjustly applied than in breaking down the moral sense of a people by forcing them to legalize this drug" in 1858.[11] The terms taxed it at a "lower rate than was paid on tea and silk entering England."[12] For the next ten years, opium traffic continued unabated. In 1881 a new law outlawed it after a new treaty with the United States had explicitly prohibited it; however, the fines were too low to be a major deterrent and, as this chapter considers, the new treaty also paved the way for U.S. federal law to restrict Chinese immigration.[13]

The second phase of the Second Opium War began in 1859 when China took a military stand to prevent the allied treaty powers of Britain and France from delivering the ratified treaty to Peking. China set up forces at the Taku Forts (大沽炮台;

Dàgū Pàotái) on the Bohai Gulf (Bóhǎi; 渤海; also known as the Gulf of Chihli, Zhílì Hǎiwān; 直隸海灣) on the way to the port city of Tianjin. In June 1859 Chinese forces initially repelled British and French forces. Williams witnessed the battle with U.S. minister John Elliot Ward from the deck of a U.S. supply ship. He later reported from the USS *Powhatan* that 452 British troops had been killed, wounded, or drowned as three vessels sank; despite the U.S. stance of neutrality, the U.S. commodore assisted the British in their retreat.[14] Williams and the U.S. entourage continued on their own to Peking—navigating the Peiho River (contemporary Hǎi Hé; 海河) inland to Tungchow (contemporary Tōngzhōu; 通州), and finally trekking fourteen miles by land to the city wall of Peking. As British and French troops continued to fight, Ward and Williams met with the Chinese officials and arranged for the exchange of treaties. Minister Ward and his delegation then left. Meanwhile, British and French forces proceeded to demolish the Chinese checkpoints and reached the outskirts of Peking. In retaliation for China's military resistance and the brutal treatment of prisoners, the troops sacked the Summer Palace (頤和園; Yíhé Yuán) and secured more concessions in the Convention of Peking (1860). France secured the freedom of missionaries to travel, live, rent, and preach throughout China—a freedom extended to Protestant missionaries of other countries; Britain made territorial demands, securing the mainland area of Kowloon across the harbor from Hong Kong island and an additional eight million taels for war reparation and compensation of British merchants.[15]

Williams was not in Peking when the British and French arrived in early October. After the treaty exchange, he had returned to South China and focused efforts on stopping the brutal traffic of Chinese laborers in what was called the Coolie trade. He published his only text in Chinese related to the effort, "Words to Startle Those Who Are Selling Their Bodies [to go] Abroad" (1859).[16] He then headed back to the United States, visiting his hometown of Utica and congregations in Boston and New York as Lincoln ran for president. Slavery disgusted Williams, and he felt that a war to purge it from the Union would fulfill the promise of the Revolution. Nevertheless, his priority continued to be helping "China's ignorant people," and he contracted a substitute to take his place in the Union army.[17] Departing with his wife and daughter for the return voyage to Hong Kong in July 1861, he was convinced that "God's hand will guide and uphold His own ark and forward His own purpose, for He sees the end from the beginning."[18]

Upon his return, Williams continued to balance dedication to spiritual mission, commerce, diplomatic duties, and print publication as an editor. Landing in Hong Kong, he was crushed to hear that his youngest son had died in the United States. Shortly thereafter his longtime collaborator and friend Rev. Elijah Bridgman passed away in Shanghai. Awaiting the arrival of the new U.S. minister, Williams channeled his grief into editorial work, revising the *Chinese Commercial Guide* (first published in the 1830s by Rev. Robert Morrison's son John Morrison) into a fifth and final edition that ran 670 pages. He also published an overview of the diplomatic record in *Treaties between the United States of America and China, Japan, Lewchew and Siam, Acts of Congress, and the Attorney-General's Opinion, with Decrees and Regulations Issued for the Guidance of Consular Courts in China* (1862).[19] This included Cushing's 1844 summary of the Treaty of Wanghia and his 1855 opinion as attorney general, both of which asserted that China had conceded "absolute and unqualified" extraterritoriality.

Minister Burlingame arrived to Macao in October 1861 to find "the American legation located in the rented house of its chargé and secretary, S. W. Williams."[20] In the spring of 1862 he and Williams traveled north to Shanghai, touring treaty ports that had opened after the First Opium War and where missionary stations struggled to operate. Williams recorded his impressions of a devastated landscape, describing the country as "everywhere open" but unsafe with the Taiping Rebellion presenting a "scene of rapine and bloodshed and suffering beyond description."[21] From Shanghai they headed to Peking, arriving in late July. Williams oversaw the renovations of a consul residence as Burlingame moved back and forth from Peking to Shanghai through Tianjin.

Williams returned to Canton for a final visit and closed down his residence. He reported to Rev. Dr. Peter Parker, his longtime collaborator and predecessor as the legation secretary, that the city was unlikely to return to its "old prosperity."[22] As centers of commerce and publishing, Canton and Macao had been eclipsed by Hong Kong and Shanghai. Looking west from Shanghai to the challenge of establishing a diplomatic residence in Peking in May 1863, Williams conjured an evangelical quest into a wilderness of Chinese sin, transposing scenes of continental Manifest Destiny in North America onto landscapes scarred by the Taiping Rebellion and Second Opium War in China. To friend and supporter Mrs. H. C. Wood in Kentucky, he wrote: "Here I am on my way to Peking with wife, children, box, bundle, and bag, all in a heap, like the big wagons that used to go through Utica on their way beyond and westward; that was going into the wilderness of nature to improve and adorn it, and make the waste places habitable, but this is going into the wilderness of sin—as bad morally as ever the one of Hagar's distress was physically. However, if God goes with me, and strengthens me, I shall not fail."[23] This pioneer nostalgia might seem out of touch with the contemporaneous Battle of Chancellorsville and General Ulysses S. Grant's long siege of Vicksburg. But Williams's reference to Hagar wrestles national redemption from an individual's exile. Hagar was an enslaved Egyptian woman serving Sarah, the first wife of Abraham. When Sarah seemed unable to conceive, Hagar bore Abraham's first son Ishmael.

After Sarah finally delivered Abraham's second son Isaac, Hagar and Ishmael were cast into the desert. Ishmael eventually rose to lead the wayward, mysterious, and eventually powerful Ishmaelite people. Alienated from the United States and his home base in South China, Williams figures himself as being in a state of similarly propitious exile, heading west to the formerly Forbidden City to establish an outpost for Burlingame's cooperative diplomacy, a mission that promised to redeem Williams's errand into a Chinese wilderness and to bring the great but wandering people of China back into the fold of Christendom.

Burlingame and the Cooperative Policy

The redemptive turn that Williams looked for in his diplomatic service to Burlingame is apparent in the biography *Anson Burlingame and the First Chinese Mission to Foreign Powers* (1912) by Williams's son Frederick Wells Williams. It presents Burlingame's life "as a romance in the stirring period of American history" that "deserves a biographer capable of giving its epic movement lasting literary form."[24] Frederick Wells Williams praises him for putting into action the biblical adage "Thou shalt love thy neighbor as thyself" and credits him with being the "father of the open-door principle."[25]

Born in upstate New York, Burlingame grew up in Detroit and attended the University of Michigan and Harvard Law School. As a dynamic member of the antislavery Free Soil Party, he represented the state of Massachusetts in the U.S. House of Representatives and denounced South Carolina representative Preston Brooks in June 1856 for beating Massachusetts senator Charles Sumner nearly to death with a cane on the floor of the U.S. Senate.[26] Burlingame campaigned hard for Lincoln but lost his own congressional seat. President Lincoln then tapped him to serve as an ambassador to Austria, but Burlingame's vocal support of the 1848 revolutions derailed the nomination. Instead, he replaced Ward, who had delivered the Senate-ratified Treaty of Tianjin to Peking in 1860. Burlingame's abolitionist convictions resonated in Peking, outside of which he "established a summer legation at Sanshannan (Temple of Three Hills)," naming it "Tremont Temple" in honor of Boston's Tremont Temple Baptist Church where he and Free Soil activists had met years before.[27]

Unlike his predecessors, Burlingame championed not a coercive but a cooperative approach to China, which would guarantee "to China her autonomy and equal treatment by the United States, on the same terms as any other independent power."[28] By "substituting fair diplomatic action for violence," Burlingame managed "an agreement on the part of the Treaty Powers to act together upon all material questions; to stand together in defence of their treaty rights, but determined at

the same time to give those treaties a generous construction; determined to maintain the foreign system of customs, and to support it in a pure administration and
upon a cosmopolitan basis; and agreement to take no cession of territory at the
treaty ports, and never to menace the territorial integrity of China."[29] In a dispatch
to Secretary of State William H. Seward, Burlingame put it this way: as minister he
would "not ask for, nor take concessions of, territory in the treaty ports, or in any
way interfere with the jurisdiction of the Chinese Government over its own people, nor ever menace the territorial integrity of the Chinese Empire"; at the same
time he pledged to uphold "our treaty right to buy and sell and hire in the treaty
ports, in respect to our rights of property and person, to the jurisdiction of our own
governments."[30] Burlingame got on well with the more powerful British minister
Frederick Bruce and helped defuse confrontations between Britain and China,
most notably in the Osborne-Lay dispute over a naval flotilla, the delivery of which
China rejected when its British commander refused either to relinquish command
or to obey Chinese authorities.[31]

Burlingame was a charismatic minister, but his success depended more on
China's postwar desperation than on his personal charms. The Second Opium War
had shaken China to the core as other revolts were breaking out in the North and
West. When the British and French forces approached Peking, the young emperor
Xianfeng fled the capital and died in exile soon after. Having lost two wars, the
imperial rulers adopted a new strategy of strategically placating Western commercial interests as a means of strengthening their military, technological capacity, and
administrative foundation. Xianfeng's brother Yìxīn (奕訢), known in English as
Prince Kung (or Prince Gong), took control of the government by collaborating with
an "exceptional group of provincial officials," including Wang Guofan, Li Hong-
zhang, and Zuo Zongtang), "who had risen to prominence fighting the Taiping"
and facing down Muslim uprisings in the west.[32] Running the government to prepare for the restoration of the emperor Xianfeng's young son, the prince Tóng Zhì
(同治帝), they set up the "Office for the Management of the Business of all Foreign
Countries" known as the Zǒnglǐ Yámén (總理衙門), which collaborated with the
British and U.S. diplomats and advisers. They appointed a British official to oversee the "Foreign-managed inspectorate of Customs." The first appointed head of
the Chinese Maritime Customs Service was Horatio Nelson Lay, who resigned after
the flotilla fiasco. Britain's second appointee, Sir Robert Hart, proved a very capable
and stabilizing force. In 1876 Hart coordinated the Chinese exhibit at the Philadelphia Centennial Exhibition.[33] His staff at the customs office included a young Hosea
Ballou Morse, who became a major historiographer of the China trade in the early
twentieth century after retiring. In 1950 the final director left from Taiwan after the
establishment of the People's Republic of China; during these decades approxi-

mately eleven thousand foreign administrators had worked under a succession of five different foreign Chief Inspectors to coordinate China's maritime customs.[34]

Prince Kung and the Zǒnglǐ Yámén pursued other initiatives of cultural collaboration including the Chinese Education Mission, which sent cadres of Chinese students to the United States from 1872 to 1881. The endeavor materialized through the efforts of Yung Wing (容閎; 1828–1912), the first person from China to graduate from Yale University. Born in a village outside of Macao, he had attended a mission school for girls run by Mrs. Mary Wanstall Gützlaff before transferring to the Morrison Education Society School in 1841. Yung's autobiography, *My Life in China and America* (1909), recounts the political tensions in Peking that contributed to the students being recalled in 1881 as China took offense at the anti-Chinese sentiment and legislation roiling the United States.[35] Other Zǒnglǐ Yámén initiatives included the commissioning of Williams's colleague and U.S. Presbyterian missionary W. A. P. Martin to translate sections of Henry Wheaton's *Elements of International Law* (1836) for dissemination to "provincial officials" who worked with the foreign missionaries, traders, and consuls. They also enlisted Martin to run the Tóngwén Guǎn (同文舘), a school dedicated to the study of foreign languages that later merged into what is now Beijing University.[36] The Tongzhi Restoration spurred other "top-down reforms" to develop military capabilities on land and sea as part of China's Self-Strengthening Movement.[37]

During his ministerial appointment, Burlingame won the confidence of Prince Kung and the Zhǒnglǐ Yámén. Upon his retirement, they enlisted him to help lead the first international embassy of Chinese officials as the "Chinese representative in treaty discussions in the United States and Europe."[38] Two Chinese ministers, Chih Kang Tajen and Sun Chia-Ku Tajen, accompanied Burlingame and shared with him the title "Envoy Extraordinary and Minister Plenipotentiary for China, Head of the Chinese Embassy." Other envoy members included the acting Chinese secretary of the British legation, Mr. J. McLeavy Brown, and the French official of the Chinese Imperial Maritime Customs service, Monsieur E. de Champs, as well as six Chinese students, four copyists and two military officers, and other servants and translators.[39] The precise nature of Burlingame's authority was ambiguous.[40] Through the English version of his directions, Burlingame claimed broad latitude of authority, including the power to negotiate on China's behalf with Secretary of State William H. Seward in Washington, DC. However, the Chinese version of his guidelines stipulated that final authorization for any negotiations would come from Peking.[41] Perhaps the ambiguity of the guidelines was Prince Kung's way of enhancing rapport with Western nations while allaying his conservative critics in Peking, who remained wary of Western assurances of peace and friendship.

Relishing his representative role in Washington, DC, in June 1868, Burlingame

"The Chinese Embassy—Photographed by Brady.; Interpreters. M. De Champs. Chih-Tajin. Sun-Tajin. J. J. MacLeavy Brown. Interpreters." *Harper's Weekly* 12.598 (18 June 1868): 376.

worked with Seward to issue a new treaty known popularly as the Burlingame Treaty or the Burlingame-Seward Treaty.[42] Article 1 reinforced China's previous concessions of access to treaty ports and extraterritoriality, while reassuring China that "in no event" would such concessions "be construed to divest the Chinese authorities of their right of jurisdiction over persons and property within said tract of land, except so far as that right may have been expressly relinquished by treaty."[43] Article 3 granted China reciprocal rights to set up consuls' residences in the United States. Article 5, entitled "Free Emigration," proved highly significant and controversial in the ensuing decade for opening U.S. citizenship to Chinese immigrants, recognizing "the inherent and inalienable right of man to change his home and his allegiance, and also the mutual advantages of free migration and immigration of their citizens and subjects respectively from one country to the other for purposes of curiosity, trade, or as permanent residents."[44] Article 6 secured for "Chinese subjects" living in or visiting the United States the "same privileges, immunities, and exceptions" as "citizens or subjects of the most favored nation."[45] The treaty was ratified by both countries and exchanged in Peking on 23 November 1869.

Today historians generally echo Frederick Wells Williams in appreciating the eponymous treaty for the ostensibly respectful tone with which it secures commercial endeavors in China.[46] However, Burlingame's "cooperative policy" still patronized China as a pagan kingdom that had come to accept the inevitability of Western commercial development in its territory and the necessity of extraterritoriality. The treaty leaves little room for China to refuse the expansive designs of U.S. commercial enterprises. The construction of networks of communication and transportation that enabled foreign access to China was not a question of "if" but of "how" and "when." Article 8 recognizes the emperor's authority in these terms:

> The United States, always disclaiming and discouraging practices of unnecessary dictation and intervention by one nation in the affairs or domestic administration of another, do hereby freely disclaim any intention or right to intervene in the construction of railroads, telegraphs, or other material internal improvements. On the other hand, His majesty and Emperor of China reserves to himself the right to decide the time, and manner, and circumstances of introducing such improvements within his dominions. With his mutual understanding it is agreed by the contracting parties that if at any time hereafter His imperial Majesty shall determine to construct or cause to be constructed works of the character mentioned within the Empire, and shall make application to the United States or any other Western power for facilities to carry out that policy, the United States will, in that case, designate and authorize suitable engineers in their persons and property, and paying them a reasonable compensation for their service.[47]

Professing to eschew "unnecessary dictation" and to honor and protect the emperor's right to rule, the treaty presents railway and telegraph construction throughout China as a foregone conclusion. It avers principles of noninterference and nonintervention in the affairs of another nation but contradictorily implies the inevitability of such intervention. In this kinder and gentler mode of free-trade imperialism, the United States promotes and encourages China's development while defending China's sovereignty against European aggression. Although a marked turn from the overt racism of Cushing's dispatches two decades before, Burlingame's agenda was not new. It echoes protective reassurances that Justice John Marshall had given to Native peoples in the Supreme Court opinions of the Marshall Trilogy (1823, 1831, 1832) and that the U.S. presidents had projected over postrevolutionary republics in the American hemisphere and the Pacific through the Monroe and Tyler doctrines.

Celebrating Burlingame's New American Romance of Civilizing Commerce

Dinner banquets in New York and Boston followed the initial signing of the Burlingame Treaty, giving the nation something to celebrate as politicians in Washington tried to turn the page from treason to Reconstruction. On 21 August 1868 at Boston's St. James Hotel, the mayor greeted distinguished guests of honor, who included Caleb Cushing, Ralph Waldo Emerson, Charles Sumner, and Oliver Wendell Holmes Jr.[48] Wealth and influence had not exempted prominent families from the grief of war. Daniel Webster's son Fletcher Webster served as Cushing's personal secretary in 1844 and was later killed at the Second Battle of Bull Run. Colonel Robert Gould Shaw, the great grandnephew of Major Samuel Shaw and a cousin of brothers John Murray and Robert Bennet Forbes, lost his life at Fort Wagner, South Carolina.[49]

In the shadow of grief and impeachment proceedings, Burlingame sounded a trumpet blast of optimism in renewing the national romance of free trade with China. He was a powerful orator—his father having been a lay preacher in Michigan—and he enthused over the progressive accomplishment of his cooperative policy. One wonders if Cushing bristled to hear Burlingame describe China as "as an equal among nations" and to praise its long history of religious toleration.[50] After sketching the empire's modes of legislation and publication, Burlingame concluded: "China is not a land of caprices,—it is a land of laws."[51] Deferring to Emerson over the philosophical import of "the ancient sages of China," he outlined the dawn of new commercial development in China—development that would not "interfere in the internal affairs of China" or "menace the territorial integrity of China."[52]

Subsequent speakers did not share Burlingame's high regard for a China. They sketched a conventional pagan foil, ruled by a barbaric despot who had marooned his subjects in the historical stagnation of monopolized trade. They rehearsed a formulaic boast that the world's youngest revolutionary nation was ushering the world's oldest empire into the brotherhood of modern nations. Such bravado relished the legacies of European imperial power that American free trade had refined. Charles Sumner compared Burlingame to Marco Polo, Vasco da Gama, and Christopher Columbus. He described Columbus's discovery of a new world as an event that had made possible the creation of United States, "destined in the history of civilization to be more than Cathay, and in the great lapse of time to welcome the Ambassador of the grand Khan."[53] Looking ahead, he asserted, "it only remains that this welcome [to the Chinese ambassadors] should be extended until it opens a pathway for the mightiest commerce of the world, and embraces within the sphere of American activity that ancient and ancestral empire, . . . on an unprecedented scale, [to] create resources and necessities on an unprecedented scale also."[54]

After Holmes recited a poem that he had written expressly for the occasion, Cushing rose to speak. He paid tribute to the special contribution of Massachusetts's "merchant princes of China" whose decades of enterprise had paved the way for the Chinese embassy.[55] At sixty-eight years of age, he referred to himself as but a "humble pioneer" of a diplomatic mission that Burlingame was expanding.[56] But Cushing did not praise the cooperative basis of Burlingame's mission. Like Sumner he invoked da Gama and Columbus to remind his audience of the ongoing "sacred, the sublime, the divine mission, to place [China's millions] in harmonious correspondence, diplomatic, political and commercial, with the nations of Christendom."[57] Emerson followed Cushing and similarly outlined a progressive turn of world-historical significance three thousand years in the making. Asserting that China had "hitherto [has been] a romantic legend to most," he acknowledged China's discovery of the magnet and inventions of "block-printing or stereotype, and lithography, and gunpowder, and vaccination, and canals."[58] Nevertheless, Western nations had taken the lead in driving historical progress as the "irresistible result of the science" enabled them to harness "the power of steam" and invent "the electric telegraph" and to open China and Japan to the world.

News of the treaty echoed triumphantly in the U.S. press. Mark Twain penned the *New York Tribune* article "The Treaty with China: Its Provisions Explained" (28 August 1868), heralding it as the "broadest, most unselfish, and the most catholic treaty yet framed by man," for presuming China's "supreme control over its own people."[59] Two years prior in 1866 Twain had met Burlingame in Hawaii while on journalistic assignment.[60] The two became friends, and Twain was even encouraged to succeed Burlingame as the next minister to China.[61] In his piece, Twain glossed each treaty article with characteristic wit, charged with pride that the world's youngest nation was civilizing China out of backward superstition. Free trade had won the day, and Article 8 won his highest praise. Later in his life he decried the U.S. war on the Philippines and lead the Anti-Imperialist League in chastising Western imperialism in China.[62] In the 1860s, however, he was of a different mind, supporting the annexation Hawai'i as a charitable national responsibility.[63] Accordingly, he characterizes Article 8 as "perhaps the most important clause of the treaty" for promising to "unlock the riches of 400,000,000 of Chinese subjects to the world."[64] He concludes with triumphal exuberance:

> [The Burlingame Treaty] looks to the opening up, in China, of a vast and lucrative commerce with the world, and of which America will have only her just share, nothing more. It looks to the lifting up of a mighty nation and conferring upon it the boon of a purer religion and of a higher and better civilization than it has known before. It is a treaty made in the broad interest of justice, enlightenment, and progress, and therefore it must stand. It bridges the Pacific, it breaks down the Tartar wall, it inspires with fresh young blood the energies of the most venerable of nations. It acquires a

grand field for capital, labor, research enterprise—it confers science, mechanics, social and political advancement, Christianity. Is it not enough?[65]

Back in Peking, Prince Kung and his allies at the Imperial Court must have been relieved to avoid a third opium war, but the foregone conclusion of Western aid and maintenance of extraterritoriality was disconcerting. The message behind the cooperative reassurances was clear: it is in the best interest of the world for the United States to oversee extraterritorial commercial development of the ancient and pagan Middle Kingdom.

Twain does acknowledge that, in the wake of the Opium Wars, it is reasonable for the Chinese people to be suspicious of foreign powers' offers of peace and friendship. But he does not regard China's suspicions as a legitimate political concern over sovereignty, extraterritoriality, or Western violations of previous treaty agreements. Rather, he depicts China's wariness as pagan superstition. He hopes for a day when China "feels that the railroad and the telegraph are not to be instruments by which she is disrupted or destroyed"; thereafter, China "will come out of her seclusion and enter upon a course of trade, the importance of which, and the amount of which, no man can compute."[66] His feminine gendering of China underscores the national hierarchy implicit in his embrace of commercial development.

Twain continues by serving up familiar stereotypes. Chinese people are primitive pagans who irrationally fear disturbance of their ancestors' graves. Of course, railway and telegraph construction required digging up the land. If Twain had credited the Chinese with having a respectable sense of spirituality, he might have registered this as a legitimate spiritual concern. Thomas David DuBois's recent overview of the political and social history of religion in China and Japan traces a general economy of spiritual, political, and religious beliefs that includes reverence for one's ancestors, involving several versions of Confucianism, several versions of Buddhism, Daoism (Chinese), and Shintoism (Japanese).[67] In contrast, Twain's article is not interested in understanding the history and nuance of spirituality in China. His Chinese are childlike in their idolatrous sensitivity to disturbing the bones of their ancestors. Here is how Twain lays out the resulting challenge of commercially developing China:

> Let us look charitably now upon a certain very serious obstacle which lies in the way of their [China's] sudden acceptance of a great railroad system. Let us remember that China is one colossal graveyard—a mighty empire so knobbed all over with graves that the level spaces left are hardly more than alleys and avenues among the clustering death mounds. Animals graze upon the grass-clad graves (for all things are made useful in China), and the spaces between are carefully and industriously cultivated. These graves are as precious as their own blood to the Chinese, for they worship their

dead as ancestors. The first railroad that plows its pitiless way through these myriads of sacred hillocks will carry dismay and distress into countless households. The railways must be built, though. We respect the griefs of the poor country people, but still the railways must be built. They will tear heartstrings out by the roots, but they lead to the sources of unimaginable wealth, and they must be built.[68]

In his call to charity Twain is not being ironic.[69] As with Jefferson's Indian mounds in *Notes on the State of Virginia* (1787), China's "sacred hillocks" dot with irrational superstition the wasteland of the primitively pagan Other who must yield to the progressive modern husbandry of Christian nations. Of course, there are major differences between Twain's China of 1868 and Jefferson's Virginia. Jefferson's idealized immigrant farmers would reject Europe's urban workshops and root themselves in the soil, inspired by noble and nomadic savages who receded into the western horizon and faded from national historical time. Possessing the land as individuals, Jefferson's farmers would then confederate a national heartland that buffered the nation from the cankerous commerce of European manufacturing. In contrast, Twain embraces an extraterritorial logic of commercial influence that liberalizes imperial China to open it to the networks of global commerce in which U.S. manufacturing companies are vying for profit by controlling the means of transportation and exchange across China's territory.

Indeed, the goal underlying Burlingame's treaty was not to possess Chinese land but to control the flow of goods and information over and through it, knocking down its Tartar walls, bridging its pagan wasteland with a world system of commerce and waking its pagan people up to the allure of purchase power. In this paradigm of civilizing commerce, railway construction would redirect the labor of China's "poor country" people into building up communicative infrastructure. Instead of sinking back and down into melancholic ancestral reflection implied by a "colossal graveyard," they would look up and out over their country as it reached to connect to the broader shared world. The Chinese would be catapulted into modernity and international comity. Twain's sentiments were not merely echoes of daydreaming merchant elites in Boston, New York, and San Francisco. As telegraph cables, the transcontinental railway, and the Suez Canal accelerated the movement of people, goods, and information across the planet, access to and through China supported celebration of the United States, rising again to world-historical prominence after its Civil War.

However, there is a historical irony to Burlingame's predictions: as the nineteenth century drew to a close, the China trade never lived up to its hype, and the optimism of his cooperative approach faded in renewed rounds of warfare. The shining crosses of Christianity and commerce failed to materialize. Williams was chagrined to meet Burlingame's diplomatic successor, J. Ross Browne, who had "a genuine loathing for the Burlingame Mission and for Burlingame's optimism."[70] An established literary author and journalist, entrepreneur, and "former federal mining commissioner" from California, Browne was committed to the development of railroads, telegraphs, and mines and sought to pursue it with or without the consent of China's governing body.[71] He registered particular concern with the Burlingame Treaty's fifth and sixth articles that recognized the inherent rights of Chinese people to reside in the United States under protection of all the rights extended to citizens of most favored nations.[72] As Burlingame continued his world tour to France and Prussia, Browne resigned and left Williams in charge of the legation in Peking.

When Browne's successor, Frederick Ferdinand Low, arrived and delivered the ratified Burlingame Treaty to Peking in November 1869, the political scene in China was changing considerably. Low accepted the mission to China after finishing a term as California's first four-year governor. (His gubernatorial predecessor was the railway magnate Amasa Leland Stanford.) In China, Low was not equipped to deal with the rising crises. Over the next few years he and Williams were caught up in the tumult of mediating between France and China after the Tianjin massacre of 21 June 1870. In 1871 Low floundered in an attempt to repeat Cushing's and Perry's exercises of gunboat diplomacy in what turned out to be a bloody and diplomatically failed confrontation involving Korea.[73] In 1875 Low left China just after the restoration of the young emperor Tongzhi, who reigned for a short time before his death sent China into another extended period of regency. Low's replacement, Benjamin Park Avery, managed an audience with the three-year-old successor emperor, Guangxu. As new hostilities broke out between Britain and China over commerce in the southwest Yunnan region of China, and as imperial administrators in Peking vied for influence, Avery was no more effective in overcoming imperial resistance to Western development of railroad and telegraph lines. He died in Peking in November 1875.[74] Williams would not be around to meet his replacement, George F. Seward, the nephew of former secretary of state William Seward. In November 1876 Williams left China for the last time and headed back to the United States.

Extraterritorial Passages to India

Today Burlingame has become a relatively minor figure in U.S. cultural history. But after the Civil War, his commercial and diplomatic accomplishment was a prominent theme in celebrations of the nation's reunification. As Burlingame's emphasis on cooperation dissipated, the softer terms of his free-trade imperialism emboldened triumphalist appeals for the United States to project its power, making the world safe for commerce as technological wonders dramatically altered senses of space and time.

Walt Whitman's "Passage to India" is a prime example. The extended lyric first appeared as the initial poem in a collection of the same name (*Passage to India*, 1871), which was itself a long appendix to the reorganized and republished fifth edition of *Leaves of Grass* (1870).[75] In reworking the volume, Whitman invokes the China trade to salve the wounds of Civil War, moving the poems concerning Lincoln ("When Lilacs Last in the Dooryard Bloom'd" and "O Captain! My Captain!") into the section retitled "President Lincoln's Burial Hymn" that follows the poem "Passage to India" in the appendix entitled *Passage of India*. So, readers in 1871 first encountered Columbus on his westward quest to the Indies. The elegies to Lincoln then follow. In his manuscript notes from 1869, Whitman reveals the "spinal Idea" of "Passage to India": "That the divine efforts of heroes, & their ideas, faithfully lived up to, will finally prevail, and be accomplished however long deferred."[76] Columbus ("the Genoese" canto 4, stanza 9, line 1) is a key hero whose "dream" finds completion in the courageous accomplishment of "captains, voyagers, explorers" and "engineers," "architects, machinists" (canto 3, stanza 6, lines 2–3), who have collaborated in creating the "modern wonders" (canto 1, stanza 1, line 4) of the Suez Canal, the transcontinental railroad, and "eloquent, gentle wires" (canto 1, stanza 1, 7) of telegraphy that span the Atlantic Ocean. Betsy Erkkila describes the poem as "Hegelian in vision and form, moving toward a dialectical union of opposites— past and present, East and West, religion and science, spirit and matter, fiction and fact—as the poet moves toward union with God."[77] As the literal earth is "spann'd, connected by net-work" (canto 3, stanza 1, line 3) of steamships crossing the oceans, and "the lands . . . welded together" (canto 3, stanza 1, line 7) by railway, humanity unites: "The people too become brothers and sisters, / The races, neighbors, to marry and be given in marriage" (canto 3, stanza 1, lines 4–5).[78] This union of space, time, and human community portends that "Nature and Man shall be disjoin'd and diffused no more" (canto 6, stanza 17, line 9) as Whitman's Poet directs the vision of spiritually transcendent union.[79] In the vehicles of technological achievement, "Whitman found a fitting symbol for his vision of history as a unitary and spiritually infused process evolving toward a global democratic community."[80] More recently Hsuan Hsu casts Whitman's synthesizing communalism in scalar terms: "If American literature is to fulfill its own democratic and aesthetic impulses toward continuity, he reasons, then its scope must encompass the entire earth—the largest, broadest scale of all."[81]

In the early twentieth-century, critical appraisals of the poem's politics and poetics were mixed as literary scholars proposed a genteel tradition of thought and a canon of American literature.[82] In *The American Renaissance*, Matthiessen did not think much of "Passage to India," preferring poems by Whitman that take in a continental American scene with the "confident vision" that "[leads] him to fulfill the most naïve and therefore natural kind of romanticism for America, the romanticism of the future."[83] Matthiessen sees Whitman crafting this sense of national future most poignantly in "When Lilacs Last in the Dooryard Bloom'd," the "tribute to Lincoln" that "best sustain[s]" his "power of giving mythical proportions to his material," with its "picture of the coffin in its night and day journey past depots and streets and over the breast of the land."[84] Conversely, Matthiessen criticizes Whitman's transnational themes for being marred by an "odd habit of introducing random words from other languages" as the poet strives "to speak not merely for Americans but for workers of all lands."[85] Muddling through French, Italian, and Spanish, Whitman devolves into "foreign jargon" "to 'eclaircise the myths of Asiatic'" in "Passage to India."[86] Matthiessen concludes that "Passage to India" lacks any discernible "myths of Asiatic," but he does not consider the cultural implications of Whitman's fascination.

The imperialist implications of Whitman's poem were apparent to Henry Nash Smith, who distrusts its synthesizing energies in *Virgin Land* (1950). In the chapter "Walt Whitman and Manifest Destiny," Smith characterizes Whitman as "the poet who gave final imaginative expression to the theme of manifest destiny."[87] "Passage to India" expands Whitman's urge to "sing the whole continent" by mobilizing "the conception of a fated course of empire leading Americans to the Shores of the Pacific and bringing them into contact with Asia."[88] He cites earlier moments in Whitman's career from *Leaves of Grass* (1860) and "Drum-Taps" (1865) when Whitman is similarly enamored with the growing influence of the United States. Smith winds up his reflections on Whitman's superficial sense of the East with the "Passage to India": "This mysticism is difficult for the twentieth century to follow, but it moves in a straight line from [Senator Thomas Hart] Benton's first intimation that the course of empire would lead the American people westward to fabulous Asia."[89] Smith does not dwell on the implications of Whitman's embrace of empire. He half-heartedly distinguishes it from "the less attractive influences that other thinkers have drawn from the notion of an American empire in the Pacific" before concluding that "one is grateful for the intrepid idealism that so triumphantly enabled Whitman to see in the march of the pioneer army a prelude to peace and the brotherhood of nations."[90] Erkkila is less compromising, interpreting Whitman's reach to the Indies of Columbian lore as his failed attempt to "save a national vision by leaping out of history toward spiritual grace"; he becomes "a prophet without a land."[91]

Reading the poem in the twenty-first century, with hindsight drawn from decades of war, covert operations, military interventions, and corporate security measures that chart United States involvement in Iran, Vietnam, Cambodia, Laos, Iraq, Afghanistan, throughout the Americas, and many other places throughout the world, we may be less inclined to trust "intrepid idealism" in justifying missions to protect and spread freedom and democracy. Given Whitman's general reputation for pushing the limits of poetic form in his pursuit of democratic expansiveness, it is surprising how conventional "Passage to India" seems when read alongside the dinner speeches that feted Burlingame. And, as Smith alerts us, the China trade had inspired similar pronouncements decades earlier. In the 1840s Asa Whitney returned from a relatively short but lucrative residence at Canton to become a major promoter of developing Pacific railways. His 1849 pamphlet *A Project for a Railroad to the Pacific, with Reports of Committees of Congress, Resolutions of State Legislatures, etc., with Other Facts Relating Thereto* (1849) boldly asserts that all humankind would benefit from the ability of the United States to project power throughout the Pacific. In proposing the Atlantic and Pacific Oceans be connected by rail, Whitney declared: "The first great object" is "to change the route for the commerce and intercourse of Europe with Asia, and from it, from interest, to pay tribute to us." Whitney continues by outlining mutually reinforcing advantages derived from the United States pursuing Far Eastern commerce and Far Western railway development: "by opening a means of transit for all our products to the markets of Asia, opening wilderness to settlement and production, connecting and binding our Pacific possessions to us, and making them the great depot for the commerce of all the world, which must pass through us from and to Europe, and our own vast country."[92] Envisioning the U.S. continent as global highway of commerce, he celebrates the rise of an American empire that completes a historical cycle and thus heralds the end of conflict in the world:

> With a naval depot on the Pacific, and with a comparatively small navy, we should command the vast Pacific, the Indian Ocean, the Chinese Seas; yes, I may say, we should command the world. How different would have been our position with the Mexican war. At a trifling expense, without hazard of life, the entire west coast of Mexico would have been under our complete control. But when the entire human family can be brought together, as they will by this road, in a free exchange of commodities, wars must then cease, as there can be no more cause for strife, and armies and navies no more wanted. It is our destiny to accomplish this vast revolution for all mankind.[93]

Whitney wrote this a decade before Commodore Matthew C. Perry, with Williams as his interpreter, set out to open Japan to free trade. The key to the United States establishing this commanding position was opening (at least at a rhetorical level) the Far West to the cross currents of world commerce. U.S. merchants would invest abroad to see the profits double back as capital for future ventures. The nation would regulate the pulsing flows of world commerce like the heart regulates the blood streaming through it.

As the prologue to this book proposed, the romance of free trade in China reverberated in images as well as words. In light of this book's previous chapters, consider again the elaborate centerfold of *Harper's Weekly* (30 May 1868) that presents the United States as the "[destined] commercial centre of the world," while silently registering the result of decades of war in China.[94] The largest engraving on the bottom is of the "City of Victoria, Hong Kong, China"; the line of sight faces north from Hong Kong Island, claimed by Britain after the First Opium War, to Kowloon on the Chinese mainland, claimed by Britain in the wake of the Second Opium War. Victoria Harbor appears as a bustling port with a skyline studded by cathedral spires, British customs and counting houses, and administrative offices. The other images encircling the map at the center offer dramatic snapshots of U.S. efforts to connect the Atlantic to the Pacific, and Europe to Asia through the American continents. With the completion of the North American railroad, the Panama Railroad's crossing of the Americas at Aspinwall would diminish in importance, at least until the last decades of the nineteenth century when the city of Aspinwall would become Colon as companies from France and then the United States raced to complete the Panama Canal.[95]

Harper's map is a tableau of the rise of the United States and of the fall of the Canton System. Coal-powered steamships and railroads have transformed the global field of transportation and communication, reworking "territorial rights and borderlines" through gunboat diplomacy.[96] *Harper's* map eclipses the logistical routes of the circuitry of previous centuries' world systems established and maintained under the influence of Portugal, Spain, the Dutch East India Company, and the British navy and East India Company. With the transcontinental rail in place, *Harper's* map relegates Cape Town to a small font; the ports in India (Calcutta or Goa), Southeast Asia (Batavia, Penang, Singapore, Manila, and Macao) and the Atlantic (St. Helena) have disappeared altogether. The map charts triangulating vectors that connect Hong Kong, Yokohama, and Melbourne, all converging on the Sandwich Islands and then reaching across the Pacific in a single vector to San Francisco, where rail passage to New York begins.

Abrogating Burlingame's Treaty

Departing Shanghai in 1876, Williams composed an essay-length response to U.S. expatriates that he then published in San Francisco as *Our Relations with China* (1877). In leaving China, he hoped to revive the optimism of the Burlingame mission. In the face of rising tide of discrimination toward Chinese in California, he offers advice on how to foster trust with China that promotes commercial progress. To distinguish the United States from other treaty powers (e.g., Britain, France, Russia) that had continued to press China militarily for concessions, Williams mentions that Article 33 of the Treaty of Wanghia had explicitly prohibited Americans from trafficking opium and credits this with shaping China's general impression that Americans had "nothing to do with the opium trade."[97] Looking ahead, Williams advises that the United States should reinforce this impression. He does not mention the treaty's articles on extraterritoriality that Cushing had summarized as conceding absolute and unqualified extraterritoriality.

As Williams well knew, China's long-held resentment of extraterritoriality was being compounded by the rising violence against Chinese people in the United States and legislative drives that lead to restrictive policies of immigration in violation of the Burlingame Treaty. In the wake of the transcontinental railroad's completion in 1869 and after the Depression of 1873 "threw many American out of work," popular "demagogues" in California had incited and channeled the rage of white laborers against Chinese people.[98] By the early 1880s, U.S. minister James B. Angell went to Peking and renegotiated Articles 5 and 6 of the Burlingame Treaty, paving the way for the federal Chinese Exclusion Act (1882). The social scene in California had seemed more promising for Chinese immigrants in the 1850s when tens of thousands emigrated to establish networks of Chinese communities, stretching across the southern provinces of China, through Hong Kong and to Hawai'i and San Francisco.[99] Today, Stanford University's Chinese Railroad Workers in North America Project presents an impressive multimedia digital archive of their experience.[100]

Returning to the United States in 1876, Williams tried to counteract racism by appreciating the Chinese not only as hardworking laborers and trustworthy potential U.S. citizens but also as part of an international network of Chinese expatriates with prestige and power. At the Social Science Association meetings in 1879, he delivered a paper on Chinese immigration, which he later published. He begins with an anecdote of the former President Ulysses S. Grant visiting Penang, the Malaccan Straits port city of contemporary Malaysia in 1878. Williams writes: "Few incidents in the last few months have had a more picturesque setting in regard to the actors, the place of meeting, and the subject talked of, than the interview held last April between General Grant and the Chinese merchants at Georgetown, in Pulo Penang."[101] In their conversation, Penang's Chinese merchants urge Grant to use his considerable "influence to secure a fair and liberal treatment for their countrymen in America, and to remove any restrictions which had been imposed on their freedom to come and go, the same as any other nations."[102]

Williams is more than simply touched that Penang's Chinese merchants were advocating on behalf of fellow Chinese emigrants living half a world away in the United States. His descriptions evince the economic influence of Penang's Chinese immigrants who built up the British-controlled port into a wealthy city; he credits the island's "commercial importance" "to the industry and skill of its twelve thousand Chinese settlers, who, under the care and control of the British Government have made it a mart for traffic of the neighboring islands and continent."[103] On the same world tour, Grant visited Canton, Hong Kong, Shanghai, and Peking, but Williams chose to focus on Penang in order to remind his U.S. readers that treatment of Chinese people ramified internationally, beyond the Forbidden City and through a global network of commerce. As the legislatures of Sacramento, California, and Washington, DC, debated the terms of Chinese citizenship and regulations of their immigration, Chinese merchants throughout the world were taking note.

At the 1878 meeting in Penang, former president Grant reassured his audience of Chinese merchants that "the hostility of which they complained did not represent the real sentiment of America; but was the work of demagogues," who "pander to prejudice against race or nationality and favor any measure of oppression that might advance their political interests."[104] Despite Grant's reassurances, the tide of racism continued to rise at the federal and state levels. Ironically, exclusionary legislation adapted earlier legislative language formulated to stop the Coolie trade in 1862 and another law that Grant had signed known as the Page Law (1875), which "prohibited involuntary immigrants from China, Japan, and other Oriental countries," focusing on Chinese women trafficked for purposes of prostitution.[105] The law's regulations ostensibly protected Chinese people from being involuntarily trafficked, but it introduced discriminatory mechanisms that obligated Chinese women to prove that they were *not* emigrating for "lewd or immoral purposes," requiring them to present a certificate and photograph and leaving them "subject to rounds of investigation" in Hong Kong and California.[106] In the election year of 1876, both the Republican and Democratic parties were sounding alarms over a deluge of Chinese immigrants, addressing the scare of "Mongolian Immigration" in their parties' platforms.[107] When in 1878 President Rutherford B. Hayes vetoed an exclusion bill that directly violated the Burlingame Treaty, it turned out to be a brief respite from an outright legislative reversal of the Burlingame Treaty's assurances.[108]

Meanwhile California pushed ahead to produce especially egregious examples of discriminatory limitations of citizenship. The state's Constitution of 1879 excluded Chinese people from equal protection under the law and the opportunity to work by asserting their categorical racial inferiority. Article I's Section 17 limited the potential for naturalization to "foreigners of the white race or African descent," and Article II's Section 1 excluded Chinese immigrants from rights of suffrage in the following terms: "no native of China, no idiot, no insane person, or person convicted of an infamous crime" or of "embezzlement or misappropriation."[109] Article 19 entitled "Chinese" dedicates four sections to protecting the state from "burdens and evils arising from presence of aliens who are or may become vagrants, paupers, mendicants, criminals, or invalids affected with contagious or infectious diseases." Such calls for protection culminated in prohibiting corporations from employing "directly or indirectly, in any capacity, any Chinese or Mongolian."[110] As Jean Pfaelzer documents, decades of devastating violence matched these legal formulations.[111]

In *Chinese Immigration* Williams attempts to debunk the case for excluding Chinese people from citizenship by pointing out certain facts. He first refutes claims that civil enfranchisement would push up the Chinese population in the United States to unmanageable numbers. Comparing the relatively slim numbers of Chinese immigrants to the much greater amount from Europe, he concludes that any fear of California or the nation being controlled by a voting block of Chinese citizens is as "baseless as the fear that the Indians are going to reunite in a league to regain their ancestral hunting-grounds."[112] Williams then addresses other California legislation that had disenfranchised Chinese people—legislation that had folded them into the racial category of "Indians" in order to justify their denial of civil protection. Saving the Chinese from the cultural quarantine of racial inferiority, Williams ridicules the presumption that "the term Indian" could reasonably include "the Chinese or Mongolian race."[113] Insulted on behalf of the Chinese, Williams asserts that Indians had never "risen above tribal relations" in their lives as hunters and nomads who were content to dig roots.[114] (In regard to Native Americans, Williams supported prejudicial federal policies of the Dawes-era that treated them as wards or children to be educated out of communal savagery and into citizenship as individuals.)[115] Williams argues that the Chinese had proved themselves worthy of enfranchisement in helping to construct the railroad—and the Senate-ratified Burlingame Treaty had honorably acknowledged Chinese peoples' contribution by securing for them civil standing. It is striking that Williams does not insist that "Heathen Chinese" first be evangelized as a condition of citizenship and instead urges his readers to "extend equal rights and protection to all races and religions."[116] After the Taiping Rebellion, Williams no longer trusted mere protestations of Christian faith as a guarantee of a person's peaceful orientation into the habits of civilized life. He did, however, trust that U.S. citizenship was implicitly a

Christianizing experience and credits the "hand of god" with bringing "the millions of China and Japan" "out of their seclusion and ignorance into a knowledge of and participation of the benefits of existing in Christian lands."[117]

To Williams's great disappointment, the Chinese Exclusion Act turned discriminatory proposals into federal law. Furthermore, there was a stinging irony in that the same treaty of 1880 by which the U.S. minister Angell recommitted the United States to outlawing the importation of opium into China also renegotiated the terms of the Burlingame Treaty to accommodate the federal exclusions.[118] In signing Chinese Exclusion into law, President Chester A. Arthur suspended "the immigration of Chinese skilled and unskilled 'laborers' for ten years, forc[ing] all Chinese then in the United States to obtain special registration certificates, and barring them from United States citizenship."[119] Chinese "merchants, students, diplomats, and travelers" were exempted, but required to prove their higher status.[120] Subsequent laws in 1884, 1888, and 1892 chipped away further on rights of laborers already in the United States while extending the restrictions.

In the final 1883 edition of *The Middle Kingdom*, William tries to mollify the significance of federal exclusion by reminding readers that Burlingame's main objective was to recognize Chinese people's civil equality as immigrants in order to eradicate the Coolie trade. But Williams's disappointment registers when he modestly characterizes the Burlingame Treaty as "simply" acknowledging the Chinese "right to immigrate like other foreigners."[121] He then follows up in a footnote reporting that "the clamor against" acknowledging and protecting the Chinese's " 'inalienable right' to freely change their residence" was "so great among the people of the Pacific coast that a special embassy of three commissioners was sent to Peking in 1880, which relegated the right of admitting Chinese as immigrants into American territory entirely to Congress."[122] Another casualty of this discriminatory legislation was Yung Wing's China Education Mission in which Williams nevertheless continued to invest great hope, anticipating the transformative impact of those returning to China with a U.S. education.[123] This juxtaposition of professed hope and footnoted disappointment pervades Williams's revised, final, and definitive edition of *The Middle Kingdom*. Its contradictions and blind spots offer a compelling conclusion to the first century of national romances of free trade in China.

Revising Faith in *The Middle Kingdom*

Despite his career as a missionary printer, diplomatic interpreter, and Sinologist that culminated in a professorship at Yale University, Williams generally faded from the scene of American Studies in the twentieth century. This is unfortunate because the scope of his experience, the shared social history it reflects, and the content of his publications evince the importance of China-U.S. commerce and diplomacy to the cultural development of the United States. By way of conclusion, this section considers Williams's final edition of *The Middle Kingdom* (1883) for the historical implications of its difference from the first edition of 1848.

The final edition is nearly twice the size and full of many additional illustrations. As Williams revised toward a definitive presentation of China for the U.S. public and for posterity, he struggled to reconcile the historical events that he had witnessed with his prior statements of faith in a divine plan to redeem China's suffering for some greater good of humanity. His decades of editing, printing, and writing about China had begun with the *Chinese Repository* in the 1830s when he was much more idealistic. As previous chapters explained, in the 1880s he was troubled by the legacies of opium smuggling and of extraterritoriality, and mystified by the Taiping Rebellion. A couple examples can serve to summarize. In the final edition he jettisons the first edition's allegory of tea by which he had aligned Providence, consumer taste, and the civilizing effects of pursuing commercial self-interest (see the introduction). In 1883 he limits the "virtue" of tea to its health benefits "in restoring the energies of the body and furnishing a drink of the gentlest and most salubrious nature."[124] He then uses tea to illustrate the massive scale of increasing commerce between China and the West, estimating that in 1670 only eighty pounds of tea had made it to England; by 1880 "one hundred and eighty million pounds" were reaching Western markets.[125] The swelling waves of tea exports had been underwritten by opium smuggling and had not resulted in the conversion of tens of millions of Chinese pagans.

Then there was the missionaries' project of extraterritorial printing. With the Taiping Rebellion haunting him, Williams qualifies his faith that printing and distributing God's word would on their own achieve socially productive ends. In 1848 Williams had written as if the mere circulation of the Gospel would result in conversion and the social and spiritual redemption of China. Celebrating the opening of treaty ports, he predicted that the "unassisted reading of books" would "wonderously open the way for the extension of commerce" and the spread of Christianity.[126] In 1883 he is more circumspect about what he phrases the "promiscuous distribution of books," placing his faith in dictionaries, rather than evangelical tracts, to nurture the "best modes of conveying the truth."[127]

Such revisions suggest his determination to recognize the historical events that he had witnessed while maintaining a general faith that God had a plan for China— a plan that would redeem the social convulsions of war and align commerce, printing, and missionary endeavors. Having grown circumspect about trading, translating, printing, and distributing the Gospel, Williams switched tracks to embrace technologies of communication and transportation as the new vehicles of civilizing instruction. But his advocacy is similarly tempered by qualifications. For example, in the preface of 1883, he predicts that "soon railroads, telegraphs, and manufacturers will be introduced" into China and "followed by whatsoever may conduce to enlightening the millions of people of China in every department of religious, political, and domestic life."[128] The passive voice of this grand pronouncement sidesteps the crucial tensions related to national agency and sovereignty, corporate ambition, and extraterritoriality.

Williams's ambivalence over the relationship between Christianity and commerce echoes in his attempt to end his revised and definitive *The Middle Kingdom* on a triumphant note. Concluding the second volume, Williams attempts to orchestrate a grand finale with two paragraphs that serially present cultural attributes that bode well for the empire's continued reform and eventual acceptance into the commercial world of civilized nations. However, a footnote on extraterritoriality interrupts the flow and detracts from the rhetorical momentum. Furthermore, as the chain of attributes unfolds, it is difficult not to recall less complementary characterizations of Chinese society in the main body of the text, let alone his earlier writings. Williams begins by lauding China's "literary institutions," even though he had criticized the patterns of political authority that these institutions perpetuated.[129] He lauds the "corps of scientific men" who had returned from the United States as part of the China Educational Mission; however, as noted, the exchange had been discontinued in 1880.[130] Williams continues by praising the "matter-of-fact habits of the Chinese, their want of enthusiasm and dislike of change," which bode well for "their development as a great community," but it is odd to claim that a *lack* of enthusiasm is conducive to the conversion and faith experiences modeled by St. Paul and David Brainerd.[131] Williams highlights traits that seem strategically stereotypical, as if reassuring readers that another Taiping Rebellion is not on the horizon. The paragraph sustains this tentative tone as Williams acknowledges that the "presentation and reception of the highest truths and motives . . . always excites thought and action" and as he posits that "the chiefest fear" in regard to approaching China "must be that of going too fast in schemes of reform and correction, and demolishing the fabric before its elements are ready for reconstruction."[132]

His list of positive characterizations also contradicts his earlier alarm over the errant allure and insidious evil of ancestral worship as it threatened to impede Christian evangelism. Instead of reinforcing the challenge of China's resistant beliefs, he outlines in this conclusion a vacuum of spiritually, noting the "non-existence of caste" in China; "the weakness of priesthood" and "the scanty influence of religion" on "the popular mind;" the "simplicity of ancestral worship"; and the "absence of gorgeous temples, splendid ritual, seductive music, gay processions, and above all, the sanctified licentiousness, to uphold and render it enticing to the depraved human nature."[133] This particular string of attributes builds evangelical hope in what China ostensibly lacks but seems more applicable as criticism of India and of Catholic nations' baroque idolatries. The paragraphs' serialized report of propitious characteristics culminates with Williams asserting that the "popular origin of government holidays" reflects "the degree of industry, loyalty, and respect for life and property"—characteristics "which furnish some grounds for trusting that the regeneration of China will be accomplished, like the operation of leaven in meal, without shivering the vessel."[134] The historical irony of the final biblical allusion is embedded in the final edition's publication date of 1883; the vessel of the Chinese government and its social framework had indeed shivered in ways that Williams had not foreseen in 1848 when he had predicted China's rise as a Christian people.

Running parallel to this final catalog of encouraging attributes is an extended footnote to the penultimate paragraph of the text that further detracts from Williams's statement of hope. Typographically it literally spills over from the penultimate page onto the final one, with the visual effect of trailing onto the bottom of the last page as the final words of the text's main body as if to outweigh his proposal of encouraging signs with the diplomatic challenges that he witnessed. It relates an anecdote in which Williams advised Prince Kung and members of the Board of Revenue to build a rail line to transport coal to Peking. Williams is met with a cool response that shows how extraterritoriality continued to frustrate enthusiasm for commercial development. The footnote deserves to be cited in full:

> The reserved force in the Chinese character was strikingly brought out in a new-year's call at Peking, which the writer [Williams] remembers, in 1870. The topic came up as to how to diminish the expense of getting coal from the mines to the city (which up to that time was carried on camels and mules), so as to put it within reach of the poor people. I [Williams] suggested a tram road as the best plan for the fifty miles of distance from the mines, and involving trifling expense. After listening to the plan, Tan Tin-siang, one of the members of the Board of Revenue, and Prince Kung, together exclaimed, "*Teih-lu lai liao! Tieh-lu lai liao!*" ('Railroads are coming in time'). The existence of the treaty principle of ex-territoriality and its consequences is constantly before the Chinese high officers, though they appreciate as well the fact that their country is preparing and will be the better for such improvements.[135]

Whereas Williams points to the "reserved force in the Chinese character" as a hopeful attribute in avoiding another Taiping Rebellion, it is also an impediment to commercial development that depends on reestablishing diplomatic trust. As Williams had put it in *Our Relations with China* (1877), his final letter to U.S. expatriates in Shanghai cited before, the issue of the "right of ex-territorial jurisdiction" endured as "a sore spot in the minds" of conservative Peking administrators who "usually oppose any demands for further privileges on the part of American representatives, and even of all foreign nations, by comparing the legal position of the two peoples in each other's territories."[136] The conclusion of the definitive edition of The Middle Kingdom is thus a vexed attempt to muster a final statement of faith in a redemptive plan—an attempt that acknowledges convulsive historical events that haunt Williams to the point of qualifying his early pursuits of extraterritorial printing. As the Day of Judgment approaches in the final pages of The Middle Kingdom, U.S. corporate goals of capitalizing on railway construction seem at odds with the evangelical and diplomatic efforts that Burlingame had touted as the cooperative premise for railroad expansion.

This discrepancy between Christianity and commerce that resonates in Williams's conclusion is historically fitting because in the 1880s and 1890s the China market never delivered the riches Burlingame had promised.[137] The Canton-based business alliances between Cohong merchants and U.S. merchants were long gone. Wrangling over contracts between various nations and companies paralyzed development plans in Peking. In 1891 an elderly John Murray Forbes was surprised to read in the morning paper that Russell & Company had gone bankrupt.[138] The fortunes generated from the old China trade continued to impact the cultural scene in the twentieth century as reflected, for example, in the writings of George Santayana and Henry James.[139]

The decade-long stalemate over railway and telegraph development was broken by the military invasion of China during the First Sino-Japanese War (1894–95). Japan's occupation tested to the point of failure China's putatively self-strengthened military capabilities, and the Qing Empire lost its economic influence over Taiwan and Korea and its territorial control over the port of Dalian and the Liaodong Peninsula.[140] In the wake of Japan's victory and the resulting "scramble for China," the U.S. commercial romance revived when the American China Development Company tried again to secure railway contracts and to extend loans in Peking.[141] Despite the efforts of J. P. Morgan and President Theodore Roosevelt, these efforts failed as China continued to wrangle over control of the constructed lines, the terms of the large loans, and the mining rights for areas near the lines.[142] New York merchants redoubled their efforts to penetrate the China market by creating the influential American Asiatic Association in 1898.[143] Meanwhile, China's territorial sovereignty was further compromised by the land grabs of Germany, Britain, France, Russia, and Japan.

The progress of missionary work in China would have been even more disappointing to Williams. In the 1880s and 1890s the numbers of missionaries living in China increased dramatically, but tensions between Western missionaries and local administrators increased substantially.[144] Catholic missionaries redoubled their efforts, the British ecumenical China Inland Mission revived the Protestant missionary corps, and the ABCFM continued to expand its operations. The ABCFM missionary Rev. William Scott Ament followed in the footsteps of Williams and Rev. Elijah Bridgman as he edited the *North China News* from Peking. However, despite Williams's appreciation of the reserved nature of the Chinese, there was another charismatic spiritual movement that started in the north of Shandong Providence and spread dramatically in an attempt to revolutionize China. The Movement of the Militia United in Righteousness (Yìhétuán yùndòng, 義和團運動; 1898–1900), or Boxer Rebellion, lasted from 1898 to 1900 as a massive popular effort to expel foreigners from the country.[145] In *Martyred Missionaries of the China Inland Mission* (1901), Marshall Broomhall of the China Inland Mission reported the killing of sixty-eight missionary family members, including twenty-six adults and children from the American Board and American Presbyterian North.[146] The *ABCFM Annual Report* of 1901 reported that all of it members at the Shangsi Mission, in an area west of Peking, had been killed, concluding: "It was the will of God. Their earthly work was done."[147] The Boxers eventually invaded Peking where the empress dowager Cixi supported them. A fifty-five-day siege of the foreign legation quarters ensued. Eventually the Eight Nation Alliance of Britain, France, Germany, Italy, Russia, Austria-Hungary, Japan, and the United States deployed twenty thousand troops to Peking and vanquished the Boxers; the seventeen hundred American troops had been redeployed from the Philippines.[148] In the international press, this was high drama. American missionary W. A. P. Martin published *The Siege in Peking: China against the World* (1900), and Buffalo Bill even integrated the Boxer siege as a sensational scene in his Wild West Show.[149]

By the 1890s, China was one piece in a larger puzzle of U.S. regional ambition across the Pacific. Before the Boxers stormed Peking, the United States had begun flexing its military muscle with a new confidence as the Spanish-American War folded into the Philippine-American War. These wars drew sharp rebuke from the Anti-Imperialist League, including Williams James, Mark Twain, Charles Francis Adams Jr., John Dewey, Henry James, and William Dean Howells. Returning from a world tour, Twain declared himself an anti-imperialist. Looking to China, he reinforced his position by allying himself with the Boxers in their goal of resisting the extractive designs of foreign powers. In taking a stand against U.S. imperialism, Twain famously criticized the ABCFM's Rev. Ament for retaliatory greed in collecting a predatory indemnity after the Boxer uprising.[150] In *North American Review* articles "To the Person Sitting in the Darkness" (1900) and "To My Missionary Critics" (1901), Twain lambasted "the hypocrisy of Christian aggression and colonial exploitation of the weak in China, the Philippines, and South Africa."[151] As Peter

Schmidt contends, Twain was mocking how rhetoric of freedom and liberation justified U.S. colonial projects abroad.[152] This later writing thus repudiates Twain's initial high praise of the Burlingame Treaty.[153]

In this climate, U.S. secretary of state John Hay wrote the two diplomatic letters of the Open Door Policy, announcing that the United States had no territorial or colonial ambitions in China and that it would ensure that no other European power, particularly Germany, would press for territory. As Paul Bové explains, the First Open Door Note (6 September 1899) asserted that Western powers should respect each other's "sphere of influence" in China, and Hay went on to outline a "new model of empire" in which "American inertia was, paradoxically, a destabilizing form of energy that expanded the U.S. arrangement of republican government and market capitalism without careful social regulation across the globe."[154] The ensuing century of nationalist revolutions in China is even further beyond the scope of Williams's underwhelming profession of faith in the Christianizing effect of railway development with which he concluded *The Middle Kingdom*.

By ending this book with Williams's ambivalent revisions, the point is not to highlight his mistakes. His struggle against disillusionment highlights his inability to reconcile Christianity and commerce as he reread his own writings in which pursuit of free trade justified opium smuggling as developing U.S. companies shielded themselves from any repercussions by claiming extraterritorial protection. Without understanding this first century of U.S.-China relations—the merchant princes' global networks, Caleb Cushing's and Commodore Matthew C. Perry's gunboat diplomacy, and the ABCFM missionaries' decades of extraterritorial printing—it might seem reasonable to regard U.S. imperialism in the Philippines as an oceanic extension of pioneer ambition looking for a new frontier. However, beginning with Major Shaw's fantastical commodity of ginseng, Far Eastern commerce had inspired conquest of the Far West in early national romances of free trade in China.

Prologue

1. "Party Terrorism," 338.
2. Twain, "The Treaty with China: Its Provisions Explained (1868)," 13, 12.
3. *Harper's Weekly* 12.596 (30 May 1868): 344.
4. Ibid., 346.
5. Ibid., 344–45.
6. Anderson, *Imagined Communities*, 24, 122.
7. See Stoler, "Intimidations of Empire," 2; and Lowe, *Intimacies of Four Continents*.

Introduction

1. Lowe, *Intimacies of Four Continents*. In regard to the U.S. orientation in the "modern world system," I follow the lead of A. Frank's *ReOrient* in broadening the geographic and historical connections supporting Immanuel Wallerstein's European-focused descriptions in, for example, *World-Systems Analysis*.
2. In regard to Chinese, I standardize Pǔtōnghuà (普通話) using traditional characters and Romanize with the phonetic system of Hànyǔ pīnyīn (漢語拼音方案) or "pinyin," in which accent marks indicate the tone of each syllable. (Pǔtōnghuà has four tones and a neutral non-tone.) Early nineteenth-century source documents offer phonetic approximations that vary considerably. An additional complication is that pinyin is one of three major alphabetic phonetic systems for Putonghua. Late nineteenth- and twentieth-century scholarship uses Romanization systems of Wade-Giles or Yale. Furthermore, Cantonese (廣東話, gwong2 dung1 waa6, Guǎngdōnghuà) was the pervasive version of Chinese spoken in South China. The Romanization system of Jyutping (粵拼, jyut6 ping3) approximates the language's nine different tones. I include Jyutping when possible in reference to key phrases.
3. Stoler's "Intimidations of Empire," 2.
4. Lowe, *The Intimacies of Four Continents*, 30.
5. See Locke, *Second Treatise on Government*, and Macpherson, *The Political Theory of Possessive Individualism*.
6. See Pocock, *The Machiavellian Moment*.
7. Maine, *Ancient Law*, 170. For further explanation of Maine's importance and the rise of contract, see Horwitz, *The Transformation of American Law*.
8. Yang, *Performing China*, 12.
9. R. Emerson, "The Young American," in *Essays and Lectures*, 213–30.
10. Ibid., 221.
11. Ibid., 228.
12. On *translatio imperii et studii* in a U.S. context, see Cheyfitz, *The Poetics of Imperialism*.
13. For example, *The American Novel and Its Tradition*, Richard Chase distinguishes between the generally middle-class realist novel (verisimilitude, development of character, continuity of plot) and the medieval precedent of romance (melodrama, action over character, astonishing events that "veer toward mythic, allegorical, and symbolic forms") to outline the romantically cast, hybrid of the "American novel (12, 13). In *Love and Death in the American*

Novel, Leslie Fiedler similarly tracks the adaptation of historical romance (Sir Walter Scott) and gothic conventions into the writing of early U.S. writers such as James Fenimore Cooper.

14. Matthiessen, *American Renaissance*, xvi, xv.

15. Ibid., xxvi.

16. Ibid.

17. McKay, *Donald McKay*, 147.

18. McKay's ships were bought and sold across various American and British trading houses that stretched across the Atlantic and Pacific, from New York to Liverpool, from Australia to China.

19. Downs, *The Golden Ghetto*.

20. For an excellent overview of Matthiessen's massive influence on subsequent scholars, his inability to bring his socialist politics and sexuality to bear on his presentation of U.S. literature in *The American Renaissance* (1941), and the significance of his career in the years after the World War II before his death in 1950, see Cain, *F. O. Matthiessen and the Politics of Criticism*. The criticism and appreciation of Matthiessen by which I have been most influenced include Arac, "F. O. Matthiessen"; Baym, *American Woman's Fiction*; Cheyfitz, "Matthiessen's American Renaissance"; Grossman, "The Canon in the Closet"; Redding, "Closet, Coup, and Cold War"; Pease, "*Moby Dick* and the Cold War."

21. The reassessment of romance as engaged with social history includes Baym, "Concepts of the Romance in Hawthorne's America"; Gilmore, *American Romanticism and the Marketplace*; Jehlen, "New World Epics"; Kaplan, *The Social Construction of American Realism*; Rogin, *Subversive Genealogy*; and many others.

22. Gilmore, *American Romanticism*, 5.

23. Jehlen, "New World Epics," 59.

24. Melville, *Moby Dick; or, the Whale*, 68.

25. Jehlen, "New World Epics," 68.

26. Berlant, *The Anatomy of National Fantasy*, 5.

27. Stoler, "Intimations of Empire," 9.

28. See Fuchs, *Romance*.

29. Casper, *Constructing American Lives*, 4.

30. Sacvan Bercovitch writes of American romanticism as long expressed in the "conflation of the private with the national dream" that emerged with Puritan "auto-American-biography"; see *Puritan Origins of the American*, 177, quoted from Rogin, *Subversive Genealogy*, 22.

31. Hayden White describes the "explanatory affect" in the essay "Interpretation in History" (58) and Romance in "Fictions of Factual Representation" (128), both in *Tropics of Discourse*. Lowe discusses White's analysis of how historical narrative is structured in *The Intimacies of Four Continents*, 138–39.

32. Seaburg and Paterson, *Merchant Prince of Boston*; Knowles, *Mastering Iron*, 120.

33. Seaburg and Paterson, *Merchant Prince*, 418.

34. See Quincy, *The History of the Boston Athenaeum*, 125–30.

35. Knowles, *Mastering Iron*, 120.

36. J. Forbes, *Letters*, 2:51–52.

37. K. Liu, *Anglo-American Steamship Rivalry*, 23–24.

38. J. Forbes, *Letters*, 2:50. Colonel Robert Gould Shaw was technically Forbes's first cousin once removed; Forbes's paternal aunt Elizabeth Perkins married Nathaniel Russell Sturgis; one their daughters married Francis George Shaw (son of the older Robert Gould Shaw). Their son was Colonel Shaw.

39. See the Massachusetts Historical Society collection guide: http://www.masshist.org/collection-guides/view/fa0225.

40. E. Emerson, "John Murray Forbes," 386.

41. Asa Whitney and Abiel A. Low also folded their China fortunes into rail investment. See Bain, *Empire Express*.

42. Christy, *The Orient in American Transcendentalism*, vii.

43. Ibid., vii. He does allude to the biographical connections that Emerson had with the "traffic in the Orient." At the end of the preface, Christy thanks "Professor Edward Waldo Forbes" for "acting in behalf of the Emerson family" to grant "permission to make use of such marginalia as I found in the Oriental books in Emerson's library" (xv). Professor Forbes who directed Harvard's Fogg Museum was the grandson of John Murray Forbes.

44. Carpenter, *Emerson and Asia*; first quoted from Weir, *American Orient*, 63.

45. Interest in Hinduism arose in part because of the work of Sir Williams Jones, founder in 1784 of the Asiatic Society of Bengal, and because of Rammohun Roy, whose articles frequently appeared in American magazines such as the Boston-based *Christian Disciple* and the *Christian Register* (Weir, *American Orient*, 53).

46. Eperjesi, *The Imperialist Imaginary*.

47. S. Williams, *The Middle Kingdom* (1848), 1:40.

48. In a general sense, Lydia Liu alerts readers to the "long history of hetero-cultural, trade relations, . . . and colonial expansion" that shaped the use of this phrase in *Clash of Empires*, 80. The word *zhōng* (中) means "central" as well as "middle," and *guó* (國) can mean "state" or "people." In *The Middle Kingdom* (1848) Williams acknowledges "Central States" and "Central Empire" as literal alternatives but adopts Middle Kingdom for its figurative capacity. He also mentions alternative names such as *"Tien Hia"* (Beneath the Sky) [Tiān xià, 天下, literally transposed as "sky under"] or the "Celestial Empire," and *"Sz' Hai"* (all within the Four Seas) [Sì hǎi, 四海, literally transposed as "four seas"]. In the editions of 1848 and 1883, Williams also notes a seemingly providential origin of the term *"China, Thina* or *Tina,* and *Sina,"* in the geographer Ptolemy from whom the Prophet Isaiah gleans the term *Sinim* in chapter 49, verse 12, that predicts their being brought into faith; see S. Williams *The Middle Kingdom* (1848), 1:3; and (1883), 2:408.

49. Williams, *Middle Kingdom* (1848), 1:xv.

50. Montesquieu's *Spirit of the Laws* offers a particularly influential formulation of "Asiatic despotism," a formulation that reverberates throughout the nineteenth century. Volume 1 introduces the concept of the "Asiatic Despot." See Ruskola, *Legal Orientalism*, 16.

51. Williams, *Middle Kingdom* (1848), 1:40.

52. Ibid., 1:1.

53. Ibid., 1:3.

54. Ibid., 1:41. For contemporary reformulations of this question that do not foreground Christian faith as the answer, see Needham, *The Grand Titration*, and Pomeranz, *The Great Divergence*.

55. Williams, *Middle Kingdom* (1848), 1:42.

56. Ibid., 1:40.

57. Ibid., 2:126.

58. Ibid.

59. Ibid.

60. Ibid., 1:299; and in the final 1883 edition, 1:299.

61. Fichter, *So Great a Profitt*, 17.

62. On the success of the U.S. traders, see Downs, *The Golden Ghetto*.

63. On the colonies' assumption of the right to charter corporations, see J. Davis, *Essays in the Earlier History of American Corporations*, 1:3–103; and Maier, "The Revolutionary Origins of the American Corporation."

64. See Van Dyke's "Bookkeeping as a Window into the Efficiencies of Early Modern Trade."

65. Morse, *The International Relations of the Chinese Empire*, 87.

66. Noble, *Beyond the Promised Land*, 101–3.

67. On the impact of Adam Smith's writings on the young American nation in the 1780s and 1790s and, specifically, on John Adams, Thomas Jefferson, and James Madison, see Fleischacker, "Adam Smith's Reception." Fleischacker argues that the founders read Smith closely and did not reduce him to the slogans of "free trade" by which Smith's theories would be foreshortened in the nineteenth century.

68. In this context, Smith regarded Britain's Navigation Acts of the 1651 as a legitimate response to Dutch threats in global trade, even if such government monopolization was generally counterproductive; see Giovanni Arrighi, *Adam Smith in Beijing*, 65, 66.

69. Adam Smith, *Wealth of Nations*.

70. Ibid., 1:31–32.

71. Ibid., 1:108, 31.

72. Ibid., 1:108. Wittfogel's *Oriental Despotism* returns to the water motif in establishing differences between hydraulic and nonhydraulic societies to revise Marx's characterization of the "Asiatic mode of production"—a phrase of significant ambiguity in Marx's oeuvre; for example, see *Capital*, vol. 1. For Wittfogel, hydraulic societies tend toward a despotic "hydraulic civilization" (centralization of power; stultifying administrative regimes) that threatens free enterprise in terms that seem to echo Adam Smith from almost two centuries before. For an overview of this phrase as it resonated in the Soviet legacy of Marxism through to Wittfogel, see S. Dunn, *The Fall and Rise of the Asiatic Mode of Production*. For criticism of the phrase "Asiatic mode of production" for its compounded inaccuracies, see Frank, *ReOrient*, 12–24.

73. Adam Smith, *Wealth of Nations*, 1:108.

74. Arrighi writes, "Smith's depictions of China are a far cry from the indictments of Montesquieu, Diderot, and Rousseau that eventually gave rise to Marx's infamous notion of an 'Asiatic mode of production.' They nonetheless are not as full of admiration as the depictions of the Sinophile faction of European Enlightenment most prominently represented by Leibniz, Voltaire, and Quesnay" (*Adam Smith in Beijing*, 58). Smith's characterizations nevertheless echo influentially, for example, in Henry Sumner Maine's description of China as legally stagnant and despotic in *Ancient Law*, 23.

75. Adam Smith, *Wealth of Nations*, 1:109.

76. Ibid., 1:108. The families to whom Smith refers are a Chinese minority ethnic group referred to in the nineteenth century as the Tanka (蜑家/疍家; Dànjiā); S. Williams mentions them briefly in *The New Middle Kingdom* (1848): "The *tankia* [*sic*], or boat-people, at Canton form a class in some respects beneath the other portions of the community, and have many customs peculiar to themselves. . . . The *tankia* came from the Miautsz' tribes, so early that their origin is unknown" (1:321). Today, the preferred name is "on-water people" or (水上人; *shuǐshàng rén*; or in Cantonese, "Nam Hoi Yan," 南海人). For an overview of their history that debunks Smith's characterizations, see E. Anderson, *The Floating World of Castle Peak Bay*. For an excellent overview of the related sociology, see http://medlibrary.org/med wiki/Tanka_(ethnic_group).

77. Adam Smith, *Wealth of Nations*, 1:145.

78. Ruskola, "Canton Is Not Boston," 868; also see Hevia, *Cherishing Men from Afar*, 238.

79. Semmel, *The Rise of Free Trade Imperialism*, 1; also see Gallagher and Robinson, "The Imperialism of Free Trade."

80. Semmel, *Rise of Free Trade Imperialism*, 11.

81. Gallagher and Robinson, "Imperialism of Free Trade," 9.

82. Carroll, *A Concise History of Hong Kong*, 23. Noble discusses the attribution of this phrase to Bowring by Karl Marx, who had attended an election speech by Bowring; see *Beyond the Promised Land*, 106–7. Amitav Ghosh weaves Bowring's quote into his novel *Sea of Poppies* (113) and the cant of free-trade imperialism through the subsequent two volumes of his Ibis Trilogy (*River of Smoke* and *Flood of Fire*).

83. John Quincy Adams, "December 1841, Lecture on the War with China," 277.

84. In the U.S. context, see Horsman, *Race and Manifest Destiny*.

85. See Ruskola, *Legal Orientalism*.

86. Echoing Ann Laura Stoler's consideration of the "common ground of conversation between United States history and postcolonial studies," this book is imbricated in the "politics of comparison" that permeated disciplines of history and literature during the formative years of area study ("Intimations of Empire," 1–22). For a useful overview of the rise of area studies in post–World War II United States, see Szanton, "The Origin, Nature, and Challenges of Area Studies in the United States"; and Cummings, "Boundary Displacement."

87. See http://www.library.yale.edu/div/spc/chinarec.htm. The Sterling Library holds the papers of Samuel Wells Williams. See also Wu, *Christianity in China*.

88. Bowra, "Obituary Notice for Hosea Ballou Morse."

89. Latourette, *The History of Early Relations between the United States and China*; and Dennett, *Americans in Eastern Asia*.

90. Greenbie and Barstow, *Gold of Ophir* (1925), xiii.

91. See K. Johnson, "Peace, Friendship, and Financial Panic." Furthermore, the American Board of Commissions of Foreign Missions was in the middle of treaty negotiations in China and in the United States; consider that Samuel Worcester, an ABCFM missionary, is the plaintiff in the third Supreme Court decision of the Marshall Trilogy, *Worcester v. Georgia* (31 US 515, 1832).

92. Fairbank, *The United States and China*. His career demonstrates sustained attention to the historical relationship between the United States and China.

93. Fairbank collaborated with many scholars as well, including Edwin O. Reischauer,

Ernest May, Paul A. Cohen, and Denis Twitchett, his coeditor in the multivolume *The Cambridge History of China* (1978–). Their scholarship has been deeply influential for many China scholars.

94. In broad terms I am referencing, Parrington's *Main Currents in American Thought*; Matthiessen's *American Renaissance*; and interdisciplinary American studies approaches that include H. Smith's *Virgin Land*, and Marx's *Machine in the Garden*.

95. Cummings, "Boundary Displacement," 8; and Holzman, "The Ideological Origins of American Studies at Yale." Also see Benedict Anderson's description of the Cold War context that shaped the area study of "Southeast Asia," in *The Spectre of Comparisons*, 8–12.

96. Holzman is quoting Yale University's 1948 Prospect of American Studies Program, in the archives of Provost Edgar S. Furniss; see "The Ideological Origins of American Studies at Yale," 84.

97. I take these terms from a small selection of the classics in American literary studies, including H. Smith's previously cited *Virgin Land*; Miller, *Errand into the Wilderness*; Lewis, *The American Adam*; Marx, *The Machine in the Garden*; Goetzmann, *Exploration and Empire*; Kolodny, *The Land before Her*; Jehlen, *American Incarnation*; and Slotkin, *Regeneration through Violence*. This partial list could extend to include the major works by Van Wyck Brooks, Richard Chase, Leslie Fielder, Philip Rahv, Robert Spiller, Richard Drinnon, Eric Sundquist, David S. Reynolds, and many others.

98. Henry Nash Smith is a bit of an exception to this generalization. He begins *Virgin Land* with "Book One: Passage to India," in which he contextualizes Jefferson's "devout agrarianism" in relation to the "[reactivation of] the oldest of all ideas associated with America— that of a passage to India," evinced in the political efforts of Missouri senator Thomas Hart Benton and the railroad promotion of the aforementioned merchant Asa Whitney. For Benton and Whitney, "access to Asia becomes a symbol of freedom and national greatness for America," in ways that Walt Whitman went on to amplify. However, for the rest of the *Virgin Land*, the importance of China fades into Smith's very insightful literary cultural discussions of the Wild West, the agrarian West, and the disappearance of the frontier (*Virgin Land*, 15, 19, 23). LeMenager considers Smith's understanding of "the West" in relation to coastal sea trade in *Manifest and Other Destinies*, 35.

99. Said writes: "This [turn toward social science] is the specifically American contribution to the history of Orientalism, and it can be dated roughly from the period immediately following World War II, when the United States found itself in the position recently vacated by Britain and France. The American experience of the Orient prior to that exceptional moment was limited. Cultural isolatos like Melville were interested in it; cynics like Mark Twain visited and wrote about it; the American Transcendentalists saw affinities between Indian thought and their own; a few theologians and Biblical students studied the Biblical Oriental languages; there were occasional diplomatic and military encounters with Barbary pirates and the like, the odd naval expedition to the Far Orient, and of course the ubiquitous missionary to the Orient. But there was no deeply invested tradition of Orientalism, and consequently in the United States knowledge of the Orient never passed through the refining and reticulating and reconstruction process, whose beginning was in philological study, that it went through in Europe. Furthermore, the imaginative investment was never made either, perhaps because the American frontier, the one that counted, was the westward one." See *Orientalism*, 290.

100. Rowe, "Edward Said and American Studies." Rowe notes: "Said's criticism of American exceptionalism was an integral part of his commitment to transnational cultural studies, and both are related to his central concern with the rise of the American Empire" (35–36). He notes Said's revised opinions in *Culture and Imperialism* (1993) and the ways in which Said's oversight of nineteenth-century colonialism "may have provided motivation for new scholarship in American studies" (37).

101. I am thinking specifically of the "New Americanist Series," for example, Kaplan and Pease, *Cultures of United States Imperialism*, and Fluck, Pease, and Rowe, *Re-framing the Transnational Turn in American Studies*. Works that have been influential to me in thinking about imperialism in relation to early national identity in the United States are Cheyfitz, *The Poetics of Imperialism*; Kaplan, *The Anarchy of Empire in the Making of U.S. Culture*; Pease, *Visionary Compacts*; and Rowe, *The New American Series*.

102. See Bauer, *The Cultural Geography of Colonial American Literatures*; Brickhouse, *Transamerican Literary Relations*; and Goudie, *Creole America*.

103. LeMenager, *Manifest and Other Destinies*, 15.

104. Richard Drinnon makes explicit connections between aggression in the "Far West," the Philippines, and the Vietnam War in the fifth part of *Facing West*. Also see Dirlik, "Chinese History and the Question of Orientalism"; Wilson, *Reimagining the American Pacific*; Schueller, *U.S. Orientalisms*; Eperjesi, *The Imperialist Imaginary*; Y. Huang, *Transpacific Imaginations*; Rifkin, "Debt and the Transnationalization of Hawai'i"; Stoler, *Haunted by Empire*; and Lowe, *The Intimacies of Four Continents*.

105. See Aldridge, *The Dragon and the Eagle*; Dolin, *When America First Met China*; Downs, *The Golden Ghetto*; Haddad, *America's First Adventure in China* and *The Romance of China*; Tchen, *New York before Chinatown*; H. Hsu, *Geography and the Production of Space in Nineteenth Century American*; Weir, *American Orient*; Egan, *Oriental Shadows*; C. Frank, *Objectifying China, Imagining America*; Yokota, *Unbecoming British*, especially chap. 3, "A Revolution Revived: American and British Encounters in Canton, China," 115–52; Ruskola, *Legal Orientalism*; Xu, *Chinese and Americans*; G. Chang, *Fateful Ties*; and Lai-Henderson, *Mark Twain in China*. Also see Block, "The Importance of the China Trade."

106. Blussé, *Visible Cities*; Goldstein, *Philadelphia and the China Trade*; Hamashita, "The Tribute Trade System and Modern Asia"; Hao, *The Commercial Revolution in Nineteenth-Century China*; He, *Macao in the Making of Early Sino-American Relations*; M. Hunt, *The Making of a Special Relationship*; Munn, "The Hong Kong Opium Revenue, 1845–1885"; Spence, *The Search for Modern China*; Wakeman, "The Canton Trade and the Opium War."

107. Fishkin offers an overview of transnational scholarship in "Crossroads of Cultures."

108. Dimock, *Through Other Continents*, 2.

109. B. Anderson, *Imagined Communities*, *The Spectre of Comparisons*, and *Under Three Flags*; and Arrighi, *The Long Twentieth Century* and *Adam Smith in Beijing*. See also Wallerstein, *World-Systems Analysis*.

110. Johannes Fabian, *Time and the Other*; and Lefebvre, *The Production of Space*.

111. Dirlik, "Chinese History and the Question of Orientalism," 401.

112. For a historical overview of the development of effective Chinese jurisprudence spanning several dynasties, see Cassel, "Excavating Extraterritoriality: The Legacies of Legal Pluralism, Subjecthood, and State-Building in China and Japan," in his *Grounds of Judgment*, 15–38.

113. Pratt, *Imperial Eyes*, 6.

114. See Dyke, *Merchants of Canton and Macao*; and J. D. Wong, *Global Trade in the Nineteenth Century*. Ngai describes Chinese participation in shaping exhibits of China as examples of "transform[ing] the figure of the 'other' from a representational construct to a social actor," and thus looking beyond "hegemonic discourse" "to understand contact, translation, exchange, negotiation, conflict, and other dynamics that attend the constitution of social relationships across cultural and national borders; see Ngai, "Transnationalism and Transformation of the 'Other,'" 60.

115. Cheyfitz, *Poetics of Imperialism*, xxii.

116. L. Liu, *Tokens of Exchange* and *Clash of Empires*.

117. P. Cohen, *Discovering History in China*, 1. In regard to work particularly illuminating for its comparative approach, see P. Cohen, *China and Christianity*; Koon, "The Face of Diplomacy in Nineteenth Century China"; and Sinn, *Pacific Crossing*.

118. Behdad, "Oriental Matters," 711.

Chapter 1 • *Characterizing the American China Trader*

1. Shaw, *Journals*, 218. For an informative account of the voyage, see P. Smith, *Empress of China*.

2. Quincy reprints the reports to John Jay from May 1785 (after the first voyage) and January and December 1787 (from Canton during the second voyage) in the appendix to *Journals*. Shaw's "Letter from Mr. Shaw," 194–97, and "Remarks on the Commerce of America with China."

3. Shaw, *Journals*, 122.

4. Casper, *Constructing American Lives*, 4. Sparks intended his biographies to be instructive for readers. Reviewing the first series in 1834, the *North American Review* described it as offering a "handful of resolute individuals, erecting in the desert, . . . firm walls of a mighty and enduring empire, destined to exert a most momentous influence over the interests of the sons of men" ("Spark's American Biography," 466). Shaw's account also appears in William Jay's biography of his father, *The Life of John Jay*.

5. Two series—the first consisting of twelve volumes (1829–30) and the second of seven (1833–34)—resulted from his editing the diplomatic record. Shaw's account of his first voyage to Canton appears in volume 7 of Jared Spark's *Diplomatic Correspondence* (1834), along with four other letters by him and John Jay's replies, including the appointment of Shaw as the American consul in Canton in November 1786.

6. The article from the *Chinese Repository* suggests that Shaw's story was not widely known. Bridgman sources Shaw's account to a review article of Spark's *Diplomatic Correspondence* in the October 1834 issue of the *North American Review* and William Jay's biography of John Jay. Bridgman prefaces Shaw's account by acknowledging the first American consul to reside in China as Samuel Snow, the father of the then consul Mr. P. W. Snow (Downs, *The Golden Ghetto*, 39–40). However, Spark's *Diplomatic Correspondence* includes Samuel Shaw's appointment in 1786, which Shaw incorporates into the title of the *Journals of Major Samuel Shaw*. It is possible that Bridgman is emphasizing the residence of Snow, rather than his appointment. Of the consuls whom Bridgman names (Samuel Snow, Carrington, Mr. Wilcox, J. H. Grosvenor, and P. W. Snow), all took part in the opium trade of

their respective companies (Downs, *The Golden Ghetto*, 364–70). [Bridgman and Williams], "Relations between the United States and China."

7. The Boston-based social register *"Our First Men"* estimated his fortune at 1 million Spanish and Mexican silver dollars and described him as "Senior partner of one of the wealthiest and largest commercial houses in the city. An accomplished merchant, and public spirited man; benevolent without ostentation or purse-proud hauteur" (42). Colonel Shaw's father Francis George Shaw (1809–92) wrote a short biography of his father Robert Gould Shaw (1776–1853) that appears in *Memorial*, 2:38–61.

8. Quincy, *History of the Boston Athenæum*.

9. Shaw, *Journals*, 129.

10. Ibid., xi.

11. Unattributed, Review of *The Journals of Major Samuel Shaw*, 250.

12. The major booster of the idea was John Ledyard (1751–89), who had spent the Revolutionary War aboard *Endeavor* on Captain James Cook's final voyage. Thomas Jefferson was even an enthusiast, but Ledyard was ahead of his time. In 1828 Jared Sparks outlined Ledyard's quixotic and ultimately frustrated global search for investors in *Memoirs of the Life and Travels of John Ledyard.*

13. The history of ginseng's export to China from North America predates the United States. In the early 1700s, the Jesuit priest Joseph-François Lafitau living near Montreal in present-day Canada saw a picture of ginseng rendered by the Jesuit Pere Jartoux in China. He surmised that it was the same plant used by the Mohawk and other Iroquois peoples. French traders began harvesting ginseng and sending it to Canton, although the North American *panax quinquefolius* is not the same as the *panax ginseng* in Asia. After the mid-eighteenth century and the French and Indian War (1756–63), the British squeezed France out of the trade. After the Revolutionary War, the United States similarly squeezed England out of the North American ginseng trade. See Knox, "The History, Geography, and Economics of North American Ginseng," 21–28.

14. Shaw, *Journals*, 134.

15. Ibid., 232.

16. Ibid., 183.

17. P. Smith, *Empress of China*, 37–39.

18. See the last page of Captain Green's "Receipts, Canton in China, 1784–1786" at the Rare Book room of Van Pelt Library, University of Pennsylvania (Ms. Coll. 499).

19. See K. Johnson, "A Question of Character," 33–56.

20. Shaw, *Journals*, 147.

21. Ibid., 136.

22. Ibid., 136–37.

23. Ibid., 139.

24. De Crèvecoeur, "Charles-Town; Letter IX," in *Letters from an American Farmer*, 213–35.

25. Lines 15, 17, 18. Freneau's poem first appeared as "On the First American Ship that Explored the Rout to China, the East-Indies, after the Revolution.—" in Freneau's *Poems Written Between the Years 1768 & 1794*, 291; it was reprinted in *Time-Piece and Literary Companion*, 17 April 1797; Yokota, *Unbecoming British*, 290; and F. Smith, "Philip Freneau and the Time-Piece Literary Companion."

26. Freneau, "On the First American Ship," line 20.

27. Shaw, *Journals*, 162.

28. Ricci, *Islam Translated*, 4, 5; also see Abu-Lughod, *Before European Hegemony*, 199–205.

29. Dolin, *When America First Met China*, 34–35.

30. For an overview of the Portuguese involvement, see Souza, *The Survival of Empire*. As for the pirates, see Anthony, *Like Froth Floating on the Sea*.

31. See Warren, *The Sulu Zone*.

32. See Blussé, *Visible Cities*.

33. Paul A. Van Dyke, "Smuggling Networks of the Pearl River Delta before 1842," in Van Dyke, *Americans and Macao*, 56.

34. Van Dyke outlines in detail the rise and life of the system in *The Canton Trade*. See also He, *Macao in the Making of Early Sino-American Relations*.

35. In *China Upside Down*, Man-houng Lin writes that "European countries exported more silver than goods to China in [the first half of the eighteenth century]. For example, some 95 percent of British payments for Chinese exports between 1721 and 1740 were made in silver dollars" (64). In the second half of the eighteenth century, "England controlled 78 percent of the value of total trade between China and the West" (64), and from 1752 to 1800 "the flow of silver from [England, Holland, France, Denmark, and Prussia] to China increased to $104,785,273" (66). James Fichter estimates that between 1760 and 1821, the East India Company alone exported roughly 150,000 pounds in silver a year to China—more than half a million ounces—the level varying annually" (32).

36. See P. Smith, *Empress of China*, 87, 154–55.

37. Shaw, *Journals*, 176. When Shaw arrived he notes that "the hoppo inquired if we had any *sing-songs*—the name they give to this sort of articles,—and, on being answered in the negative, seemed rather displeased. However, when we told them that we were from a new country, for the first time, and did not know that it was customary to bring such things, he appeared satisfied, but did not forget to enjoy it." The situation was smoothed over by the Cohong Pankekoa, who "caused [the American vessel] to be registered in the hoppo's books as an English country ship," with the implication that the expected cumshaw would be paid by other British arrivals. The American's oversight and Pankekoa's pragmatic fix would cause trouble when at the end of the trading season the Americans tried to get final permission to leave and found out that they had been legally registered as British; Shaw, *Journals*, 192–93.

38. Shaw, *Journals*, 176.

39. Ibid., 120.

40. Downs, *The Golden Ghetto*.

41. Perdu, "Rise & Fall of the Canton Trade System-III," 4.

42. Cheong, *Hong Merchants of Canton*; Van Dyke, *Merchants of Canton and Macao*.

43. Shaw, *Journals*, 347. Shaw worked with "Pankekoa" (Pokenhua) and Chowqua, whose garden estate he visited and admired (174).

44. Fairbank, *History of China*, 10:9.

45. Haddad, *Romance of China*, 46.

46. The historical work on Houqua is extensive. See Van Dyke, *Merchants of Canton and Macao*; and John D. Wong's *Global Trade in the Nineteenth Century*.

47. Frederic D. Grant Jr., "The April 1820 Debt Settlement between Conseequa and Benjamin Chew Wilcocks."

48. For descriptions of a garden, see Shaw, *Journals*, 178–79. For consideration of the implications of Shaw's description, see Johnson, "A Question of Character," 46–47.

49. Shaw, *Journals*, 152.

50. Ibid., 227–28. For Shaw's reading of Lord Kames and Goldsmith, see K. Johnson, "A Question of Character."

51. Ibid., vi.

52. Ibid., 162.

53. Ibid.

54. Ibid., 246.

55. Ibid.

56. Ibid.

57. Ibid.

58. Ibid.

59. Ibid., 250–51.

60. Ibid.

61. Ibid., 261–62.

62. Seaburg and Paterson, *Merchant Prince of Boston*, 53.

63. Ibid., 155–56.

64. Howay, "Early Days of the Maritime Fur-Trade on the Northwest Coast," quoted from Gibson, *Otter Skins, Boston Ships, and China*, 52–53; also see Dolin, *Fur, Fortune, and Empire*, 148–65. For the journals of the *Columbia* expeditions, see Howay, *Voyages of the "Columbia" to the Northwest Coast*.

65. Trocki, *Opium, Empire and the Global Political Economy*, 76.

66. [Williams], "The fur trade."

67. Ibid., 551, 553.

68. Shaw, *Journals*, 553.

69. Dolin, *Fur, Fortune, and Empire*, 281–82.

70. Delano, *Narrative*.

71. Trocki, *Opium, Empire and the Global Political Economy*, 58.

72. Shaw, *Journals*, 154.

73. Dikötter, Laamann, and Xun, *Narcotic Culture*, 3.

74. Trocki, *Opium, Empire and the Global Political Economy*, 22.

75. Van Dyke, *The Canton Trade*, 11–12, 120–26.

76. Lin, *China Upside Down*, 64.

77. Blue, "Opium for China," 32.

78. Ibid., 33.

79. Van Dyke, *The Canton Trade*, 125. Forty years later, Rev. Elijah Bridgman, one of the first two American missionaries to arrive in Canton in 1830, corroborated Shaw's account in articles appearing in the *Chinese Repository* before the First Opium War. In "The traffic in opium carried on with China: its early history, and the present mode of conducting it, from the delivery of the drug by the cultivators to its reception by the consumers" (April 1837), he begins the account of the EIC opium trade with its "small adventure from Bengal to China,"

where it set up a station outside of Macao to facilitate its sale and circumvent the Portuguese brokerage in Macao; see [Bridgman], "The traffic in opium carried on with China," 547.

80. Van Dyke, *The Canton Trade*, 125.

81. This is a reductive summary of the triangle; for more careful discussion of the various commodities involved and the nature of the investors in India and China, as well as the Chinese investors in Canton, see Wakeman, "The Canton Trade and the Opium War."

82. Trocki, *Opium, Empire and the Global Political Economy*, 61.

83. Ibid., 94.

84. Ibid., 98. Trocki quotes these figures from Man-huong Lin's *China Upside Down*.

85. Shaw, *Journals*, 169.

86. Ibid.

87. Ibid., 238.

88. Ibid., 238–39.

89. Stelle, "American Trade in Opium."

90. For an example of how U.S. trading firms capitalized on this relative regulatory flexibility, see Van Dyke, "Bookkeeping as a Window into Efficiencies of Early Modern Trade."

91. Goldstein, *Stephen Girard's Trade with China*, 72.

92. Ibid., 74.

93. Ibid.

94. Ibid., 91.

95. Stelle in "American Trade in Opium" notes that Astor was an "important rival of J. & T. H. Perkins in the opium trade for a brief period after the close of the War of 1812" (440).

96. Ibid., 429. The *Memoir of Thomas Handasyd Perkins* by Perkins's son-in-law Thomas Cary documents the early Perkins & Company interest in Turkish opium. In 1796 Thomas H. and James wrote to their cousin in Smyrna that "the deranged state of the European trade, consequent on the existing war between Great Britain and continental powers, have opened some new channels for the American commerce in the Mediterranean, and experiments which have been made in those seas exciting further spirit of enterprise, we avail ourselves of a conveyance by way of Naples to make a few inquires respecting the commerce of your city" (282).

97. Roberts, "Commercial Philanthropy," 29.

98. Ibid., 31. Roberts is quoting from the Perkins papers, vol. 37, 23 September 1805, Massachusetts Historical Society.

99. Roberts, "Commercial Philanthropy," 31.

100. Stelle, "American Trade in Opium," 433.

101. Ibid., 442.

102. Ibid.

103. Trocki, *Opium, Empire and the Global Political Economy*, 95.

104. See Melville, "Israel Potter." The book editions are *Israel Potter: His Fifty Years of* (1855) and (1855).

105. Freeman Hunt included an abbreviated version of Perkins's biography by Cary in volume 1 of *Lives of American Merchants*, 33–101.

106. Cary, *Memoir of Thomas Handasyd Perkins*.

107. Ibid., 244–45.

108. [Peabody], "Art. XI.—1. *Memoir of Thomas Handasyd Perkins*," 218–19.

109. Ibid., 232.

110. Cary, *Memoir of Thomas Handasyd Perkins*, 201–2.

111. Ibid., 219, 222, 223.

112. Ibid., 222.

113. Ibid.

114. H. Cohen, "Israel Potter," 287, 314.

115. Rogin explains the swing from Major Thomas Melvill's military heroism to his son Allan Melvill's business failure as reflecting a broader cultural shift from the "household order of eighteenth-century America to the divided realms of work and conjugal family in the nineteenth." By going to New York, Herman Melville's father "shattered traditional ties" of family association that had been reinforced in the national heroism of his father and father-in-law and put himself and his family on the "wheel of fortune"; see *Subversive Genealogy*, 23–24.

116. Bellis, "Israel Potter," 607.

117. Potter, *Life and Remarkable Adventures of Israel R. Potter*.

118. Bellis, "Israel Potter," 609; Chacko and Kulcsar, "Israel Potter: Genesis of a Legend."

119. H. Cohen, "Israel Potter," 305. Cohen notes that Trumbull borrowed freely from other sources and invented the adventure. For more, see the appendix to *Israel Potter: His Fifty Years of Exile* (1850), in *The Writings of Herman Melville*.

120. Casper, *Constructing American Lives*.

121. Bellis, "Israel Potter," 608, 622.

122. Melville, *Israel Potter*, New York edition, 4.

123. Bellis, "Israel Potter," 608.

124. Melville, *Israel Potter*, New York edition, 4.

125. Ibid., 5.

126. Ibid., 3.

127. Ibid.

128. Ibid.

129. Ibid., 5.

130. Ibid.

131. H. Cohen, "Israel Potter, 322.

132. Quincy, *Figures of the Past From the Leaves of Old Journals*, 129–130. For an account of the Bunker Hill memorial, see Seaburg and Patterson, *Merchant Prince of Boston*, 318–44.

133. Rogin, *Subversive Genealogies*, 33.

134. Seaburg and Patterson, *Merchant Prince of Boston*, 331.

135. Cary, *Memoir of Thomas Handasyd Perkins*, 342.

136. Ibid., 423.

137. Ibid., 408.

138. Cushing, "Mr. Cushing at the Bunker Hill Dinner," 94.

139. Ibid., 95.

140. Ibid.

Chapter 2 • Captain Amasa Delano, China Trader

1. Delano, *Narrative*.

2. "Benito Cereno" first appeared as three installments (October, November, and Decem-

ber 1855) in *Putnam's Monthly Magazine of American Literature, Science and Art* and the following year in the book *The Piazza Tales*, 109–270. In "Melville's *Benito Cereno* and Captain Delano's Voyages," Horace Scudder pointed out that Melville derived his story from an episode in chapter 18.

3. Scudder, "Melville's *Benito Cereno* and Captain Delano's Voyages."

4. Greg Grandin offers a poignant overview of what the rebelling Africans would have suffered before boarding the *Tryal*, tracing brutalizing itineraries of transport across the Atlantic Ocean from West Africa to Buenos Aires, and across the South American continent to the Pacific coastal town of Valparaiso (121–22). He also notes the diversity of the enslaved people who would have spoken Wolof, Mandinka, Fulani, and Spanish; some of them would have been Muslim, including the leaders Babo and his son Muri (2, 171–73). Grandin, *Empire of Necessity*.

5. Melville, "Benito Cereno," *The Piazza Tale*, 136.

6. To summarize the interpretive method: this chapter focuses on the object of the Spanish dollar as described by Delano in *Narrative of Voyages* in order to establish a new interpretative context in which to consider the characters and plot of Melville's story. To echo Elaine Freedgood's formulation, the chapter approaches dollars as a collector, probing their metonymic associations in order to offer a new allegorical interpretation of Melville's story; see *The Ideas in Things*, 3–4.

7. Grandin, *Empire of Necessity*, 311.

8. Delano, *Narrative*, 106.

9. Warren, *Sulu Zone*, 43.

10. Ibid., xix.

11. For a compelling overview of the geopolitical dynamics of piracy and slave raiding in Southeast Asia deserve, see Warren's *Sulu Zone*. In addition, see Bose's *A Hundred Horizons*, which adopts the term "interregional arena" to describe areas that "lie between the generalities of a 'world system' and the specificities of particular regions" (6).

12. Warren, *Sulu Zone*, 151.

13. Delano, *Narrative*, 165.

14. See Warren, *Sulu Zone*, xxiii.

15. Delano, *Narrative*, 165. As proof he cites David Woodard's account, the descriptive title of which conveys the dramatic impact of being captive by "Malays": *The Narrative of Captain Woodard and Four Seamen, who lost their ship while in a boat at sea, and surrendered themselves up to the Malays, in the island of Celebes.*

16. Warren, *Sulu Zone*, xii.

17. Delano, *Narrative*, 81.

18. Ibid., 69.

19. Ibid., 45.

20. Stuckey and Leslie, "Captain Delano's Claim," 267.

21. Grandin, *Empire of Necessity*, 72.

22. Delano, *Narrative*, 211.

23. Ibid., 250.

24. Ibid., 388.

25. Ibid., 307.

26. Ibid., 306.

27. Ibid.

28. Ibid.

29. Ibid., 414.

30. Ibid., 320.

31. It is a bit confusing in the original because Delano narrates the *Tryal* episode in chapter 18 of *Narrative of Voyages* as a topical digression (related to Chili and Peru) from the chronological account of his second voyage from 1799 to 1802. However, it is clear from Delano's account and the court documents that appear in the account that the date of the encounter is 1805.

32. Ibid., 329.

33. Ibid., 327.

34. Ibid., 329. On these proceedings, see Stuckey and Leslie, "Captain Delano's Claim."

35. Stuckey and Leslie delve into the court documents related to Delano's litigation; see "Captain Delano's Claim."

36. Grandin, *Empire of Necessity*, 246.

37. Ibid.

38. Delano, *Narrative*, 350–51.

39. Ibid.

40. Ibid., 350.

41. Ibid., 351.

42. Grandin, *Empire of Necessity*, 263.

43. Melville, "Benito Cereno," 136, 110, 150.

44. Ibid., 115.

45. Ibid., 113.

46. Ibid., 115.

47. Ibid., 254.

48. Ibid., 126, 141.

49. Ibid., 131.

50. Ibid., 133.

51. Ibid., 197–98.

52. Ibid., 203.

53. Ibid., 204.

54. Ibid., 201.

55. Ibid., 203.

56. Ibid.

57. Ibid., 209.

58. Ibid., 116, 254.

59. Ibid., 254.

60. Ibid., 270.

61. Ibid., 267.

62. Ibid.

63. Ibid., 268.

64. Ibid.

65. Ibid., 155–56.

66. Warren Delano Jr. (1809–98), the maternal grandfather of President Franklin Delano

Roosevelt, started with Russell & Company after a term in Manila where he directed the allied firm of Russell, Sturgis & Company. In Canton he directed Russell & Company from 1840 to 1844 and from 1861 to 1866. His brother Edward Delano took a turn as director from 1844 to 1846. See the preface to *Delano's Voyages of Commerce and Discovery*, xxii; Downs, *The Golden Ghetto*, 365.

67. Melville, "Benito Cereno," 117.

68. Ibid., 128–29.

69. Ibid., 161, 162–63.

70. Ibid., 199, 201.

71. Ibid., 175.

72. Ibid., 188–89.

73. Jordan, *White over Black*.

74. Melville, "Benito Cereno," 188–89.

75. Ibid., 197.

76. Ibid., 197–98.

77. Ibid., 260.

78. Ibid., 211.

79. Ibid., 212.

80. Ibid.

81. Ibid., 213.

82. Ibid.

83. Ibid.

84. Ibid., 115.

85. For example, Jean Fagan Yellin contends that the story disrupts prevalent stereotypes of "the negro" as exotically primitive, happily enslaved, pathetically victimized, or ruthlessly violent in a long legacy of American letters, stretching from Thomas Jefferson's *Notes on the State of Virginia* (1782) to nineteenth-century "plantation fiction." For Yellin, the "Yankee, Slaveholder and Negro" are Melville's "shifting triad of figures" through which the story exposes the artificiality and social utility of racial masks (682). See Yellin, "Black Masks," 678, 681. Also see Karcher, *Shadow over the Promised Land*; Rogin, *Subversive Genealogy*.

86. Sundquist, "'Benito Cereno' and New World Slavery 101–2. Sundquist expanded this essay in *To Wake the Nations*.

87. Sundquist, "'Benito Cereno' and New World Slavery," 101–2.

88. Ibid., 94, 95.

89. Ibid., 108.

90. Sunquist phrases it this way in *To Wake the Nations*, 28.

91. DeLombard, "Salvaging Legal Personhood: Melville's *Benito Cereno*."

92. Ibid., 44. This echoes a more general condition of Western identity, what Joan Dayan calls *retractable personhood* or the "alternation between person and thing" that "occurs not just within but across individuals and races in a kind of reciprocal contractual exchange run amok"; Dayan's "Legal Slaves and Civil Bodies." See also Balibar, "Subjection and Subjectivation."

93. DeLombard, "Salvaging Legal Personhood," 43. See Dimock, *Residues of Justice*, 207, 196.

94. DeLombard, "Salvaging Legal Personhood," 52.

95. Ibid.

96. Ibid., 53–54. DeLombard's interpretation complements other readings that consider the legal complexity of a captain's maritime authority, manifested in his power to flog members of his crew arbitrarily, in ways that motivated sailors to liken themselves to slaves at the mercy of ship captain tyrants; for example, see Rogin, *Subversive Genealogy*, 157.

97. Ralph Waldo Emerson, "The Young American," in Emerson, *Essays and Lectures*, 221.

98. Ibid., 221–22.

99. Herman Melville, "Bartleby," in Melville, *The Piazza Tales*, 33.

100. Seaburg and Paterson, *Merchant Prince of Boston*, 37.

101. Ibid., 38.

102. Stoddard is a discredited eugenicist whom Tom Buchanan recommends in F. Scott Fitzgerald's *The Great Gatsby* (1925). In regard to Stoddard's book on the Haitian Revolution, *The French Revolution in San Domingo*, he dedicates it to his mother and begins by declaring "the world-wide struggle between the primary races of mankind . . . bids to be the fundamental problem of the twentieth century." He exemplifies this by noting that the "French Revolution in San Domingo" "erased some of the finest European colonies from the map of the white world" (vii).

103. Seaburg and Paterson, *Merchant Prince of Boston*, 41; the parenthetical quotations in the citation are taken from the letter book and correspondence of T. H. Perkins (from 24 July 1786 and 27 July 1786), in the manuscript materials held at the Massachusetts Historical Society.

104. Cary, *Memoir of Thomas Handasyd Perkins*, 10.

105. Seaburg and Paterson, *Merchant Prince of Boston*, 160–61.

106. Ibid., 145, 451.

107. Cary, *Memoir of Thomas Handasyd Perkins*, 146.

108. The appendix of Cary's *Memoir of Thomas Handasyd Perkins* includes a letter dated 1 November 1799 in which Colonel Perkins advises Captain Stephen Hall of the brig "Sally" to go first through the Indian Ocean to take seal skins, moving from Kergulen's Island to St. Paul's, and then to the Isle of Amsterdam. After collecting the skins, Captain Hall is to go straight to Macao to learn of the price. If the price is low, Hall is to entrust the skins to the American consul at Canton Samuel Snow (the successor of Major Samuel Shaw), who will store them until market conditions improve. Perkins then directs his Captain Hall to the Northwest Coast for sea-otter pelts.

109. Ibid., 19, 20.

110. Ibid.

111. Ibid., 31.

112. Ibid.

113. Delano, *Narrative*, 256.

114. Ibid.

115. Ibid., 328.

116. Ibid.

117. Ibid.

118. Ibid., 255.

119. Ibid., 327.

120. Melville, "Benito Cereno," 115; also see Fisher, *Hard Facts*.

121. Rogin notices that in *The Piazza Tales*, the stories "The Piazza" and "The Encantadas: or the Enchanted Isles" relegate the exotic South Sea maidens of *Typee* to *Mardi* to "tedious domesticity" and dispel auras of gothic mystery as the picturesque landscape descriptions resolve into "static, frozen designs" that are drained of adventure. Rogin, *Subversive Genealogy*, 157. In explaining the stories' presentation of "static, frozen design," Rogin draws from Brodhead's *Hawthorne, Melville, and the Novel*.

122. Rogin, *Subversive Genealogy*, 157.

123. Ibid., 208, 209.

124. Melville, "Benito Cereno," 161.

125. Ibid.

126. Delano, *Narrative*, 414.

127. Fichter, *So Great a Profitt*, 30. On the systemic impact of Spanish American silver dollars, also see A. Frank, *ReOrient*, 4–5 and 143–49.

128. Fichter, *So Great a Profitt*, 32.

129. Stelle, "American Trade in Opium to China, Prior to 1820"; Downs, *The Golden Ghetto*, 358–63.

130. Stelle, "American Trade in Opium," 442.

131. Hunter, *The "Fan Kwae" at Canton*, 54–55.

132. Lin, *China Upside Down*, 2.

133. S. Williams, *Middle Kingdom* (1848), 2:395.

134. Ibid.

135. See Louis Jordan, "The Coins of Colonial and Early America," at Coin and Currency Collections, Department of Special Collections University of Notre Dame Libraries, http://www.coins.nd.edu/ColCoin/ColCoinText/Sp-milled.5.html. He cites Josep Pellicer I Bru, *Glosario de Maestros de Ceca y Ensayadores* (Madrid: Asociacion Numismatica Espanola, 1975).

136. Hunter, *The "Fan Kwae" at Canton*, 58–59. The Carolus III (3) Spanish dollar preceded the Carolus III and was an older and less familiar coin than the preferred "Old Head" Carolus IIII during the first two decades of the nineteenth century.

137. Downs, *Golden Ghetto*, 107.

138. S. Williams, *The Middle Kingdom* (1848), 2:156–57.

139. Delano, *Narrative*, 498.

140. Ibid.

141. Ibid.

142. Ibid.

143. Ibid.

144. Ibid., 500.

145. Ibid.

146. Ibid.

147. Ibid., 501.

148. Ibid.

149. Ibid.

150. Ibid.

151. Ibid., 502.

152. Ibid., 503.

153. Ibid.

154. Ibid.

155. Ibid.

156. Adam Smith, *Wealth of Nations*, 1:319.

157. Ibid., 1:291.

158. Ibid., 1:298–99.

159. Before workers took the silver to the mint, Spanish mine operators relied on Indians and enslaved Africans to extract silver, but the goal was to do more than scrape specie out of the earth. See Bowser, *The African in Colonial Peru*. Bower provides an overview of the sixteenth century in which Spain debated how best to mine the silver, either by investing money in the importation of enslaved people from Africa or through "Indian labor" (13). He explains that "Spanish mine operators were concerned with mortality rates in the labor force in relation to profits" (14). Thus, Spanish mines tended to be worked by native peoples who were pressed into service through various tactics but whose death did not mean a loss of "capital investment" (14). This mix of Indian and enslaved African labor continued into the nineteenth century.

160. Grandin, *Empire of Necessity*, 28.

161. Grandin mentions the 1781 massacre aboard the *Zong* in which slaves were thrown overboard and their owners eventually reimbursed through insurance claims (ibid., 28). For further analysis of this incident and its aesthetic, financial, and philosophical implications, see Baucom, *Specters of the Atlantic*.

162. Melville, "Benito Cereno," 168. A doubloon is a Spanish gold coin worth thirty-two reales and equivalent to four Spanish silver dollars (eight reales apiece). Its front bore the image of the Spanish king; the reverse was a complex variation of the Spanish coat of arms.

163. Ibid.

164. Ibid., 115.

165. Ibid., 270.

Chapter 3 • *The Troubled Romance in Harriett Low's Picturesque Macao*

1. In regard to Harriett Low, this chapter cites *Light and Shadows of a Macao Life: The Journal of Harriett Low, Travelling Spinster*, edited by Hodges and Hummel. Low is one of several American women to visit and write about China in the 1830s and 1840s. Arriving in Manila, she received word that her friend from Salem, Lucy Hiller Lambert Cleveland (1780–1866), was in Batavia and on her way to Macao with her husband Captain William Cleveland. Cleveland stayed in Macao nearly three months and kept a journal that includes color sketches of Macao; see Lucy Cleveland, Voyage of the *Zephyr* 1829, MS 656 1829Z, and Sketchbook, M1237, Phillips Library at the Peabody Essex Museum. Harriett's longer-term friend was Caroline Shillaber, whom she had known in Salem. She accompanied her brother moving from Batavia (Jakarta) to Macao in December 1832. A few years after Harriett had left Macao, Caroline Hyde Butler (1804–92) lived there with her merchant husband Edward Butler from February to March 1837 and kept a diary; see Puga, "Representing Macao in 1837." In the 1840s Rebecca Kinsman (1804–92) was also in Macao with her husband Nathaniel Kinsman, a merchant with Wetmore & Company. She sent letters back to her family in Salem. For other women writing, see H. Hsu's "Cultural Orphans: Domesticity, Missionaries, and China from Stowe to Sui Si Far," in his *Geography and the Production of Space*, 94–128; and Susan E.

Schopp, "Five American Women's Perceptions of China 1829–1941." For general overviews of women in Macao and China, see Ford, *Troubling American Women*; and Isabel Morais, "Henrietta Hall Shuck."

2. Low's diaries are in the Library of Congress. The most complete published edition is Hodges and Hummel's *Light and Shadows of a Macao Life*; this book follows their example in spelling Harriett with two t's. Harriett's daughter Katharine Hilliard edited her letters into the abbreviated and filtered *My Mother's Journal*. Harriett's letters feature in *The China Trade Post-Bag*. Rosemarie W. N. Lamas has recently published an account of Low's life in Macao by editing Low's letters and journals; see *Everything in Style*. Harriett's sister Mary Ann wrote a journal as well, but it has not survived.

3. Hodges and Hummel, *Lights and Shadows*, 1:2.

4. Gikandi, *Maps of Englishness*, 123; Sharpe, *Allegories of Empire*; Suleri, *The Rhetoric of English India*; and Mills, *Discourses of Difference*.

5. Stoler, "Tense and Tender Ties," 2.

6. Lowe, *The Intimacies of Four Continents*.

7. For an overview of Low's journal as it relates to opium, see Taketani, "Colonial Violence via Opium Addiction: Harriett Low's Macao," in her *U.S. Women Writers*, 93–124.

8. I use the term *homosocial* in the context of Sedgwick's *Between Men*. My point is not to characterize U.S. China traders as heterosexual men but rather to posit a continuum of intimacies between men that the conventional biographies of early national merchant patriarchs elide.

9. Downs, *The Golden Ghetto*, 61. For more on Russell, see Lange, "The Forgotten Connection."

10. On the endurance of this relationship, J. Forbes, *Letters and Recollections*, 1:77–80. For an interpretative overview of this connection in regard to U.S.-China commerce, see J. D. Wong's, *Global Trade*.

11. See Downs, *The Golden Ghetto*; and Haddad, *America's First Adventure in China*.

12. Hodges and Hummel, *Lights and Shadows*, 1:372–73.

13. Downs, *Golden Ghetto*, 369.

14. Ibid., 161.

15. Hodges and Hummel, *Lights and Shadows*, 1:185.

16. See He, *Macao*, 98–120.

17. Hodges and Hummel, *Lights and Shadows*, 1:410.

18. In Belmont, Massachusetts, he married Mary Louise Gardner and started a family. His granddaughters by his daughter Mary Louisa Cushing Boit are the models for the four girls depicted in a French drawing room with the two giant Japanese vases in John Singer Sargent's *Daughters of Edward Darley Boit* (1882). J. P. Cushing's estate would become famous for its sumptuous gardens that were regularly open to the public. As for Samuel Russell, he returned to Middleton, Connecticut, and established the Russell Manufacturing Company, a very successful textile company.

19. Hodges and Hummel, *Lights and Shadows*, 1:146.

20. Coates, *The Old "Country Trade,"* 113. The ship's name has no connection to the Forbes brothers.

21. Coates, *Country Trade*, 114.

22. Ibid.

23. Hodges and Hummel, *Lights and Shadows*, 1:161.

24. Ibid., 1:390.

25. Downs, *The Golden Ghetto*, 365.

26. Hunter, *The "Fan Kwae" at Canton*. A. C. Hunter, son of W. C. Hunter, writes the preface to the Shanghai edition of 1911 (vi).

27. Wood Sr. acted and directed theaters in Philadelphia, Baltimore, and Washington; his *Personal Recollections of the Stage* conveys the impressive extent of his transatlantic social connections.

28. Hodges and Hummel, *Lights and Shadows*, 1:411.

29. Hunter, *The "Fan Kwae" at Canton*, 109.

30. Hunter, *Bits of Old China*, 270. Timothy Mo's novel *An Insular Possession* centers on these figures in a fictional account of the 1830s Canton trade leading to the First Opium War.

31. Clarke, "The Development of the English Language Press," 492–93.

32. Hodges and Hummel, *Lights and Shadows*, 1:197.

33. King and Clarke, *A Research Guide to China-Coast Newspapers*, 160.

34. Hodges and Hummel, *Lights and Shadows*, 1:5.

35. Ibid., 1:374.

36. For an account of the Portuguese in Macao and of Harriett Low's representation of them, see Puga, "Images of Nineteenth-Century Macao."

37. Taketani in *U.S. Women Writers* notes that Harriett shows very "little respect for this [Chinese] servant class" (101–2).

38. Hodges and Hummel, *Lights and Shadows*, 1:69.

39. Ibid., 1:77, 100; see Van Dyke, *Merchants of Canton and Macao*.

40. Hodges and Hummel, *Lights and Shadows*, 1:190–94.

41. Ibid., 1:193.

42. Ibid., 1:194.

43. Ibid.

44. Ibid., 1:196.

45. Ibid.

46. Ibid., 2:730, 768.

47. Ibid., 2:789.

48. Ibid., 1:370.

49. See C. Low, *Some Recollections by Captain Charles P. Low*, 32–33, 165.

50. Holloway, *Famous American Fortunes*, 418.

51. "Abiel Abbot Low is Dead: A Merchant Prince of the City Passes Away," *New York Times*, 8 January 1893; see McKay, *Donald McKay and His Famous Sailing Ships*, 242.

52. Holloway, *Famous American Fortunes*, 418.

53. Hodges and Hummel, *Lights and Shadows*, 1:19. Low's emphasis.

54. Ibid., 2:540.

55. Ibid., 1:217; also 2:457.

56. Ibid., 1:28. Low's emphasis.

57. Ibid., 1:95.

58. Ibid., 2:525.

59. Ibid., 2:426.

60. Ibid., 1:351.

61. Ibid., 1: 578, 805.

62. Ibid., 2:600.

63. Ibid., 1:283. Low's emphasis.

64. Ibid., 1:293.

65. Ibid., 2:551. Low's emphasis.

66. Ibid., 1:217.

67. Ibid., 1:77.

68. Horsman, *Race and Manifest Destiny*.

69. Hodges and Hummel, *Lights and Shadows*, 1:163.

70. Davison. "E. W. Clay and the American Political Caricature Business."

71. Hodges and Hummel, *Lights and Shadows*, 1:339. Low's emphasis.

72. Ibid., 1:111. Low's emphasis.

73. Ibid., 2:572.

74. Ibid., 2:573.

75. Seaburg and Paterson, *Merchant Prince of Boston*, 165.

76. Robert Bennet, his brothers, and his uncles all maintained a strong pride in their Scottish heritage. Perhaps this pride helped in negotiating with the major competing British firms founded by Scotsmen. Richard J. Grace describes the political and social turmoil in the aftermath of the failed Jacobite rising of 1745—turmoil that motivated many young Scottish men to seek fortunes in the East Indies trade; see the chapter "Prelude: The Scotland of Their Birth," in *Opium and Empire*, 3–12.

77. Hodges and Hummel, *Lights and Shadows*, 1:293.

78. Ibid., 1:305.

79. Kerr, *Letters from China*, 119.

80. Ibid., July 1839, 142.

81. Hodges and Hummel, *Lights and Shadows*, 1:291, 199, 302.

82. Ibid., 2:470.

83. Hunter, *The "Fan Kwae" at Canton*, 110.

84. Hodges and Hummel, *Lights and Shadows*, 1:251.

85. Ibid., 2:478. Low's emphasis.

86. Wood, *Sketches*.

87. Ibid., 8.

88. Ibid., 201, 141.

89. See Gombrich, *Art and Illusion*; J. Hunt and Willis, *The Genius of Place*; Novak, *Nature and Culture*; Bermingham, *Landscape and Ideology*; Boime, *The Magisterial Gaze*; A. Miller, *Empire of the Eye*; and Conron, *American Picturesque*. Conron's work is brilliant and has been very important to my understanding of the texture of the picturesque as it transformed in different periods throughout the nineteenth century. Finally, Suleri's *The Rhetoric of English India* offers insight on the colonial context of visual aesthetics that inform this reading of Wood and Low.

90. William Gilpin, Uvedale Price, and Richard Payne Knight each wrote several essays of importance; in summary, consider Gilpin's *An Essay on Prints, Containing Remarks upon Principles of Picturesque Beauty* (1768); Price's *Essays on the Picturesque, as Compared to the Sublime and Beautiful: and, on the Use of Studying Pictures for the Purpose of Improving Real Landscape* (1794); and Richard Payne Knight's *An Analytical Inquiry into the Principles of Taste*

(1805). Contemporary scholarship on these concepts is copious and overlaps with the previous citations. In regard to the picturesque, see Price, "The Picturesque Moment"; Robinson, *Inquiry into the Picturesque*; Copley and Garside, *The Politics of the Picturesque*; Marshall, *The Frame of Art*; Conron, *American Picturesque*; and K. Johnson, *Henry James and the Visual*.

91. Sara Suleri offers a more capacious discussion of Burke's sense of the sublime in "Edmund Burke and the Indian Sublime," chapter 2 of *The Rhetoric of English India*, 24–48.

92. Coleridge, *Biographia Literaria*, 309.

93. Chambers, *Designs of Chinese Buildings*; and *A Dissertation on Oriental Gardening*.

94. See Conron, *American Picturesque*, 7; and Price, "Picturesque Moment," for further explanation of the "drama of composition."

95. Wood, *Sketches*, 54–56.

96. Ibid., 22.

97. Hodges and Hummel, *Lights and Shadows*, 2:457–58. Low's emphasis.

98. Wood, *Sketches*, 26.

99. Ibid.

100. Hodges and Hummel, *Lights and Shadows*, 2:437. Low's emphasis.

101. Ibid., 1:374, 375.

102. Ride and Ride, *An East India Company Cemetery*.

103. Suleri, *Rhetoric of English India*, 75, 80.

104. Hodges and Hummel, *Lights and Shadows*, 2:454.

105. Ibid., 2:455.

106. Wood, *Sketches*, 34.

107. Hodges and Hummel, *Lights and Shadows*, 2:455.

108. Ibid., 2:459–61. Low's emphasis.

109. Ibid., 2:607.

110. Ibid., 2:497. Low's emphasis.

111. Ibid., 2:513.

112. Adam Smith, *The Theory of Moral Sentiments*, 192.

113. Ibid., 193.

114. Ibid., 2:513–14.

115. Ibid., 2:647. Low's emphasis.

116. Ibid., 2:647–48.

117. Ibid., 2:648.

118. Ibid. Low's emphasis.

119. Ibid. Low's emphasis.

120. *Heathen* is the term that Eliza J. Gillett Bridgman uses throughout her book *Daughters of China*.

121. Ibid., 120.

122. Shuck's former pastor memorialized her in *A Memoir of Mrs. Henrietta Hall Shuck*, edited by Jeremiah Bell Jeter.

123. Shuck, *Scenes in China*, 151.

124. Ibid., 148.

125. Jeter, *A Memoir*, 222.

126. Eliza Bridgman, *Daughters of China*, 3.

127. Sukjoo Kim writes: "Liang was known generally as Liang Gongfa or Liang Aa. . . .

The affixed 'A' commonly preceding the name 'Fa' is added in the Cantonese style" and adopted by the missionaries (1). See Kim, "Liang Fa's Quanshi liangyan."

128. Eliza Bridgman, *The Pioneer of American Missions in China*, 55.

129. Ibid., 194.

130. Eliza Bridgman, *Daughters of China*, 138.

131. Ibid., epigraph.

132. The collection of essays that came to be known as "Suspiria de Profundis" (Sighs from the Depths) extended over several issues of *Blackwood's* and other periodicals. These essays were not published in book form until decades after De Quincey's death. The quote that Bridgman uses as the epigraph for *Daughters of China* is from the subsection "Levana and Our Lady of Sorrows" (746); see De Quincey, "Suspiria de Profundis."

133. Hodges and Hummel, *Lights and Shadows*, 2:41.

134. Eliza Bridgman, *Daughters of China*, 27.

Chapter 4 • The Sacred Fount of the ABCFM

1. For a nineteenth-century description of the *Chinese Repository*, see Holt, "The Mission Press in China." For a more recent overview of the journal, see Malcolm, "The Chinese Repository."

2. In the magisterial *A History of American Magazines*, Frank Luther Mott does not mention the *Chinese Repository*, although he insightfully differentiates the terms *journal, newspaper, paper, periodical,* and *review* (1:5–9).

3. Malcolm, "The Chinese Repository," 172.

4. [Bridgman], "European Periodicals Beyond the Ganges," 160; see Malcolm, "The Chinese Repository," 165–78.

5. Bridgman and Williams, *General Index*, v, viii.

6. Jonathan Spence, *God's Chinese Son*, 170. For a more about Catholic and Protestant missionaries in China, see P. Cohen, *China and Christianity*.

7. S. Williams, *The Middle Kingdom* (1883), 2:624. For an account of the events, see Spence's *God's Chinese Son*.

8. Sukjoo Kim writes: "Liang was known generally as Liang Gongfa (梁恭發) or Liang Afa (梁阿發). . . . The affixed 'A' commonly preceding the name 'Fa' is added in the Cantonese style" and adopted by the missionaries," in "Liang Fa's Quanshi liangyan," 1. For a list of Liang Fa's publications and short biography, see Alexander Wylie, *Memorials of Protestant Missionaries*, 21–25.

9. Hall, *Cultures of Print*, 5.

10. Contemporary historiography extends the legacy of their publications in frequent citations. Influential accounts of the Opium War such as Greenberg, *British Trade and the Opening of China*; Waley, *The Opium War through Chinese Eyes*; Chang, *Commissioner Lin and the Opium War*; Fay, *The Opium War*; and Wakeman, *Strangers at the Gate* all cite its pages. More recently Lovell in *The Opium War* describes the *Chinese Repository* as "Canton's leading English-language publication" of the era (4).

11. Article 19 of the United Nation's "Universal Declaration of Human Rights" (1948) puts it this way: "Everyone has the right to freedom of opinion and expression; this right

includes freedom to hold opinions without interference and to seek, receive and impart information and ideas through any media and regardless of frontiers."

12. See Field, *The Crisis of Standing*; and D. King, "The New Divinity and the Origins of the American Board of Commissioners for Foreign Missions."

13. Karen Sánchez-Eppler looks at an 1824 friendship album "from a Chinese youth" named Wu Lan who was enrolled at the Foreign Mission School in Cornwall, Connecticut; see "Copying and Conversion."

14. H. Hsu, *Geography and the Production of Space*, 3.

15. Brückner, *The Geographic Revolution*, 1.

16. Ibid., 41.

17. Ibid., 107.

18. Ibid., 151, 163.

19. Richard. J. Moss, "Republicanism, Liberalism, and Identity," 215; cited in Livingstone, "Geographical Inquiry," 111.

20. H. Hsu, *Geography and the Production of Space*, 27.

21. Morse, *Geography*, 327.

22. Wylie, *Memorials of Protestant Missionaries*, 68.

23. The definitive biography on Bridgman is Michael C. Lazich's *E. C. Bridgman*.

24. Ibid., 81.

25. Reed, *Gutenberg in Shanghai*, 42.

26. F. Williams, *Life and Letters*, 78; also see Edwards, *The Missionary Gazetteer*, 79.

27. Unattributed, "China-Extracts from the General Letter of the Mission [8 September 1836]," 263.

28. [Bridgman], "Crisis in Opium Traffic," (June 1839). The process of destruction involved breaking up tens of thousands of opium balls in a water-filled trench and mixing the opium with lime and salt.

29. [Bridgman], "Reminiscences of a trip up the river of Canton."

30. Cushing in "Message from the President of the United States," 2.

31. Wylie, *Memorials of Protestant Missionaries*, 70.

32. F. William, *Life and Letters*, 247.

33. Ibid., 181.

34. Ibid., 47.

35. Ibid., 49.

36. For a definitive overview, see Phillips, *Protestant America and the Pagan World*.

37. Lazich, *E. C. Bridgman*, 78.

38. Gulick, *Peter Parker and the Opening of China*.

39. Tracy, *History of the American Board of Commissioners for Foreign Missions*, 276, 308. In the final issue of the *Chinese Repository*, Williams gives an overview of all missionaries to China in the lead article "List of Protestant Missionaries to the Chinese"; he mentions many other Americans, including Stephen Johnson, Samuel Munson, and Stephen Tracy (514).

40. See Jeter, *A Memoir of Mrs. Henrietta Shuck*; Ford, *Troubling American Women*.

41. Spence, *God's Chinese Son*, 92–93; Y. Teng, "Reverend Issachar Jacox Roberts and the Taiping Rebellion."

42. Haddad, *America's First Adventure in China*, 189.

43. Britton, *The Chinese Periodical Press*, 23; quoted from Zhang, *Origins of the Modern Chinese Press*, 39. On Gützlaff's fascinating life and travels through China and Southeast Asia, see Lutz, *Opening China*.

44. Eisenstein, *The Printing Press*, 24.

45. [Bridgman], "Literary Notices: Chinese Printing," 418.

46. Ibid., 419.

47. Christopher A. Daily tracks the metalinguistic rationale back to the academic training for London Missionary Service at Gosport Academy under Rev. David Bogue (1750–1825). Drawing on the Scottish Realism of Thomas Reid as well as American Reformed Theology (Jonathan Edwards, Samuel Hopkins) and the missionary examples of colonial missionaries John Eliot and David Brainerd, Bogue laid a foundation for foreign ministry in the study of Latin, Hebrew, Greek, and French. The curriculum then expanded to train for proficiency in the indigenous language of the destination station. Missionaries hoped to craft simple and engaging conversion parables and translate biblical passages into the mother tongue of the auditors and readers, appealing to the innate common sense of the potential converts. Bridgman and Williams likewise envisioned opening the minds of Chinese people through the organic print production of the Chinese language. See Daily, *Robert Morrison and the Protestant Plan for China*, 59.

48. Marshman's book *Elements of Chinese Grammar* was an important influence and inspiration on young missionaries for generations. See Zhang, *Origins of the Modern Chinese Press*, 36.

49. William Milne's *China Monthly Magazine* (察世俗每月統記傳; Chá shìsú měi yuè tǒng jì chuán; 1815–22) first appeared in August 1815, printed in Malacca by "traditional Chinese woodblock." It ran for seven years with a monthly run of five hundred, "circulat[ing] through the Chinese communities in South East Asia and some parts of China." Zhang, *Origins of the Modern Chinese Press*, 36.

50. Ibid., 36.

51. Ibid., 38.

52. [Bridgman], "European Periodicals Beyond the Ganges."

53. Zhang, *Origins of the Chinese Press*, 101–5.

54. Milne, *A Retrospect of the First Ten Years of the Protestant Mission to China*, 226–28.

55. [Bridgman], "Literary Notices: Chinese Printing," 420.

56. Ibid.

57. Evan Davies quoting Dyer's letter to the directors of the London Missionary Society in *Memoir of the Rev. Samuel Dyer*, 89; see Su, "The Printing Presses of the London Missionary Society among the Chinese," 262–63.

58. Dyer from Davies, *Memoir of the Rev. Samuel Dyer*, 84.

59. F. Williams, *Life and Letters*, 110.

60. For example, in a letter to his brother 23 July 1863, Williams refers to himself similarly: "Little by little the work goes on, however, and God uses the tools and the men which are likely to carry it further, as they are at hand"; F. Williams, *Life and Letters*, 344.

61. S. Williams, *Middle Kingdom* (1848), 2:354.

62. 2:355.

63. [Bridgman], "Introduction," 1.

64. Ibid., 3–4.

65. Ibid., 5.

66. [Bridgman], "Periodical literature," 1.

67. [Bridgman], "Introductory remarks," 2.

68. [Bridgman], "The Chinese language," 6.

69. [Bridgman], "Periodical literature,"1.

70. Ibid., 12.

71. Ibid.

72. Ibid., 2.

73. Ibid., 12.

74. Ibid., 6.

75. Ibid.

76. Ibid.

77. Ibid.

78. Ibid.

79. Ibid., 3.

80. Ibid.

81. Ibid., 11.

82. [Stevens], "Promulgation of the Gospel in China."

83. Ibid., 434, 435.

84. [Bridgman], "The Chinese language," 13.

85. Ibid., 9–10.

86. Songchuan Chen follows up the military connotations of the print endeavor in "An Information War Waged by Merchants and Missionaries at Canton."

87. [Bridgman], "The Chinese Language," 8.

88. Ibid., 7.

89. [Bridgman], "European Periodicals Beyond the Ganges," 145.

90. W. Hunter, *Fan Kwae*, 109.

91. Le Pichon, *China Trade and Empire*.

92. *Canton Register* 1.1 (8 November 1827): 1.

93. *Canton Register* 1.2 (24 November 1827): 5.

94. *Canton Register* 1.4 (14 December 1827): 13.

95. Ibid.

96. *Canton Register* 1.7 (4 February 1828): 21.

97. *Canton Register* 1.7 (11 February 1828): 25.

98. Ibid.

99. *Canton Register* 1.7 (11 February 1828): 27.

100. Ibid. The *Canton Register* continued operations for more than ten years, ending its run in 1843 after the First Opium War. See Britton, *The Chinese Periodical Press*, 27; King and Clarke, *A Research Guide to China-Coast Newspapers*, 160.

101. [Bridgman], "Remarks on the present crisis in the opium traffic," 8.

102. In the late 1830s Gützlaff's collaborated with the opium traders Jardine, Matheson, & Co., voyaging up the China coast on its opium vessels, translating for the traders as he distributed evangelical tracts, whose print production the company funded. During the final phase of the First Opium War, Gützlaff served under Henry Pottinger as the chief of secret police and the administrating magistrate at the British-occupied port city of Ningpo. See

Bickers, *The Scramble for China*, 51; Lazich, *E. C. Bridgman*, 98–99; and Songchuan Chen, "An Information War Waged by Merchants and Missionaries at Canton."

103. [Bridgman], "Cultivation of the poppy."

104. G. H. Smith, "Abstract of a paper on opium-smoking in Penang."

105. [Bridgman], "Retrospection," (February 1842): 66.

106. [Bridgman], "Retrospection," (April 1842): 189.

107. Ibid., 196.

108. [Bridgman], "Suspension of trade," 454.

109. [Bridgman], "Remarks on the present crisis in the opium traffic," 2.

110. Ibid.

111. Ibid., 6.

112. Charles W. King as "CR," "Review of the difficulties between the English and Chinese authorities."

113. Editorial preface to Forbes as "Non Sine Causa," "Reply to article second, in the Repository for January," 532.

114. John Quincy Adams, "December 1841, Lecture on the War with China."

115. Ibid., 289.

116. Ibid.

117. [Bridgman], "Imperial edict," 405.

118. [Morrison], "Opium."

119. Ibid., 138.

120. [Morrison], "Memorial of Choo Tsun on Opium."

121. Ibid., 390.

122. Ibid., 391.

123. [Bridgman], "Imperial edict," 405.

124. S. Williams, *Middle Kingdom* (1848), 2:509.

125. S. Williams, *Middle Kingdom* (1883), 2:482.

126. [Bridgman], "Retrospection," (August 1842), 404, 406.

127. S. Williams, *Middle Kingdom* (1848), 2:633.

128. Ibid., 2:518.

129. Ibid., 2:514.

130. Lazich, *E. C. Bridgman*, 187.

131. [Bridgman], "Crisis in Opium Traffic," (June 1839), 77. See L. Liu, *The Clash of Empires*, 93, 169; and Lazich, *E. C. Bridgman*, 187.

132. [Bridgman], "Crisis in Opium Traffic," (June 1839), 77; L. Liu, *Clash of Empires*, 169.

133. [Bridgman], "Crisis in Opium Traffic," (June 1839), 77; Lazich, *E. C. Bridgman*, 187; and L. Liu, *Clash of Empires*, 169.

134. [Bridgman], "Crisis in Opium Traffic," (June 1839), 77; Lazich, *E. C. Bridgman*, 187; and L. Liu, *Clash of Empires*, 93, 169.

135. Lazich, *E. C. Bridgman*, 187.

136. L. Liu, *Clash of Empires*, 119.

137. Ibid., 92.

138. Gulick, *Peter Parker and the Opening of China*, 88–91.

139. [Parker], "Hospital Reports of the Medical Missionary Society for China, for the year 1839," 634; see L. Liu, *Clash of Empires*, 118–20.

140. Parker, "Hospital Reports of the Medical Missionary Society for China, for the year 1839," 635.

141. Ibid.

142. [Bridgman and Thom], "Letter to the Queen of England," (May 1939), and "Letter to the queen of England," (February 1840).

143. In regard to original Chinese sources, see S. Teng and Fairbank, *China's Response to the West*, 5. They track back to *Ch-ou-pan i-wu shi-mo* (A complete account of the management of barbarian affairs), 260 chün (Peking: printed by the Palace Museum in 1929–31), 7.33–36b; Lin Tse-hsü, *Lin Wen-chung-kung cheng-shu* (Collection of memoirs by Lin Tse-hsü), 37 chüan (printed by the author's family), part II, 4.16–20; and *Ch'ing shih-lu, Ta-Ch'ing li-ch'ao shih-lu* (Veritable records of successive reigns of the Ch'ing dynasty), photographic edition, 1220 ts'e (Changchun, 1937), 324.25b–26; Lydia Liu, *Clash of Empires*, takes the original from the collected writing of Lin Zexu, by Lin Zexu et al., *Lin Zexu Nianpu xinbian* (Revised chronicles of Lin Zexu's life), ed. Lai Xinxia (Tianjin: Nankai daxue chubanshe, 1997), viz. p. 269, n. 65, of *Clash of Empires* (2004).

144. [Bridgman and Thom], "Letter to the Queen of England," (May 1839), 9.

145. Ibid.

146. S. Teng and Fairbank, *China's Response to the West*, 24.

147. Fay, *The Opium War*, 143. Arthur Waley translated the letter from the original Chinese in *The Opium War*, 28–31. Fay (380) compliments Waley's version, criticizing as stilted the translation that Hsin-pao Chang offers in *Commissioner Lin and the Opium War*.

148. L. Liu, *Clash of Empires*, 93–94; W. Hunter, *Bits of Old China*, 262–63.

149. Fay, *The Opium War*, 206.

150. L. Liu, *Clash of Empires*, 269.

151. Liu, in *Clash of Empire*, 229–41, juxtaposes the "original [1840 letter from the] document titled 'Ni yu yingjili guowang xi' (A draft declaration to the sovereign of England) jointly submitted by Lin Zexu, Deng Tingzhen, and Yi Liang," with the contemporary translation that appeared in the *Chinese Repository* (February 1840), and the 1954 translation by Teng and Fairbank.

152. [Bridgman and Thom], "Letter to the Queen of England," (February 1840), 502.

153. Ibid., 501.

154. Ibid., 502–3.

155. Wakeman, *The Opium War through Chinese Eyes*, 209.

156. [Williams]," Treaty between her Majesty the Queen of Great Britain and the Emperor of China."

157. *Chinese Repository* 13.5 (September 1844): 9.

158. The quote is from January 1842, 1.

159. Bridgman, "Retrospect," (November 1842), 586.

160. Ibid., 688.

161. F. Williams, *Life and Letters*, 121.

162. Ibid.

163. Ibid.

164. Ibid., 122.

165. Unattributed, "Journal of Occurrences," (October 1844), 560.

166. F. Williams, *Life and Letters*, 127–28.

167. "Chinese Stereotype-Printing," *Missionary Herald* 30.7 (July 1834): 268, quoted by S. Williams in "Chinese Metallic Types," 530. In his article, he refutes the efficacy of stereotype printing and embraces the project of manufacturing metallic type.

168. Lazich, *E. C. Bridgman*, 194–96.

169. F. Williams, *Life and Letters*, 172.

170. Ibid., 178.

171. Ibid., 174. Letter is dated 22 June 1850.

172. S. Williams and Bridgman, *General Index*, vii.

173. Ibid., v, viii.

174. F. Williams, *Life and Letters*, 230.

175. For an overview, see Hevia, *English Lessons*, 31–48.

176. F. Williams, *Life and Letters*, 242.

177. Ibid.

178. Ibid., 245–46.

179. Ibid.

180. Ibid., 173.

181. For an excerpt of this tract, see Cheng and Lestz, *The Search for Modern China*, 132–36.

182. Kim, "Liang Fa's Quanshi liangyan," 65. Also see Boardman, *Christian Influence*.

183. Jonathan Spence, *God's Chinese Son*; Cheng, *Chinese Sources for the Taiping Rebellion*, 62 and 93; and Y. Teng, "Reverend Issachar Jacox Roberts and the Taiping Rebellion."

184. Kim, "Liang Fa's Quanshi liangyan," 14.

185. Jonathan Spence, *God's Chinese Son*, 232.

186. Kim, "Liang Fa's Quanshi liangyan," 7, 65.

187. S. Williams, *Middle Kingdom* (1883), 2:589.

188. Jonathan Spence, *God's Chinese Son*, 184, 220.

189. F. Williams, *Life and Letters*, 179–80.

190. S. Williams, *The Middle Kingdom* (1883), 2:585.

191. S. Williams, *The Middle Kingdom* (1848), 2:400–401.

192. Ibid., 1:501.

193. S. Williams, *The Middle Kingdom* (1883), 2:499.

194. F. Williams, *Life and Letters*, 446.

195. S. Williams, *The Middle Kingdom* (1883), 2:600, 446, 624.

196. S. Williams, *A Syllabic Dictionary of the Chinese Language*, x.

197. F. Williams, *Life and Letters*, 393.

198. Ibid.

199. Ibid.

200. Ibid., 326.

Chapter 5 • *Caleb Cushing's Print Trail of Legal Extraterritoriality*

1. In regard to the treaty language, see Miller, "China: 1844 (Document 109)," 626.

2. Cushing, *Opinion of the Attorney General*, 6. In the opinion, Cushing is quoting his own "Dispatch 97 (to Secretary of State Calhoun, 29 September 1844)."

3. According to Wesley R. Fishel, "The first reference to extraterritoriality came in the

General Regulations of Trade, which were incorporated into the Treaty of the Bogue, October 8, 1843," Article 13 of which "stated that British subjects involved in criminal cases were to be tried by officials according to British law"; see *End of Extraterritoriality*, 5.

4. To elucidate the nuance of legal authority in China, Pär Kristoffer Cassel takes a broad view on legal authority in regard to the development of jurisdiction over persons and territories, from the Tang, Yuan, Ming, and Qing dynasties; see "Codifying Extraterritoriality: The Chinese Unequal Treaties," chapter 2 in *Grounds of Judgment*. As for the internal dynamics of Qing legal culture, see Cassel's chapter 1: "Excavating Extraterritoriality: The Legacies of Legal Pluralism, Subjecthood, and State-Building in Japan."

5. The complex legal workings of consular jurisdiction soon disproved Cushing's claim. As Eileen P. Scully describes the legacy of U.S. extraterritoriality, from 1906 to 1942 the Ninth Circuit Court of Appeals in San Francisco maintained oversight of the U.S. Court in Shanghai—a court with jurisdiction that included Korea; see *Bargaining with the State from Afar*. On the end of this arrangement, see Fishel, *Grounds of Judgment*, 207–15; and Kayaoğlu, *Legal Imperialism*, 181–85.

6. Cushing was the most influential although not the first diplomat to push for extraterritoriality in a commercial treaty with a country in the East Indies; in 1833 Edmund Roberts had signed the Treaty of Amity and Commerce between Siam and the United States, which stipulates that U.S. consuls would use U.S. law in adjudicating conflicts between U.S. citizens in Siam. See Welch, "Celeb Cushing's Chinese Mission and the Treaty of Wanghia: A Review," 350. For the limits of U.S. constitutional guarantees to U.S. citizens tried in China, see Raustiala, *Does the Constitution Follow the Flag?*, 69–72.

7. Ruskola, *Legal Orientalism*, 130.

8. Ruskola, "Canton Is Not Boston" and *Legal Orientialism*, 114; Ruskola is quoting Chief Justice John Marshall's decision *Schooner Exc. v. McFadden* (1812).

9. Cassel, *Grounds of Judgment*, 7.

10. Sexton, *The Monroe Doctrine*, 248.

11. For example, see Cushing's "Dispatch 71 (to Secretary of State Calhoun, 5 July 1844)"; "Dispatch 76 (to Secretary of State Calhoun, 15 July 1844)"; "Dispatch 86 (to Secretary of State Calhoun, 29 September 1844)"; "Dispatch 97 (to Secretary of State Calhoun, 29 September 1844)." For demonstration of these dispatches' impact on the presentation of the treaty to Congress, see President Tyler's "To the Senate of the United States (22 January 1845)," 1–2.

12. Cushing, *Opinion of the Attorney General*, 6; he is quoting his own "Dispatch 97 (to Secretary of State Calhoun, 29 September 1844)."

13. The definitive biography on Cushing is Belohlavek's, *Broken Glass*; in regard to Cushing's return through Mexico to New York, see 178–80.

14. For a general overview of how race became a concept that framed cultural identity in the United States, see Horsman, *Race and Manifest Destiny*; and Jordan, *White over Black*.

15. Belohlavek estimates John Perkins Cushing's fortune at $7 million, making him "the wealthiest man in New England" (*Broken Glass*, 3).

16. Ibid., 152.

17. For a contemporary overview of Everett's life, see *Tribute of the Massachusetts Historical Society*, 9–18.

18. See Foletta, *Coming to Terms with Democracy*, 73–75.

19. Belohlavek, *Broken Glass*, 14.

20. Cushing, *Review, Historical and Political, of the Late Revolution in France.*

21. Belohlavek, *Broken Glass*, 54.

22. Webster, "Intercourse with China," 468.

23. Ibid., 468.

24. Ibid., 469.

25. Webster, "The President's Letter to the Emperor," 476.

26. Ibid., 477.

27. Belohlavek, *Broken Glass*, 156.

28. Haddad, *America's First Adventure in China*, 145.

29. Belohlavek, *Broken Glass.*, 160.

30. Ibid., 159.

31. Webster, "The President's Letter to the Emperor," 476.

32. Lazich, *E. C. Bridgman*, 129; and Dennett, *Americans in Eastern Asia*, 557.

33. S. Teng and Fairbank, *China's Response to the West: A Documentary Survey*, 37.

34. See Mann and Kuhn, "Dynastic Decline and the Roots of Rebellion."

35. D. Miller, "China: 1844 (Document 109)," 627.

36. Downs, *Golden Ghetto*, 365–66.

37. Lazich, *E. C. Bridgman*, 237.

38. "Journal of Occurrences," *Chinese Repository* (December 1845), 590.

39. Hale, *Sketches of the Lives of the Brothers Everett*; "Journal of Occurrences," *Chinese Repository* (June 1847), 367.

40. Belohlavek, *Broken Glass*, 147.

41. Ibid., 14; O'Sullivan, "Annexation"; and "The Great Nation of Futurity."

42. Fuess, *Caleb Cushing, a Memoir*, 7; Fuess also wrote a two-volume biography, *The Life of Caleb Cushing.*

43. Wisconsin Historical Society, http://www.wisconsinhistory.org/hp/register/viewSummary.asp?refnum=05000955.

44. Belohlavek, *Broken Glass*, 355–56.

45. See Kayaoğlu, *Legal Imperialism*, 27; and Raustiala, *Does the Constitution Follow the Flag?*.

46. Scully, *Bargaining with the State*, 23–28. Fishel similarly distinguishes between *extraterritoriality* and *exterritoriality* in his *End of Extraterritoriality*, 2. Taking a broader view across the decades of nineteenth-century and early twentieth-century extraterritoriality in China and Japan, Cassel eschews the term *system* for *practice* by those interacting in a "legally pluralistic environment" (*Grounds of Judgment*, 6).

47. In *End of Extraterritoriality*, Fishel writes that the Treaty of Wanghia "provided in explicit language for extraterritorial jurisdiction in civil as well as in criminal cases, and the terminology of the treaty became a model for those which were concluded by other countries with China" (6).

48. S. Williams, *Treaties between the United States of America and China*, 16. Williams published this as the secretary of the U.S. Legation directed by Anson Burlingame. It includes Cushing's abstract of the treaty (September 1845) and Cushing's 1855 opinion as the U.S. attorney general; also, D. Miller, "China: 1844," 566.

49. S. Williams, *Treaties between the United States of America and China*, 17; D. Miller, "China: 1844," 567.

50. S. Williams, *Treaties between the United States of America and China*, 17; D. Miller, "China: 1844," 566.

51. S. Williams, *Treaties between the United States of America and China*, 17; D. Miller, "China: 1844," 570.

52. This goes back to the early twentieth-century historiography by H. B. Morse and T. Dennett and echoes to this day. The biography by Fuess, *The Life of Caleb Cushing* does not delve in to the opium question. Neither does Belohlavek's *Broken Glass*.

53. Cushing's "Abstract of the Treaty," 3.

54. Ibid., 4.

55. Gulick, *Peter Parker*, 114; for account of the negotiations, see 113–23.

56. Ibid., 121, 98–99. Also see the U.S. Department of State, Office of the Historian website on "Chiefs of Mission for China," https://history.state.gov/departmenthistory/people/chiefsofmission/china.

57. Cushing's "Abstract of the Treaty," 4.

58. D. Miller, "China: 1844," 628.

59. Ibid., 630. Cushing, "Dispatch 86 (to Secretary of State Calhoun, 19 August 1844)," 91–92.

60. Cushing, "Dispatch 76 (to Secretary of State Calhoun, 15 July 1844)," 60.

61. Cushing, "Dispatch 97 (to Secretary of State Calhoun, 29 September 1844)," 5.

62. Ibid.

63. Ibid., 10.

64. Ibid., 12–13.

65. Ibid., 12.

66. Ibid., 13.

67. Ruskola, *Legal Orientalism*, 151.

68. Ibid., 119.

69. Ruskola, *Legal Orientalism*, 114.

70. Prucha, *American Indian Treaties*.

71. Ruskola, *Legal Orientalism*, 116.

72. Marshall's decision tasks the U.S. federal government with protecting these indigenous savages, but only in mere occupation of land—an occupation that will cease at some undetermined point when the land will become part of the United States. Marshall's majority opinion in *Cherokee Nation v. Georgia* (1831) reinforced this first decision. He expresses sympathy for the Cherokee who had sued the state of Georgia for violating a treaty with the United States that had secured land for the Cherokee, but Marshall then claims that the court lacks jurisdiction over the case by infamously defining the Cherokee as a "domestic dependent nation," without rights as either U.S. citizens or foreign nationals. For concise statement of these principles, see "Chapter V: Of Property" in John Locke's *Second Treatise of Government*.

73. Ruskola, *Legal Orientalism*, 116.

74. Cushing, "Art. VIII—*An Address to the Whites*."

75. In the 1830s Boudinot argued for compromise with the federal government when

removal seemed unstoppable. He resigned his editorship in 1832 of the *Cherokee Phoenix.* He later capitulated to federal demands of the Treaty of New Echoata (1835), contradicting the Cherokee's principal chief John Ross, who refused to sign it. Boudinot paid for this signature with his life when he was assassinated in removal territory. "Ancient Cherokee law" deems "land cession" to be "a capital crime." See Perdue and Green, *The Cherokee Removal: A Brief History with Documents,* 161.

76. Cushing, "Art. VIII—*An Address to the Whites,*" 471.

77. Ibid., 474.

78. Wallace, *Jefferson and the Indians.* It is worth mentioning that in the third case of the Marshall Trilogy *Worcester v. Georgia* (1832), the Supreme Court ruled for the plaintiff Rev. Samuel Worcester, an ABCFM missionary and U.S. citizen, who claimed that Georgia had no jurisdiction over Cherokee land and had arrested him unlawfully. Nevertheless, the administrations of Andrew Jackson and Martin Van Buren went on to support Georgia's usurpation of Cherokee land. Of course, the Chinese were not Cherokees, and Cushing was not scheming to speculate on Chinese land as real estate.

79. Sexton, *Monroe Doctrine,* 53.

80. Collaborating with the Nazi government in the 1930s, Carl Schmitt fixated on the Monroe Doctrine, Theodore Roosevelt's reinterpretation of it as an interventionist corollary in 1904, and President Woodrow Wilson's preservation of it in Article 21 of the Covenant League of Nations. See two essays he wrote in 1933 and 1939 to justify Hitler's controlling oversight of Europe as a *Großraum,* recently translated into English in Legg, *Spatiality, Sovereignty and Carl Schmitt.*

81. John Quincy Adams (Secretary of State), "President's Annual Address (Monroe Doctrine)," 13–14, col. 14.

82. Ibid., 23.

83. Ibid., 22–23.

84. Ibid., 23–24.

85. Onuf, *Jefferson's Empire,* 2, 56.

86. Ibid., 51.

87. Ibid., 121. Also see Pocock, "Chapter XV: The Americanization of Virtue: Corruption, Constitution and Frontier," in *The Machiavellian Moment,* 506–52.

88. Padgen, *Lords of All the World,* 58.

89. Cushing, "[Hayti 1821]; Art VI" and "[Hayti 1829]; Art. VIII."

90. Cushing, "[Hayti 1821]; Art VI," 112.

91. Ibid., 115.

92. Ibid., 119.

93. Ibid., 129, 130.

94. Cushing, "[Hayti 1829]; Art. VIII."

95. Caleb Cushing, "Art. V.—Insurrection of Paez in Columbia," 89.

96. Cushing, "Art. III.—*Ensayo de la Historia Civil del Paraguay, Buenos Ayres y Tucuman,*" 286.

97. Ibid., 288.

98. Cushing, "Art. V.—Insurrection of Paez in Columbia," 90.

99. Cushing, "Art. V.—1. *A Statistical and Commercial History of the Kingdom of Guatemala in Spanish America.*"

100. Ibid., 127, 128.

101. Ibid., 129.

102. Ibid.

103. Ibid.

104. Cushing, "Dispatch 97 (to Secretary of State Calhoun, 29 September 1844)," 12.

105. Cushing, "Art. II—Modern Law of Nations," 287 and 289. This essay refines the ideas he first laid out in this two-volume *Review of the Late Revolution in France*.

106. Cushing, "Art. II—Modern Law of Nations," 294.

107. Cushing, *Review of the Late Revolution in France*, xi.

108. Ibid.

109. Ibid.

110. Ibid., xii.

111. Ibid., xiii.

112. Cushing, "Art. II—Modern Law of Nations," 295.

113. Ibid., 299.

114. Ibid., 290.

115. Ibid., 301.

116. Ibid., 302.

117. Ibid., 303.

118. Ibid., 297.

119. Ibid.

120. Ibid., 304.

121. Ibid., 303.

122. Ibid., 304.

123. Ibid., 290.

124. Cushing, *Review of the Late Revolution in France*, lxviii.

125. Cushing, "Art. II—Modern Law of Nations" (1835), 306.

126. Ibid., 302.

127. Ibid.

128. Webster, "Message from the President of the United States, on the Subject of the Trade and Commerce of the United States with the Sandwich Islands."

129. Ibid., 464.

130. Ibid.

131. Ibid.

132. Mark Rifkin explains that Hawai'i's debt obligation to the United States "function[ed] as a mechanism for materially constituting the domestic policy, one could say the political and economic identity of Hawai'i" but in ways that, rather than expressing a Hawaiian national identity, facilitated the influence of the United States in "stabilizing [Hawai'i's] multidimensional role as a pivot in US commercial geographies (especially the China trade)." See Rifkin, "Debt and Transnationalization of Hawai'i," 43, 56.

133. Webster, "Message from the President of the United States, on the Subject of the Trade and Commerce of the United States with the Sandwich Islands," 467.

134. Cushing, "Mr. Cushing at the Bunker Hill Dinner," 94.

135. Wilkes published the multivolume works, including *Voyage Round the World*.

136. Cushing, *Speech of Mr. Cushing*, 13.

137. Caleb Cushing, "Art. IV—1. *Journal of an Exploring Tour beyond the Rocky Mountains.*"

138. Cushing, *Speech of Mr. Cushing* (1838), 8.

139. Ibid.

140. Ibid., 9.

141. Ibid., 7.

142. Ibid., 9.

143. Ibid., 1.

144. Ibid., 4.

145. Ibid., 5.

146. Ibid., 7.

147. Ibid., 2.

148. The first American edition by Carey, Lea, & Blanchard appeared as two volumes in 1836 and was followed by British and French editions and translations into French, German, Dutch, and Swedish. The British edition slightly altered the title, removing "Anecdotes of": *Astoria; or, Enterprise Beyond the Rocky Mountains.* In 1849, Irving published a revised edition as volume 8 in *The Works of Washington Irving* with the original American-edition title, relatively few changes, and an additional final paragraph celebrating that, before his death in 1848, Astor knew that "the flag of his country waved over 'Astoria.'" (501).

149. Irving, *Astoria* (1836), 1:38, 41.

150. Ibid., 2:247.

151. Ibid., 1: 6.

152. Cushing, *Speech of Mr. Cushing*, 7.

153. Ibid.

154. Ibid., 2.

155. Ibid., 6.

156. S. Williams, "The fur trade."

157. Seaburg and Paterson, *Merchant Prince of Boston*, 316.

158. Cushing, *Speech of Mr. Cushing*, 9.

159. Ibid.

160. Ibid., 13.

161. Cushing, "Mexico," 435.

162. Ibid.

163. Ibid.

164. Ibid.

165. Ibid.

166. Ibid.

167. Davids, *American Diplomatic and Public Papers*, 1:13. Kearney also argues the importance of suppressing the opium trade in Dispatch 44 to the secretary of the navy, 21 April 1843 (ibid., 1:8).

168. Ibid., 1:15.

169. Ibid., 1:13 (22 April 1843); 1:17 (12 June 1843).

170. Ibid., 1:17. (12 June 1843); also see Downs, *Golden Ghetto*, 186–89.

171. [Bridgman], "Reminiscences of a trip up the river of Canton."

172. [Cushing], "Language of Communication between Chinese and European governments," 281.

173. Ibid., 286.

174. Ibid., 293.

175. S. Williams, *Middle Kingdom* (1848), 1:498.

176. Ibid., 1:499.

177. [Bridgman], "Message from the President" (August, September, October, November 1845).

178. Ibid. (September 1845), 410; (August 1845), 354.

179. Ibid. (September 1845), 417.

180. Ibid., 418.

181. See [Bridgman], "A List of thirty-four articles," 40.

182. [Bridgman], "Journal of Occurrences: treaties with Great Britain, France, and the United States."

183. The *Chinese Repository* printed a version of the final treaty with Chinese and English on the same page: "Treaty between the United States of America and the Chinese Ta Tsing Empire."

184. L. Liu, *Clash of Empires* and *Tokens of Exchange*.

185. Cassel writes that "maintaining Qing legal order was not simply a matter of rigidly applying legal codes on both native and foreign criminals; it was a normative legal order that laid down Confucian ideals to which all members of society were supposed to conform, although certain concessions could be made to foreigners with the aim of ultimately integrating them into this legal order" (*Grounds of Judgment*, 47). Cassel goes on to describe the pliability of juridical treatment of foreigners in relation to the mention of extraterritoriality in the Treaty of Bogue (52).

186. [Bridgman], "A List of Thirty-four articles," 37.

187. Scully, *Bargaining with the State*, 2.

188. Belohlavek, *Broken Glass*, 178.

189. S. Williams, *Middle Kingdom* (1883), 2:659.

190. Ibid.

191. This is true of *The Middle Kingdom* (1848; 1883) and other writings; in an article he published upon returning to the United States, he never mentions Cushing and attributes extraterritoriality to the Treaty of Tianjin (1860); see S. Williams, "Our Treaties with China."

192. Samuel Williams writes: "The treaty of Wanghia embodied all the important stipulations of the two English treaties and commercial regulations; and provided further for the erection of hospitals, chapels, and cemeteries at the five ports, and visits of the ship-of-war to any part of the coast. The duty on lead and ginseng was reduced, and tonnage duty was not to be demanded a second time from a vessell [sic] going to another port to clear off her cargo. These privileges also extended to all nations as well as the United States. Mr. Cushing, having accomplished the object of his mission, left China without seeing the other ports, making only a transient visit at Canton and Hongkong, and embarked in the U.S. brig Perry, Aug. 28th, direct for San Blas" (*The Middle Kingdom*, 1848, 2:591).

193. Ibid., 2:594.

194. Ibid., 2:598, 600.

195. Ibid., 2:657.

196. Ibid.

197. Ibid., 2:523.

198. Unattributed, "Riot in Canton," 46.

199. S. Williams, *Middle Kingdom* (1848), 1:363. On John Peters's Chinese Museum, see chapter 7, "The Cultural Fruits of Diplomacy: A Chinese Museum and Panorama," in Haddad, *The Romance of China*. Peters, *Miscellaneous Remarks*.

200. These five characters are only part of the concluding phrase: 自與詩書結靜緣 ("Zì yǔ Shīshū jié jìng yuán); or in literal English terms: oneself, gives, poem, book, to form, quiet, connection. Tang Yin's 山水畫 focuses on the self as a sense of being coming into fuller realization by engaging a legacy of books. Williams's interpretation of the quote recontextualizes the verse to imply cross-cultural friendships forged through shared scholarly interests, as personified in Kíying's ostensibly friendly willingness to negotiate with the Americans and French.

201. S. Teng and Fairbank retranslate from source documents that they describe in *Research Guide for China's Response to the West*, 6. For the document itself, see S. Teng and Fairbank, *China's Response to the West: A Documentary Survey*, 36–42. The translation by Thomas Wade appeared in the article "A New War on China."

202. Wade, "A New War with China."

203. F. Williams, *Life and Letters*, 267; journal entry from 10 March 1858.

204. Ibid. Combining the description Williams gives in the *Middle Kingdom* with this one from his biography, the frontispiece seems to be an engraving of a daguerreotype taken by West of a painting that Peters had acquired from a Chinese painter.

205. F. Williams, *Life and Letters*, 267–68.

206. Ibid.

207. Ibid., 269.

208. Ibid.

209. Koon, "The Face of Diplomacy in Nineteenth-Century China," 131.

210. S. Williams, *Middle Kingdom* (1883), 2:654. Kíying's portrait appears as a plate between pages 654 and 655.

Chapter 6 • *Extraterritorial Burial and the Visual Aesthetics of Free-Trade Imperialism*

1. Blum, *View from the Masthead*.

2. Ibid., 156. The account of Perry's expedition was nominally authored by Francis L. Hawks, D.D., L.L.D. This chapter refers to this first edition of the House of Representatives, published by congressional order in 1856. Researching this material, I have often consulted the Dover reprint of volume 1 (2000). Volume 2 also includes two essays by Perry on the future of U.S. commerce in Asia.

3. Hawks, *Narrative of the Expedition*, 1:256.

4. Ibid., 1:75.

5. Ibid.

6. Freeman writes that by the mid-nineteenth century "steel-hulled vessels using steam propulsion had joined the fleets of sail-powered, wooden, or iron-hulled merchantmen plying the eastern seas, and the dependence on wind power for navigation was reduced. With it went the need to follow the ancient dictates of the monsoons"; see *The Straits of Malacca*, 13.

7. Ibid., 183–84.

8. Preble, *The Opening of Japan*, 17.

9. Ibid., 22. Preble's editor Szczesniak misidentifies the island as Prince Edward's Island in the Indian Ocean (21).

10. Ibid., 22.

11. Wiley *Yankees in the Land of the Gods*, 1:475.

12. B. Anderson, *Imagined Communities*, 30.

13. Hawks, *Narrative of the Expedition*, 1:3.

14. Ibid., 1:74.

15. Ibid., 1:5.

16. Ibid., 1:4.

17. Ibid., 2:176.

18. Ibid., 2:176.

19. Feifer, *Breaking Open Japan*, 106.

20. Hawks, *Narrative of the Expedition*, 1:136.

21. S. Williams, *Journal of the Perry Expedition to Japan*, 2.

22. Preble, *Opening Japan*.

23. Hawks, *Narrative of the Expedition*, 1:145.

24. Wiley, *Yankees in the Lands of Gods*, 282.

25. Hawks, *Narrative of the Expedition*, 1:382.

26. See Dower, "Black Ships & Samurai," 4; and Wiley, *Yankees in the Land of the Gods*.

27. See Jansen, *The Making of Modern Japan*.

28. Hawks, *Narrative of the Expedition*, 1:264.

29. Ibid., 1:197.

30. Feifer, *Breaking Open Japan*, 126; Wiley notes in *Yankees in the Lands of Gods* that Perry never mentions the white flags in his journal or the *Narrative*. Wiley anchors the source in Tokyo Teikoku Daigaku, Bunka Daigaku, Shiryo Hensangakari, eds., *Dai Nihon Komonjo: Bakumatsu Kaikoku Kankei Monjo* (Tokyo: Tokyo Imperial University, Shiryo Henan Kyoku, 1912), 1:169–70, translated in *Meiji Japan through Contemporary Sources*, vol. 2, *1844–1882* (Tokyo: Centre for East Asian Cultural Studies, 1970), 15–16. See Wiley, *Yankees in the Lands of Gods*, 320, 529.

31. Hawks, *Narrative of the Expedition*, 1:74.

32. Ibid., 1:76.

33. Dower, "Black Ships & Samurai," 10. For an overview explanation of the rise of the Shogun, the expulsion of foreigners, prohibition of Christianity, and quarantine of Dutch trade to Dejima, see Wiley, *Yankees in the Lands of Gods*, 232–56.

34. Wiley, *Yankees in the Lands of Gods*, 175–76; for a brief synopsis of Abe's life and rise to prominence in the Bakufu and Roju, see Wiley, 258–81.

35. Preble, *Opening Japan*, 49; Hawks, *Narrative of the Expedition*, 1:288.

36. Hawks, *Narrative of the Expedition*, 1:49.

37. Ibid., 1:54.

38. See ibid., 1:288; and Ride and Ride, *An East India Company Cemetery*.

39. F. Williams, *Life and Letters*, 211.

40. Hawks, *Narrative of the Expedition*, 1:353.

41. S. Williams, *Journal of the Perry Expedition to Japan*, 166.

42. Wiley, *Yankees in the Hands of Gods*, 402.

43. Hawks, *Narrative of the Expedition*, 1:475.

44. F. Williams, *Life and Letters*, 212–13.

45. Wiley, *Yankees in the Lands of Gods*, 433.

46. Ibid., 480.

47. Feifer, *Breaking Open Japan*, 281; also see Griffis, *Townsend Harris*. Griffis also wrote the first biography of Perry, *Matthew Calbraith Perry*.

48. In regard to Wilkes, see Block, "The Importance of the China."

49. Preble, *The Opening of Japan*, 49. In addition to Preble's account, see the journal of Williams S. Speiden Jr., who served as a pursuer's clerk aboard the *Mississippi*; his account was recently published as *With Commodore Perry to Japan*. Samuel Wells Williams also kept a journal of the expedition that his son later edited and published; Perry tried without success to pull Williams into the editing project. The only other accounts published contemporaneous to the *Narrative* were by the expedition's sketch artist Heine; Bayard Taylor, a reporter who accompanied Perry on the first phase and whose journalistic accounts created a buzz about Perry in the United States; and Robert Tomes, who published *The Americans in Japan*, an abridged account of the expedition.

50. Dower, "Black Ships & Samurai," chap. 4.

51. Heine's work was published separately as *Graphic Scenes in the Japan*. He also published his account in German; see Heine, *With Perry to Japan*, originally published as *Reise um die Erde nach Japan an Bord der Expeditions-Escadre unter Commodore M. C. Perry*, 2 vols. (Leipzig: Hermann Costenoble, 1856). Heine's first trip as an expedition sketch artist was to Central America and his next was with Perry. After the expedition, William Heine returned to the United States. He became a citizen in 1855, started a family, and continued traveling, including to Germany, where he published his drawings and accounts of his travels. During the U.S. Civil War, he "held three commands and finished as a brigadier general in the Civil War" (Heine, *With Perry to Japan*, xi–xii; Moore, "More about the Events," 83). Adapting his landscape sketching skills to the battlefield proved a major challenge; he was arrested and detained at Fortress Monroe after drawings appeared in *Harper's Weekly* in 26 April 1862, revealing information about the Union defenses at Yorktown. However, he had not drafted them and was later exonerated. After the war, he served as a consular clerk in Florence, Paris, and Liverpool and died in Dresden, Germany in 1885.

52. Feifer, *Breaking Open Japan*, 356.

53. See "Perry in Japan, a Visual History," Brown University Center for Digital Scholarship, http://library.brown.edu/cds/perry/.

54. See Hawthorne, *The English Notebooks*, 147–48. Quoted in Kleitz, "Herman Melville, Matthew Perry." Also see Wiley, *Yankees in the Land of the Gods*, 462.

55. F. Williams, *Life and Letters*, 231, 232.

56. Hawks, *Narrative of the Expedition*, 1:v.

57. Ibid., 1:iv, v.

58. In *Art and Illusion* Ernst Hans Gombrich writes that "the correct portrait, like the useful map, is an end product of a long road through schema and correction. It is not a faithful record of visual experience but the faithful construction of a relational model" (90).

59. See http://www.MorrisonChapel.com/history/.

60. Shaw, *Journals*, 241.

61. [Bridgman], "Art. III. Obituary notices of the late Mrs. Marshman and Mrs. Morrison," 299.

62. [Bridgman], "Article V. "British burial ground in Macao," 48.

63. Ibid., 49.

64. Macao's "Protestant Grave Yard" holds other graves of prominent Americans, including General George Washington's godson and namesake George Washington Biddle (?–1811) whose father Clement Biddle (1740–1814) served as commissary general under Washington in the Revolutionary War. Biddle died before the cemetery opened, and his body was later moved to its present location; Biddle's grave is the earliest death memorialized in the cemetery (Ride and Ride, *An East Indian Company Cemetery*, 40). Also buried there is Edmund Roberts (1784–1836), the first U.S. envoy to the Far East who drew up the Treaty of Amity and Commerce between Siam and the United States (1833) (ibid., 168–69). As mentioned in chapter 3, Thomas T. Forbes was initially buried in the Protestant Grave Yard after he drowned in the typhoon of 1829; his younger brothers Robert Bennet and John Murray later took the body back to Boston.

65. On the far left is that of the Right Honorable Lord Henry John Spencer Churchill, 4th Son of George V, Duke of Marlborough who died on 2 June 1840 commanding the *Druid* in the Macao Roads (great-grand-uncle of Winston Churchill). The obelisk next to it honors the sacred memory of Captain Sir Humphrey Le Fleming Senhouse, who died of fever in Hong Kong after "arduous duties at the capture of the Heights of Canton, 1841" during the First Canton War (1839–42).

66. Ride and Ride, *An East Indian Company Cemetery*, 150.

67. Ibid., 117.

68. Preble, *Opening Japan*, 50.

69. Ibid., 54–55.

70. Ibid., 63.

71. Hawks, *Narrative of the Expedition*, 1:164.

72. Ibid., 1:475.

73. Ibid., 1:411, 425.

74. Downing, "Public Cemeteries and Public Gardens."

75. Ibid., 9.

76. Ibid., 12.

77. Downing, *A Treatise*.

78. Ibid., 26.

79. Ibid., 25.

80. Ibid., 28.

81. Ibid., 38, 40–41, 45.

82. Downs, *The Golden Ghetto*, 245–51.

83. Downing, *A Treatise*, 52.

84. Ibid., 54.

85. Ibid., 55.

86. Ibid., 87.

87. Ibid., 61.

88. Shaw, *Journals*, 197–98.

89. In regard to Japan, see DuBois, *Religion and the Making of Modern East Asia*, 53–71, 105–22.

90. Hawks, *Narrative of the Expedition*, 2:173–82.

91. Ibid., 2:173.

92. Ibid., 2:187.

93. Ibid.

94. Ibid., 2:175.

95. Ibid., 2:176.

96. Ibid.

97. Ibid.

98. Ibid.

99. Ibid.

100. Ibid.

101. Ibid., 2:180.

102. Ibid., 2:181.

103. Ibid.

104. Ibid., 2:187.

105. Ibid., 1:357. See F. Williams, *Life and Letters*, 209–12, for Samuel Williams's description of the railroad and telegraph demonstrations.

106. Hawks, *Narrative of the Expedition*, 1:357.

107. Ibid.

108. Ibid.

109. Ibid.

110. Ibid., 1:357–58.

111. Ibid., 2:186.

112. Ibid.

113. Ibid.

114. For an account of the network developed by A. A. Low & Bros., see C. Low, *Some Recollections*.

115. R. Forbes, *Personal Reminiscences*, 357.

116. Haddad, *America's First Adventure in China*, 171; R. Forbes, *Personal Reminiscences*, 364.

117. Haddad, *America's First Adventure in China*, 169. Opium remained a considerable part of the Russell & Company income stream; in 1864 $1.1 million worth went inland, with an apex in 1867 of $2.4 million, and $1.48 million in 1871 when $5.7 million worth of cotton and textiles made up the main haul; see K. Liu, *Anglo-American Steamship Rivalry in China*, 66, 87.

118. Haddad, *America's First Adventure in China*, 170.

119. K. Liu, *Anglo-American Steamship Rivalry in China*, 29, 31.

120. Ibid., 15.

121. In his memoir *Personal Reminiscences*, Robert Bennet Forbes summarizes the success: in four years, the SSNC had bought out all rivals and "flourished for seven to eight years, growing up to a capital of £2,200,000 and a fleet of eighteen steamers" (366). In 1877 Russell & Company lost control of the lucrative SSNC, selling the steamer fleet to Li Hung-Chang, governor general of Chihli and owner of the China Merchants Steam Navigation

Company, who rose to prominence in the decade of collaboration with Western powers; Russell & Company bought the fleet back in the 1880s as China protected it from French confiscation during the Sino-French War (1884–85). See Ji, *History of Modern Shanghai Banking*, 61. On Russell & Company's reacquisition of the fleet, see D. Anderson, *Imperialism and Idealism*, 140.

122. R. Forbes, *Personal Reminiscences*, 293.

123. Ibid.

124. Ibid., 294.

125. Pearson, *An American Railroad Builder*, v.

126. Haddad, *America's First Adventure in China*, 211.

127. Ibid., 178.

128. See Larson, *Bonds of Enterprise*, 212.

Chapter 7 • *Passages to India from the Newly United States*

1. F. Williams, *Life and Letters*, 328.

2. P. Cohen, *China and Christianity*, 128.

3. The treaty appears as an appendix in F. Williams, *Anson Burlingame*, 275–80.

4. *Banquet to His Excellency Anson Burlingame*, 17.

5. Ibid.

6. F. Williams, *Life and Letters*, 421.

7. S. Williams, *Middle Kingdom*, 2:xiii. The publication history began with the first edition by New York and London publisher Wiley and Putnam in 1848. In the first year it went through three editions, and the third edition was republished through the 1850s and translated into German. In 1857 a fourth edition appeared that was republished over the next two decades. In 1883 Charles C. Scribner's Sons published the fifth and final edition.

8. See Harris, *God's Arbiters*, 36, 144–45.

9. F. Williams, *Life and Letters*, 122.

10. See Hevia, *English Lessons*, 70–73. Also see "Treaties and Documents Concerning Opium 253.

11. S. Williams, *Middle Kingdom* (1883), 2:657.

12. Ibid.

13. On the Treaty of 1880, see D. Anderson, *Imperialism and Idealism*, 123. In 1881 the opium trade was again outlawed, but the "penalties were a miniscule fine of $50–$250," short imprisonment, and confiscation, which did little to discourage the traffic. See Scully, *Bargaining with the State from Afar*, 78.

14. F. Williams, *Life and Letters*, 302–13.

15. On China's concession regarding missionaries, see P. Cohen, *China and Christianity*, 68–69. On the concessions secured by the British, see Carroll, *A Concise History of Hong Kong*, 23–24.

16. F. Williams, *Life and Letters*, 325–26. In 1862 the United States passed into law "an Act to Prohibit the Coolie Trade," but its enforcement in South China was lax and complicated by increasingly racist attitudes toward Chinese people in California. See Sinn, *Pacific Crossing*, 240–42.

17. F. Williams, *Life and Letters*, 329.

18. Ibid.

19. S. Williams, *Treaties between the United States of America and China.*

20. F. Williams, *Anson Burlingame,* 20.

21. F. Williams, *Life and Letters,* 335.

22. Ibid., 342.

23. Ibid., 343.

24. F. Williams, *Anson Burlingame,* v, viii.

25. Ibid., vi.

26. Ibid., 13.

27. D. Anderson, *Imperialism and Idealism,*19.

28. F. Williams, *Life and Letters,* 358–59.

29. Ibid., 359.

30. F. Williams, *Anson Burlingame,* 33.

31. D. Anderson, *Imperialism and Idealism,* 30–32.

32. Jonathan D. Spence, *Search for Modern China,* 191–93.

33. Haddad, "Traditional China and Chinese Yankees: The Centennial Exposition of 1876," in *Romance of China,* http://www.gutenberg-e.org/haj01/frames/fhaj10.html; and Ngai, "Transnationalism and Transformation of the 'Other.'"

34. Bickers, *The Scramble for China,* 1, 3.

35. See Rhoads, *Stepping Forth into the World;* and Xu, *Chinese and Americans,* chap. 2. Yung Wing writes of supervising the mission in his autobiography, *My Life in China and America.*

36. Spence, *Search for Modern China,* 191, 194.

37. Pong, *Shen Pao-Chen.* Also see G. Chang, *Fateful Ties,* 92–93.

38. Jonathan D. Spence, *The Search for Modern China,* 196.

39. Biggerstaff, "The Official Chinese Attitude toward the Burlingame Mission," 687.

40. Biggerstaff, "A Translation of Anson Burlingame's Instructions from the Chinese Foreign Office." S. W. Williams describes the assumptions of Burlingame's authority: "Though Mr. Burlingame was invested with full powers, it was not expected that he would negotiate new treaties," in *Our Relations with the Chinese Empire,* 10. Also see D. Anderson, *Imperialism and Idealism,* 41–42.

41. D. Anderson, *Idealism and Imperialism,* 40–42.

42. The treaty's official name is the "Additional Article to the Treaty of Commerce between the United States and China, of June 18, 1858. Signed at Washington, 28 July, 1868." The treaty appears as an appendix in F. Williams, *Anson Burlingame,* 275–80.

43. Twain, "The Treaty with China," 1.

44. Ibid., 7.

45. Ibid.

46. Schrecker, "'For the Equality of Men—For the Equality of Nations'"; Chang, *Fateful Ties,* 96.

47. F. Williams, *Anson Burlingame,* 279–80.

48. *Reception.*

49. For the ancestry of Samuel Shaw, see Goldfeld, *The North End,* 85–86.

50. *Reception,* 26, 22.

51. Ibid., 22.

52. Ibid., 23, 24.

53. Ibid., 37–40.

54. Ibid., 40.

55. Ibid., 43.

56. Ibid., 44.

57. Ibid., 50.

58. Ibid., 52, 53.

59. Twain, "The Treaty with China," 13.

60. Lai-Henderson, *Mark Twain in China*, 39.

61. Ibid., 41–42.

62. Zwick, *Mark Twain's Weapons of Satire*; Harris, *God's Arbiters*; H. Hsu, *Sitting in Dark-ness*; and Lai-Henderson, *Mark Twain in China*.

63. See Wilson, "Exporting Christian Transcendentalism."

64. Twain, "Treaty with China," 12.

65. Ibid.

66. Ibid., 28.

67. DuBois, *Religion and the Making of Modern East Asia*.

68. Twain, "Treaty with China," 11.

69. Wilson, "Exporting Christian Transcendentalism," 521–52.

70. D. Anderson, *Imperialism and Idealism*, 52.

71. Ibid., 53.

72. F. Williams, *Anson Burlingame*, 284.

73. D. Anderson, *Imperialism and Idealism*, 74–75.

74. Ibid., 80–89.

75. Luke Mancuso explains the confusion of the copyright dates in the fifth edition, which has three different versions: "Whitman reissued [the fifth edition of] *Leaves* with the *Passage to India* annex, adding 120 pages with 74 poems, 24 of which were new texts, while the others were culled from earlier editions of his work. In 1872, this bifurcated edition was reissued, directly from Washington, D.C., dated 1872 but copyrighted in 1870. Still another issue of the book contained the *Passage to India* annex, with separate pagination, as well as the additional supplement *After All, Not to Create Only* (later "Song of the Exposition"), with 24 additional pages, also published as a separate pamphlet with separate pagination. In short, the fifth edition of *Leaves* contained in its format three separate books of poetry, as well as the related publication of a pamphlet called *As a Strong Bird on Pinions Free, and Other Poems* in 1872. The latter *As a Strong Bird* booklet also contained the significant prose Preface, now known as the 1872 Preface"; see Mancuso, "*Leaves of Grass*, 1871–72 edition"; and The Walt Whitman Archive, http://www.whitmanarchive.org/criticism/current/encyclopedia/entry_25.html. This chapter references the second version of the fifth edition of *Leaves of Grass* (Washington, DC, 1872).

76. See page three of Whitman's manuscript, http://digitalgallery.nypl.org/nypldigital/id?m_1248854. The New York Public Library's Oscar Line Collection holds the 1869 manuscript and has page images of its twenty-three pages, http://exhibitions.nypl.org/treasures/items/show/103; also see Bowers, "The Earliest Manuscript of Whitman's 'Passage to India' and Its Notebook."

77. Erkkila, *Whitman the Political Poet*, 267.

78. Whitman, *Leaves of Grass*, appendix, stanza 3, 6. For an enthusiastic appreciation of Whitman's poem, see Doudna, " 'The Essential Ultimate Me.' "

79. Whitman, *Leaves of Grass*, appendix, line 114; Ahluwalia, "A Reading of Whitman's 'Passage to India.' "

80. Erkkila, *Whitman the Political Poet*, 269.

81. H. Hsu *Geography*, 135.

82. In *Whitman the Political Poet*, Erkkila summarizes the reception, 343–44; also see Paryz, *Postcolonial and Imperial Experience in American*, 179–184.

83. Matthiessen, *American Renaissance*, 543.

84. Ibid., 618.

85. Ibid., 529.

86. Ibid., 530.

87. H. Smith, *Virgin Land*, 44.

88. Ibid., 45.

89. Ibid., 47–48.

90. Ibid., 48.

91. Erkkila, *Whitman the Political Poet*, 273.

92. Whitney, *A Project for a Railroad to the Pacific*, 13, 16.

93. Ibid., 39.

94. *Harpers' Weekly* 12.596 (30 May 1868): 346.

95. On the Panama Canal, see Maurer and Yu, *The Big Ditch*.

96. Brückner, *The Geographic Revolution in Early America*, 106.

97. S. Williams, *Our Relations with China*, 7.

98. Haddad, *The Romance of China*, sec. 5.

99. M. Hsu, "Trading with Gold Mountain"; and Sinn *Pacific Crossings*.

100. See Chinese Railroad Worlds in North America Project, http://web.stanford.edu/group/chineserailroad/cgi-bin/wordpress/.

101. S. Williams, *Chinese Immigration*, 4.

102. Ibid.

103. Ibid.

104. Ibid.

105. Sinn, *Pacific Crossing*, 248.

106. Ibid., 252.

107. D. Anderson, *Imperialism and Idealism*, 107.

108. Ibid., 110.

109. *The Statues of California*, xxiii, xxiv.

110. Ibid., xli.

111. Pfaelzer, *Driven Out*.

112. S. Williams, *Chinese Immigration*, 11.

113. Ibid., 32.

114. Ibid., 31.

115. Ibid., 46.

116. Ibid., 46–47.

117. Ibid., 45–46.

118. D. Anderson, *Imperialism and Idealism*, 123–24.

119. Spence, *The Search for Modern China*, 207; Sinn, *Pacific Crossing*, 261.

120. Sinn, *Pacific Crossing*, 261.

121. S. Williams, *Middle Kingdom* (1883), 2:699.

122. Ibid.

123. Ibid., 2:739.

124. Ibid., 2:39. Compare with *The Middle Kingdom* (1848), 2:126.

125. S. Williams, *Middle Kingdom* (1883), 2:373.

126. S. Williams, *Middle Kingdom* (1848), 2:380, 378.

127. Ibid., 2:371, 370.

128. S. Williams, *Middle Kingdom* (1883), 2:xv.

129. Ibid., 2:741.

130. Ibid.

131. Ibid., 2:742.

132. Ibid.

133. Ibid.

134. Ibid.

135. Ibid., 2:741–42.

136. S. Williams, *Our Relations*, 12.

137. D. Anderson, *Imperialism and Idealism*, 153. Also see McCormick, *China Market*.

138. J. Forbes, *Letters and Recollections*, 2:225.

139. See, for example, K. Johnson, "Henry James and the China Trade."

140. Bickers, *Scramble for China*, 324.

141. See Ibid., 324–29.

142. Braisted, "The United States and the American China Development Company."

143. Eperjesi, "The American Asiatic Association."

144. P. Cohen, *China and Christianity*.

145. P. Cohen, *History in Three Keys*.

146. Broomhall, *Martyred Missionaries*.

147. *Ninety-First Annual Report of the American Board of Commissioners for Foreign Missions*, 110.

148. Lai-Henderson, *Mark Twain in China*, 58.

149. See Martin, *The Siege in Peking*; and Haddad, "The Wild West Turns East."

150. See Lai-Henderson, *Mark Twain in China*, 53–74.

151. Ibid., 60. See Twain, "To the Person Sitting in the Darkness" and "To My Missionary Critics."

152. Schmidt, *Sitting in the Darkness*, 142–43.

153. As further example: Twain began the story "Extract from Captain Stormfield's Visit to Heaven" in 1868 and published it in 1909. As Stephanie LeMenager argues in *Manifest and Other Destinies*, in "making the domain of Heaven large enough to contain the multiple histories of colonization and imperialism that inform modernity," Twain "foresees the future of Manifest Destiny" as "a situation on the North American continent in which competing nations and diasporic nationalities vie for recognition in the wake of the exposure of European or 'white' hegemony" (216).

154. Bové, "To Make a Way," 152–53.

Articles from the Chinese Repository *(1832–1851)*

Articles were generally published anonymously or attributed to a pseudonym. Samuel Wells Williams and Elijah Bridgman produced the *General Index of Subjects Contained in the Twenty Volumes of the Chinese Repository: with an Arranged List of the Articles* (Canton, 1851) that attributes authorship. The first nine annual volumes from 1832 to 1840 ran from May to April. Beginning in January 1841, the next eleven volumes ran from January to December. There are typographical errors in some of the issues dates, which the following bibliography corrects without indication.

Adams, John Quincy. "December 1841, Lecture on the War with China, Delivered before the Massachusetts Historical Society." *Chinese Repository* 11.5 (May 1842): 274–89.

[Bridgman, Elijah]. "Article 1. Portuguese in China: Contribution to an Historical Sketch of the Roman Catholic Church at Macao; and the domestic and foreign relations of Macao. By A. L., Knt. Canton, China 1834. Pp. 53." *Chinese Repository* 3.7 (November 1834): 289–303.

———. "British burial ground in Macao: notices of the first interment there, and of recent erection of monuments: Parsee graves on the seashore." *Chinese Repository* 11.1 (January 1842): 48–54.

———. "The Chinese language: its antiquity, extensive use, and dialects; its character and value; attention paid to it by Europeans; and the aids and inducements to study it at the present time." *Chinese Repository* 3.1 (May 1834): 1–14.

———. "Crisis in Opium Traffic: orders from Lin high imperial commissioner for the surrender of the drug to the Chinese government; all foreigners forbidden to leave Canton; their whole trade suspended; port clearances denied to their ships at Whampoa; with a narrative of proceedings relative thereto." *Chinese Repository* 7.12 (April 1839): 609–56.

———. "Crisis in Opium Traffic; continuation of the narrative, with official papers, &c. (Continued from vol. VII, page 656)." *Chinese Repository* 8.1 (May 1839): 12–37.

———. "Crisis in Opium Traffic; continuation of the narrative, with official papers, &c. (Continued from 37)." *Chinese Repository* 8.2 (June 1839): 70–83.

———. "Cultivation of the poppy, in Europe, China, and India: extent and quality of the land so occupied; time and mode of culture; and the amount of population and capital engaged therein." *Chinese Repository* 5.10 (February 1837): 470–75.

———. "European Periodicals Beyond the Ganges: Prince of Wales' Island Gazette; Malacca Observer; Periodical Miscellany; Singapore Chronicle; Singapore Free Press; Chronica de Macao; Macaista Imparcial; Canton Register; Canton Press; and Chinese Repository." *Chinese Repository* 5.4 (August 1836): 145–60.

———. "Imperial edict, referring the memorials of Choo Tusn and Heu Kew to the chief provincial officers of Canton; with brief remarks on the present state of the question." *Chinese Repository* 5.9 (January 1837): 405–6.

———. "Introduction." *Chinese Repository* 1.1 (May 1832): 1–5.

———. "Introductory remarks." *Chinese Repository* 2.1 (May 1833): 1–9.

———. "A List of thirty-four articles, deliberated and determined upon, for the trade of the merchants of the United States of America, at the five ports in China. Translated from the Chinese." *Chinese Repository* 14.1 (January 1845): 30–40.

———. "Literary intelligence: Foreign presses in China: Poetry of the Chinese, &c.; Contribution to an Historical Sketch of the Romanists at Macao; and the Anglochinese Kalendar for 1834." *Chinese Repository* 3.1 (May 1834): 43–44.

———. "Literary Notices: Chinese Printing." *Chinese Repository* 1.10 (February 1833): 414–22.

———. "Message from the President of the United States to the senate, transmitting the treaty concluded between Mr. Cushing and Kíying in behalf of their respective governments." *Chinese Repository* 14.8 (August 1845): 353–77; 14.9 (September 1845): 410–23.

———. "Message from the President of the United States to the senate, transmitting the treaty concluded between Mr. Cushing and Kíying in behalf of their respective government. Death of Sue Aman, a Chinese shot by an American in Canton." *Chinese Repository* 14.10 (October 1845): 487–93; 14.11 (November 1845): 525–39.

———. "Miscellanies: The Press." *Chinese Repository* 2.2 (June 1833): 92–93.

———. "Obituary notices of the late Mrs. Marshman and Mrs. Morrison, both among the first missionary laborers, the one to India, the other to China." *Chinese Repository* 16.7 (June 1847): 297–300.

———. "Obituary of the [sic] Edwin Stevens, Late Seamen's Chaplain in the Port of Canton." *Chinese Repository* 5.11 (March 1837): 513–18.

———. "Periodical literature: Chinese Almanacs; imperial Court Calendar; the provincial Court Circular of Canton; the Peking Gazette; with remarks on the condition of the press in China." *Chinese Repository* 5.1 (May 1836): 1–12.

———. "A picture of the Precious Porcelain pagoda in the Recompensing Favor monastery of Kiángnán (commonly known as the Porcelain Tower)." *Chinese Repository* 13.5 (May 1844): 261–65.

———. "Remarks on the present crisis in the opium traffic, with inquiries respecting its causes, and the best course to be pursued by those now connected with it." *Chinese Repository* 8.1 (May 1839): 1–8.

———. "Reminiscences of a trip up the river of Canton, on board the U.S. Frigate Constellation, in the spring of 1842." *Chinese Repository* 11.6 (June 1842): 329–35.

———. "Retrospection, or a review of public occurrences in China during the last ten years, from January 1st, 1832, to December 31st, 1841." *Chinese Repository* 11.1 (January 1842): 1–28.

———. "Retrospection, or a review of public occurrences in China during the last ten years, from January 1st, 1832, to December 31st, 1841. (Continued from page 28)." *Chinese Repository* 11.2 (February 1842): 65–81.

———. "Retrospection, or a review of public occurrences in China during the last ten years, from January 1st, 1832, to December 31st, 1841. (Continued from page 81)." *Chinese Repository* 11.3 (March 1842): 121–32.

———. "Retrospection, or a review of public occurrences in China during the last ten years, from January 1st, 1832, to December 31st, 1841. (Continued from page 132)." *Chinese Repository* 11.4 (April 1842): 185–201.

———. "Retrospection, or a review of public occurrences in China during the last ten years, from January 1st, 1832, to December 31st, 1841. (Continued from page 201)." *Chinese Repository* 11.5 (May 1842): 241–66.

———. "Retrospection, or a review of public occurrences in China during the last ten years, from January 1st, 1832, to December 31st, 1841. (Continued from page 266)." *Chinese Repository* 11.6 (June 1842): 297–307.

———. "Retrospection, or a review of public occurrences in China during the last ten years, from January 1st, 1832, to December 31st, 1841. (Continued from page 307)." *Chinese Repository* 11.7 (July 1842): 345–74.

———. "Retrospection, or a review of public occurrences in China during the last ten years, from January 1st, 1832, to December 31st, 1841. (Continued from page 374)." *Chinese Repository* 11.8 (August 1842): 401–10.

———. "Retrospection, or a review of public occurrences in China during the last ten years, from January 1st, 1832, to December 31st, 1841. (Continued from page 410)." *Chinese Repository* 11.9 (September 1842): 447–70.

———. "Retrospection, or a review of public occurrences in China during the last ten years, from January 1st, 1832, to December 31st, 1841. (Continued from page 470)." *Chinese Repository* 11.10 (October 1842): 521–28.

———. "Retrospection, or a review of public occurrences in China during the last ten years, from January 1st, 1832, to December 31st, 1841. (Continued from page 528)." *Chinese Repository* 11.11 (November 1842): 577–86.

———. "Sü Amún: annual provision for the support of his widow and mother, voluntarily made by the person who caused his death during the riots in June 1844." *Chinese Repository* 15.1 (January 1846): 307–10.

———. "Suspension of trade, occasioned by the smuggling of opium, within the Bogue, on the river at Whampoa, and into the foreign factories at Canton, with notices of public execution, riot, &c., connected therewith." *Chinese Repository* 7.8 (December 1838): 437–56.

———. "Toleration of Christianity, intimated by the emperor Tánkwáng, December 28th, 1844, in reply given to a memorial from the imperial commissioner Kíying." *Chinese Repository* 14.4 (April 1845): 195–99.

———. "The traffic in opium carried on with China: its early history, and the present mode of conducting it, from the delivery of the drug by the cultivators to its reception by the consumers." *Chinese Repository* 5.12 (April 1837): 546–53.

[Bridgman, Elijah, and R. Thom]. "Letter to the Queen of England, from the high imperial commissioner Lin, and his colleagues. From the Canton Press." *Chinese Repository* 8.10 (February 1840): 497–503.

———. "Letter to the Queen of England from the imperial commissioner and the provincial authorities requiring interdiction of opium." *Chinese Repository* 8.1 (May 1939): 9–12.

[Bridgman, Elijah, and Samuel Wells Williams]. "Relations between the United States and China; narrative of the Empress, the first American ship which visited this port; trial of Terranova; treatment of national ships." *Chinese Repository* 5.5 (September 1836): 218–31.

[Cushing, Caleb]. "Art. I. Language of Communication between Chinese and European governments.—Communicated for the Repository." *Chinese Repository* 13.6 (June 1844): 281–300.

———. "Art. 1. *Legatio Batavica ad Magnum Tartariae Chamum Sungteium, modernum Sinae Imperatorem, &c. Conscripta vernacule per Joannem Nieuhovium, Primum Leationis Aulae Magistrum, &c. Latinitate donatum per clarissmum virum Georgium Hornium, Historiarum in celeberrima Lugd. Batav. Acad. Prof.* Amstelodami (cicicclxviii [1668]). Reviewed by Correspondent." *Chinese Repository* 13.8 (August 1844): 393–407.

Dyer, Samuel. "Miscellanies: Chinese Metal Types." *Chinese Repository* 2.10 (February 1834): 477–78.

[Forbes, Robert Bennet] as "Non Sine Causa." "Reply to article second, in the Repository for January, in a letter addressed to the editor, dated Canton February 14th, 1840." *Chinese Repository* 8.10 (February 1840): 532–43.

[Gützlaff, Karl A.] as Philosinensis. "Propagation of the Gospel in China: little progress hitherto made; difficulties to be encountered; encouragements to perseverance." *Chinese Repository* 3.6 (October 1834): 244–46.

[King, Charles W.] as CR. "Review of the difficulties between the English and Chinese authorities." *Chinese Repository* 8.9 (January 1840): 446–78.

[Medhurst, Walter] as Typographus Sinensis. "Estimate of the proportionate expense of Xylography, Lithography, and Typography, as applied to Chinese printing; view of advantages and disadvantages of each." *Chinese Repository* 3.6 (October 1834): 246–52.

[Morrison, John R.]. "Hong merchant's Report on Commerce: 1st, respecting the exportation of sycee; 2d, the interchange of merchandise; 3d, measures to prevent illegalities; and 4th, the transit of opium and the coasting trade in it." *Chinese Repository* 5.9 (January 1837): 385–90.

[————]. "Memorial of Choo Tsun on Opium: character of the trade in it; impolicy of sanctioning it; its baneful effects on property and on the physical and moral character, of the people. Dated October, 1836." *Chinese Repository* 5.9 (January 1837): 390–98.

[————]. "Opium: memorial to the emperor proposing to legalize the importation of it; some of the probable results of such a measure; translation of the memorial." *Chinese Repository* 5.3 (July 1836): 138–44.

[————]. "Report in reference to the Circulation of dollars in China; necessity of retaining them in the provinces; their weight and standard objectionable; precautions against the exportation of sycee silver." *Chinese Repository* 5.9 (January 1837): 419–22.

[Parker, Peter]. "Hospital Reports of the Medical Missionary Society for China, for the year 1839." *Chinese Repository* 8.12 (April 1840): 624–39.

Smith, G. H. "Abstract of a paper on opium-smoking in Penang. By G. H. Smith, surgeon in Penang.—Mode of preparing opium for smoking; causes of the prevalence of the habit; mode of smoking; description of a smoking-shop; effects of the opium on the smoker; influence of the habit on the health, vigor, and conformation of the Chinese. Extracted from Johnson's Medico-Chirurgical Review for April, 1842." *Chinese Repository* 11.11 (November 1842): 587–92.

[Stevens, Edwin]. "Promulgation of the Gospel in China: I. Obstacles to it:—1. laws against foreigners; 2. against foreign religions; 3. system of education; 4. the language: II. Facilities;—1. limited intercourse practicable; 2. knowledge of reading; 3. no ruling priesthood; 4. disposition of the people; 5. foreign interest felt for China." *Chinese Repository* 3.9 (January 1835): 428–38.

[Webster, Daniel]. "Letter to the Emperor of China from the president of the United States of America, written at Washington, 12th July, 1843." *Chinese Repository* 14.11 (November 1845): 542–43.

[Williams, Samuel Wells]. "Chinese metallic types: proposals for casting a font of Chinese types by means of steal punches in Paris; attempt made in Boston to stereotype from wooden blocks." *Chinese Repository* 3.11 (March 1835): 528–33.

———. "The fur trade: animals which produce fine furs; those producing hairy skins; the progress of the fur trade in Asia, America, and Europe; imports into China." *Chinese Repository* 3.12 (April 1835): 548–59.

———. "List of Protestant Missionaries to the Chinese, with the present position of those now among them." *Chinese Repository* 20.8–12 (August–December 1851): 513–45.

———. "Pagodas in and near Canton; their names and times of their erection." *Chinese Repository* 19.10 (October 1850): 535–43.

Unattributed. "Characters formed by the divisible type belonging to the Chinese mission of the Board of foreign missions of the Presbyterian Church in the United States of America. Macao, Presbyterian press, 1844." *Chinese Repository* 14.3 (March 1845): 124–29.

———. "Christian Missions in China: remarks on the means and measures for extending and establishing Christianity; namely, the preaching of the gospel, schools, publication of books, charities, &c." *Chinese Repository* 3.12 (April 1835): 559–68.

———. "Free intercourse with China; present situation of the country; remarks on it, by Staunton, Majoribanks, Auber, and by the writers in the Quarterly and Westminster Reviews, Spectator (London Newspaper), and Alexander's East India Magazine." *Chinese Repository* 3.3 (July 1834): 128–38.

———. "Free Trade with the Chinese." *Chinese Repository* 2.1 (December 1833): 355–74.

———. "Intercourse with the Chinese." *Chinese Repository* 1.4 (August 1832): 141–47.

———. "Journal of Occurrences: Peking Gazette; Peking; Shanse; Hoonan; Tibet; imperial commissioners; Canton Court Circular." *Chinese Repository* 5.1 (May 1836): 44.

———. "Journal of Occurrences: removal of the office of the Chinese Repository to Hongkong: notices of the colony; return of his excellency, governor Davis, from the northern ports; Canton; growth of opium; state of the Chinese Empire." *Chinese Repository* 13.10 (October 1844): 559–60.

———. "Journal of Occurrences: treaties with Great Britain, France, and the United States; affairs at Peking Shánghai, Ningpo, Kúláng sú, Canton, Macao, and Hong Kong; Protestant missions in China." *Chinese Repository* 14.1 (January 1845): 55–56.

———. "Journal of Occurrences: U.S.A. Squadron, commodore Biddle; exchange of treaties; stipulations of the Nanking treaty not completed; reference to Peking; French Mission; Commissioner Lin; Mr. Fortune; Castle Huntley; a junk run down; Horsburgh light-house; health of Hongkong; close of the year." *Chinese Repository* 14.12 (December 1845): 590–92.

———. "Journal of Occurrences: general remarks; the late expedition; notice of the decease of Mr. Everett; death of Mr. Clopton; French mission; negotiations for obtaining rent; Pwan Sz'shing; robbers in Tungkwan Hien." *Chinese Repository* 16.7 (June 1847): 366–68.

———. "Journal of Occurrences: Act of Congress conferring powers on the American commissioners and consuls in China." *Chinese Repository* 17.11 (November 1848): 597–600.

———. "Men and Things in Shánghái: number and character of its population; tything system; taxation; sickness, and pauperism; distribution of food; use of opium and prospect of traffic being legalized; increase of the general commerce; the number of foreign residents; new churches dedicated; converts to Christianity; committee of Delegates for revision of the Old and New Testaments in Chinese." *Chinese Repository* 19.2 (February 1850): 105–10.

———. "Promulgation of the Gospel in China." *Chinese Repository* 3.9 (January 1835): 428–37.

———. "Riot in Canton; proclamation allowing foreigners to enter the city; counter proclamations by the gentry and people; placard before the prefect's gate; demolition and burning of his office by the populace; further proclamations from the high authorities to quiet the people." *Chinese Repository* 15.1 (January 1846): 46–54.

———. "Treaty between her Majesty the Queen of Great Britain and the Emperor of China, signed in the English and Chinese languages, at Nanking, August 29th." *Chinese Repository* 13.8 (August 1844): 437–46.

———. "Treaty between the United States of America and the Chinese Ta Tsing Empire, concluded and signed at Wánghiá, July third in the year of our Lord one thousand eight hundred and forty-four, by their excellencies Caleb Cushing and Kíying, in Chinese and English." *Chinese Repository* 14.12 (December 1845): 555–83.

———. "Treaty with the Chinese, a great desideratum; probability of forming one, with remarks concerning the measures by which the object may be gained." *Chinese Repository* 4.10 (February 1835): 441–49.

———. "Universal Peace; obstacles to it in the character and government of nations, particularly of China and Japan; with remarks on the means best fitted to remove these obstacles." *Chinese Repository* 3.11 (March 1835): 516–27.

Articles from the North American Review

Cushing, Caleb. "Art. VIII—*An Address to the Whites; delivered in the First Presbyterian Church of Philadelphia, on 26th of May, 1826*. By Elias Boudinot, a Cherokee Indian. Philadelphia. 8vo. pp. 16." *North American Review* 23.53 (October 1826): 470–74.

———. "Art. VII.—*Codice diplomatico Colombo-Americano, ossia Raccolta di Documenti originali e inediti, spettanti a Cristoforo Colombo, alla Scoperta ed al Governo dell' America, publicato per Orine degl' Ill^{mi} Decurioni della Città de Genova*. Genova, 1823. 4to. Pp. 80–348." *North American Review* 21.49 (October 1825): 398–429.

———. "Art. I.—*Coleccion de los Viages y Déscubrimientos, que hicieron por Mar los Españoles desde Fines del Siglo XV, con varios Documentos inéditos concernientes a la Historia de la Marina Castellana y de los Establecimientos Españoles en Indias, coorinada é ilustrada por Don Martin Fernandez de Navarrete*. Madrid, 1825. Tom. I. *Viages de Colon: Almirantazgo de Castilla.—*Tom. II. *Documentos de Colon y de las primeros Poblaciones*. (8vo. pp. CLI. 455 and 455)." *North American Review* 24.55 (April 1827): 265–94.

———. "Art. III.—*Ensayo de la Historia Civil del Paraguay, Buenos Ayres y Tucuman*. Libro VI. Capituli 1–3, vol. III, p. 242–333. (Published in Buenos Ayres, 1817. The three chapters here specified contain the History of the Insurrection, which broke out in Peru in the year 1780.)" *North American Review* 20.47 (April 1825): 283–308.

———. "2.—*Florula Bostoniensis. A Collection of Plants of Boston and its Vicinity, with their generic and specific Characters, principal Synonyms, Descriptions, Places of Growth, and time of Flowering; and occasional Remarks*. By Jacob Bigelow, M.D. &c. Second Edition, greatly enlarged; to which is added a Glossary of the Botanical Terms employed in the Work. 8vo.

Cummings, Hilliard, & Co. Boston. 1824." *North American Review* 20.46 (January 1825): 221–24.

———. "[Hayti 1829]; Art. VIII—1. *The Present State of Hayti, with Remarks on its Agriculture, Commerce, Laws, Religion, Finances and Population.* By James Franklin. London. 1828. 2.—*Histoire d'Hayti, depuis sa Découvert, jusqu'en 1824.* Par M. Charles Malo. Nouvelle Edition. Paris. 1825." *North American Review* 28.62 (January 1829): 150–65.

———. "[Hayti 1821]; Art VI.—1. *Reflexions Politiques sur quelques Ouvrages et Journaux Français concernant Hayti, par M. Le Baron de Vastey, Secrétaire du Roi, Chevalier de l'ordre Royal et Militaire de Saint Henry, Prépteur de Son Altesse royale Monseigneur le Prince Royale d'Hayti &c.* A Sans-Souci, de l'Imprimerie Royale, 1817, 8vo. Pp. xx. 206. 2. *Reflexions sur le Noirs et les Blancs &c. par le Baron de Vastey.* Au Cap-Henry, chez P. Roux, Imprimeur du Roi, 1816, 8vo. pp. 112. 3. *Acte de l'independance d'Hayti.* Au Cap-Henry, 4to. 4. *Code Henry.* Au Cap-Henry, chez P. Roux, Imprimeur du Roi, 1912, 8vo. pp. 754. 5. *Gazette Royale d'Hayti.* 6. *Des Almanachs Royals d'Hayti,* 8vo. 7. *Des Ordonnances, Declarations, Proclamations, &c. du Roi d' Hayti.* 8. *Relation de La Fête de S. M. la Reine d'Hayti avec un Coup-d'oeil Politique sur la Situation actuelle du Royaume d'Hayti.* Au Cap-Henry, chez P. Roux, Imprimeur du Roi, 1816, 8vo. pp. 76. 9. *L'Entrée du Roi en sa Capitale, Opera Vaudeville, par M. le Comte de Rosiers.* A Sans-Souci, de l'Imprimerie Royale, 1818, 8vo. pp. 43." *North American Review* 12.30 (January 1821): 112–34.

———. "Art. V.—Insurrection of Paez in Columbia: 1. *Manifiesto que el Poder Ejecutivo de Colombia presenta a la Republica, y al Mundo sobre los Acontecimentos de Venezuela, desde el 30 de Abril del presente Año de 1826—16.* Bogotá. 1826; 2. *Documento Curioso sobre los Acontecimientos de Venezuela, etc. Carta Confidencial del Vice-presidente de la Republic al Jeneral José Antonio Paez.* Bogotá. 1826; 3. *Respuesta al Jeneral José Antonio Paez a la Carta Confidencial, que le dirigio Vice-presidente de la Republica, etc.* Bogotá. 1826; 4. *Ejecucion del Decreto del Poder Ejecutivo, para Alistamiento en las Milicias, que motive la Acusacion del Jeneral en Jefe José Antonion Paez, ante el Senado.* Valencia. 1826." *North American Review* 25.56 (June 1827): 89–112.

———. "Art. IV.—1. *Journal of an Exploring Tour beyond the Rocky Mountains, under the Direction of the American Board of Commissioners for Foreign Missions, performed in the Years 1835, 1836, and 1837; containing a Description of the Geography, Geology, Climate, and Productions, and the Number, Manners, and Customs of the Natives. With a Map of Oregon Territory.* By the Rev. Samuel Parker, A.M. Ithaca, N.Y.: 1838. 12 mo. Pp. 371. 2. *Narrative of a Journey across the Rocky Mountains to the Columbia River, and a Visit to the Sandwhich Islands, Chili, &c. With a Scientific Appendix.* By John K. Townsend, Member of the Academy of Natural Sciences of Philadelphia. Philadelphia and Boston: 1839. 8. Vo. pp. 352." *North American Review* 50.106 (January 1840): 75–144, 288.

———. "Art. V.—*The Life of John Ledyard, the American Traveller; comprising Selections from his Journals and Correspondence.* By Jared Sparks. Cambridge. Hilliard & Brown. 8vo. pp. 325." *North American Review* 27.61 (October 1828): 360–71.

———. "Art. II—*Modern Law of Nations.* 1. *Ward's Law of Nations.* 8vo. 2 vols. 1795. 2. *Vattel's Law of Nations, by Chitty.* 8vo. 1829." *North American Review* 41.89 (October 1835): 287–306.

———. "Art. V.—1. *A Statistical and Commercial History of the Kingdom of Guatemala in Spanish America, containing important Particulars relative to its Productions, Manufacturers, Cus-

toms, &c. with an Account of its Conquest by the Spaniards, and a Narrative of the principal Events down to the present Time. By D. Domingo Juarros. Translated by J. Baily. 8vo. pp. 502. London, 1823; 2. *Contitucion de la Republica Federal de Centro-América, dada por la Samblea Nacional Constituyente en 22 de Noviembre de 1824.* Guatemala. 1825; 3. *Constitucion del Estado del Salvador.* S. Salvador. 1824; 4. *Constitucion Politica del Estado de Nicaragua, decretada y sancionada por la Asambléa Constituyente en el Año de 1826.* Gutemala. 1826; 5. *Mensage del C. Manuel José Arce, Presidente de la Republica de Centro-América de 1826.* Guatemala; 6. *Discursos de* José del Valle, *en el Congreso Federal de Centro-América de 1826.* Guatemala; 7. *El Liberal. El Indicador. El Centinela del Salvador. Redactor General.* (Newspapers printed in Central America.); 8. *Proyecto de Reforma del Sistema de Hacienda y Erecion de un Banco Nacional de Centro-América, por J.M.R.* (S. Juan Manuel Rodriguez.) Guatemala. 1827; 9. *Manfestos y Decretos del Gefe del Estado de Guatemala y del Presidente de Centro-América; Cartas de los Gobiernos del Salvador, de Honduras, Nicaragua y Costa Rica, &c. &c. 1826–27.*" *North American Review* 26.57 (January 1828): 127–45.

———. "Art. II.—*Storia dell' America, in Continuazione del Compendio della Storia Universale, del Sig. Conte di Segur. Opera originale Italiana.* Milano, presso la Società Tipographica de' Classici Italiani (Fusi, Stella, e Compani.) Tom. 29, in 18mo. 1820–1823." *North American Review* 27.60 (July 1828): 30–42.

———. "Art. XVIII.—*Viaggi d'Amerigo Vespucci, con la Vita, l'Elogio e la Disserlazione giustificativa di questo celebre Navigatore, del Padre Stanislao Canovai delle Scuole Pie, pubblico Professore di Matèmatica. Opera postuma.* Firenze, 1817, 8vo, pp. 392." *North American Review* 12.31 (April 1821): 318–40.

[Peabody, Andrew Preston]. "Art. XI.—1. *Memoir of Thomas Handasyd Perkins; containing Extracts from his Diaries and Letters. With an Appendix.* By Thomas G. Cary. Boston: Little, Brown & Co. 1856. 8vo. pp. 304. 2.—*Lives of Eminent Merchants.* By Freeman Hunt, A. M. Editor of the Merchant's Magazine. Vol. 1. New York, 1856. pp. 576." *North American Review* 83.172 (July 1856): 217–33.

Twain, Mark. "To My Missionary Critics." *North American Review* 172.533 (April 1901).

———. "To the Person Sitting in the Darkness." *North American Review* 172.531 (February 1901).

Unattributed. "Critical Notices: *The Journals of Major Samuel Shaw, the first American Consul at Canton. With a Life of the Author, by Josiah Quincy.* Boston: Crosby & Nichols. 1847. 8vo. pp. 360." *North American Review* 66.138 (January 1848): 250–53.

———. "Spark's American Biography. The Library of American Biography. Conducted by Jared Sparks. Volume 1. Boston. 1834." *North American Review* 38.83 (April 1834): 466–86.

Articles from Other British and U.S. Eighteenth- and Nineteenth-Century Periodicals

Cushing, Caleb. "English and French Intervention in the Rio De La Plata." *United States Magazine and Democratic Review* 18.93 (March 1846): 163–85.

———. "Mexico." *United States Magazine and Democratic Review* 18.93 (June 1846): 426–44.

———. "Mr. Cushing at the Bunker Hill Dinner." *Advocate of Peace (1837–1845)* 5.8 (August 1843): 94–95.

De Quincey, Thomas. "Opium and the China Question." *Blackwood's Edinburgh Magazine* 97.296 (June 1840): 717–38.

———. "Postscript to the Opium and the China Question." *Blackwood's Edinburgh Magazine* 97.296 (June 1840): 847–53.

———. "Suspiria de Profundis: Being a Sequel to the Confessions of an English Opium-Eater." *Blackwood's Edinburg Magazine* 107.356 (June 1845): 739–51.

———. "War with China, and the Opium Question." *Blackwood's Edinburgh Magazine* 97.293 (March 1840): 368–83. New York: Published by Jemima M. Mason.

Downing, Andrew Jackson. "Public Cemeteries and Public Gardens." *Horticulturalist Journal of Rural Art and Rural Taste. Devoted to Horticulture, Landscape Gardening, Rural Architecture, Botany, Pomology, Entomology, Rural Economy, &c.* 4.1 (July 1849): 9–12.

Emerson, Edward Waldo. "John Murray Forbes." *Atlantic Monthly* 84.503 (September 1899): 382–96.

Holt, W. S. "The Mission Press in China." *Chinese Recorder and Missionary Journal* 10.3 (May–June 1879): 207–19.

Kipling, Rudyard. "The White Man's Burden: The United States and the Philippine Islands." *McClure's Magazine* 12.4 (5 February 1899): 290–91.

O'Sullivan, John L. "Annexation." *United States Magazine and Democratic Review* 17.85 (July–August 1845): 5–10.

———. "The Great Nation of Futurity." *United States Magazine and Democratic Review* 6.23 (November 1839): 426–30.

[Shaw, Samuel]. "Letter from Mr. Shaw, agent for the owners of the ship *Empress of China*, in her voyage to Canton, addressed to John Jay, esq, New York, May 19, 1785." *American Museum, or, Repository of Ancient and Modern Fugitive Pieces, &c., Prose and Poetical* 1.3 (March 1787): 194–97.

———. "Remarks on the Commerce of America with China." *American Museum, or, Universal Magazine: Containing essays on agriculture, commerce, manufactures, politics, morals, and manners. Sketches of natural characters, natural and civil history, and biography. Law information, public papers, proceedings of Congress, intelligence; Moral tales, ancient and modern poetry, &c. &c.* 7.3 (March 1790): 126–28.

———. "Statement of the Ships Employed in the Trade to Canton." *American Museum or, Universal Magazine: Containing essays on agriculture, commerce, manufactures, politics, morals, and manners. Sketches of natural characters, natural and civil history, and biography. Law information, public papers, proceedings of Congress, intelligence; Moral tales, ancient and modern poetry, &c. &c.* 7.3 (March 1790): 128.

Twain, Mark. "The Treaty with China: Its Provisions Explained (1868)." *Journal of Transnational American Studies* 2.1 (2010): 1–12. Originally published in the *New York Tribune*, 28 August 1868.

Unattributed and unidentified. "China-Extracts from the General Letter of the Mission, [8 September 1836]." *Missionary Herald* 33.6 (June 1837): 261–63.

———. "General Letter of the Mission [7 March 1837]." *Missionary Herald* 33.11 (November 1837): 459–61.

———. "A New War with China." *The Spectator*, no. 1629 (17 September 1859): 942–44.

———. "Party Terrorism." *Harpers Weekly* 12.596 (30 May 1868): 338.

Wade, Thomas. "A New War on China." *The Spectator*, no. 1629 (17 September 1859): 944.

Williams, Samuel Wells. "Our Treaties with China." *New Englander* 38 (May 1879): 301–24.

———. "Present Position of the Chinese Empire in Relation to Intercourse with Other Nations." *Transactions of the American Ethnological Society* 2 (1845): 265–81. New York: Bartlett & Welford, 1848.

Primary Book Sources

Abeel, David. *Journal of a Residence in China, and the Neighboring Countries, from 1829 to 1833.* New York: Leavitt, Lord, 1834.

Adams, Henry. *The Education of Henry Adams.* 1918; New York: Library of America, 1983.

Adams, John Quincy. "President's Annual Address [Monroe Doctrine (December 1823)]." In *The Debates and Proceedings in the Congress of the United States; with an Appendix, containing Important State Papers and Public Documents, and all the Laws of a Public Nature; with a Copious Index,* 12–24. Eighteenth Congress.—First Session: Comprising the Period from December 1, 1823 to May 27, 1824, Inclusive. Washington, DC: Printed and Published by Gales and Seaton, 1856.

American Board of Foreign Missions for the Presbyterian Church. *Seventh Annual Report of the Board of Foreign Missions of the Presbyterian Church, in the United States of America, May, 1844.* New York: Published for the Board, 1844.

———. *The Eighth Annual Report of the Board of Foreign Missions of the Presbyterian Church, in the United States of America, May, 1845.* New York: Published for the Board, 1845.

———. *Ninetieth Annual Report of the American Board of Commissioners for Foreign Missions, Presented at the Meeting Held at St. Louis, Mo. October 10–12, 1900.* Boston: Beacon Press, 1901.

———. *Ninety-First Annual Report of the American Board of Commissioners for Foreign Missions, Presented at the Meeting Held at Hartford, Conn., October 8–11, 1901.* Boston: Beacon Press, 1902.

Banquet to His Excellency Anson Burlingame, and His Associates of the Chinese Embassy, by the Citizens of New York, on Tuesday, June 23, 1868. New York: Sun Book and Job Printing House, 1868.

Bridgman, Elijah Coleman, and Samuel Wells Williams. *General Index of Subjects in the Twenty Volumes of the Chinese Repository: with an Arranged List of Articles.* Canton: Mission Press, 1851.

Bridgman, Eliza J. Gillet. *Daughters of China; or, Sketches of Domestic Life in the Celestial Empire.* New York: Robert Carter & Brothers, 1853.

———. *The Pioneer of American Missions in China: The Life and Labors of Elijah Coleman Bridgman.* New York: Anson D. F. Randolph, 1864.

Broomhall, Marshall. *Martyred Missionaries of the China Inland Mission with a Record of the Perils and Sufferings of Some Who Escaped.* London: Morgan & Scott, 1901.

Butler (Laing), Caroline Hyde. "Journal of Caroline H. Butler (Laing) on a trip to China (1836–1837) [Journal of a voyage to China in the year 1836–7 on the ship *Roman*, Capt. Benson]." Typescript (198 pp.), 1836–37. New-York Historical Society, New York City.

Cary, Thomas G. *Memoir of Thomas Handasyd Perkins: Containing Extracts from His Diaries and Letters. With an Appendix.* Boston: Little, Brown, 1856.

Chambers, William. *Designs of Chinese Buildings, Furniture, Dresses Machines and Utensils, Engraved by the Best Hands, From the Originals Drawn in China by Mr. Chambers, Architect,* member of the Imperial Academy of Arts at Florence, To Which is Annexed, A Description of their Temples, Houses, Gardens, &c. London, 1757.

———. *A Dissertation on Oriental Gardening*. London: Printed by W. Griffin, Printer to the Royal Academy, 1772.

Clay, E. W. *Life in Philadelphia*. Philadelphia: Published by Wm. Simpson, 1829.

Coleridge, Samuel Taylor. *Biographia Literaria*. Edited by John Shawcross. Oxford: Clarendon Press, 1907.

Cushing, Caleb. "Abstract of the Treaty." In *Message from the President of the United States, Communicating An Abstract of the Treaty between the United States of America and the Chinese Empire, January 22, 1845. Read, referred to the Committee on Foreign Relations, and order to be printed*. U.S. Congressional Serial Set. 28th Congress, 2nd Session. Senate Document 58 (Serial Set 450, Number 2; Washington, DC, 1845): 2–4.

———. "Dispatch 71 (to Secretary of State Calhoun, 5 July 1844)." In *Senate of the United States, January 28, 1845. Ordered, That the documents communicated by the President of the United States in relation to the treaty with the Ta Tsing Empire, from which the injunction of secrecy has been removed, be printed for the use of the Senate*. U.S. Congressional Serial Set. 28th Congress, 2nd Session. Senate Document 67 (Serial Set 450, Number 2; Washington, DC, 1845): 77–80.

———. "Dispatch 76 (to Secretary of State Calhoun, 15 July 1844)." In *Senate of the United States, January 28, 1845. Ordered, That the documents communicated by the President of the United States in relation to the treaty with the Ta Tsing Empire, from which the injunction of secrecy has been removed, be printed for the use of the Senate*. U.S. Congressional Serial Set. 28th Congress, 2nd Session. Senate Document 67 (Serial Set 450, Number 2; Washington, DC, 1845): 58–61.

———. "Dispatch 86 (to Secretary of State Calhoun, 19 August 1844)." In *Senate of the United States, January 28, 1845. Ordered, That the documents communicated by the President of the United States in relation to the treaty with the Ta Tsing Empire, from which the injunction of secrecy has been removed, be printed for the use of the Senate*. U.S. Congressional Serial Set. 28th Congress, 2nd Session. Senate Document 67 (Serial Set 450, Number 2, Washington, DC, 1845): 91–93.

———. "Dispatch 97 (to Secretary of State Calhoun, 29 September 1844)." In *Message from the President of the United States, Communicating An Abstract of the Treaty between the United States of America and the Chinese Empire, January 22, 1845. Read, referred to the Committee on Foreign Relations, and order to be printed*. U.S. Congressional Serial Set. 28th Congress, 2nd Session. Senate Document 58 (Serial Set 450; Number 2; Washington, DC, 1845): 4–14.

———. *Opinion of the Attorney General Concerning the Judicial Authority of the Commissioner or Minister and of Consuls of the United States in China and Turkey*. Washington, DC: A. O. P. Nicholson, Public Printer, 1855.

———. *Reminiscences of Spain, the Country, Its People, History, and Monuments*. 2 vols. Boston: Carter, Hendee and Company and Allen and Ticknor, 1833.

———. *Review, Historical and Political, of the Late Revolution in France, and the Consequent Events in Belgium, Poland, Great Britain, and other parts of Europe*. 2 vols. Boston: Carter, Hendee; Newburyport: Thomas B. White, 1833.

————. *Speech of Mr. Cushing, of Massachusetts, on the Subject of Oregon Territory. Delivered in the House of Representatives, May 17 and 22, 1838.* Washington, DC: Printed by Gales and Seaton, 1838.

Davies, Evan. *Memoir of the Rev. Samuel Dyer, Sixteen Years Missionary to the Chinese.* London: John Snow, 1846.

de Crèvecoeur, J. Hector St. John [Michel Guillaume St. Jean]. *Letters from an American Farmer.* 1782; London, 1783.

Delano, Amasa. *Delano's Voyages of Commerce and Discovery: Amasa Delano in China, the Pacific Islands, Australia, and South America, 1789–1807.* Edited by Eleanor Roosevelt Seagraves. 1817; Stockbridge, MA: Berkshire House Publishers, 1994.

————. *A Narrative of Voyages and Travels in Northern and Southern Hemispheres: Comprising Three Voyages Round the World; Together with a Voyage of Survey and Discovery, in the Pacific Ocean and Oriental Islands.* Boston: Printed by E. G. House, for the Author, 1817.

Downing, Andrew Jackson. *A Treatise on the Theory and Practice of Landscape Gardening, Adapted to North America; with a View to the Improvement of Country Residences. Comprising Historical Notices and General Principles of the Art, Directions for Laying Out Grounds and Arranging Plantations, the Description and Cultivation of Hardy Trees, Decorative Accompaniments to the House and Grounds, the Formulation of Pieces of Artificial Water, Flower Gardens, etc. With Remarks on Rural Architecture.* 2nd ed. 1841; New York and London, 1844.

Du Halde, Jean Baptiste. *A Description of the Empire of China and Chinese-Tartary, Together with the Kingdoms of Korea and Tibet: Containing the Geography and History (Natural as well as Civil) of those Countries. Enrich'd with General and Particular Maps, and Adorned with a Great Number of Cuts.* From the French of P. J. B Du Halde, Jesuit: with Notes Geographical, Historical, and Critical; and Other Improvements, particularly in Maps, By the Translator [R. Brookes]. 2 vols. London: Printed by T. Gardner in Bartholomew-Close, for Edward Cave, at St. John's Gate, 1738, 1741.

————. *The General History of China. Containing a Geographical, Historical, Chronological, Political and Physical Description of the Empire of China, Chinese-Tartary, Corea and Thibet. Including and Exact and Particular Account of their Customs, Manners, Ceremonies, Religion, Arts and Sciences. The Whole Adorn'ed with Curious Maps, and Variety of Copper Plates.* Done from the French of Du Halde [by R. Brookes]. 3rd edition corrected 4 vols. London: Printed for J. Watts and Sold by B. Dod at the Bible and Key in Ave-Mary Lane, near Stationers-Hall, 1741. 1735; London: Printed for J. Watts, 1741.

Dunn, Nathan. *Ten Thousand Chinese Things: A Descriptive Catalogue of the Chinese Collection in Philadelphia, with Miscellaneous Remarks Upon the Manners, Customs, Trade, and Government of the Celestial Empire.* Philadelphia, 1839.

Edwards, B[ela] B[ates]. *Biography of Self-Taught Men. With an Introductory Essay.* Boston: Perkins & Marvin, 1832.

————. *The Missionary Gazetteer: Comprising a Geographical and Statistical Account of the Various Stations of the American and Foreign Protestant Missionary Societies of All Denominations, with their Progress in Evangelization and Civilization.* Boston: Published by William Hyde & Co., 1832.

Emerson, Edward Waldo. *The Early Years of the Saturday Club, 1855–1870.* Boston: Houghton Mifflin, 1898.

Emerson, Ralph Waldo. *Essays and Lectures: Nature; Addresses and Lectures; Essays: First and*

Second Series; Representative Men; English Traits; The Conduct of Life. Edited by Joel Porte. New York: Library of America, 1983.

Forbes, John Murray. *Letters and Recollections of John Murray Forbes.* Edited by Sarah Forbes Hughes. 2 vols. Boston: Houghton, Mifflin, 1899.

Forbes, Robert Bennet. *Letters from China: The Canton-Boston Correspondence of Robert Bennet Forbes, 1838–1840.* Edited by Sarah Forbes Hughes. Mystic, CT: Mystic Seaport Museum, 1996.

———. *Personal Reminiscences. Second Edition, Revised, to Which Is Added Rambling Recollections Connected with China.* 1876; Boston: Little, Brown, 1882.

———. *Remarks on China and the China Trade.* Boston: Samuel N. Dickinson, 1844.

Freneau, Philip. *Poems Written Between the Years 1768 & 1794.* Monmouth, NJ: Philip Freneau, 1795.

Gilpin, William. *An Essay upon Prints, Containing Remarks upon the Principles of Picturesque Beauty.* London: J. Robson, 1768.

Goldsmith, Oliver. *An History of the Earth and Animated Nature.* 4 vols. Philadelphia: Printed for Mathew Carey, 1773.

———. *An History of the Earth and Animated Nature.* 5 vols. Philadelphia: Thomas T. Ash, 1823.

Griffis, William Elliot. *Matthew Calbraith Perry: A Typical American Naval Officer.* Boston: Cupples and Hurd, 1887.

———. *Townsend Harris, First American Envoy in Japan.* Boston: Houghton, Mifflin, 1895.

Hale, Edward E. *Sketches of the Lives of the Brothers Everett.* Boston: Little, Brown, 1878.

Hawkes, Francis L. *Narrative of the Expedition of an American Squadron to the China Seas and Japan, performed in the years 1852, 1853, and 1854, under the Command of Commodore M. C. Perry, United States Navy by the Order of the Government of the United States, Compiled from the original notes and journals of the Commodore Perry and his officers, at his request and under his supervision.* 3 vols. Washington, DC: A. O. P. Nicholson, Printer, 1856; Beverly Tucker, Senate Printer, 1856. Vol. 1, reprinted, Mineola, NY: Dover, 2000.

Hawthorne, Nathaniel. *The English Notebooks, 1853–1856.* Edited by Thomas Woodson and William Ellis. Columbus: Ohio State University Press, 1997.

Hay, John. *Letters of John Hay and Extracts from Diary.* Edited by Henry Adams. 3 vols. New York: Gordian Press, 1969.

Heine, Wilhelm. *Graphic Scenes in the Japan Expedition.* New York: Putnam, 1856.

———. *Reise um die Erde nach Japan an Bord der Expeditions-Escadre unter Commodore M. C. Perry.* 2 vols. Leipzig: Hermann Costenoble, 1856.

———. *With Perry to Japan: A Memoir by William Heine.* Translated with an introduction by Frederic Trautmann. Honolulu: University of Hawaii Press, 1990.

Holloway, Laura C. *Famous American Fortunes and the Men Who Have Made Them: A Series of Sketches of Many of the Notable Merchants, Manufacturers, Capitalists, Railroad Presidents, Bonanza and Cattle Kings of the Country.* Philadelphia: Bradley, 1884.

Hunt, Freeman. *Lives of American Merchants.* New York: Derby & Jackson; Cincinnati: H. W. Derby, 1857.

Hunter, William C. *Bits of Old China.* London: Kegan Paul, Trench, 1885.

———. *The "Fan Kwae" at Canton Before Treaty Days, 1825–1844.* 1882; Shanghai: Kelly and Walsh, 1911.

Irving, Washington. *Astoria; or, Anecdotes of an Enterprise Beyond the Rocky Mountains.* 2 vols. Philadelphia: Carey, Lea, & Blanchard, 1836.

———. *Astoria; or, Anecdotes of an Enterprise beyond the Rocky Mountains. Author's Revised Edition.* Vol. 8 of *The Works of Washington Irving.* New York: George P. Putnam, 1849.

———. *Three Western Narratives: A Tour on the Prairies* (1835); *Astoria; or, Anecdotes of an Enterprise Beyond the Rocky Mountains* (1836); *The Adventures of Captain Bonneville* (1837). Edited by James P. Ronda. New York: Library of America, 2004.

Jay, William. *The Life of John Jay: with Selections from his Correspondence and Miscellaneous Papers.* 2 vols. New York: J. & J. Harper, 1833.

Jefferson, Thomas. *Notes on the State of Virginia.* Philadelphia: R. T. Rawle Publisher, 1801.

Jeter, Jeremiah Bell. *A Memoir of Mrs. Henrietta Shuck, the First American Female Missionary to China.* Boston: Gould, Kendall, and Lincoln, 1850.

Kinsman, Rebecca Chase. "Daily Life of Mrs. Nathaniel Kinsman in Macao, China. Excerpts from Letters of 1844." *Essex Institute Historical Collection* 86 (October 1950): 311–30.

———. "Journal of Rebecca Chase Kinsman kept on her voyage to China in 1843." Typescript, [1958, by Mrs. Storer P. Ware]. Baker Library, Harvard Business School, Boston.

———. "Journal of Rebecca Chase Kinsman Kept on Her Voyage to China in 1843." *Essex Institute Historical Collection* 90.3 (July 1954): 289–308; 90.4 (October 1954): 389–409.

———. "Life in Macao in the 1840's: Letters of Rebecca Chase Kinsman to Her Family in Salem. From the Collection of Mrs. Rebecca Kinsman Munroe." *Essex Institute Historical Collection* 86.1 (January 1950): 15–40.

———. "Life in Macao in the 1840's: Letters of Rebecca Chase Kinsman to Her Family in Salem. From the Collection of Mrs. Rebecca Kinsman Munroe." *Essex Institute Historical Collection* 86.1 (April 1950): 106–43.

Knight, Richard Payne. *An Analytic Inquiry into the Principles of Taste.* 1805; Bristol: Thoemmes Press, 1999.

Ledyard, John. *A Journal of Captain Cook's Last Voyage to the Pacific Ocean.* New Haven, CT, 1783.

Locke, John. *Second Treatise on Government.* 1690; New York: Macmillan, 1952.

Low, Charles P. *Some Recollections by Captain Charles P. Low, Commanding the Clipper Ships "Howqua," "Jacob Bell," "Samuel Russell," and "N. B. Palmer," in the China Trade 1847–1873.* Boston: Geo. H. Ellis, 1906.

Maine, Henry Sumner. *Ancient Law: Its Connection with the Early History of Society, and Its Relation to Modern Ideas.* London: John Murray, 1861.

Marshman. Joshua. *Elements of Chinese Grammar, with a Preliminary Dissertation on the Characters, and the Colloquial Medium of the Chinese, and an Appendix Containing the Ta-Hyoh of Confucius with a Translation.* Serampore: Mission Press, 1814.

Martin, W. A. P. *The Siege in Peking: China against the World.* New York: Fleming H. Revell Company, 1900.

Memorial Biographies of the New England Historic Genealogical Society. 9 vols. Boston: Published by the Society, 1881.

Melville, Herman. *Israel Potter: His Fifty Years of Exile.* New York: Putnam's, 1855; London: G. Routledge, 1855.

———. *Israel Potter: His Fifty Years of Exile* (1850). In *The Writings of Herman Melville,* edited by Harrison Hayford, Hershel Parker, and G. Thomas Tanselle. Chicago: Northwestern University Press and the Newberry Library, 1982.

————. "Israel Potter; or, Fifty Years of Exile, A Fourth of July Story." *Putnam's Monthly Magazine of American Literature, Science and Art*, July 1854–March 1855.

————. *Moby Dick; or, the Whale*. New York: Harper & Brothers, 1851.

————. *The Piazza Tales*. New York: Dix & Edwards, 1856.

Milne, William. *A Retrospect of the First Ten Years of the Protestant Mission to China (Now, in Connection with the Malay, Denominated, the Ultra-Ganges Missions) Accompanied with Miscellaneous Remarks on the Literature, History, and Mythology of Chine, &c.* Malacca: Printed at the Anglo-Chinese Press, 1820.

Montesquieu, Baron de. *The Spirit of the Laws*. Translated from the French. 3 vols. London: J. Nourse and P. Vaillant, 1750.

Morrison, John Robert. *A Chinese Commercial Guide: Consisting of Collection of Details Respecting Foreign Trade in China*. Printed at the Albion Press, 1834.

Morrison, Mary. *Memoirs of the Life and Labours of Robert Morrison*. London, 1839.

Morrison, Robert. *Vocabulary of the Canton Dialect* (廣東省土話字彙). Macao: Printed at the Honorable East India Company's Press, 1828.

Morse, Jedidiah. *Geography Made Easy: Being an Abridgment of the American Universal Geography. To which are prefixed Elements of Geography. For the use of schools and academies in the United States of America*. 1784; Boston: J. T. Buckingham, 1814.

Ninety-First Annual Report of the American Board of Commissioners for Foreign Missions, Presented at the Meeting Held at Hartford, Conn., October 8–11, 1901. Boston: Beacon Press, 1902.

Nye, Gideon. *British Opium Policy and Its Results to India and China*. Printed at Macao, 1874.

————. *The Gage of Two Civilizations: Shall Christendom Waver?* Printed at Macao, 1860.

————. *The Morning of My Life in China*. Canton, 1873 and 1877.

————. *Peking the Goal,—the Sole Hope of Peace. Comprising an Inquiry into the Origin of the Pretensions of Universal Supremacy by China, and into the Causes of the First War; With Incidents of the Imprisonment of the Foreign Community and of the First Campaign of Canton. 1841*. Canton, 1873.

————. *The Rationale of the China Question "by an American."* Macao, 1857 and 1873.

————. *Tea and the Tea Trade*. Canton, 1850. Originally published in *Hunt's*, January and February 1850.

Other Merchants and Sea Captains of Old Boston. Boston: State Street Trust, 1919.

"Our First Men": A Calendar of Wealth Fashion and Gentility; Containing a List of Those Person Taxed in the City of Boston, Credibly Reported to Be Worth One Hundred Thousand Dollars, with Biographical Notes of the Principal Persons. Boston: Published by All the Book Sellers, 1846.

Pearson, Henry Greenleaf. *An American Railroad Builder: John Murray Forbes*. Boston: Houghton Mifflin, 1911.

Peters, John R., Jr. *Miscellaneous Remarks upon the Government, History, Religions, Literature, Agriculture, Arts, Trades, Manners, and Customs of the Chinese*. Philadelphia: G. B. Zieber, 1847.

Potter, Israel R. *Life and Remarkable Adventures of Israel R. Potter (A Native of Cranston, Rhode-Island.) Who Was a Soldier in the American Revolution, And took a distinguished part in the Battle of Bunker Hill (in which he received three wounds) after which he was taken Prisoner by the British, conveyed to England, where for 30 years he obtained a livelihood for himself and family, by crying "Old Chairs to Mend" through the Streets of London.—In May last, by the assistance of the American Consul, he succeeded (in the 79th year of his age) in obtaining a passage to his native country, after an absence of 48 years.* Providence: Printed by Henry Trumbull, 1824.

Preble, George Henry. *The Opening of Japan: A Diary of Discovery in the Far East, 1853–1856; from the original manuscript in the Massachusetts Historical Society.* Edited by Boleslaw Szezesniak. Norman: University of Oklahoma Press, 1962.

Price, Uvedale. *An essay on the picturesque, as compared with the sublime and the beautiful; and, on the use of studying pictures, for the purpose of improving real landscape* (1794). London: Printed for J. Robson, 1796.

Quincy, Josiah. *Figures of the Past From the Leaves of Old Journals.* Boston: Roberts Brothers, 1883.

———. *The History of Harvard University.* Cambridge, MA: Published by John Owen, 1840.

———. *The History of the Boston Athenaeum, with Biographical Notices of Its Deceased Founders.* Cambridge, MA: Metcalf, 1851.

———. *Memoir of the Life of John Quincy Adams.* Boston: Phillips, Sampson, 1859.

Reception and Entertainment of the Chinese Embassy, by the City of Boston. Boston: Alfred Mudge & Son, City Printers, 1868.

Shaw, Samuel. *The Journals of Major Samuel Shaw, the First American Consul at Canton, with a Life of the Author by Josiah Quincy.* Edited by Josiah Quincy. Boston: Wm. Crosby and H. P. Nichols, 1847.

Shuck, Henrietta Hall. *A Memoir of Mrs. Henrietta Hall Shuck, the First American Female Missionary to China.* Edited by Jeremiah Bell Jeter. Boston: Gould, Kendall, and Lincoln, 1850.

———. *Scenes in China; or, Sketches of the Country, Religion, and Customs of the Chinese.* Philadelphia: American Baptist Publication Society, 1851.

Smith, Adam. *An Inquiry into the Nature and Causes of the Wealth of Nations.* 5th ed. 3 vols. 1776; London: A. Strahan and T. Cadell, 1789.

———. *The Theory of Moral Sentiments; or, an Essay Towards an Analysis of the Principles by which Men Naturally Judge Concerning the Conduct and Character, First of their Neighbors, and afterwards of Themselves.* 1759; Dublin: Printed by J. Beatty and C. Jackson, 1777.

Sparks, Jared, ed. *The Diplomatic Correspondence of the United States of America, from the Signing of the Definitive Treaty of Peace, 10th September, 1783, to the Adoption of the Constitution, March 4, 1789. Being the Letters of the Presidents of Congress, the Secretary for Foreign Affairs—American Ministers at Foreign Courts, Foreign Ministers near Congress—Reports of Committees of Congress, and Reports of the Secretary for Foreign Affairs on Various Letters and Communications; together with Letters from Individuals on Public Affairs. Published under the direction of the Secretary of State, from the original Manuscripts in the Department of State, conformably to an Act of Congress, approved May 5, 1832.* 7 vols. Washington, DC: Francis Preston Blair, 1833–34.

———. *Memoirs of the Life and Travels of John Ledyard.* London: Henry Colburn, 1828.

Speer, William. *The Oldest and the Newest Empire: China and the United States.* Cincinnati, Ohio: National Publishing, 1870.

Speiden, William. *With Commodore Perry to Japan: The Journal of William Speiden Jr., 1852–*

1855. Edited by John A. Walter, David A. Ranzan, and John J. McDonough. Annapolis, MD: Naval Institute Press, 2013.

Spence, Joseph. "A Particular Account of the Emperor of China's Gardens Near Pekin" (1752). In *Fugitive Pieces, on Various Subjects. By Several Authors,* 1:61–88. London: R. and J. Dodsley, 1761.

State Street Trust Company. *Old Shipping Days in Boston.* Boston: Walton Advertising and Printing, 1918.

———. *Other Merchants and Sea Captains of Old Boston: Being More Information about the Merchants and Sea Captains of Old Boston Who Played Such an Important Part in Building Up the Commerce of New England Together with some Quaint Stories of the Sea.* Boston: Walton Advertising and Printing, 1919.

———. *Some Merchants and Sea Captains of Old Boston: Being a Collection of Sketches of Notable Mean and Mercantile Houses Prominent During the Half of the Nineteenth Century in the Commerce and Shipping of Boston.* Boston: Walton Advertising and Printing, 1918.

The Statues of California Passed at the 23rd Session of the Legislature, 1880. Began on Monday, January 5th, and ended on Friday, April 16th, 1880. Sacramento: State Office, J. D. Young, Supt. State Printing, 1880.

Stoddard, T. Lothrop. *The French Revolution in San Domingo.* Boston: Houghton Mifflin, 1914.

Tomes, Robert. *The Americans in Japan: An Abridgement of the Government Narrative of the U.S. Expedition to Japan, under Commodore Perry.* New York: D. Appleton, 1857.

Tracy, Joseph. *History of the American Board of Commissioners for Foreign Missions. Compiled Chiefly from the Published and Unpublished Documents of the Board.* 1840; New York: M. W. Dodd, 1842.

Tribute of the Massachusetts Historical Society to the Memory of Edward Everett, January 30, 1865. Boston: Massachusetts Historical Society, 1865.

Tyler, John. "To the Senate of the United States (22 January 1845)." In *Message from the President of the United States, Communicating An Abstract of the Treaty between the United States of America and the Chinese Empire, January 22, 1845. Read, referred to the Committee on Foreign Relations, and order to be printed.* U.S. Congressional Serial Set. 28th Congress, 2nd Session. Senate Document 58 (Serial Set 450, Number 2; Washington, DC, 1845): 1–2.

Walton Advertising and Printing Company. *Old Shipping Days in Boston.* Boston: State Street Trust Company, 1918.

Webster, Daniel. "Intercourse with China (Mr. Webster to Mr. Cushing [8 May 1843])." In *The Works of Daniel Webster,* 6:467–72. 7th ed. Boston: Little, Brown, 1853.

———. "Message from the President of the United States, on the Subject of the Trade and Commerce of the United States with the Sandwich Islands, and of Diplomatic Intercourse with their Government; also, in Relation to the new Position of Affairs in China, growing out of the Late War between Great Britain and China, and recommending Provision for a Diplomatic Agent, December 31, 1842." In *The Works of Daniel Webster,* 6:463–67. 7th ed. Boston: Little, Brown, 1853.

———. "Mr. Webster to Mr. Cushing [8 May 1843]." *The Works of Daniel Webster,* 6:472–75. 7th ed. Boston: Little, Brown, 1853.

———. "The President's Letter to the Emperor." In *The Works of Daniel Webster,* 6:475–77. 7th ed. Boston: Little, Brown, 1853.

Whitman, Walt. "Passage to India." In *Leaves of Grass*. Washington, DC, 1872.

Whitney, Asa. *A Project for a Railroad to the Pacific, with Reports of Committees of Congress, Resolutions of State Legislatures, etc., with Other Facts Relating Thereto*. New York: Printed by George W. Wood, 1849.

Wilkes, Charles. *Narrative of the United States Exploring Expedition: during the years 1838, 1839, 1840, 1841, 1842*. London: Ingram, Cooke, 1852.

———. *Voyage Round the World, Embracing the Principal Events of the Narrative of the United States Exploring Expedition*. 1849; New York: G. P. Putnam, 1851.

Williams, Frederick Wells. *Anson Burlingame and the First Chinese Mission to Foreign Powers*. New York: Charles Scribner's Sons, 1912.

———. *The Life and Letters of Samuel Wells Williams, LL.D.: Missionary, Diplomatist, Sinologue*. New York: G. P. Putnam's Sons, 1889.

Williams, Samuel Wells. *Chinese Commercial Guide, Consisting of a Collection of Details and Regulations Respecting Foreign Trade with China, Sailing Directions, Tables, &c.* 4th ed., revised and enlarged. Canton: Printed at the Office of the Chinese Repository, 1856.

———. *Chinese Immigration: A Paper Read before the Social Science Association, at Saratoga, September 10, 1879*. New York: Charles Scribner's Sons, 1879.

———. *Easy Lessons in Chinese (Shiji Dacheng)*. Macau: Xiangshan Shuyuan, 1842.

———. *A Journal of the Perry Expedition to Japan (1853–54) by S. Wells Williams, First Interpreter of the Expedition, Edited by His Son F. W. Williams*. Edited by Frederick Wells Williams. Yokohama, Japan: Kelley & Walsh, 1910.

———. *The Middle Kingdom: A Survey of the Geography, Government, Education, Social Life, Arts, Religion, &c., of the Chinese Empire and Its Inhabitants. With a New Map of the Empire, and Illustrations, Principally Engraved by J. W. Orr*. 2 vols. New York: Wiley and Putnam, 1848.

———. *The Middle Kingdom: A Survey of the Geography, Government, Literature, Social Life, Arts, and History of the Chinese Empire and Its Habitants: Revised Edition, with Illustrations and a New Map of the Empire*. 2 vols. New York: Charles Scribner's Sons, 1883.

———. *Our Relations with the Chinese Empire*. San Francisco, 1877.

———. *A Syllabic Dictionary of the Chinese Language; Arranged According to the Wu-fang Yuen Yin, with the Pronunciation of the Characters as Heard in Peking, Canton, Amoy, and Shanghai*. Shanghai: American Presbyterian Mission Press, 1874.

———. *Treaties between the United States of America and China, Japan, Lewchew and Siam, Acts of Congress, and the Attorney-General's Opinion, with the Decrees and Regulations Issued for the Guidance of the U.S. Consular Courts In China. Published by Authority*. Hong Kong, 1862.

Wood, William W. *Sketches of China: with Illustrations from Original Drawings*. Philadelphia: Carey & Lea, 1830.

Wood, William W., Sr. *Personal Recollections of the Stage, Embracing Notices of Actors, Authors, and Auditors, during a Period of Forty Years*. Philadelphia: Henry Carry Baird, 1855.

Woodard, David. *The Narrative of Captain Woodard and Four Seamen, who lost their ship while in a boat at sea, and surrendered themselves up to the Malays, in the island of Celebes; containing an interesting account of their sufferings from Hunger and various Hardships, and their Escape from the Malays, after a Captivity of Two Years and a Half; Also an Account of the Manners and Customs of the Country, And a Description of the Harbours and Coast, &c. together with an Introduction, And an Appendix, containing Narratives of various Escapes from Shipwrecks, under great Hardships and Abstinence; A Valuable Seaman's Guide, And the*

Importance of Union, Confidence, and Perseverance, in the Midst of Distress. Edited by William Vaughn. London: Printed for J. Johnson, 1804.

Wylie, Alexander. *Memorials of Protestant Missionaries to the Chinese: Giving A List of Their Publications, and Obituary Notices of the Deceased.* Shanghai: American Presbyterian Missionary Press, 1867.

Yung, Wing. *My Life in China and America.* New York: Holt, 1909.

Secondary Critical and Historical Sources

Abu-Lughod, Janet. *Before European Hegemony: The World System, A.D. 1250–1350.* Oxford: Oxford University Press, 1989.

Agamben, Giorgio. *State of Exception.* Translated by Kevin Attell. Chicago: University of Chicago Press, 2005. Originally published as *Stato di eccezione* (Turin: Bollati Boringhieri editore, 2003).

Ahluwalia, Harsharan Singh. "A Reading of Whitman's 'Passage to India.'" *Walt Whitman Quarterly Review* 1.1 (1983): 9–17.

Aldridge, Alfred Owen. *The Dragon and the Eagle: The Presence of China in the American Enlightenment.* Detroit: Wayne State University Press, 1993.

Anderson, Benedict. *Imagined Communities: Reflections on the Origin and Spread of Nationalism.* London: Verso, 1983.

———. *The Spectre of Comparisons: Nationalism, Southeast Asia and the World.* London: Verso, 1998.

———. *Under Three Flags: Anarchism and the Anti-Colonial Imagination.* London: Verso, 2005.

Anderson, David L. *Imperialism and Idealism: American Diplomats in China, 1861–1898.* Bloomington: Indiana University Press, 1985.

Anderson, Eugene N. *The Floating World of Castle Peak Bay.* Ann Arbor, M: University Microfilms International, 1978. Originally published by the American Anthropological Association, 1970.

Anthony, Robert J. *Like Froth Floating on the Sea: The World of Pirates and Seafarers in Late Imperial South China.* Berkeley, CA: Institute of East Asian Studies, 2003.

Arac, Jonathan. "F. O. Matthiessen: Authorizing an American Renaissance." In *The American Renaissance Reconsidered*, edited by Walter Benn Michaels and Donald Pease, 90–112. Baltimore: Johns Hopkins University Press, 1985.

Arrighi, Giovanni. *Adam Smith in Beijing: Lineages of the Twenty-First Century.* London: Verso, 2007.

———. *The Long Twentieth Century: Money, Power, and the Origins of Our Times.* London: Verso, 1994.

Bain, David Haward. *Empire Express: Building the First Transcontinental Railroad.* New York: Viking, 1999.

Bald, R. C. "Sir William Chambers and the Chinese Garden." *Journal of the History of Ideas* 11.3 (June 1950): 287–320.

Balibar, Étienne. "Subjection and Subjectivation." In *Supposing the Subject*, edited by Joan Copjec, 1–15. London: Verso, 1994.

Banner, Stuart. *Possessing the Pacific: Land, Settlers, and Indigenous People from Australia to Alaska.* Cambridge, MA: Harvard University Press, 2007.

Baucom, Ian. *Specters of the Atlantic: Finance Capital, Slavery, and the Philosophy of History.* Durham, NC: Duke University Press, 2005.

Bauer, Ralph. *The Cultural Geography of Colonial American Literatures: Empire, Travel, Modernity.* Cambridge: Cambridge University Press, 2003.

Baym, Nina. *American Woman's Fiction: A Guide to Novels by and about Women in America, 1820–1870.* 1978; Champaign: University of Illinois Press, 1993.

———. "Concepts of the Romance in Hawthorne's America." *Nineteenth-Century Fiction* 38.4 (March 1984): 426–43.

Behdad, Ali. "Oriental Matters." *MFS: Modern Fiction Studies* 56.4 (Winter 2010): 709–28.

Bellis, Peter J. "Israel Potter: Autobiography as History as Fiction." *American Literary History* 2.4 (Winter 1990): 607–26.

Belohlavek, John M. *Broken Glass: Caleb Cushing and the Shattering of the Union.* Kent, OH: Kent State University Press, 2005.

Bercovitch, Sacvan. *Puritan Origins of the American Self.* New Haven: Yale University Press, 1975.

Berlant, Lauren. *The Anatomy of National Fantasy: Hawthorne, Utopia, and Everyday Life.* Chicago: University of Chicago Press, 1991.

Bermingham, Ann. *Landscape and Ideology: The English Rustic Tradition, 1740–1860.* Berkeley: University of California Press, 1986.

Bickers, Robert. *The Scramble for China: Foreign Devils in the Qing Empire, 1832–1914.* London: Allen Lane, 2011.

Biggerstaff, Knight. "The Official Chinese Attitude toward the Burlingame Mission." *American Historical Review* 41.4 (July 1936): 682–702.

———. "A Translation of Anson Burlingame's Instructions from the Chinese Foreign Office." *Far Eastern Quarterly* 1.3 (May 1942): 277–79.

Block, Michael. "The Importance of the China Trade in American Exploration and Conquest of the Pacific, 1830–1850." In *Americana and Macao: Trade, Smuggling, and Diplomacy on the South China Coast,* edited by Paul A. Van Dyke, 95–103. Hong Kong: Hong Kong University Press, 2012.

Blue, Gregory. "Opium for China: The British Connection." In *Opium Regimes: China, Britain, and Japan, 1839–1952,* edited by Timothy Brook and Bob Tadashi Wkabayashi, 31–54. Berkeley: University of California Press, 2000.

Blum, Hester. *View from the Masthead: Maritime and Antebellum American Sea Narratives.* Chapel Hill: University of North Carolina Press, 2008.

Blussé, Leonard. *Visible Cities: Canton, Nagasaki, and Batavia and the Coming of the America.* Cambridge, MA: Harvard University Press, 2008.

Boardman, Eugene Powers. *Christian Influence upon the Ideology of the Taiping Rebellion, 1851–1864.* 1952; New York: Octagon Books, 1972.

Boime, Albert. *The Magisterial Gaze: Manifest Destiny and the American Landscape Painting, c. 1830–1865.* Washington, DC: Smithsonian Institution, 1991.

Bose, Sugata. *A Hundred Horizons: The Indian Ocean in the Age of Global Empire.* Cambridge, MA: Harvard University Press, 2006.

Bové, Paul. "To Make a Way: Telling a Story of US-China Union through the Letters of Henry Adams and John Hay." In *Narratives of Free Trade: The Commercial Cultures of US-China*

Relations, edited by Kendall Johnson, 149–62. Hong Kong: Hong Kong University Press, 2012.

Bowers, Fredson. "The Earliest Manuscript of Whitman's 'Passage to India' and Its Notebook." *Bulletin of the New York Public Library* 61 (1957): 319–52.

Bowra, C. A. V. "Hosea Ballou Morse." *Journal of the Royal Asiatic Society of Great Britain and Ireland*, no. 2 (April 1934): 425–30.

Bowser, Frederick P. *The African in Colonial Peru, 1524–1650*. Stanford, CA: Stanford University Press, 1974.

Braisted, William R. "The United States and the American China Development Company." *Far Eastern Quarterly* 11.2 (February 1952): 147–65.

Braudel, Fernand. *Civilization and Capitalism, 15th–18th Century*. 3 vols. New York: Harper & Row, 1982–84.

———. *The Mediterranean and the Mediterranean World in the Age of Philip II*. Vol. 1. Translated from the French by Siân Reynolds. Berkeley: University of California, 1995. Originally published as *La Mediterranée et le monde mediterranéen à l'époque de Philippe II* (1949).

Brickhouse, Anna. *Transamerican Literary Relations and the Nineteenth-Century Public Sphere*. Cambridge: Cambridge University Press, 2004.

Britton, Roswell S. *The Chinese Periodical Press, 1800–1912*. Shanghai: Kelly & Walsh, 1933.

Brodhead, Richard. *Hawthorne, Melville, and the Novel*. Chicago: University of Chicago Press, 1976.

Brook, Timothy. *Opium Regimes: China, Britain, and Japan, 1839–1952*. Edited by Timothy Brook and Bob Tadashi Wakabayashi. Berkeley: University of California Press, 2000.

Brückner, Martin. *The Geographic Revolution in Early America: Maps, Literacy, & National Identity*. Chapel Hill: University of North Carolina, 2006.

Byrd, Cecil K. *Early Printing in the Straits Settlements, 1806–1858: A National Library Special Publication*. Singapore: Singapore National Library, 1970.

Cain, William E. *F. O. Matthiessen and the Politics of Criticism*. Madison: University of Wisconsin Press, 1988.

Callahan, James Morton. *American Relations in the Pacific and the Far East, 1784–1900*. Baltimore: Johns Hopkins Press, 1901.

Carpenter, Frederic Ives. *Emerson and Asia*. Cambridge, MA: Harvard University Press, 1930.

Carroll, John M. *A Concise History of Hong Kong*. Lanham, MD: Rowman & Littlefield, 2007.

Carter, Thomas Frances. *The Invention of Printing in China and Its Spread Westward*. 2nd ed. Revised by L. Carrington Goodrich. 1925; New York: Ronald Press, 1955.

Casper, Scott E. *Constructing American Lives: Biography and Culture in Nineteenth-Century America*. Chapel Hill: University of North Carolina Press, 1999.

Cassel, Pär Kristoffer. *Grounds of Judgment: Extraterritoriality and Imperial Power in Nineteenth-Century China and Japan*. New York: Oxford University Press, 2012.

Chacko, David, and Alexander Kulcsar. "Israel Potter: Genesis of a Legend." *William and Mary Quarterly*, 3rd ser., 31 (1984): 365–89.

Chakrabarty, Dipesh. *Provincializing Europe: Postcolonial Thought and Historical Difference*. Princeton: Princeton University Press, 2000.

Chan, Sucheng. "Against All Odds: Chinese Female Migration and Family Formation on

American Soil during the Early Twentieth Century." In *Chinese American Transnationalism: The Flow of People, Resources, and Ideas between China and America during the Exclusion Era*, edited by Sucheng Chan, 34–135. Philadelphia: Temple University Press, 2006.

———, ed. *Chinese American Transnationalism: The Flow of People, Resources, and Ideas between China and America during the Exclusion Era*. Philadelphia: Temple University Press, 2006.

Chang, Gordon H. *Fateful Ties: A History of America's Preoccupation with China*. Cambridge, MA: Harvard University Press, 2015.

Chang, Hsin-pao. *Commissioner Lin and the Opium War*. Cambridge, MA: Harvard University Press, 1964.

Chase, Richard. *The American Novel and Its Tradition*. 1957; Baltimore: Johns Hopkins University Press, 1980.

Chatterjee, Partha. *Nationalism Thought and the Colonial World*. Minneapolis: University of Minnesota Press, 1993.

Chaudhuri, K. N. *The Trading World of Asia and the English East Indian Company, 1600–1760*. Cambridge: Cambridge University Press, 1978.

Ch'en, Anthony Kuo-tung. *The Insolvency of the Chinese Hong Merchants, 1760–1843*. Taipei: Institute of Economics, Academia Sinica, 1990.

Chen, Shehong. "Republicanism, Confucianism, Christianity, and Capitalism in American Chinese ideology." In *Chinese American Transnationalism: The Flow of People, Resources, and Ideas between China and America during the Exclusion Era*, edited by Sucheng Chan, 174–93. Philadelphia: Temple University Press, 2006.

Chen, Songchuan. "An Information War Waged by Merchants and Missionaries at Canton: The Society of Diffusion of Useful Knowledge in China, 1834–1839." *Modern Asia Studies* 46.6 (2012): 1705–35.

Cheng, J. C. *Chinese Sources for the Taiping Rebellion, 1850–1864*. Hong Kong: Hong Kong University Press, 1963.

Cheng, Pei-Kai, and Michael Lestz, with Jonathan D. Spence. *The Search for Modern China, a Documentary Collection*. New York: W. W. Norton, 1999.

Cheong, W. E. *Hong Merchants of Canton: Chinese Merchants in Sino-Western Trade*. London: Curzon Press, 1997.

Cheyfitz, Eric. "Matthiessen's American Renaissance: Circumscribing the Revolution." *American Quarterly* 41.2 (June 1989): 341–61.

———. *The Poetics of Imperialism: Translation and Colonization from* The Tempest *to* Tarzan. Expanded ed. 1991; Philadelphia: University of Pennsylvania Press, 1997.

Chittenden, Hiram Martin. *The American Fur Trade of the Far West*. 2 vols. 1935; Lincoln: University of Nebraska Press, 1986.

Christman, Margaret C. S. *Adventurous Pursuits: Americans and the China Trade, 1784–1844*. Washington, DC: Smithsonian Institution Press, 1984.

Christy, Arthur. *The Orient in American Transcendentalism: A Study of Emerson, Thoreau, and Alcott*. New York: Columbia University Press, 1932.

Clark, William Bedford. "How the West Won: Irving's Comic Inversion of the Westering Myth in *A Tour on the Prairies*." *American Literature* 50.3 (November 1978): 335–47.

Clarke, Prescott. "The Development of the English Language Press on the Chinese Coast, 1827–1881." MA thesis, School of Oriental and African Studies, University of London, 1981.

Clunas, Craig. *Pictures and Visuality in Early Modern China*. Princeton: Princeton University Press, 1997.

Clyde, Paul H., ed. *United States Policy toward China: Diplomatic and Public Documents, 1839–1939*. New York: Russell and Russell, 1964.

Coates, W. H. *The Old "Country Trade" of the East Indies*. London: Imray, Laurie, Norie & Wilson, 1911.

Coe, Andrew. *Eagles & Dragons: A History of Americans in China & the Origins of the American Club Hong Kong*. Hong Kong: American Club, 1997.

Cohen, Hennig. "Israel Potter: Background and Foreground." In *Israel Potter: His Fifty Years of Exile*, by Herman Melville, 283–342. New York: Fordham University Press, 1991.

Cohen, Paul. *China and Christianity: The Missionary Movement and the Growth of Chinese Antiforeignism, 1860–1870*. Cambridge, MA: Harvard University Press, 1963.

———. *Discovering History in China: American Historical Writing on the Recent Chinese Past*. New York: Columbia University Press, 1984.

———. *History in Three Keys: The Boxers as Event, Experience, and Myth*. New York: Columbia University Press, 1997.

Conron, John. *American Picturesque*. University Park: Pennsylvania State University Press, 2000.

Cooke, C. A. *Corporation, Trust and Company: A Legal History*. Manchester: Manchester University Press, 1950.

Copley, Stephen, and Peter Garside, eds. *The Politics of the Picturesque: Literature, Landscape and Aesthetics since 1770*. Cambridge: Cambridge University Press, 1994.

Cummings, Bruce. "Boundary Displacement: Area Studies and International Studies during the Cold War." *Bulletin of Concerned Asian Scholars* 29.1 (January–March 1997): 6–26.

Daily, Christopher. *Robert Morrison and the Protestant Plan for China*. Hong Kong: University of Hong Kong Press, 2013.

Dary, David. *The Oregon Trail: An American Saga*. Oxford: Oxford University Press, 2005.

Davids, Jules, ed. *American Diplomatic and Public Papers: The United States and China. Series 1: The Treaty System and the Taiping Rebellion, 1842–1860*. 21 vols. Wilmington, DE: Scholarly Resources, 1973.

Davies, Stephen. *East Sails West: The Voyage of the Keying, 1846–1855*. Hong Kong: University of Hong Kong Press, 2014.

Davis, David Brion. *The Problem of Slavery in Western Culture*. New York: Oxford University Press, 1966.

Davis, Joseph Stancliffe. *Essays in the Earlier History of American Corporations, Numbers I–III; Number IV*. 2 vols. Cambridge, MA: Harvard University Press, 1917.

Davison, Nancy R. "E. W. Clay and the American Political Caricature Business." In *Prints and Printmakers of New York State, 1825–1940*, edited by David Tatham, 91–110. Syracuse: Syracuse University Press, 1986.

Dayan, Joan. "Legal Slaves and Civil Bodies." In *Materializing Democracy: Toward a Revitalized Cultural Politics*, edited by Russ Castronovo and Dana D. Nelson, 53–94. Durham, NC: Duke University Press, 2002.

DeLombard, Jeannine Marie. "Salvaging Legal Personhood: Melville's *Benito Cereno*." *American Literature* 81.1 (March 2009): 35–64.

Dennett, Tyler. *Americans in Eastern Asia: A Critical Study of United States' Policy in the Far East in the Nineteenth Century*. New York: Macmillan, 1922.

Desmond, Jane C., and Virginia R. Domínguez. "Resituating American Studies in a Critical Internationalism." *American Quarterly* 48.3 (September 1996): 475–90.

Dewey, John. "The Historical Background of Corporate Legal Personality." *Yale Law Journal* 35.6 (1926): 655–73.

Dikötter, Frank, Lars Laamann, and Zhou Xun. *Narcotic Culture: A History of Drugs in China.* Chicago: University of Chicago Press, 2004.

Dimock, Wai Chee. *Residues of Justice: Literature, Law, Philosophy.* Berkeley: University of California Press, 1997.

———. *Through Other Continents: American Literature across Deep Time.* Princeton: Princeton University Press, 2006.

Dirlik, Arif. "Bringing History Back In: Of Diasporas, Hybridities, Places, and Histories." In *Beyond Dichotomies: Histories, Identities, Cultures, and the Challenge of Globalization,* edited by Elisabeth Mudimbe-Boyi, 93–127. Albany: State University of New York Press, 2002.

———. "Chinese History and the Question of Orientalism." In *Genealogies of Orientalism: History, Theory, Politics,* edited by Edmund Burke III and David Prochaska, 384–413. Lincoln: University of Nebraska Press, 2008.

———. "Timespace, Social Space, and the Question of Chinese Culture." *boundary2* 35 (Spring 2008): 1–22.

Dirlik, Arif, ed., with the assistance of Malcolm Yeung. *Chinese on the American Frontier.* Lanham, MD: Rowman & Littlefield, 2001.

Dolin, Eric Jay. *Fur, Fortune and Empire: The Epic History of the Fur Trade in America.* New York: W. W. Norton, 2010.

———. *When America First Met China: An Exotic History of Tea, Drugs, and Money in the Age of the Sail.* New York: W. W. Norton, 2012.

Donahue, William J. "The Caleb Cushing Mission." *Modern Asian Studies* 16.2 (1982): 193–216.

Doudna, Martin K. "'The Essential Ultimate Me': Whitman's Achievement in 'Passage to India.'" *Walt Whitman Quarterly Review* 2.3 (1984): 1–9.

Dower, John W. "Black Ships & Samurai." Chapter 4, "Encounters: Facing 'East.'" Massachusetts Institute of Technology, 2008. http://visualizingcultures.mit.edu.

Downs, Jacques M. *The Golden Ghetto: The American Commercial Community at Canton and the Shaping of American China Policy, 1784–1844.* Bethlehem, PA: Lehigh University Press, 1997.

Drinnon, Richard. *Facing West: The Metaphysics of Indian-Hating and Empire Building.* Minneapolis: University of Minnesota Press, 1980.

DuBois, Thomas. *Religion and the Making of Modern East Asia.* Cambridge: Cambridge University Press, 2011.

Dulles, Foster Rhea. *The Old China Trade.* Boston: Houghton Mifflin, 1930.

Dunn, Stephen P. *The Fall and Rise of the Asiatic Mode of Production.* 1982; New York: Routledge, 2011.

Egan, Jim. *Oriental Shadows: The Presence of the East in Early American Literature.* Columbus: Ohio State University Press, 2011.

Eisenstein, Elizabeth. *The Printing Press as an Agent of Change: Communications and Cultural Transformations in Early-Modern Europe.* Vols. 1 and 2. 1979; Cambridge: Cambridge University Press, 2009.

Eperjesi, John R. "The American Asiatic Association and the Imperialist Imaginary of the American Pacific." *boundary2* 28.1 (Spring 2001): 195–219.

———. *The Imperialist Imaginary: Visions of Asia and the Pacific in American Culture.* Hanover, NH: Dartmouth College Press, 2005.

Erkkila, Betsy. *Whitman, the Political Poet.* New York: Oxford University Press, 1989.

Fabian, Johannes. *Time and the Other: How Anthropology Makes Its Object.* New York: Columbia University Press, 1983.

Fairbank, John K., ed. *The Cambridge History of China.* Vol. 10, *Late Ch'ing, 1800–1911, Part I.* Cambridge: Cambridge University Press, 1978.

———. *Chinese-American Interactions: A Historical Summary.* New Brunswick, NJ: Rutgers University Press, 1975.

———. *China Perceived: Images and Policies in Chinese-American Relations.* New York: Knopf, 1974.

———. *The Great Chinese Revolution, 1800–1985.* New York: Harper & Row, 1986.

———. *Trade and Diplomacy on the China Coast: The Opening of the Treaty Ports, 1842–1854.* Cambridge, MA: Harvard University Press, 1953.

———. *The United States and China.* Cambridge, MA: Harvard University Press, 1948.

Fay, Peter Ward. *The Opium War, 1840–1842: Barbarians in the Celestial Empire in the Early Port of the Nineteenth Century and the War by Which They Forced Her Gates Ajar.* Chapel Hill: University of North Carolina Press, 1975.

Febvre, Lucien Paul, and Henri Jean Martin. *The Coming of the Book: The Impact of Printing, 1450–1800.* Translated by David Gerard. 1976; London: New Left Books, 1976. Originally published as *L'apparition du livre* (1976).

Feifer, George. *Breaking Open Japan: Commodore Perry, Lord Abe, and American Imperialism.* New York: HarperCollins, 2006.

Fichter, James R. *So Great a Profit: How the East Indies Trade Transformed Anglo-American Capitalism.* Cambridge, MA: Harvard University Press, 2010.

Fiedler, Leslie A. *Love and Death in the American Novel.* 1960; New York: Stein and Day, 1982.

Field, Peter S. *The Crisis of Standing Order: Clerical Intellectuals and Cultural Authority in Massachusetts, 1780–1833.* Amherst: University of Massachusetts Press, 1998.

Fishel, Wesley R. *The End of Extraterritoriality in China.* Berkeley: University of California Press, 1952.

Fisher, Philip. *Hard Facts: Setting and Form in the American Novel.* Oxford: Oxford University Press, 1985.

Fishkin, Shelley Fisher. "Crossroads of Cultures: The Transnational Turn in American Studies. Presidential Address to the American Studies Association, November 12, 2004." *American Quarterly* 57.1 (March 2005): 17–57.

Fleischacker, Samuel. "Adam Smith's Reception among the American Founders, 1776–1790." *William and Mary Quarterly* 59.4 (October 2002): 897–924.

Fluck, Winfried, Donald E. Pease, and John Carlos Rowe, eds. *Re-framing the Transnational Turn in American Studies.* Hanover, NH: Dartmouth University Press, 2011.

Foletta, Marshall. *Coming to Terms with Democracy: Federalist Intellectuals and the Shaping of an American Culture.* Charlottesville: University Press of Virginia, 2001.

Fontenoy, Paul E. "An 'Experimental' Voyage to China, 1785–1787." *American Neptune* (1996). http://www.pem.org/sites/neptune/voyage1.htm.

————. "Ginseng, Otter Skins, and Sandalwood: The Conundrum of the China Trade." *The Northern Mariner / Le Marin du nord* 7.1 (January 1997): 1–16.

Ford, Stacilee. *Troubling American Women: Narratives of Gender and Nation in Hong Kong.* Hong Kong: Hong Kong University Press, 2011.

Foster, John W. *American Diplomacy in the Orient.* Boston: Houghton Mifflin, 1903.

Frank, Andre Gunder. *ReOrient: Global Economy in the Asian Age.* Berkeley: University of California Press, 1998.

Frank, Caroline. *Objectifying China, Imagining America: Chinese Commodities in Early America.* Chicago: University of Chicago Press, 2011.

Franklin, H. Bruce. "'Apparent Symbol of Despotic Command': Melville's *Benito Cereno.*" *New England Quarterly* 34.4 (December 1961): 462–77.

Freedgood, Elaine. *The Ideas in Things: Fugitive Meaning in the Victorian Novel.* Chicago: University of Chicago Press, 2006.

Freeman, Donald B. *The Straits of Malacca: Gateway or Gauntlet.* Montreal and Kingston: McGill-Queen's University Press, 2003.

Fuchs, Barbara. *Romance.* New York: Routledge, 2004.

Fuess, Claude M. *Caleb Cushing, a Memoir.* Boston: Massachusetts Historical Society, 1932.

————. *The Life of Caleb Cushing.* 2 vols. New York: Harcourt, Brace, 1923.

Gallagher, John, and Ronald Robinson. "The Imperialism of Free Trade." *Economic History Review,* 2nd ser., 6.1 (1953): 1–15.

Garrett, Valery M. *Heaven Is High, the Emperor Far Away: Merchants and Mandarins in Old Canton.* New York: Oxford University Press, 2002.

Ghosh, Amitav. *Food of Fire.* New York: Picador, 2015.

————. *River of Smoke.* New York: Picador, 2011.

————. *Sea of Poppies.* New York: Picador, 2008.

Gibson, James R. *Otter Skins, Boston Ships, and China Goods: The Maritime Fur Trade of the Northwest Coast, 1785–1841.* Seattle: University of Washington Press, 1992.

Gikandi, Simon. *Maps of Englishness: Writing Identity in the Culture of Colonialism.* New York: Columbia University Press, 1996.

Gilmore, Michael T. *American Romanticism and the Marketplace.* Chicago: University of Chicago Press, 1985.

Glazener, Nancy. *Reading for Realism: The History of a U.S. Literary Institution, 1850–1910.* Durham, NC: Duke University Press, 1997.

Goetzmann, William H. *Exploration and Empire: The Explorer and the Scientist in the Winning of the American West.* 1966; New York: Norton, 1978.

Goldfeld, Alex R. *The North End: A Brief History of Boston's Oldest Neighborhood.* Charleston, SC: History Press, 2009.

Goldstein, Jonathan. *Philadelphia and the China Trade, 1682–1846.* University Park: Pennsylvania State University Press, 1978.

————. *Stephen Girard's Trade with China, 1787–1824: The Norms versus the Profits of Trade.* Portland, ME: MerwinAsia, 2011.

Goldstein, Jonathan, Jerry Israel, and Hilary Conroy, eds. *America Views China: American Images of China Then and Now.* Bethlehem, PA: Lehigh University Press, 1991.

Gombrich, E. H. *Art and Illusion: A Study in the Psychology of Pictorial Representation.* 1960; Princeton: Princeton University Press, 1972.

Gordon, Andrew. *The Modern History of Japan: From Tokugawa Times to the Present.* New York: Oxford University Press, 2003.

Goudie, Sean. *Creole America: West Indies and the Formation of Literature and Culture in the New Republic.* Philadelphia: University of Pennsylvania Press, 2006.

Grace, Richard J. *Opium and Empire: The Lives and Careers of William Jardine and James Matheson.* Montreal and Kingston: McGill-Queen's University Press, 2014.

Grandin, Greg. *The Empire of Necessity: Slavery, Freedom, and Deception in the New World.* New York: Henry Holt, 2014.

Grant, Frederic Delano. "The April 1820 Debt Settlement between Conseequa and Benjamin Chew Wilcocks." In *Americans in Macao: Trade, Smuggling, and Diplomacy on the South China Coast,* edited by Paul A. Van Dyke, 73–94. Hong Kong: Hong Kong University Press, 2012.

———. "Hong Merchant Litigation in the American Courts." *Proceedings of the Massachusetts Historical Society* 99: 44–62. Boston: Northeastern University Press, 1988.

Gray, Edward G. *The Making of John Ledyard: Empire and Ambition in the Life of an Early American Traveler.* New Haven: Yale University Press, 2007.

Greenberg, Michael. *British Trade and the Opening of China, 1800–42.* Cambridge: Cambridge University Press, 1951.

Greenbie, Sydney, and Marjorie Barstow. *Gold of Ophir; or, The China Trade in the Making of America.* New York: Wilson-Erickson, 1937. Originally published as *Gold of Ophir: The Lure That Made America* (Garden City, NY: Doubleday, Page, 1925).

Grossman, Jay. "The Canon in the Closet: Matthiessen's Whitman, Whitman's Matthiessen." *American Literature* 70.4 (December 1998): 799–832.

Gulick, Edward V. *Peter Parker and the Opening of China.* Cambridge, MA: Harvard University Press, 1973.

Habermas, Jürgen. *Structural Transformation of the Public Sphere: An Inquiry into a Category of Bourgeois Society.* Translated by Thomas Burger and Frederick Lawrence. 1989; Cambridge, MA: MIT Press, 1991. Originally published as *Strukturwandel der Öffentlichkeit: Untersuchungen zu einer Kategorie der bürgerlichen Gesellschaft* (1962).

Haddad, John Rogers. *America's First Adventure in China: Trade, Treaties, Opium and Salvation.* Philadelphia: Temple University Press, 2013.

———. "China of the American Imagination: The Influence of Trade on US Portrayals of China, 1820–1850." In *Narratives of Free Trade: The Commercial Cultures of Early US-China Relations,* edited by Kendall Johnson, 57–82. Hong Kong: Hong Kong University Press, 2012.

———. *The Romance of China: Excursions to China in U.S. Culture: 1776–1876.* New York: Columbia University Press, 2008. http://www.gutenberg-e.org/haj01/index.html.

———. "The Wild West Turns East: Audience, Ritual, and Regeneration in Buffalo Bill's Boxer Uprising." *American Studies* 49.3 (Fall–Winter 2008): 5–38.

Hall, David D. *Cultures of Print: Essays in the History of the Book.* Amherst: University of Massachusetts Press, 1996.

Hamashita, Takeshi. "The Tribute Trade System and Modern Asia." In *Japanese Industrialization and the Asian Economy,* edited by A. J. H. Latham and Heita Kawakatsu, 91–107. New York: Routledge.

Hao, Yen'ping. "Chinese Teas to America: A Synopsis." In *America's China Trade in Historical*

Perspective: The Chinese and American Performance, edited by Ernest R. May and John K. Fairbank, 11–31. Cambridge, MA: Harvard University Press, 1986.

———. *The Commercial Revolution in Nineteenth-Century China: The Rise of Sino-Western Mercantile Capitalism*. Berkeley: University of California Press, 1986.

———. *The Comprador in Nineteenth-Century China: Bridge between East and West*. Cambridge, MA: Harvard University Press, 1979.

Harris, Susan K. *God's Arbiters: Americans and the Philippines, 1898–1902*. New York: Oxford University Press, 2011.

He, Sebing. *Macao in the Making of Early Sino-American Relations, 1784–1844*. Macao: Cultural Affairs Bureau of the Macao S.A.R Government, 2015.

———. "Russell and Company and American Trade with Canton in the Nineteenth Century" [Qichang Yanghang yu shijiu shiji Meiguo dui Guangzhou maoyi]. *Academic Research* [Xueshu yanjiu] 6 (2005): 109–16.

Hevia, James. *Cherishing Men from Afar: Qing Guest Ritual and the Macartney Embassy of 1793*. Durham, NC: Duke University Press, 1995.

———. *English Lessons: The Pedagogy of Imperialism in Nineteenth-Century China*. Durham, NC: Duke University Press, 2003.

Holzman, Michael. "The Ideological Origins of American Studies at Yale." *American Studies* 40.2 (Summer 1999): 71–99.

Horsman, Reginald. *Race and Manifest Destiny: Origins of American Racial Anglo-Saxonism*. Cambridge, MA: Harvard University Press, 1986.

Horwitz, Morton J. *The Transformation of American Law, 1780–1860*. Cambridge, MA: Harvard University Press, 1979.

Howard, David Sanctuary. *New York and the China Trade*. New York: New-York Historical Society, 1984.

Howay, Frederic William. "Early Days of the Maritime Fur-Trade on the Northwest Coast." *Canadian Historical Review* 4.1 (1923): 26–44.

———, ed. *Voyages of the "Columbia" to the Northwest Coast, 1787–1790 and 1790–93*. 1941; Oregon Historical Society Press, in cooperation with the Massachusetts Historical Society, 1990.

Hsu, Hsuan L. *Geography and the Production of Space in Nineteenth-Century American Literature*. Cambridge: Cambridge University Press, 2010.

———. *Sitting in Darkness: Mark Twain, Asia, and Comparative Racialization*. New York: New York University Press, 2015.

Hsu, Madeline. "Trading with Gold Mountain, *JinShanZhuang* and Networks of Kinship and Native Place." In *Chinese American Nationalism: The Flow of People, Resources, and Ideas between China and America during the Exclusion Era*, 22–33. Philadelphia: Temple University Press, 2006.

Huang, Yunte. *Transpacific Displacement: Ethnography, Translation, and Intertextual Travel in Twentieth-Century American Literature*. Berkeley: University of California Press, 2002.

———. *Transpacific Imaginations: History, Literature, Counterpoetics*. Cambridge, MA: Harvard University Press, 2008.

Huang, Zisheng and Sibing He. *Feilübin Huaqiao Shi* [History of the Philippine Chinese]. Rev. and enlarged ed. Guangzhou: Guangdong Gaodeng Jiaoyü Chubanshe [Guangdong Higher Education Press], 2009.

Hummel, Arthur W., ed. *Eminent Chinese of the Ch'ing Period (1644–1912)*. 2 vols. Washington, DC: Government Printing Office, 1943–44.

Hunt, John Dixon. *The Picturesque Garden in Europe*. London: Thames & Hudson, 2003.

Hunt, John Dixon, and Peter Willis, eds. *The Genius of Place: The English Landscape Garden, 1620–1820*. London: Elek, 1975; Cambridge, MA: MIT Press, 1988.

Hunt, Michael H. *The Making of a Special Relationship: The United States and China to 1914*. New York: Columbia University Press, 1983.

Isaacs, Harold. *Scratches on Our Minds: American Images of China and India*. New York: J. Day, 1958.

James, C. L. R. *Mariners, Renegades & Castaways: The Story of Herman Melville and the World We Live In*. 1953; Hanover, NH: University Press of New England for Dartmouth College, 2001.

Jameson, Frederic. "Culture and Finance Capital." *Critical Inquiry* 24.1 (Autumn 1997): 246–65.

Jansen, Marius B. *The Making of Modern Japan*. Cambridge, MA: Harvard University Press, 2000.

———. "Obituary: John King Fairbank (1907–1991)." *Journal of Asian Studies* 51.1 (February 1992): 237–42.

Jefferson, Thomas. *The Writings of Thomas Jefferson*, Vol. 12. Edited by Andrew A. Lipscomb and Albert Ellery Bergh. Washington, DC: Issued under the auspices of the Thomas Jefferson Memorial Association of the United States, 1903–4.

Jehlen, Myra. *American Incarnation: The Individual, the Nation, and the Continent*. Cambridge, MA: Harvard University Press, 1986.

———. "New World Epics." *Salmagundi* 36 (Winter 1977): 49–58.

Ji, Zhaolin. *History of Modern Shanghai Banking: The Rise and Decline of China's Finance Capitalism*. London: M. E. Sharpe, 2003.

Johannson, Kristin. *Ginseng Dreams: The Secret World of America's Most Valuable Plant*. Lexington: University of Kentucky Press, 2006.

Johnson, Kendall. "Henry James and the China Trade." *Modern Fiction Studies* 60.4 (Winter 2014): 677–710.

———. *Henry James and the Visual*. Cambridge: Cambridge University Press, 2007.

———. "Peace, Friendship, and Financial Panic: Reading the Mark of Black Hawk in *Life of Ma-Ka-Tai-Me-She-Kia-Kiak*." *American Literary History* 19.4 (Winter 2007): 771–99.

———. "A Question of Character: The Romance of Early Sino-American Commerce in *The Journals of Major Samuel Shaw, the First American Consul at Canton* (1847)." In *Narratives of Free Trade: The Commercial Cultures of Early US-China Relations*, edited by Kendall Johnson, 33–56. Hong Kong: Hong Kong University Press, 2012.

———. "Reading for Contexts of American Orientalism from the Far East to the Far West." *American Literary History* 25.3 (Fall 2013): 638–59.

Johnson, Rossiter, ed., and John Howard Brown, managing ed. *The Twentieth Century Biographical Dictionary of Notable Americans*. 10 vols. Boston: Biographical Society, 1904.

Johnston, Patricia, and Caroline Frank, eds. *Global Trade and Visual Arts in Federal New England*. Durham, NH: University of New Hampshire Press, 2014.

Jordan, Winthrop D. *White over Black: American Attitudes toward the Negro, 1550–1812*. Chapel Hill: University of North Carolina Press, 1968.

Jung, Moon-Ho. *Coolies and Cane: Race, Labor, and Sugar in the Age of Emancipation.* Baltimore: Johns Hopkins University Press, 2006.

———. "Outlawing 'Coolies': Race, Nation, and Empire in the Age of Emancipation." *American Quarterly* 57.3 (September 2005): 677–701.

Kaplan, Amy. *The Anarchy of Empire in the Making of U.S. Culture.* Cambridge, MA: Harvard University Press, 2005.

———. *The Social Construction of American Realism.* Chicago: University of Chicago Press, 1988.

Kaplan, Amy, and Donald E. Pease, eds. *Cultures of United States Imperialism.* Durham, NC: Duke University Press, 1993.

Karcher, Carolyn L. *Shadow over the Promised Land: Slavery, Race, and Violence in Melville's America.* Baton Rouge: Louisiana State University Press, 1980.

Kayaoğlu, Turan. *Legal Imperialism: Sovereignty and Extraterritoriality in Japan, the Ottoman Empire, and China.* Cambridge: Cambridge University Press, 2010.

Keliher, Macabe. "Anglo-American Rivalry and the Origins of U.S. China Policy." *Diplomatic History* 31.2 (April 2007): 227–57.

Kerr, Phyllis Forbes. *Letters from China: The Canton-Boston Correspondence of Robert Bennet Forbes, 1838–1840.* Compiled and edited by Phyllis Forbes Kerr. Mystic, CT: Mystic Seaport Museum, 1996.

Kim, Sukjoo. "Liang Fa's Quanshi liangyan and Its Impact on the Taiping Movement." PhD dissertation, Baylor University, 2011.

King, David W. "The New Divinity and the Origins of the American Board of Commissioners for Foreign Missions." In *North American Foreign Missions, 1810–1914: Theology, Theory, and Policy,* edited by Wilbert R. Shenk, 1–34. Grand Rapids, MI: William B. Eerdman's, 2004.

King, Frank H. H., and Prescott Clarke. *A Research Guide to China-Coast Newspapers, 1822–1911.* Cambridge, MA: Harvard University Press, 1965.

Kleitz, Dorsey. "Herman Melville, Matthew Perry, and the *Narrative of the Expedition of an American Squadron to the China Seas and Japan.*" *Leviathan: A Journal of Melville Studies* 8.3 (2006): 25–32.

Knowles, Anne Kelly. *Mastering Iron: The Struggle to Modernize an American Industry, 1800–1868.* Chicago: University of Chicago Press, 2013.

Knox, Jerry Bradley. "The History, Geography, and Economics of North American Ginseng." MA thesis, California State University, Fullerton, 1999.

Kolodny, Annette. *The Land before Her: Fantasy and Experience of the American Frontiers, 1630–1860.* Chapel Hill: North Carolina Press, 1984.

Koon, Yeewan. "The Face of Diplomacy in Nineteenth-Century China: Qiying's Portrait Gifts." In *Narratives of Free Trade: The Commercial Cultures of Early US-China Relations,* edited by Kendall Johnson, 131–48. Hong Kong: Hong Kong University Press, 2012.

Lai, Walton Look. *Indentured Labor, Caribbean Sugar: Chinese and Indian Migrants to the British West Indies, 1838–1918.* Baltimore: Johns Hopkins University Press, 1993.

Lai-Henderson, Selina. *Mark Twain in China.* Stanford, CA: Stanford University Press, 2015.

Lamas, Rosemarie W. N. *Everything in Style: Harriet Low's Macau.* Hong Kong: Hong Kong University Press, in conjunction with Instituto Cultural do Governo da R.A.E. de Macau, 2006.

Lange, Amanda E. "The Forgotten Connection: The Connecticut River Valley and the China

Trade." In *Global Trade and Visual Arts in Federal New England*, edited by Patricia Johnston and Caroline Frank. Durham, 71–98. Hanover, NH: University of New Hampshire Press.

Larson, John Lauritz. *Bonds of Enterprise: John Murray Forbes and Western Development in America's Railway Age*. Expanded ed. 1984. Iowa City: University of Iowa Press, 2001.

Latourette, Kenneth Scott. *The History of Early Relations between the United States and China, 1784–1844*. New Haven: Yale University Press, 1917.

Lauer, Uta. "China Studies: Landscape Painting." *Oxford Bibliographies*. http://www.oxfordbib liographies.com/view/document/obo-9780199920082/obo-9780199920082-0051.xml#.

Lazich, Michael C. "American Missionaries and the Opium Trade in Nineteenth-Century China." *Journal of World History* 17 (Spring 2006): 197–223.

———. *E. C. Bridgman, 1801–1861: America's First Missionary to China*. Lewiston, NY: E. Mellen Press, 2000.

Lee, E. "Defying Exclusion: Chinese Immigrants and Their Strategies during the Exclusion Era." In *Chinese American Transnationalism: The Flow of People, Resources, and Ideas between China and America during the Exclusion Era*, edited by Sucheng Chan, 1–22. Philadelphia: Temple University Press, 2006.

Lee, Jean Gordon. *Philadelphians and the China Trade, 1784–1844*. Philadelphia: Philadelphia Museum of Art, 1984.

Lefebvre, Henri. *The Production of Space*. Translated by Donald Nicholson-Smith. 1974; Malden, MA: Blackwell, 1991.

Legg, Stephen. *Spatiality, Sovereignty and Carl Schmitt: Geographies of the Nomos*. New York: Routledge, 2011.

LeMenager, Stephanie. *Manifest and Other Destinies: Territorial Fictions of the Nineteenth-Century United States*. Lincoln: University of Nebraska Press, 2004.

———. "Trading Stories: Washington Irving and the Global West." *American Literary History* 15.4 (Winter 2003): 683–708.

Le Pichon, Alain, ed. *China Trade and Empire: Jardine, Matheson & Co. and the Origins of British Rule in Hong Kong, 1827–1843*. Oxford: Published for the British Academy by Oxford University Press, 2006.

Lewis, R. W. B. *The American Adam: Innocence, Tragedy, and Tradition in the Nineteenth Century*. Chicago: University of Chicago Press, 1955.

Lin, Man-houng. *China Upside Down: Currency, Society, and Ideologies, 1808–1856*. Cambridge, MA: Harvard University Press, 2006.

Linebaugh, Peter, and Marcus Rediker. *The Many-Headed Hydra: Sailors, Slaves, Commoners and the Hidden History of the Revolutionary Atlantic*. London: Verso, 2000.

Liu, Kwang-Ching. *Anglo-American Steamship Rivalry in China, 1862–1874*. Cambridge, MA: Harvard University Press, 1962.

Liu, Lydia H. *Clash of Empires: The Invention of China in Modern World Making*. Cambridge, MA: Harvard University Press, 2004.

———, ed. *Tokens of Exchange: The Problem of Translation in Global Circulation*. Durham, NC: Duke University Press, 1999.

Livingstone, David N. "Geographical Inquiry, Rational Religion, and Moral Philosophy: Enlightenment Discourses on the Human Condition." In *Geography and Enlightenment*, edited by David N. Livingstone and Charles W. J. Withers, 93–124. Chicago: University of Chicago Press, 1999.

Loines, Elma, ed. *The China Trade Post-Bag of the Seth Low Family of Salem and New York.* Manchester, ME: Falmouth Publishing House, 1953.

Lovejoy, Arthur O. "The Chinese Origin of Romanticism." In *Essays in the History of Ideas,* 99–135. Baltimore: Johns Hopkins University Press, 1948.

Lovell, Julia. *The Opium War: Drugs, Dreams and the Making of China.* London: Picador, 2011.

Low, Harriett. *Light and Shadows of a Macao Life: The Journal of Harriett Low, Travelling Spinster.* 2 vols. Edited by Nan P. Hodges and Arthur W. Hummel. Woodinville, WA: History Bank, 2002.

———. *My Mother's Journal: A Young Lady's Diary of Five Years Spent in Manila, Macao, and the Cape of Good Hope from 1829–1834.* Edited by Katherine Hilliard. Boston: G. H. Ellis, 1900.

Lowe, Lisa. "The Intimacies of Four Continents." In *Haunted by Empire: Geographies of Intimacy in North American History,* edited by A. L. Stoler, 191–212. Durham, NC: Duke University Press, 2006.

———. *The Intimacies of Four Continents.* Durham, NC: Duke University Press, 2015.

Lutz, Jessie Gregory. *Opening China: Karl F. A. Gützlaff and Sino-Western Relations, 1827–1852.* Grand Rapids, MI: William B. Eerdmans, 2008.

Macpherson, C. B. *The Political Theory of Possessive Individualism: Hobbes to Locke.* Oxford: Oxford University Press, 1962.

Maier, Pauline. "The Revolutionary Origins of the American Corporation." *William and Mary Quarterly* 50.1 (January 1993): 51–84.

Malcolm, Elizabeth. "The *Chinese Repository* and Western Literature on China 1800 to 1850." *Modern Asia Studies* 7.2 (1972): 165–78.

Malley, R., et al. "Constructing the State Extraterritorially: Jurisdictional Discourse, the National Interest, and Transnational Norms." *Harvard Law Review* 103.6 (April 1990): 1273–1305.

Mancuso, Luke. "*Leaves of Grass,* 1871–72 Edition." In *Walt Whitman: An Encyclopedia,* edited by J. R. LeMaster and Donald D. Kummings. New York: Garland Publishing, 1998.

Mann, Susan, and Philip A. Kuhn. "Dynastic Decline and the Roots of Rebellion." In *The Cambridge History of China,* vol. 10, *Late Ch'ing, 1800–1911, Part I,* edited by John K. Fairbank, 107–62. Cambridge: Cambridge University Press, 1978.

Marshall, David. *The Frame of Art: Fictions of Aesthetic Experience, 1750–1815.* Baltimore: Johns Hopkins University Press, 2005.

Marx, Leo. *The Machine in the Garden: Technology and the Pastoral Ideal in America.* Oxford: Oxford University Press, 1964.

Matthiessen, F. O. *American Renaissance: Art and Expression in the Age of Emerson and Whitman.* New York: Oxford University Press, 1941.

Maurer, Noel, and Carlos Yu. *The Big Ditch: How America Took, Built, Ran, and Ultimately Gave Away the Panama Canal.* Princeton: Princeton University Press, 2010.

May, Ernest R. *American Imperialism: A Speculative Essay.* 1968; Chicago: Imprint Publications, 1991.

May, Ernest R., and John K. Fairbank. *America's China Trade in Historical Perspective: The Chinese and American Performance.* Committee on American-East Asia Relations, in collaboration with the Council on East Asian Studies, Harvard University. Cambridge, MA: Harvard University Press, 1986.

Mazumdar, Sucheta. "Locating China, Positioning America: Politics of Civilizational Model of World History." In *From Orientalism to Postcolonialism: Asia, Europe and the Lineages of Difference*, edited by Sucheta Mazumdar, Vasant Kaiwar, and Thierry Labica, 43–82. London: Routledge, 2009.

Mazumdar, Sucheta, Vasant Kaiwar, and Thierry Labica. *From Orientalism to Postcolonialism: Asia, Europe and the Lineages of Difference*. London: Routledge, 2009.

McCormick, Thomas J. *China Market: America's Quest of Informal Empire, 1893–1901*. Chicago: Quadrangle Books, 1967.

McKay, Richard C. *Donald McKay and His Famous Sailing Ships*. 1928; Mineola, NY: Dover Publications, 1995.

Mehta, Uday Singh. *Liberalism and Empire: A Study in Nineteenth-Century British Liberal Thought*. Chicago: University of Chicago Press, 1989.

Miller, Angela. *Empire of the Eye: Landscape Representation and American Cultural Politics, 1825–1875*. Ithaca, NY: Cornell University Press, 1993.

Miller, David Hunter, ed. "China: 1844 (Document 109)." In *Treaties and Other International Acts of the United States of America*, vol. 4, *Documents 80–121: 1836–1846*. Washington, DC: Government Printing Office, 1934.

———. *Treaties and Other International Acts of the United States of America*. 8 vols. Washington, DC: Government Printing Office, 1931–34.

Miller, Perry. *Errand into the Wilderness*. Cambridge, MA: Harvard University Press, 1956.

Miller, Stuart Creighton. "The American Trader's Image of China, 1785–1882." *Pacific Historical Review* 36.4 (November 1967): 375–95.

———. "Ends and Means: Missionary Justification of Force in Nineteenth Century China." In *The Missionary Enterprise in China and America*, edited by John K. Fairbank, 249–82. Cambridge, MA: Harvard University Press, 1974.

———. *The Unwelcome Immigrant: The American Image of the Chinese, 1785–1882*. Berkeley: University of California Press, 1969.

Mills, Sara. *Discourses of Difference: An Analysis of Women's Travel Writing and Colonialism*. London: Routledge, 1991.

Mo, Timothy. *An Insular Possession*. London: Chatto and Windus, 1986.

Molloy, William M., ed. *Treaties, Conventions, International Acts, Protocols and Agreements between the United States of America and Other Powers, 1776–1909*. 2 vols. Washington, DC: Government Printing Office, 1910.

Moore, Merl M., Jr. "More about the Events Surrounding the Suppression of *Harper's Weekly*, April 26, 1862." *American Art Journal* 12 (Winter 1980): 82–85.

Morais, Isabel. "Henrietta Hall Shuck: Engendering Faith, Education, and Culture in Nineteenth-Century Macao." In *Americans and Macao: Trade, Smuggling, and Diplomacy on the South China Coast*, edited by Paul A. Van Dyke, 105–24. Hong Kong: Hong Kong University Press, 2012.

Morse, Hosea Ballou. *Chronicles of the East India Company Trading to China, 1635–1834*. Edited by Patrick Tuck. 3 vols. New York: Routledge, 2000.

———. *The Gilds of China: With an Account of the Gild Merchant or Co-Hong of Canton*. London: Longmans, Green, 1909.

———. *The International Relations of the Chinese Empire*. 3 vols. London: Longmans, Green, 1910–18.

———. *The Trade and Administration of the Chinese Empire.* Shanghai: Kelley and Walsh, 1908.

Moss, Richard J. "Republicanism, Liberalism, and Identity: The Case of Jedidiah Morse." *Essex Institute Historical Collections* 126 (1990): 209–36.

Mott, Frank Luther. *A History of American Magazines.* 5 vols. Cambridge, MA: Harvard University Press, 1938–68.

Munn, Christopher. *Anglo-China: Chinese People and British Rule in Hong Kong, 1841–1880.* Richmond, Surrey: Curzon, 2001.

———. "The Hong Kong Opium Revenue, 1845–1885." In *Opium Regimes: China, Britain, and Japan, 1839–1952,* edited by Timothy Brook and Bob Tadashi Wakabayashi, 105–26. Berkeley: University of California Press, 2000.

Murphy, Gretchen. *Hemispheric Imaginings: The Monroe Doctrine and Narratives of U.S. Empire.* Durham, NC: Duke University Press, 2005.

Needham, Joseph. *The Grand Titration: Science and Society in East and West.* London: Allen & Unwin, 1969.

Ngai, Mae N. "Transnationalism and Transformation of the 'Other': Response to the Presidential Address." *American Quarterly* 57.1 (March 2005): 59–65.

Nield, Robert. *The China Coast: Trade and the First Treaty Ports.* Hong Kong: Joint Publishing, 2010.

Noble, David F. *Beyond the Promised Land: The Myth and the Movement.* Toronto: Between the Lines, 2005.

Novak, Barbara. *Nature and Culture: American Landscape and Painting, 1825–1875.* 1980; Oxford: Oxford University Press, 1995.

Onuf, Peter S. *Jefferson's Empire: The Language of American Nationhood.* Charlottesville: University Press of Virginia, 2000.

Padgen, Anthony. *Lords of All the World: Ideologies of Empire in Spain, Britain, and France, c.1500–c.1800.* New Haven: Yale University Press, 1995.

Parrington, Vernon. *Main Currents in American Thought: An Interpretation of American Literature from the Beginnings to 1920.* New York: Harcourt, Brace, 1927, 1930.

Paryz, Marek. *Postcolonial and Imperial Experience in American Transcendentalism.* New York: Palgrave Macmillan, 2012.

Pease, Donald E. "*Moby Dick* and the Cold War." In *The American Renaissance Reconsidered,* edited by Walter Benn Michaels and Donald E. Pease, 113–55. Baltimore: Johns Hopkins University Press, 1985.

———. "US Imperialism: Global Dominance without Colonies." In *A Companion to Postcolonial Studies,* edited by Henry Schwartz and Sangeeta Ray, 203–20. Malden, MA: Blackwell, 2000.

———. *Visionary Compacts: American Renaissance Writings in Cultural Context.* Madison: University of Wisconsin Press, 1987.

Perdu, Peter C. "Rise & Fall of the Canton Trade System, III." Massachusetts Institute of Technology, 2008. http://ocw.mit.edu/ans7870/21f/21f.027/rise_fall_canton_01/pdf/cw03_essay.pdf.

Perdue, Theda, and Michael D. Green, eds. *The Cherokee Removal: A Brief History with Documents.* Boston: Bedford Books, 1995.

Pfaelzer, Jean. *Driven Out: The Forgotten War against Chinese Americans.* New York: Random House, 2007.

Phillips, Clifton Jackson. *Protestant America and the Pagan World: The First Half Century of the American Board of Commissioners for Foreign Missions, 1810–1860.* 1968; Cambridge, MA: East Asian Research Center, Harvard University Press, 1969.

Pickowicz, Paul. "William Wood in Canton: A Critique of the China Trade before the Opium War." *Essex Historical Collections* 107 (1971): 3–32.

Pocock, J. G. A. *The Machiavellian Moment: Florentine Political Thought and the Atlantic Republican Tradition.* 1975; Princeton: Princeton University Press, 2003.

———. *Virtue, Commerce, History: Essays on Political Thought and History, Chiefly in the Eighteenth Century.* Cambridge: Cambridge University Press, 1985.

Pomeranz, Kenneth. *The Great Divergence: China, Europe, and the Making of the Modern World Economy.* Princeton: Princeton University Press, 2000.

Pong, David. *Shen Pao-Chen and China's Modernization in the Nineteenth Century.* Cambridge: Cambridge University Press, 1994.

Poovey, Mary. *A History of the Modern Fact: Problems of Knowledge in the Sciences of Wealth and Society.* Chicago: University of Chicago Press, 1998.

Pratt, Mary Louise. *Imperial Eyes: Travel Writing and Transculturation.* London: Routledge, 1992.

Price, Martin. "The Picturesque Moment." In *From Sensibility to Romanticism,* edited by Frederick Hilles and Harold Bloom, 259–92. New York: Oxford University Press, 1965.

Prucha, Francis Paul, ed. *American Indian Treaties: The History of a Political Anomaly.* Berkeley: University of California Press, 1994.

———. *Documents of United States Indian Policy.* 3rd ed. Lincoln: University of Nebraska Press, 2000.

———. *Indian Peace Medals in American History.* Madison: State Historical Society, 1971.

Puga, Rogério. "'A gem of a place': Macau após a guerra do ópio: o diário de Rebecca Chase Kinsman." In *Estudos sobre a China VI,* vol. 2, edited by Ana Maria Amaro, 903–55. Lisbon: Centro de Estudos Chineses-Instituto Superior de Ciências Sociais e Políticas, 2004.

———. "Imagens de Macau oitocentista: a visão intimista de uma jovem americana. O diário de Harriett Low (Hillard) (1829–33)." In *Estudos sobre a China V,* vol. 2, edited by Ana Maria Amaro, 713–67. Lisbon: Centro de Estudos Chineses-Instituto Superior de Ciências Sociais e Políticas, 2003.

———. "Images of Nineteenth-Century Macau in the Journals of Harriett Low (1829–1834) and Rebecca Chase Kinsman (1843–1847)." *Oriente* 14 (April 2006): 90–104.

———. "Interpreting Macau through the Journals of Harriett Low and Rebecca Chase Kinsman." *Journal of Sino-Western Cultural Studies* 6.1 (June 2008): 605–64.

———. "Macau and Timor in 1829: The Journal and the Unpublished Drawings of Lucy Cleveland." *Oriente* 18 (2007): 3–33.

———. "Macau nos anos (18)30: o diário de Caroline Hyde Butler Laing (1837)." *Revista portuguesa de estudos chineses (Zhongguo yanjiu)* 1.2 (2007): 71–112.

———. "O primeiro olhar norte-americano sobre Macau: os diários de Samuel Shaw (1754–1794)." In *Intertextual dialogues, travel & routes: actas do XXVI encontro da APEAA,* edited by Ana Gabriela Macedo et al., 227–51. Braga: University of Minho, 2007.

———. "Representing Macao in 1837: The Unpublished Peripatetic Diary of Caroline Hyde Butler (Laing)." In *Narratives of Free Trade: The Commercial Cultures of Early US-China Relations*, edited by Kendall Johnson, 117–30. Hong Kong: Hong Kong University Press, 2012.

———. *A World of Euphemism: Representações de Macau na obra de Austin Coates; City of Broken Promises enquanto Romance Histórico e Bildungsroman Feminino*. Lisbon: Fundação para a Ciência e a Tecnologia-Ministério da Ciência, Tecnologia e Ensino Superior/Fundação Calouste Gulbenkian, 2009.

———. "A vivência social do género na Macau oitocentista: o diário de Harriet Low (Hillard)." *Administração: revista de administração pública de Macau* 15 (56) (2002): 605–64.

Putzel, Max. "The Source and the Symbols of Melville's 'Benito Cereno.'" *American Literature* 34.2 (May 1962): 191–206.

Qiao, Mingshun. *The First Page of Sino-US Relations: The Signing of the Wangxia Treaty of 1844* [Zhongmei guangxi de diyi ye: 1844 nian wangxia tiaoyue qianding de qianqian houhou]. Beijing: Shehui kexue wenxian chubanshe [Social Sciences Documentation Press], 1991.

Raustiala, Kal. *Does the Constitution Follow the Flag? The Evolution of Territoriality in American Law*. Oxford: Oxford University Press, 2009.

Redding, Arthur. "Closet, Coup, and Cold War: F. O. Matthiessen's *From the Heart of Europe*." *boundary2* 33.1 (Spring 2006): 171–201.

Rediker, Marcus. *Between the Devil and the Deep Blue Sea*. Cambridge: Cambridge University Press, 1987.

Reed, Christopher A. *Gutenberg in Shanghai: Chinese Print Capitalism, 1876–1937*. Hong Kong: University of Hong Kong Press, 2004.

Reynolds, Michael. *Beneath the American Renaissance: The Subversive Imagination in the Age of Emerson and Melville*. Cambridge, MA: Harvard University Press, 1988.

Rhoads, Edward J. M. *Stepping Forth into the World: The Chinese Education Mission to the United States, 1872–81*. Hong Kong: Hong Kong University Press, 2011.

Ricci, Ronit. *Islam Translated: Literature, Conversion, and the Arabic Comopolis of South and Southeast Asia*. Chicago: University of Chicago Press, 2011.

Ride, Lindsay, and May Ride. *An East India Company Cemetery: Protestant Burials in Macao*. Edited by Bernard Mellor. Hong Kong: Hong Kong University Press, 1995.

Rifkin, Mark. "Debt and the Transnationalization of Hawai'i." *American Quarterly* 60.1 (March 2008): 43–66.

Robert, Dana L. *American Women in Mission: A Social History of Their Thought and Practice*. Macon, GA: Mercer University Press, 1996.

Roberts, Timothy Mason. "Commercial Philanthropy: ABCFM Missionaries and the American Opium Trade." In *The Role of the American Board in the World: Bicentennial Reflections on the Organization's Missionary Work, 1810–2010*, edited by Clifford Putney and Paul T. Burlin, 27–48. Eugene, OR: Wipf & Stock, 2012.

Robinson, Sidney. *Inquiry into the Picturesque*. Chicago: University of Chicago, 1991.

Rogin, Michael Paul. *Subversive Genealogy: The Politics and Art of Herman Melville*. Berkeley: University of California Press, 1985.

Rowe, John Carlos. "Edward Said and American Studies." *American Quarterly* 56.1 (March 2004): 33–47.

———. *The New American Studies*. Minneapolis: University of Minnesota Press, 2002.

Ruskola, Teemu. "Canton Is Not Boston: The Invention of American Imperial Sovereignty." *American Quarterly* 57.3 (September 2005): 859–84.

———. *Legal Orientalism: China, the United States, and Modern Law.* Cambridge, MA: Harvard University Press, 2013.

Said, Edward. *Orientalism.* New York: Vintage Books, 1979.

———. "Orientalism Reconsidered." In *Literature, Politics and Theory: Papers from the Essex Conference, 1976–84,* edited by Francis Barker, Peter Hulme, Margaret Iversen, and Diana Loxley, 210–29. London: Methuen, 1986.

Sánchez-Eppler, Karen. "Copying and Conversion: An 1824 Friendship Album 'from a Chinese Youth.'" *American Quarterly* 59.2 (June 2007): 301–39.

Schmidt, Peter. *Sitting in the Darkness: New South Fiction, Education, and the Rise of Jim Crow Colonialism, 1865–1920.* Jackson: University of Mississippi, 2008.

Schopp, Susan E. "Five American Women's Perceptions of China, 1829–1941: 'A Yard-Stick of Our Own Construction.'" In *Americans and Macao: Trade, Smuggling, and Diplomacy on the South China Coast,* edited by Paul A. Van Dyke, 125–42. Hong Kong: Hong Kong University Press, 2012.

Schrecker, John. "'For the Equality of Men—For the Equality of Nations': Anson Burlingame and China's First Embassy to the United States, 1868." *Journal of American-East Asian Relations* 17 (2010): 9–34.

Schroeder, John H. *Matthew Calbraith Perry: Antebellum Sailor and Diplomat.* Annapolis, MD: Naval Institute Press, 2001.

Schueller, Malini Johar. *U.S. Orientalisms: Race, Nation, and Gender in Literature, 1790–1890.* Ann Arbor: University of Michigan Press, 2001.

Scudder, Harold H. "Melville's *Benito Cereno* and Captain Delano's Voyages." *PMLA* 43.2 (June 1928): 502–32.

Scully, Eileen P. *Bargaining with the State from Afar: American Citizenship in Treaty Port China, 1844–1942.* New York: Columbia University Press, 2001.

Seaburg, Carl, and Stanley Paterson. *Merchant Prince of Boston, Colonel T. H. Perkins, 1764–1854.* Cambridge, MA: Harvard University Press, 1971.

Sedgwick, Eve Kosofsky. *Between Men: English Literature and Male Homosocial Desire.* New York: Columbia University Press, 1985.

Semmel, Bernard. *The Rise of Free Trade Imperialism: Classical Political Economy, the Empire of Free Trade and Imperialism, 1750–1850.* Cambridge: Cambridge University Press, 1970.

Sexton, Jay. *Debtor Diplomacy: Finance and American Foreign Relations in the Civil War Era, 1837–1873.* Oxford: Clarendon, 2005.

———. *The Monroe Doctrine: Empire and Nation in Nineteenth-Century America.* New York: Hill and Wang, 2011.

Sharpe, Jenny. *Allegories of Empire: The Figure of Woman in the Colonial Text.* Minneapolis: University of Minnesota Press, 1993.

Shaw, Damian. "Harriett Low: An American Spinster at the Cape, 12 January to 4 May 1834." *South African Historical Journal* 62.2 (2010): 287–302.

Shewmaker, Kenneth E. "Forging the 'Great Chain': Daniel Webster and the Origins of American Foreign Policy toward East Asia and the Pacific, 1841–1852." *Proceedings of the American Philosophical Society* 129.3 (1985): 225–59.

Sinn, Elizabeth. *Pacific Crossing: California Gold, Chinese Migration, and the Making of Hong Kong.* Hong Kong: University of Hong Kong Press, 2013.

Slotkin, Richard. *Regeneration through Violence: The Mythology of the American Frontier, 1600–1869.* Middleton, CT: Wesleyan University Press, 1973.

Smith, Frank. "Philip Freneau and the Time-Piece Literary Companion." *American Literature* 4.3 (November 1932): 270–87.

Smith, Henry Nash. *Virgin Land: The American West as a Symbol and Myth.* Cambridge, MA: Harvard University Press, 1950.

Smith, Philip Chadwick Foster. *The Empress of China.* Philadelphia: Philadelphia Maritime Museum, 1984.

Snow, Jennifer C. *Protestant Missionaries, Asian Immigrants, and Ideologies of Race in America, 1850–1924.* New York: Routledge, 2006.

Sommer, Doris. *Foundational Fictions: The Novel Romance of Latin America.* Berkeley: University of California Press, 1991.

Souza, George Bryan. *The Survival of Empire: Portuguese Trade and Society in China and the South China Sea, 1630–1754.* Cambridge: Cambridge University Press, 1986.

Spence, Jonathan. *God's Chinese Son: The Taiping Heavenly Kingdom of Hong Xiuquan.* New York: W. W. Norton, 1996.

———. *The Search for Modern China.* 3rd ed. 1990; New York: W. W. Norton, 2013.

Stelle, Charles Clarkson. *Americans and the China Opium Trade in the Nineteenth-Century.* New York: Arno Press, 1981.

———. "American Trade in Opium to China, Prior to 1820." *Pacific Historical Review* 9.4 (December 1940): 425–44.

Stern, Madeleine B. *William Williams: Pioneer Printer of Utica, New York, 1787–1850.* Charlottesville: Bibliographical Society of the University of Virginia, 1951.

Stoler, Ann Laura, ed. *Haunted by Empire: Geographies of Intimacy in North American History.* Durham, NC: Duke University Press.

———. "Intimations of Empire: Predicaments of the Tactile and Unseen." In *Haunted by Empire: Geographies of Intimacy in North American History*, edited by Ann Laura Stoler, 1–22. Durham, NC: Duke University Press, 2006.

———. "Tense and Tender Ties: The Politics of Comparison in North American History and (Post) Colonial Studies." In *Haunted by Empire: Geographies of Intimacy in North American History*, edited by Ann Laura Stoler, 23–70. Durham, NC: Duke University Press, 2006.

Stuckey, Sterling, and Joshua Leslie. "Captain Delano's Claim against Benito Cereno." *Modern Philology* 85.3 (February 1988): 265–87.

Su, Ching. "The Printing Presses of the London Missionary Society among the Chinese." PhD dissertation, University of London, 1996.

Suleri, Sara. *The Rhetoric of English India.* Chicago: University of Chicago Press, 1992.

Sundquist, Eric. "'Benito Cereno' and New World Slavery." In *Reconstructing American Literary History*, edited by Sacvan Bercovitch, 93–122. Cambridge, MA: Harvard University Press, 1986.

———. *To Wake the Nations: Race in the Making of American Literature.* Cambridge, MA: Harvard University Press, 1993.

Swisher, Earl. *China's Management of the American Barbarians: A Study of Sino-American Re-*

lations, 1841–1861, with Documents. New Haven: Far Eastern Publications, Yale University Press, 1953.

Szanton, David L. "The Origin, Nature, and Challenges of Area Studies in the United States." In *The Politics of Knowledge: Area Studies and the Disciplines*, edited by David Szanton, 1–33. Berkeley: University of California Press, 2004.

Takaki, Ronald. *A Different Mirror: A History of Multicultural America*. Boston: Little Brown, 1993.

Taketani, Etsuko. *U.S. Women Writers and the Discourses of Colonialism, 1825–1861*. Knoxville: University of Tennessee Press, 2003.

Tchen, John Kuo Wei. *New York before Chinatown: Orientalism and the Shaping of American Culture, 1777–1882*. Baltimore: Johns Hopkins University Press, 1999.

Teng, Ssu-yü S. *Historiography of the Taiping Rebellion*. 1962; Cambridge, MA: East Asian Research Center, Harvard University Press, 1972.

Teng, Ssu-yü S., and John K. Fairbank, with E-tu Zen Sun, Chaoying Fang, et al. *China's Response to the West: A Documentary Survey, 1839–1923*. Cambridge, MA: Harvard University Press, 1954.

———. *Research Guide for China's Response to the West: A Documentary Survey, 1839–1923*. Cambridge, MA: Harvard University Press, 1954.

Teng, Yuan Chung. "Reverend Issachar Jacox Roberts and the Taiping Rebellion." *Journal of Asian Studies* 23.1 (1963): 55–67.

Thomas, Brook. *American Literary Realism and the Failed Promise of Contract*. Berkeley: University of California Press, 1997.

———. "China Men, United States v. Wong Kim Ark, and the Question of Citizenship." *American Quarterly* 50.4 (December 1998): 689–717.

Todd, David. "John Bowring and the Global Dissemination of Free Trade." *Historical Journal* 51.2 (2008): 373–97.

Tong, Te-kong. *United States Diplomacy in China, 1844–60*. Seattle: University of Washington Press, 1964.

"Treaties and Documents concerning Opium." *American Journal of International Law*, Suppl.; Official Documents 3.3 (July 1909): 253–75.

Trocki, Carl A. *Opium, Empire and the Global Political Economy: A Study of the Asian Opium Trade, 1750–1950*. London: Routledge, 1999.

United States Department of State. *Despatches from United States Consuls in Macao, 1849–1869*. Record group 59. Microcopy no. 109. Washington, DC: National Archives 1947.

Van Dyke, Paul A. *Americans and Macao: Trade, Smuggling, and Diplomacy on the South China Coast*. Hong Kong: Hong Kong University Press, 2012.

———. "Bookkeeping as a Window into the Efficiencies of Early Modern Trade: Europeans, Americans and Others in China Compared, 1700–1842." In *Narratives of Free Trade: The Commercial Cultures of Early US-China Relations*, edited by Kendall Johnson, 17–31. Hong Kong: Hong Kong University Press, 2012.

———. *The Canton Trade: Life and Enterprise on the China Coast, 1700–1845*. Hong Kong: Hong Kong University Press, 2005.

———. *Merchants of Canton and Macao: Politics and Strategies of the Eighteenth-Century Chinese Trade*. Hong Kong: Hong Kong University Press, 2011.

Wakeman, Frederic, Jr. "The Canton Trade and the Opium War." In *The Cambridge History of China*, vol. 10, *Late Ch'ing, 1800–1911. Part 1*, edited by Denis Twitchett and John K. Fairbank, 163–212. Cambridge: Cambridge University Press, 1978.

———. *Strangers at the Gate: Social Disorder in South China, 1839–1861*. Berkeley: University of California Press, 1966.

Waley, Arthur. *The Opium War through Chinese Eyes*. Stanford, CA: Stanford University Press, 1958.

Wallace, Anthony C. F. *Jefferson and the Indians: The Tragic Fate of the First Americans*. Cambridge, MA: Harvard University Press, 1999.

Wallerstein, Immanuel. *World-Systems Analysis: An Introduction*. Durham, NC: Duke University Press, 2004.

Ward, Edith Nevill Smythe. *Caroline Hyde Butler Laing (1804–1892): A Family Heritage; Letters and Journals of Caroline Hyde Butler Laing, 1804–1892*. East Orange, NJ: Abbey Printers, 1957.

Warner, Michael. *Letters of the Republic: Publication and the Public Sphere in the Eighteenth-Century America*. Cambridge, MA: Harvard University Press, 1990.

Warren, James Francis. *The Sulu Zone, 1768–1898: The Dynamics of External Trade, Slavery, and Ethnicity in the Transformation of a Southeast Asian Maritime State*. 1981; Singapore: National University of Singapore Press, 2007.

Weir, David. *American Orient: Imagining the East from the Colonial Era through the Twentieth Century*. Amherst: University of Massachusetts Press, 2011.

Welch, Richard E., Jr. "Celeb Cushing's Chinese Mission and the Treaty of Wanghia: A Review." *Oregon Historical Quarterly* 57.4 (December 1957): 328–57.

White, Hayden. *Metahistory: The Historical Imagination in Nineteenth-Century Europe*. Baltimore: Johns Hopkins University Press, 1975.

———. *Tropics of Discourse: Essays in Cultural Criticism*. Baltimore: Johns Hopkins University Press, 1978.

Wiley, Peter Booth, with Korogi Ichiro. *Yankees in the Land of the Gods: Commodore Perry and the Opening of Japan*. New York: Penguin Books, 1990.

Williams, John Camp. *An Oneida County Printer: William Williams, Printer, Publisher, Editor with a Bibliography of the Press at Utica, Oneida County New York, from 1803–1838*. New York: Charles Scribner's Sons, 1906.

Wills, John E. *Pepper, Guns, and Parleys: The Dutch East India Company and China, 1662–1681*. Cambridge, MA: Harvard University Press, 1974.

———. "Tribute, Defensiveness, and Dependency: Uses and Limits of Some Basic Ideas about Mid-Qing Dynasty Foreign Relations." *American Neptune* 48.4 (Fall 1988): 225–29.

Wilson, Rob. "Exporting Christian Transcendentalism, Importing Hawaiian Sugar: The Trans-Americanization of Hawai'i." *American Literature* 72.3 (September 2000): 521–52.

———. *Reimagining the American Pacific: From* South Pacific *to* Bamboo Ridge *and Beyond*. Durham, NC: Duke University Press, 2000.

Wittfogel, Karl A. *Oriental Despotism: A Comparative Study of Total Power*. New Haven: Yale University Press, 1957.

Wong, John D. *Global Trade in the Nineteenth Century: The House of Houqua and the Canton System*. Cambridge: Cambridge University Press, 2016.

Wong, K. Scott, and Sucheng Chan, eds. *Claiming America: Constructing Chinese American Identities during the Exclusion Era*. Philadelphia: Temple University Press, 1998.

———. "The Transformation of Culture: Three Chinese Views of America." *American Quarterly* 48.2 (June 1996): 201–32. Reprinted in *Locating American Studies: The Evolution of a Discipline* (Baltimore: Johns Hopkins University Press, 1998).

Woodhouse, Samuel W. "The Voyage of the Empress of China." *Pennsylvania Magazine of History and Biography* 63.1 (1939): 24–36.

Wu, Xiaoxin. *Christianity in China: A Scholar's Guide to Resources in the Libraries and Archives of the United States*. 2nd ed. New York: Routledge, 2015.

Xu, Guoqi. *Chinese and Americans: A Shared History*. Cambridge, MA: Harvard University Press, 2014.

Yang, Chi-ming. *Performing China: Virtue, Commerce, and Orientalism in Eighteenth-Century England, 1660–1760*. Baltimore: Johns Hopkins University Press, 2011.

Yellin, Jean Fagan. "Black Masks: Melville's 'Benito Cereno.'" *American Quarterly* 22 (Autumn 1970): 578–89.

Yokota, Kariann Akemi. *Unbecoming British: How Revolutionary America Became a Postcolonial Nation*. Oxford: Oxford University Press, 2011.

Zhang, Xiantao. *The Origins of the Modern Chinese Press: The Influence of the Protestant Missionary Press in Late Qing China*. New York: Routledge, 2007.

Zheng, Yangwen. *The Social Life of Opium in China*. Cambridge: Cambridge University Press, 2005.

Zo, Young Kil. "Chinese Emigration into the United States, 1850–1880." PhD dissertation, Columbia University, 1971.

Zug, James. *American Traveler: The Life and Adventures of John Ledyard, the Man Who Dreamed of Walking the World*. New York: Basic Books, 2005.

Zwick, Jim, ed. *Mark Twain's Weapons of Satire: Anti-imperialist Writings on the Philippine-American War*. Syracuse, NY: Syracuse University Press, 1992.

The letter *f* following a page number denotes a figure.